————————— ITE METROPOLIS —————————

WHITE METROPOLIS

*Race, Ethnicity, and Religion
in Dallas, 1841–2001*

BY MICHAEL PHILLIPS

UNIVERSITY OF TEXAS PRESS
Austin

Chapter one appeared previously as "White Violence, Hegemony, and Slave Rebellion in Dallas, Texas, before the Civil War," in *East Texas Historical Journal* 37, no. 2 (fall 1999). Courtesy of East Texas Historical Association and Dr. Archie P. McDonald, editor.

Requests for permission to reproduce material from this work should be sent to:
Permissions
University of Texas Press
P.O. Box 7819
Austin, TX 78713-7819
www.utexas.edu/utpress/about/bpermission.html

⊗ The paper used in this book meets the minimum requirements of ANSI/NISO Z39.48-1992 (R1997) (Permanence of Paper).

Library of Congress Cataloging-in-Publication Data

Phillips, Michael, 1960–
White metropolis : race, ethnicity, and religion in Dallas, 1841–2001 / by Michael Phillips. — 1st ed.
p.   cm.
Includes bibliographical references and index.
ISBN 0-292-70968-4 (cl. : alk. paper) —
ISBN 0-292-71274-x (pbk. : alk. paper)
1. Dallas (Tex.) — Race relations — History.   2. Dallas (Tex.) — Ethnic relations — History.   I. Title.
F394.D219A25   2006
305.8′009764′2812 — dc22
2005008255

CONTENTS

Illustrations follow Acknowledgments

ACKNOWLEDGMENTS

This book represents a tribute to the patience and commitment of my parents, Joseph Touart Phillips and Marie Louise Phillips. Both endured poverty in the Depression-era Deep South, yet they devoted their full energies to seeing that their children enjoyed a life filled with greater opportunity. My mother generously supported every step of my education both financially and emotionally and even served as a typist when I indulged in my short-lived career as an overwrought teenage novelist. My father, Joseph Phillips, was a true working-class hero. His father had abandoned him and five siblings during the depths of the Great Depression, and my father spent part of his childhood in a Catholic-run orphanage in Mobile, Alabama. Inspired by patriotism and a desire to find work, he enlisted in the Marine Corps, where he served for twenty-two years, seeing combat action in both Korea and Vietnam. My father was the ultimate history buff, and I think that in his sixty-eight-year life he read every book published on the Civil War and World War II. I hold an enduring image of him returning from the library on Saturdays with huge stacks of books under each arm. He inspired both my love of reading and my fascination with history. I must also thank my sister, Marie Diane Pugh, who served as my first literary audience and who patiently plowed through some of the worst fiction and poetry ever written, all scrawled in my unreadable calligraphy.

My deepest appreciation goes to John Dycus, the extraordinary editorial adviser to *The Shorthorn,* the University of Texas at Arlington student newspaper, where I worked as an undergraduate. Dycus more than any person helped me discover my voice as a writer and honed my skills so that all my profound insights were not lost in a flood of clumsy verbiage. I must also thank friends who read portions of my dissertation and gave advice: Carman C. Curton, Patrick Cox, Lee Thompson, Lore Kuehnert, Mary Shomon, Kelly Bender, Steve Bender, Linda Van Ingen, Janet Neff, and my uncle Patrick Phillips. Julia Hickman's support was of incalculable value. Special thanks go to my siblings-in-law Stephanie Camfield for being a patient and kind listener, Sara Weeks for running down Dallas crime statistics while I was still living in California, and Ben Shub for his crucial legal advice. I also owe a debt to Jerome Weeks for his discussions of Dallas cultural life and the State-Thomas neighborhood.

I want to thank Jon Weist for always being there as a friend. Lacey Veal, you are a beloved daughter to me. You have been an invaluable support for our family as well as a shining example and cool older sister for my son. I want to express my love for Danny Pugh, Jeremy Pugh, Suzanna Weeks, Will Camfield, Olivia Camfield, Celeste Camfield, Laura Shub, Allison Shub, Toby Symonds, and Noah and Will Bender, whose smiles and spirits have turned a curmudgeon into an optimist.

Alice Shub, Bill Neff, and Jeff West all shared memories of Dallas and its natural setting and pointed me toward important primary sources. William Farmer, Donald Payton, Darwin Payne, Becky Spicer, Rebecca Bennett, Lewis Johnson, and Debra Bryant offered hours of their time in answering questions about Dallas history, helping with translations, or guiding me to archives and newspaper accounts of Dallas' past.

I used twelve archives while conducting this research and owe much to the staffs at these fine institutions. I would like to thank Gaylon Polatti and Rachel Roberts for their extensive assistance at the Dallas Historical Society. I would like to also thank Steve Landregan, the archivist at the Roman Catholic Diocese in Dallas; Gerry Cristol, the archivist at Dallas' Temple Emanu-El; Katherine R. Goodwin of the Labor Archives at the University of Texas at Arlington; the staff at the Dallas/Texas History and Archives Division at the J. Erik Jonsson Library in Dallas, especially Carol Roark and Sarah Ewald; the staff at the Center for American History at the University of Texas at Austin; Grace G. Charles, the talented library assistant at the Hector P. Garcia Collection at Texas A&M University at Corpus Christi; and the staff at the Texas State Library Archives Division. I am especially grateful to Paul Dehaven, pastor of communications, Rae Lamburton, executive secretary, and Meg Ackley, administrative assistant, at Scofield Memorial Church in Dallas. Pastor Dehaven was courteous and extremely generous as he guided me through C. I. Scofield's papers and shared his knowledge about this important Dallas minister.

The following professors provided invaluable aid, by writing recommendation letters, by answering research questions, or by above-and-beyond work as educators: Sarah Stage, Sterling Stuckey, Sharon Salinger, Robert Patch, and Brian Lloyd at the University of California at Riverside; and Richard Graham, David Montejano, Peter Jelavich, Brian Levack, Joan Nueberger, and Norman Brown at the University of Texas at Austin; Patricia Evridge Hill of San Jose State; Walter Buenger of Texas A&M University; Randolph B. "Mike" Campbell of the University of North Texas; Donald E. Reynolds, formerly of Texas A&M University at Commerce; and Donald S. Frazier of McMurry University, all of whom thoughtfully responded to email queries regarding nineteenth- and twentieth-century Texas. Harvey Graff of the University of Texas at San Antonio granted me an entire afternoon to discuss Dallas' "Origin Myth" and the city's uneasy relationship with its history. Dr. Graff was friendly and accessible and offered a treasure of information; I owe him my deep gratitude.

I was lucky to work with a dissertation committee made up of some of the preeminent scholars in the nation. My committee, Douglas E. Foley, Gunther Peck, James Sidbury, Mauricio Tenorio, and particularly my dissertation director, Neil Foley, diligently critiqued long-winded drafts and corrected faulty reasoning. I cannot completely express my gratitude to Neil Foley for being an enthusiastic supporter of this project from the beginning. He encouraged me to take chances and never lost faith in my ability to produce what I hope will be an important contribution to scholarship on the Southwest. I thank him for being a tireless mentor, coach, and friend who turned a clueless former journalist into a professional historian. I also have to give great credit for whatever success this book has to my editor at the University of Texas Press, William Bishel, who expertly guided me through the rocky terrain of academic publishing.

I would have given up on this project long ago if it were not for my ever-forgiving and always loving wife, Samantha Shub. Samantha was not just a thoughtful partner and eagle-eyed editor but was also a cheerleader in times of despair, an advocate in times of insecurity, and a friend in times of loneliness. Samantha steered me through computer meltdowns, emotional crises, and moments of physical fatigue. I cannot imagine having written this book without her.

Finally, I would like to dedicate this work to my son, Dominic Shehan Phillips. Almost all of the research, writing, rewriting, tears, laughter, exhaustion, and celebration that went into this work happened before your birth, but the joy your parents felt at its completion was made richer by your unexpected, miraculous, and ecstatically celebrated arrival. In your beautiful eyes I see the answer. You represent the future and make the battle for social justice worth the struggle.

1. In 1941 the *Dallas Morning News* ran a series of cartoons on Dallas' history to commemorate the city's centennial. The above cartoon, depicting the search for who started an 1860 fire that destroyed much of Dallas and was blamed on rebellious slaves, captures the contradictory views white residents held toward African Americans. Whites told themselves that blacks had been childlike and happy as slaves but that they were easily manipulated into violence, particularly by malevolent regional outsiders. Courtesy: Dallas Historical Society.

2. The "plantation myth" portrayed slaves as well cared for and loved as family members by their white masters until political radicals upset the natural racial order. This myth thrived throughout the twentieth century. The above photograph, taken in 1909 and featuring a generation of Dallas' powerful Cockrell family surrounding their smiling former slave William Winn, captures this pastoral imagery. Courtesy: Dallas Historical Society.

3. John Henry Brown, elected as mayor in both Galveston and Dallas, fanned fears of a slave revolt in Texas with publication in 1860 of the so-called Bailey Letter. Later, as Dallas County's first published historian, Brown cast the city's past as a tale of superior whites triumphing over dark-skinned savages. Courtesy: Dallas Historical Society.

4. Though he possessed shaky theological credentials, Dallas minister Cyrus I. Scofield published a reference Bible that became perhaps the most important document in fundamentalist Protestantism and profoundly influenced how American Gentiles viewed Jews. Courtesy: Scofield Memorial Church.

5. Dallas businessman and "Merchant Prince" Philip Sanger worried that Dallas schools fostered in working-class children "foolish yearning after political prominence." He called for a more strictly industrial curriculum to dampen incipient labor radicalism. Courtesy: Texas/Dallas History and Archives Division, Dallas Public Library.

6. Dallas' Deep Ellum became "the gathering place of blacks from all over the country, for Mexicans fleeing oppression in Mexico, for Jews who established businesses and poor whites looking for 'action,' " wrote local historian Robert Prince. Whorehouses, blues joints, and this pawn shop at 2524 Elm, owned by "the Loan Ranger," Honest Abe Goldstein, dotted the multiracial, multi-ethnic Deep Ellum landscape. Courtesy: Texas/Dallas History and Archives Division, Dallas Public Library.

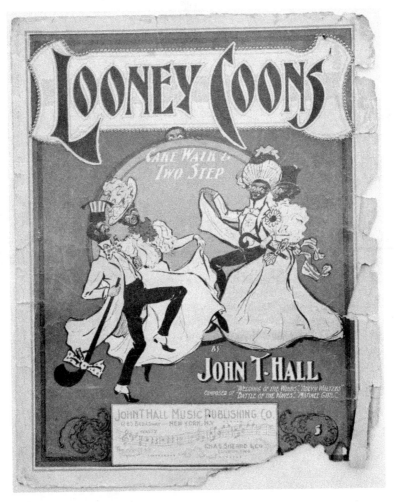

7. Oblivious to the suffering and fear blacks experienced, music sheets for songs like "Looney Coons" sold at Dallas-area stores and appealed to white audiences, combining patronizing contempt for African Americans with an envy for the imagined simplicity of their lives. Photo by Missy Schuelke. From the author's private collection.

8. Fear joined envy when whites contemplated their black neighbors. While white Dallas told itself that blacks were docile and content with political inequality, they paradoxically portrayed black men as raping beasts who could not truly be civilized, as demonstrated in the 1910 lynching of Allen Brooks. Courtesy: Texas/Dallas History and Archives Division, Dallas Public Library.

Will The Federal Suffrage Amendment Complicate The Race Problem?

A little study will prove that the national enfranchisement of women will IN NO WAY complicate the race problem.

In all of the fifteen Southern States, except Mississippi and South Carolina, THE WHITE WOMEN GREATLY OUTNUMBER THE NEGRO WOMEN.

In nine of these States, THE WHITE WOMEN OUTNUMBER THE TOTAL NEGRO POPULATION.

There are in the Southern States 2,017,286 MORE WHITE WOMEN THAN NEGRO MEN AND WOMEN PUT TOGETHER.

The following table taken from the Census of 1910 proves this statement. The figures are for the total population of the States named. They may be found on page 100 of the Abstract of the 1910 Census.

STATES	Total Negro Population	White Women	Negro Woman	Preponderence of White over Negro Women
Maryland	232,250	533,567	117,501	416,066
Virginia	671,096	685,446	340,554	344,892
North Carolina	697,843	745,659	358,262	387,397
South Carolina	835,843	335,617	427,765	−92,148
Georgia	1,176,987	707,314	596,724	110,590
Florida	308,669	211,089	147,307	63,782
Mississippi	1,009,487	384,055	506,691	−122,636
Alabama	908,282	602,941	460,488	142,453
Tennessee	473,088	841,810	239,378	602,432
Kentucky	261,656	997,918	130,164	867,754
Arkansas	442,891	544,606	219,568	325,038
Louisiana	713,874	460,626	360,050	100,576
Texas	691,049	1,533,411	345,108	1,188,303
Missouri	157,452	1,528,376	76,963	1,451,413
West Virginia	64,173	549,491	27,566	521,925
Total	8,644,640	10,661,926	4,354,089	6,307,837

In Mississippi and South Carolina, where negro women outnumber white women, negro men outnumber white men. There is no more reason why the presence of negro women should debar women from voting, than the presence of negro men debars men from voting.

Mississippi imposes a heavy educational qualification; South Carolina both an educational and a property qualification. If women voted, these qualifications would apply to women exactly as to men.

A FEDERAL SUFFRAGE AMENDMENT MERELY FORBIDS THE DISFRANCHISEMENT OF A WOMAN ON THE SOLE GROUND THAT SHE IS A WOMAN.

There are to-day, in all our States, widely-varying voting qualifications—some wise; some unwise. Women did not frame these qualifications; and since women are disfranchised, they cannot change them. They merely ask that where a woman measures up to the standard required of a man, she may not be debarred from voting because she is a woman.

This will not make our electoral arrangements perfect, but it will remedy THEIR MOST GLARING INJUSTICE, THE ALMOST COMPLETE DISCRIMINATION AGAINST WOMEN.

NATIONAL LITERATURE HEADQUARTERS,
CONGRESSIONAL UNION FOR WOMAN SUFFRAGE,
213 HALE BUILDING, PHILADELPHIA

9. White feminists in Texas sometimes utilized negrophobia to marshal support for women's suffrage, as shown in this Pennsylvania-printed leaflet purportedly based on 1910 Census figures. Enfranchising women would increase white voting power, some suffragists argued, especially if time-tested methods of racial discrimination barred black women from the ballot box. Courtesy: Dallas Historical Society.

10. In his play *Judge Lynch, Dallas Daily Times-Herald* theater critic John William Rogers, pictured here standing between two unidentified women, portrayed poor white trash as the creators of violence, disorder, and bigotry, even though some of his elite peers had rushed to join the revived Klan of the 1920s. Courtesy: Texas/Dallas History and Archives Division, Dallas Public Library.

The Knights of the
KU KLUX KLAN
Are Continuing Their Fight
Started 18 Years Ago

For:-	**Against:-**
Christianity	Atheism
Individualism	Dictatorship
Liberty	Anarchy
Justice	Bolshevism
Education	Communism
Patriotism	*Facism
Fraternity	*Naziism
Nationalism	Internationalism
Representative	and all other
Government	Anti-American "Isms"

*Facism and Naziism are new names for the old world schemes to destroy
Liberty-Freedom-Individualism.

The KLAN leads the way
Back to the Constitution and
the REPUBLIC it Guarantees.
JOIN NOW! The Ku Klux Klan Program is Action!

If Interested, address, P. O. Box 2072, Dallas, Texas

11. The largest Ku Klux Klan chapter in the country in the early 1920s called Dallas home, but by the time this leaflet was issued in the 1930s, the order had been marginalized due to scandal and the lower-class image some city elites held of the organization. The heated opposition of the *Dallas Morning News* and other powerful institutions to the 1920s Klan allowed the city to later gloss over its racist past. Courtesy: Dallas Historical Society.

12. Early in the twentieth century, African Americans would stop by a studio at 2212 Elm Street and pose for novelty postcard portraits. In spite of the implication of this picture, Dallas was more of a destination for African Americans than a point of departure, and they accounted for 15 percent of the city's population in the late 1920s. Courtesy: Dallas Historical Society.

13. African Americans gather for a baptism in Denton, just north of Dallas, in 1908. Black Christianity in North Texas retained many aspects of West African folk religion and emphasized the obligation each individual had to the entire African American community. Courtesy: Dallas Historical Society.

14. African American educators like John Leslie Patton used the opportunity created by segregated schools to recapture the black past for his students. Patton's students learned that Africa had not been a "dark continent" but a creator of civilizations. Courtesy: Dallas Historical Society.

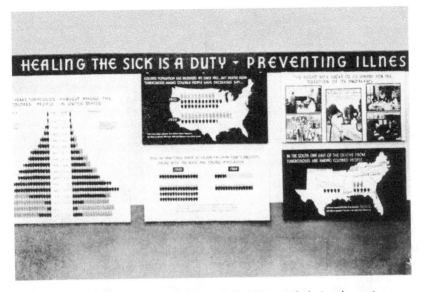

15. The African Americans who planned the Hall of Negro Life during the 1936 state centennial at Fair Park emphasized black progress in America since the end of slavery, such as in this health care display. Some whites visiting the exhibit expressed discomfort at evidence of black intelligence and creativity. Courtesy: Texas/Dallas History and Archives Division, Dallas Public Library.

16. An African American woman dresses as a "mammy" as part of an advertising promotion at the state fair. In this imagery, black women symbolize servitude, while the state itself is represented by the towering image of a white man, seen in the form of the "Big Tex" statue in the background. Big Tex represented not only white male supremacy but the attempts of Texas elites to carve out a Western identity for the state as separate from the rest of the Old South. Courtesy: Texas/Dallas History and Archives Division, Dallas Public Library.

17. As Dallas increasingly segregated not only by race but by class in the late nineteenth and early twentieth centuries, the symbolic compensation of white privilege became more important to the Anglo poor and working classes. Residents of the slum shown here insisted on being paid what scholar W. E. B. DuBois once called "the wages of whiteness." Courtesy: Dallas Public Library.

18. Dallas Republican Congressman Bruce Alger, who represented the city in Washington from 1954 through 1964, rode the wave of social and demographic changes the city experienced as a result of World War II. Alger's rhetoric on segregation and race proved more nuanced and sophisticated than that of his predecessors. Courtesy: Texas/Dallas History and Archives Division, Dallas Public Library.

19. Not everyone living in Dallas accepted the racial status quo, as indicated by this interracial demonstration through the streets of Dallas on March 14, 1965. By the mid-1960s, many white Dallas residents had concluded that segregation was immoral and provided propaganda to the Soviet Union in the Cold War struggle to win allies in places like Africa. Courtesy: Texas/Dallas History and Archives Division, Dallas Public Library.

20. Even if men like Bruce Alger gave racism a more polished veneer, the core sentiments of many white Dallasites remained unchanged from the days of slavery: African Americans represented physically repulsive primitives who could taint whites through any form of physical contact, even metaphorical contact through political alliance. Here, in a Bill McClanahan cartoon that appeared in the March 5, 1960, *Dallas Morning News,* a figure representing "politics" leans over to kiss a baby labeled "organized minorities." Courtesy: *Dallas Morning News* and Texas/Dallas History and Archives Division, Dallas Public Library.

WHITE METROPOLIS

THROUGH A GLASS DARKLY

Memory, Race, and Region in Dallas, Texas

To historians, Dallas remains the undiscovered country. The city's creation features a racial dynamic of such complexity that the topic should have interested scholars long ago. To date only one book, journalist Jim Schutze's 1986 work *The Accommodation: The Politics of Race in an American City,* attempted a comprehensive view of racial issues in Dallas, and even that is a simplified model of black-white conflict in which Schutze renders the city's Mexican American community invisible.[1] Schutze's fellow journalists, cut off from larger intellectual trends in the social sciences, have produced most book-length studies on Dallas. Such writers shied away from analyzing how ideologies of race, gender, and class shaped the city. The result is endless debate on trivia, such as who Dallas was named after, while substantial issues like power and wealth distribution are neglected.[2]

Too small in the 1860s and 1870s to merit extensive consideration in histories of the Civil War and Reconstruction, too Southern to be placed in the context of the great labor battles of the late nineteenth century, and too Western to be incorporated into monographs on the Southern desegregation struggle in the mid-twentieth century, Dallas stands as a postmodern Potemkin Village—a façade behind which nothing stands. Set against the image of brutal Southern sheriffs and angry mobs in other communities, the often quiet, more private freedom struggles in Dallas faded from view, moving one Dallas historian, W. Marvin Dulaney, to pose the question, "Whatever happened to the civil rights movement in Dallas, Texas?"[3]

Judging from American history texts, even those focused on the South and the Southwest, one might believe the answer to Dulaney's question is "Nothing much." Dallas does not merit a single mention in Taylor Branch's 1,064-page study of the civil rights movement, *Parting the Waters: America in the King Years, 1954–1963.* Robert Weisbrot, in his 1990 monograph *Freedom Bound: A History of America's Civil Rights Movement,* tells the Dallas story in a paragraph: "The sit-ins reached Dallas only in 1961, but white leaders adjusted with astonishing rapidity and goodwill, desegregating forty stores and major hotels with minimal resistance." The city then takes a polite bow and exits Weisbrot's narrative. Even when an author broadens the topic, Dallas maintains its invisibility. A photo of the famous Dallas skyline graces the cover of John Boles' 569-page *The South through Time: A History of an American Region,* but the city appears nowhere in the index.[4]

Logically, Dallas should present a tantalizing target for academics. For much of the twentieth century, Dallas represented the second-largest metropolis in the former Confederacy.[5] The city claimed one of the largest African American populations in the United States (with the twelfth-highest percentage of African Americans of major American cities in 1990).[6] The city had the fifteenth-highest percentage of Hispanics among major metropolitan areas in 1996 (15.1 percent in the Dallas–Fort Worth area).[7] The prominent position of a small but activist Jewish population in city politics and business starting in the 1870s and an influx of immigrants from Southeast Asia in the 1970s and 1980s added more dimensions to the city's diversity. Dallas, with its ambiguous geographic position on the hinge of the South, the West, and the Mexican borderlands, provides a fascinating opportunity for historians to consider not just race and ethnicity but the formation of regional identities as well.

Dallas yearly ranks as one of the Southwest region's economic powerhouses. At different times, the Dallas–Fort Worth area has represented a financial center for the cotton industry, the turf of oil barons, a banking capital, a center of high-tech firms such as Ross Perot's Electronic Data Systems, and the home base of the aviation giant American Airlines. Several firms relocated to Dallas after World War II, bringing a migration of highly trained, technically skilled Easterners and Midwesterners with no cultural or political ties to traditional Dixiecrat politics, thus anticipating the emergence of a transregional Sunbelt in the 1970s and 1980s.[8] The political realignment of the South, in which one-party rule by an ultraconservative, segregationist Democratic Party gave way to an ascendant, increasingly racist Republican Party, began in Dallas, eventually choking off many of the gains made by the civil rights movement in the 1950s and 1960s.[9]

Dallas' churches played a substantial role in this transformation. W. A. Criswell's First Baptist Church provided leadership and critical support for television evangelist Jerry Falwell's right-wing Moral Majority organization in the late 1970s and early 1980s. Criswell's church also served as the headquarters for the conservative takeover of the Southern Baptist Convention, the nation's largest Protestant denomination, and became a key backer of the GOP in what had been a Democratic city. "To say that First Baptist had a high identity with the Republican Party is to say that fish have a high identity with the ocean," wrote Joel Gregory, a one-time minister at the church. Starting in Dallas, a solid axis formed between an increasingly reactionary Republican Party and politically active Christian conservatives, a marriage that dominated American politics in the last two decades of the twentieth century.[10]

Dallas' unique geographical position, its place as a major American city, and its importance in national political and religious life should have spawned a lively tradition of serious scholarship. Academic neglect of Dallas, however, represents amnesia by design. In this obsessively image-conscious city, elites feared that a conflict-marred past filled with class and racial strife represented a dangerous model for the future. City leaders transformed the community into a laboratory of forgetfulness.[11]

Throughout its past, Dallas' leaders faced a series of pitched battles for political supremacy with a long line of dissenters. In each case, elites ultimately prevailed, but they controlled official memory more completely than they did the city's populace. In place of history, a myth of consensus arose in which a white male elite, ruling for the good of the "city as a whole," created a community "with no reason for being" as an act of macho will. Past acts of political resistance contradicting this story line got cast into an Orwellian memory hole.[12] This Origin Myth justifies a continued political dominance by white business elites and insinuates that African Americans, Mexican Americans, and others directly challenging the city's power structure are embarking on a dangerous deviation from past success.

Rather than dealing with the messiness of the past, many opinion makers in Dallas chose to pretend the city had no history. In 1999, *Dallas Morning News* reporter Bryan Woolley glanced at decades past and found little worth recalling. "Until 1963 and that fateful day in Dealey Plaza [when President John Kennedy was assassinated], the history of Dallas had been a quiet one . . . ," Woolley wrote. "No bloody Alamo battle had been fought in it . . . The cowboys and gunslingers of the frontier era had preferred Fort Worth. Dallas had Bonnie and Clyde, and that was about it in the way of historical drama."[13] The unimportance of the past lay at the heart of the city's self-image, argues Harvey Graff, a history professor formerly at the University of Texas at Dallas. "Dallas has *no* history—*no* reason to exist," he wrote, mocking the Origin Myth. "Residents and visitors are told this incessantly . . . Dallas fears its own past, fears history in general, as threats to its present and possible futures."[14] To Dallas elites, Graff writes, history "suggests . . . an anchor of corpses whose recognition and admittance might drag as a deadweight against the unlimited rise of the city on the southern prairies." In addition,

Dallas remains marked by the lasting trauma of the Kennedy assassination, which "stimulates a desire to escape from, transcend, and leave behind—all of course impossible without real loss and great costs—the city's . . . history."[15]

If city leaders insisted that Dallas' past was an irrelevant, unhealthy impediment to the future, this did not stop them from nurturing a mythology of ceaseless progress. John Henry Brown, a newspaper editor, author, state legislator, mayor of Galveston and then of Dallas, became Dallas' first historian and began this dominant Whiggish tradition in Dallas historiography.[16] Starting with Brown's *History of Dallas County, Texas: From 1837 to 1887*, such "boosters" portrayed the city's history as beginning with the arrival of John Neely Bryan, the first Anglo settler, in 1841.[17] This narrative thus erases some 14,000 years of Native American history in the Dallas area.[18] Dallas emerged, Brown said, when the first Texans conquered not only Indians but Mexicans, "a nation of mixed blooded people, who had been held, for three hundred years, in abject subjection to a foreign, absolute monarchy."[19]

Brown already fully articulated a central feature in Dallas mythology, that whites represented progress and that people of color represented savagery.[20] In the twentieth century, local historians continued to use race as one explanation for the success of white colonizers in Dallas. "The Anglo-Saxon element, which penetrated the North East section of Texas, was of the same strain as King Alfred the Great, who wrote the charter of English liberty, and of the same blood that coursed through the veins of Oliver Cromwell," wrote one Dallas chronicler, Mattie Jacoby Allen. Like Brown, she saw liberty as grounded in whiteness. Allen described independence as innate in the conquering Anglo-Saxons. "These pioneers, who blazed the way into a savage and unfriendly country . . . relied on . . . the physical strength which they possessed, and their own individualism."[21]

Brown's themes were reiterated twenty-two years later by the second major local historian, prominent attorney Philip Lindsley. In his 1909 work *A History of Greater Dallas and Vicinity*, Lindsley described the Anglo conquest of Texas in 1836 as "the reassertion of the inherent superiority of the Anglo-Saxon over the Latin races." The hatred of "oppression and misrule" and "the universal longing for freedom" all derived from Anglo-Saxon racial traits, Lindsley argued.[22] Other early chroniclers, like Brown and Lindsley, crafted most elements of the city's Origin Myth. A fertile land lay wasted in the hands of colored peoples. A group of brave and determined white businessmen took the crude but favorable elements and fashioned from them a meritocracy on the plains. With *Fortune* magazine's publication of Holland McCombs' 1949 article "The Dydamic [*sic*] Men of Dallas," the Ur text of the Dallas Origin Myth, the Dallas Citizens Council (a cabal of business leaders who called the political shots behind the scenes) was transformed into a collection of near-demigods.[23]

Dallas, McCombs' *Fortune* article declared, should never have been a city. Dallas "sat astride no natural routes of trade." Yet, McCombs declared, Dallas was the "Athens of the Southwest, the undisputed leader of finance, insurance, distribution, culture, and fashion for this land of the super-Americans." There was nothing Dallas business leaders could not do, according to McCombs. "Everything in Dallas is bigger and better; the parties are plushier, the buildings more air-conditioned, the women better dressed, and the girls more fetching," he gushed. "And in all of these things it is, finally, a monument to sheer determination. Dallas doesn't owe a thing to accident, nature, or inevitability. It is what it is—even to the girls—because the men of Dallas damn well planned it that way." To McCombs, non-whites lacked any role in making Dallas, as did women, who appear as the passive witnesses to male ambition.[24]

McCombs tells a good story, but it's fantasy. Business demigods did not magically summon Dallas from the prairie. Dallas' early white immigrants found the area ideally located atop potential riches. In 1843, just two years after the town's founding, the *Houston Telegraph and Texas Register* predicted that Dallas "will soon be one of the most desirable situations of Texas, and . . . the center of flourishing settlements."[25] City founder John Neely Bryan built his cabin near a natural ford crossing the Trinity River called Kikapo Trace, which was earmarked as part of a military road the Texas Republic planned from Austin to the Red River. Native Americans and buffalo had so often used the ford that the banks had worn down on both sides of the river. The land readily lent itself to agriculture. Martin A. Gauldin, a visitor to Dallas in 1845, said, "The prairies is the richest looking soil I ever saw . . . This country has plenty of water and mill privileges."[26] Contrary to the legend, from the beginning Dallas was the logical place for an important commercial settlement.

A myth concocted mostly by journalists became part of municipal propaganda. A flyer for a 1985 bond issue boldly proclaimed on its cover, "There is no real reason for a place called Dallas. No harbor drew people here, no oceans, no mountains, no great natural beauty. Yet . . . people made out of Dallas what it is today: the shining city of the Sunbelt, a city of opportunity, a great place in which to live and work."[27] It seemed foolish to challenge an undeniable, almost miraculous record of success, and Dallas oligarchs undoubtedly hoped the myth would head off any challenge to their rule.

The Origin Myth and its believers' view of the past as unremitting progress generally overlooked the high human costs of conquest and development. If this narrative makes for poor history, however, at least it is coherent. It remains a tale broadly disseminated through the *Dallas Morning News*, Chamber of Commerce brochures, and tourist pamphlets. For the most part, even harsh critics of Dallas' leadership accepted that white elites alone determined the course of Dallas history. Non-elites were simply the passive victims or beneficiaries of elite actions.

If McCombs praised the politically prominent Citizens Council as unified and efficient, Warren Leslie, previously a reporter and an executive at Neiman-Marcus, charged in his 1964 book, *Dallas Public and Private*, that the council represented government "by private club." Written in the aftermath of the Kennedy assassination, Leslie's book asserted that Dallas society had a violent, oppressive side, but the author allowed for the possibility of reform. "Nothing in Dallas will change tomorrow, or even soon after that . . . ," Leslie wrote, "[but the] Citizens Council is reassessing itself to see whether or not a business elite is the best ruling group, or whether the good minds of the city, unaccompanied by money, should be asked to supply a conscience to the cash."[28] However, as the closing comments to Leslie's book indicate, he could only conceive of reform generated by the white, all-male ruling bloc. The population outside the corporate boardrooms remained as voiceless in Leslie's nightmare vision as in McCombs' puffery.

Former *Dallas Times Herald* reporter Jim Schutze's *The Accommodation* gives marginal Dallasites a voice but ends up partly blaming the victims of Dallas' racial and class hierarchies for their oppression. Schutze's pioneering work savaged the undemocratic nature of the local ruling class and identified racism as a poison continually infused into Dallas' body politic. So explosive were these charges in the mid-1980s that Taylor Publishing, a Dallas firm that generates most of its profits from publishing high school yearbooks, cancelled publication of the book. In *The Accommodation* Schutze describes the Citizens Council as a shadowy, undemocratic elite that held the city in its authoritarian grasp throughout the civil rights era.[29] By the 1950s, this monolithic leadership, dominated by banking and real estate interests, conceived of a master plan for development of the "worthless" Trinity floodplain. Leaders planned dam construction and the clearing of land inconveniently populated by low-income African Americans. The Citizens Council, Schutze says, hoped to muscle blacks out of the area through eminent domain. As the *coup de grace*, the council planned to convince the federal government to pay for the Trinity River redevelopment in the name of urban renewal.

In order to succeed, this cynical scheme required keeping bad press to a minimum. Elites detested overt racial conflict, Schutze suggests. As for the black community, Schutze's view can be summarized by the hardcover dust jacket, which depicts black and white hands locked in a Faustian grasp. Following a series of bombings in 1950 targeting blacks buying homes in previously all-white neighborhoods in South Dallas, Schutze argued, African Americans made a political deal with the devil. Outnumbered, with "white families around them . . . capable of banding together to murder them," African American leaders reached a decision with the Citizens Council to "live with what was, with reality, the alternative—the accommodation."[30]

Schutze ignores conflict among elites when it contradicts his picture of a Citizens Council in complete control. His Citizens Council is demonic but no less "dydamic" than McCombs' heroic oligarchs. Schutze's portrayal of African Americans as relentlessly victimized practically erases the lengthy history of a Dallas civil rights movement that assumed a dominant position in the state starting in the 1930s. In the 1950s, the Dallas chapter of the NAACP provided most of the leadership and money to fight landmark desegregation cases in Texas, such as *Sweatt v. Painter,* which led to integration of the University of Texas.[31]

If Schutze rushes to depict African Americans as collaborators in their own oppression, he also virtually neglects a key third dimension to the city's racial politics: the substantial Mexican American population. By the mid- to late twentieth century, race was no longer a matter of black and white. African Americans occupied the city's bottom social rung. Leaders of the Mexican American civil rights movement feared that a too-close identification with the black freedom struggle would cause Hispanics' status to sink to a similar level.

In January 1996, Dallas' first African American county commissioner, John Wiley Price, staged protests at Parkland Memorial Hospital, contending that Parkland discriminated against black and brown job applicants. Price's outrage focused on one hospital board member, Jaime Ramon, calling him a "coconut"—brown on the outside but white inside. Price accused his Mexican American nemesis of collaborating with whites against blacks and Latinos. Price himself faced accusations of racism when he held aloft a sign telling Ramon to go "back to old Mexico." Price asserted that Ramon identified himself as white, and he sought to categorize the hospital official as a foreign outsider threatening blacks who shared an "American" identity with their white oppressors. Latino civil rights organizations then led protests calling for Price's resignation.[32]

The controversy surrounding Price and Ramon reveals the persistent power of "whiteness" in Dallas. Racial categories proved fluid, but Dallasites solidly associated success with a white identity. Since Dallas' founding in the 1840s, the uncertain promise of whiteness made to Mexican Americans, Jews, and working-class Anglos proved a powerful tool of division, effectively blocking coalitions for social justice. No historian should assume the naturalness of an alliance of African Americans with Mexican Americans and other marginalized groups that (with the exception of Native Americans) did not endure slavery. The racial bottom line in the United States remains the division between black and everything else. Nevertheless, cross-racial alliances have occasionally occurred, and one should avoid dismissing the possibility of black and brown cooperation. The developing African American conflict with Mexican Americans, Jews, and the white working class in Dallas reveals much about the broader contours of American racial politics.

Marginalized groups such as Mexican Americans won only partial acceptance as white, occupying an uncomfortable middle ground in the city's racial hierarchy between wealthy Anglos at the top and poor African Americans at the bottom. Latino and African American leaders wrestled for the second rung on the city's ladder of power.[33] Population projections prophesied diminished African American influence. The city split into three major racial camps in the 1990s, with 48 percent of the city's population classified as white, 28 percent as African American and 21 percent as Hispanic. Demographers projected that in the first three decades of the twenty-first century the Hispanic population could grow more than four times faster than the African American population.[34] Yet, many Hispanic leaders claimed that the demands of African American firebrands like Price overshadowed the needs of Dallas' Latino community.

In December 1997, Dallas hosted the first of a series of community forums on American race relations called for by President Bill Clinton. Municipal Judge Vonceil Hill drew up the guest list, which excluded members of the white, Hispanic, and Asian American communities. Even before the forum, Hispanic activists aimed their ire at blacks, complaining that African Americans monopolized the local dialogue on race. "There has been only one racial agenda in this town—a black agenda," said Adelfa Callejo, a lawyer and longtime activist. "But that's about to change."[35]

Mainstream Mexican American politicians like Jesse Diaz viewed black gains in administrative appointments at the Dallas Independent School District (DISD) as coming at the expense of Mexican Americans, claiming that "[t]he oppressed have become the oppressor."[36] Meanwhile, many African Americans saw Hispanics as riding on the coattails of previous hard-fought civil rights battles won by blacks. "This is about people fighting for the polluted pie—for a piece of it," school trustee Yvonne Ewell said. "The district didn't provide what black people needed when we were the majority. I doubt it is going to do it now for Hispanics." The dialogue between the two communities often degenerated into name-calling. "I call them vultures," Dallas

NAACP President Lee Alcorn said of the city's Hispanic leaders in a *Washington Post* interview.[37]

Having buried the past with a mythology of progress and consensus, Dallas' leadership viewed the contentious present as comparatively dreadful. Even boosters expressed despair over the confrontational politics of the 1990s. The mythological past provided no model of a city in which quarrelsome, even furious debate could clarify issues or improve policy. The Dallas of old triumphed, the myth said, because there were no disagreements and few factions. Boosters contended that the strife marking the end of the civil rights movement denoted the first stride into chaos as they lost confidence in the future and wistfully praised the undemocratic past.

By the 1990s, Dallasites literally waited for their city to explode. Sordid conflicts between blacks and Latinos at Dallas school board meetings and an ugly February 1993 riot during a downtown rally "celebrating" the Dallas Cowboys' Super Bowl victory made many long for the fictional good old days when the Dallas Citizens Council called the shots.[38] The Origin Myth formerly promoted pride and optimism about the city and its limitless future. Now it became an unbearable burden, a rebuke to the messy present. Longtime *Dallas Times Herald* reporter Darwin Payne best summed up the sad yearning of boosters in the late 1990s. In his history of twentieth-century Dallas, *Big D,* he characterizes the city as "coming apart in the 90s," as if a city that had rested on a foundation of white supremacy and segregation somehow experienced unity in the good old days.[39] "Few [public leaders] . . . valued [Dallas] as something whose whole was greater than its separate parts," Payne wrote of the 1990s.[40] To Payne, the bitter divisions in that decade represented an aberration of the Dallas experience. Influenced, unconsciously or not, by the Origin Myth's privileging of consensus, Payne associated division with decline. As Payne's own books suggest, however, conflict has been the rule rather than the exception in the Dallas past.

The Dallas power structure, in fact, always depended on divisiveness. Skin color split the city, and winning acceptance as part of the white ruling caste consistently represented the surest means of social advancement. Such a system depended on the notion that the black and white "races" represent distinct entities with innate qualities. Harvard biologist Stephen Jay Gould argued that race has no real scientific meaning. There is more genetic variation—deviations in skin pigment, hair texture, inherited disorders, etc.—*within* the arbitrary racial boxes used to divide humanity than *between* them. Since miscegenation has proved as certain in human history as death, war, and taxes and since the purity of each group is a fiction, the definitions of these supposedly distinct categories change each time a child is born.[41] As sociologist Howard Winant points out, "in the United States, hybridity is universal: most blacks have 'white blood,' and many millions of whites have 'black blood'... colonial rule, enslavement, and migration have dubious merits, but they are all effective 'race mixers.'"[42] Regardless of how arbitrarily these classifications are defined, however, placement in a racial category held real-life consequences.[43]

"Becoming white meant gaining access to a whole set of public and private privileges that materially and permanently guaranteed basic subsistence needs and, therefore, survival," wrote Cheryl I. Harris in a 1993 essay in the *Harvard Law Review*. "Becoming white increased the possibility of controlling critical aspects of one's life rather than being the object of others' domination."[44] To be classified as "non-white" in cities like Dallas, on the other hand, was to be assigned low-wage jobs and to have few opportunities for economic advancement. At the opening of the last decade of segregation in the 1960s, non-whites in Dallas County annually earned about one-fourth the yearly wages of whites, while non-white males suffered twice the unemployment rate of their white peers and were far more likely to be imprisoned.[45] Economic disparities along racial lines survived the dismantling of Jim Crow in the mid-twentieth century.

Material motives abounded for seeking inclusion within whiteness. If such racial lines had proved unmovable, living conditions might have proven so desperate as to spark violent resistance by people of color. The definition of racial identities such as white, black, and brown, however, vary over time and by location. Millions of Mexican Americans, for instance, magically ceased to be white in 1930 by virtue of the U.S. Census Bureau, which in its population statistics separated those of Hispanic descent from the white population and placed them in a separate "Mexican" category.[46] Such legal definitions had little to do with the reality of racial categories and more to do with preventing the transfer of wealth from a white master class to a population of color through inheritance by mixed-race children. In Dallas, the flexibility of such categories lent the idea of race special power. The lure of whiteness often left potential collaborators, the city's brown and black populations, at loggerheads.

Drawing inspiration from earlier scholars such as W. E. B. DuBois, historian David R. Roediger utilized whiteness to explain the persistent racism of politically oppressed white workers in America. Why, Roediger and other whiteness scholars ask, do such workers respond to the racially divisive appeals of politicians from George Wallace to Ronald Reagan when their interests are more logically served by forging common cause with blacks, Latinos, and other economically oppressed groups in challenging the privileges of wealthy whites?[47]

The answer, Roediger and allied historians say, is that racial thought in nineteenth-century America defined many immigrant groups, such as the Irish, as non-whites. These immigrants, because of differences in language, religion, and culture, did not jibe with the concept of whiteness held by well-entrenched Anglo-Saxon elites. Many elites, such as in the scientific community, concocted ever more complex racial schemas that categorized southern and eastern Europeans, Middle Easterners, and Asians as not black, but not quite white. Some argued that rather than three or four "great" races, there were sixty or more, each with its own inherent traits. As non-whites, the Irish and other immigrants have experienced their own taste of discrimination, though one considerably less bitter than that endured by African Americans.

As labor radicalism began to rise, these groups, consciously or not, struck a metaphorical bargain with traditional "native" Anglo-Saxon elites. Immigrants would gain membership within the white race provided they surrendered their ethnic identities, accepted white supremacy, and disavowed radicalism. In return, they would receive material benefits such as better housing and schools than their black peers in addition to the "psychological" wage of membership in a superior caste. Yet, immigrant groups paid the wages of whiteness by alienating themselves from possible allies in their struggle for genuine political and economic power.

Non-black workers remain invested in whiteness because of the impermanence of racial status. If a group never faced racial demotion, the urge to embrace white supremacy would diminish over time. Neil Foley, in *The White Scourge: Mexicans, Blacks, and Poor Whites in Texas Cotton Culture*, demonstrates that poor white sharecroppers in nineteenth- and twentieth-century Texas faced the loss of their racial position. Wealthy cotton growers, eager to promote Mexican and black sharecroppers as cheaper pools of labor and concerned over signs of incipient radicalism among white farm workers, promoted the notion that "white trash" descended from inferior stock. Such implied threats of racial demotion give whiteness its power as a ruling ideology.[48]

This book defines whiteness as the creation of white identity. As such, whiteness represents a subjective abstraction receiving a wide variety of interpretations from historical actors. Much of nineteenth- and twentieth-century political and social dialogue centered on the meaning of white identity, on who was white and who was not, and on the ways in which whites differed from other people. This dialogue extended far beyond issues of color or phenotype and incorporated consideration of whether white and non-white groups had innately different racial personalities, priorities, and polities. The fact that individuals defined whiteness in wildly different ways does not mitigate the usefulness of whiteness as an analytical tool, as some historians have recently argued. The debates over the meaning of white identity, as scholars like Matthew Frye Jacobson and Alexander Saxton have suggested, center on the overarching theme of who deserves citizenship in a "white republic" and how that republic would reflect white racial traits.

In Dallas, whiteness represented a merger of physical characteristics and political beliefs. Based on the premise that northern and western Europeans alone were the creators of civilization, this ideology contended that only these peoples and their descendents could manage a free republic. Blackness, in the minds of many Dallasites, equaled savagery, license, and irresponsibility. Most Dallasites fell between the extremes of whiteness and blackness. For those so marginalized, such as Mexican Americans and Jews, social acceptability depended on moving closer to the white ideal. Being white required not just a European ancestry and a relatively pale skin. Race was also attitude. As will be argued in the following chapters, whiteness rested on a steadfast belief in racial differences, support for capitalism, faith in rule by the wealthy, certitude that competition and inequality arose from nature, and rejection of an activist government that redistributed political or economic power. Whiteness was most clearly defined by what it was not: it was not black, communal, or socialist.

Because most whiteness scholars focus on regions outside the South, they neglect an important way in which whiteness evolved differently in the former Confederacy. North of the Mason-Dixon line, the clear racial division imagined between white and black grew murkier with successive waves of immigrants in the eighteenth and nineteenth centuries. This book argues that in Southern cities such as Dallas, Houston, and Atlanta that emerged as independent and international economic centers in the late 1800s, regional identity initially complicated whiteness more than immigration. Only after 1900 did the racial identity of other whites, such as Jews and Italians, become a major concern to the Anglo majority in New South cities.

In formulating whiteness over the past 160 years, Dallas elites held sway, but they did not dictate. Mostly Anglo and Protestant, the city's early elite consisted of slaveholders, large landowners, and merchants. The power of the merchant class expanded when a rail line reached the city in the early 1870s. As historian Patricia Evridge Hill points out, by the late 1800s the city's politics were dominated by unstable coalitions of small business owners, bankers, industrial leaders, and newspaper publishers. These ruling blocs vied with growing trade unions, populists, and socialists for control of city hall. By the mid-1930s, elites formed the Dallas Citizens Council, a clique of real estate magnates, downtown department store owners, bankers, manufacturers, insurance company executives, and owners of utilities and media outlets that for three decades determined who held political office in the city.[49] Wealth and power alone did not grant one elite status, however, as suggested by the exclusion in the 1950s and 1960s of oilman H. L. Hunt or right-wing Congressman Bruce Alger from Dallas' inner circle. Membership in the city's elite also required tempered conservative values that balanced rhetoric calling for limited federal government with the desire to attract federal support for urban development projects benefiting the wealthy. To be elite one in addition had to command a constituency that could successfully push elite political and economic projects and yet be humble enough to accept the collective leadership style provided by the Citizens Council.[50]

In spite of its durability, however, its small size kept the city's leadership class from simply imposing its will: it had to manufacture the consent of the lower classes. Dallas' white elites achieved power through a rough-and-tumble process of cultural hegemony. Dallas' leaders formed a complex and shifting system of alliances to maintain a grip on power. These ruling blocs fragmented, then reformulated, in the face of repeated crises: the loss of the Civil War, Reconstruction, increased regional and ethnic diversity in the late nineteenth century, the splintering of the national Democratic Party after World War II, and the social pressures of the Cold War.

Dallas's leadership class stood on shifting sands. The efforts of white elites to form a permanent ruling structure were complicated not only by changing historical conditions, but also by divisions along regional and religious lines. Residents of Northern and Southern origin fiercely battled over secession, slavery, Reconstruction policies, and Jim Crow laws. Members of the Jewish and Catholic faiths were suspected of having alien racial origins and struggled to win a place among the city's decision makers, with some non-Protestants, such as the Sanger family, winning a tenuous place in the city's inner circle. The city's most prosperous capitalists often depended on middle- and working-class support to achieve their political and economic agenda.

The battle of wealthy whites in Dallas to form permanent cross-class alliances with white workers and the middle class and the compromises forced upon elites by these groups form the heart of this book. Elites created these unsteady ruling cliques through an elaborate, contradictory, and not always successful cultural war of position, the front lines of which included the news media, the pulpit, music, theater, literature, the schools, and even architecture. Elites battled to convince a skeptical population that the interests of the wealthy were synonymous with the needs of the entire city.[51]

In the first two chapters I argue that even before the Civil War, Dallas attracted a substantial number of immigrants from free states such as Illinois. Conflicts erupted between Dallas residents of Southern and Northern origin over race, the meaning of citizenship, and the status of the Union, with Southerners racializing their Northern neighbors as "black Republicans." From the 1850s to the 1870s, newspapers like the *Dallas Herald* accused Northerners, particularly Republicans, of supporting abolitionism and plotting to spread miscegenation to destroy the South. Northerners were deemed race traitors, blurring the natural boundary between white and black, and, it was implied, frequently engaging in interracial sex themselves. As true whites, loyal Southerners defended the color line even to the point of death, the *Herald* suggested.[52]

Wealthy Dallasites of Northern origin briefly ruled Dallas after the Civil War and modified the status quo regarding black civil rights, but soon lynch mobs ensured conformity to the prior racial order in North Central Texas. Upon the Northern surrender of African American civil rights at the end of Reconstruction, elites no longer saw bloodshed as a necessary means of enforcing political control. Like other urban Southerners, Dallas elites worried that pandemic violence might frighten away the Northern capital needed for their city to rise as a regional economic empire. From Atlanta to Dallas, Southern urban leaders reconfigured local memories of the Civil War from a conflict between racial orders to a tragic but noble clash of Anglo-Saxons who achieved brotherhood through combat heroism. "Black Republicans" thus dissolved into the white mass along with Jews and others formerly perceived as outsiders. Whiteness proved unstable, however. Anglos displaced by a new, rising economic order blamed their dislocation on Jews and other new immigrants to the South, scapegoats who suddenly found their whiteness challenged.

Other historians have examined the so-called Cult of the Lost Cause as a means by which the powerful in the North and South constructed regional reconciliation on the backs of African Americans. This book will examine the Lost Cause mythology as it shaped the ideology of whiteness. Studying Dallas provides a window into how regional identity influenced the urban construction of whiteness across the South. The Origin Myth implies Dallas' uniqueness, yet the Dallas story is less important because of its differences than because of its resemblance to the racial drama unfolding in cities like Houston and Atlanta, which also rose as key transportation hubs with lucrative links to the global economy. These cities won over Northern investors by consciously diluting their Southern identities, transforming themselves into economic colossi supposedly too busy to hate and too forward-looking to have a past worth remembering.

Houston, for instance, cut itself loose entirely from its Southern roots and even the planet, as, by the 1970s, its boosters proclaimed it "the international city" and "Space City, USA." In a region where colleges and high schools named their sports teams Rebels or Colonels in homage to antebellum nostalgia, these New South cities labeled their professional franchises the Cowboys, Mavericks, Rangers, Oilers, Rockets, Astros, Braves, Hawks, and Falcons, names that evoked the West, the modern economy, or nature—anything but the slave past. De-Southernization, however, met considerable resistance. Periodic strikes and violent tragedies like the 1915 Leo Frank lynching reveal the deep resistance to the Northern economic colonization of the South and the post–Civil War effort to dilute Southern identity.[53]

In the end, the struggle over regional identity in cities like Dallas represented a class struggle. Southern urban elites finally united behind an economic agenda but left unresolved the battle between rich and poor. A more specifically Southern identity faded in these cities, especially with the end of *de jure* segregation, but this conflict merely gave way to often violent class war, a process which fragmented white identity just as immigration had complicated whiteness in the North.

As argued in the second, third, and fourth chapters, a specter haunted the imagination of white elites throughout Dallas history: a revolt of poor and working-class whites allied with African Americans and other marginalized groups. Elites warned of the dangers created by a radical democracy that gave the masses a substantial voice. The rise of labor unions in the urban South, which elites often claimed sprang from a Jewish conspiracy, added special urgency to the dread of class rebellion. The rise of lower-class "undermen" threatened social chaos, elites warned, and this fear of revolt provided a special theological significance to whiteness in Dallas. Largely lacking in previous studies of whiteness by scholars such as Roediger, Matthew Frye Jacobson, and Theodore W. Allen has been the role that pre-millennial dispensationalism, so important among conservative Protestants in the South, played in shaping white identity for both Jews and Gentiles. Even as they welcomed Northern Jewish capital, Southern elites disdained the rise of a radical Jewish working class. White Southern workers in the early twentieth century often depicted the division between capitalists and workers as a divide between Christians and Jews. Groups like the Ku Klux Klan, which was resurrected in the 1920s, exploited this sentiment, racializing as non-whites the Jews, Italians, and others who began to migrate to the urban South in the early 1900s.

Elites accused these groups of spawning radicalism, while workers often saw them as competition for jobs.

Anti-Semitic Klansmen, however, had to contend with dispensationalists who interpreted the Bible as a prophetic text announcing the imminent Second Coming of Christ and gave Jews a special role in ensuring the establishment of a godly millennium of peace on earth. In spite of the persistence of anti-Semitism among Dallas elites, dispensationalism allowed Jews to be post-Calvary theological heroes. The leading Dallas dispensationalist, Cyrus Scofield, even suggested that Jews could win a place in heaven without conversion to Christianity. Dispensationalism thus allowed Jews, just as they became an economically significant population in post–Civil War Dallas, a chance to achieve conditional whiteness not only in the city but also, as this theology came to dominate much of fundamentalist Protestantism, across America.[54]

This book argues that dispensationalism shaped whiteness beyond altering Gentile perceptions of Jews. Dispensationalism defined Christians and Jews as over and against all other religions, just as racists depicted the white race as over and against a world of color. Whiteness, like dispensationalism, is also a form of eschatology, a Manichean struggle between spiritual and racial light and darkness. Some of the twentieth century's leading white supremacist writers, such as Madison Grant and Lothrop Stoddard, in some ways paralleled Scofield's predictions of a future war between Christians and a literal Antichrist. Eugenicist books such as *The Passing of the Great Race, The Revolt against Civilization: The Menace of the Under Man,* and *The Rising Tide of Color against White World Supremacy* (which evokes images of a Noachian-style racial deluge) suggest a secular analog to Scofield's literal interpretation of Revelation.[55] These white supremacists also depicted history as heading toward an Armageddon in which white civilization squared off against colored savagery. To understand whiteness, one must appreciate the immediacy and drama that dispensationalism lends to this ideology.

Dispensationalism also admirably served the political needs of the Dallas leadership as it shed theological doubt on political reform. Lower-income whites were encouraged to believe that political resistance was not just futile but sinful. Through elite control of the schools, the media, the pulpit, and political institutions, the twin notions of whiteness and dispensationalism entered the common sense of Dallas' workers and their poor neighbors. The remainder of this book describes this hegemonic process.

In response to the pressures of whiteness, African Americans developed an alternative culture that valued blackness and insisted that Dallas live up to its ostensible republican values. Africanized Christianity prepared the black community for a long-term struggle against Jim Crow. Because they did not question the economic system at the root of whiteness, however, such civil rights leaders found themselves ill prepared when the dismantling of Jim Crow laws failed to end racism and blacks continued to suffer economic disenfranchisement.

As noted in Chapters 5, 6, and 7, the civil rights campaign achieved a string of legal successes in the late 1940s and early 1950s, yet Dallas proved resistant to change. White union members continued to see African Americans as a cheap labor source exploited by management to drive down wages. The pressures of whiteness drove a wedge between African Americans and their peers in the Jewish and Mexican American communities.

At the same time, philosophical splits among Gentile whites further paralyzed the city. If fractures among blacks, white workers, Jews, and Latinos prevented the formation of an effective coalition for change, the collapse of consensus in the Anglo middle and upper classes after World War II blocked elites from rolling back already hard-won reforms. A wave of immigrants from other regions of the country to Dallas from the 1940s, coupled with Cold War angst, produced further political fragmentation in Dallas. No group became powerful enough to achieve ideological dominance. Deep divisions frustrated elite attempts to preserve Jim Crow while also keeping civil rights activists from joining forces to significantly change the city's economic structure.

Dallas' racism remained largely invisible to the outside world because of its sophistication and subtlety. The city had no cartoon villains as clearly repressive as Birmingham's Sheriff Bull Connor, and Dallas avoided the troubles that characterized so many American cities in the 1960s. Nevertheless, the divisive power of whiteness meant that African Americans, Mexican Americans, Jews, and labor would have to carry on fractured struggles for social justice that left Dallas as something less than a city and more a disjointed collection of parts. Alienated from each other and divided within, factions seeking greater status, let alone the more chimerical goal of racial democracy, found their dreams drifting into an ever-receding future.

ONE

THE MUSIC OF CRACKING NECKS

Dallas Civilization and Its Discontents

Toward the end of her life, Lizzie Atkins looked back on the days since Texas Emancipation and, despite the abolition of slavery, believed that the African American community had degenerated. The Federal Writers' Project of the Works Progress Administration in the 1930s sent a host of interviewers across the South to collect anecdotes from former slaves. Interviewed at her home in Madisonville, Texas, 144 miles southeast of Dallas, Atkins insisted that something bad had happened to black Texans since the end of the Civil War. Blacks grew lazy, becoming liars and thieves, Atkins said, because "they are mixing with the white people too much, so many half-breeds, and this shows they are going backwards instead of forwards."[1]

Atkins, who grew up as a slave in Washington County, about 204 miles southeast of Dallas, believed that before the Civil War a solid color line existed between black and white. On one side, blackness equaled dignity, honesty, and thrift. On the other, whiteness meant degeneracy. Atkins could not hide her contempt for white people or their culture. In spite of the inequality it generated, Texas' color line allowed a separate black society to develop in which African Americans judged the world and their peers on their own terms. Seven decades after slavery, Atkins saw this separation as natural and miscegenation violated this fundamental order.

Atkins' comments reflect one basic truth. Much of East and North Central Texas before the Civil War had a simpler black-white racial structure. As this chapter will argue, soon after Anglo Texas' separation from Mexico in the 1835–1836 revolution, white elites created a society rooted in the absolute legal separation of the white and black worlds. In order to prevent the development of a mulatto population that might inherit the political and economic wealth of the racial ruling class, white leaders promulgated harsh legal penalties in the 1840s and 1850s attached to blackness. Blacks faced slavery, the death penalty for many crimes punished less severely for whites, and laws defining the offspring of mixed-race parents as enslaved bastards ineligible for inheritance. Whiteness was defined simply as the absence of blackness, Indian blood, or other racial "pollution," although many who were socially accepted as white had been polluted in this manner. Elites hoped that the social superiority all whites ostensibly enjoyed over blacks ameliorated disparities of power and wealth within the white community.

To the dismay of elites, however, frequently severe weather and a cash-strapped economy made life insecure for the non-slaveholding majority. In Dallas, divisions developed along economic and regional lines, leading to outbursts of violence that disturbed elite confidence and security. When a fire destroyed downtown Dallas in 1860, elite suspicions settled on white abolitionists born outside the South. The violence of 1860 created the terrain on which postwar racial ideology developed. Elites labeled those opposed to their notions of race and class hierarchy as uncivilized and therefore not fully white. After Reconstruction, the city leadership embraced a more fluid concept of race in which white status could be gained or lost based on acceptance of elite social norms. This more flexible definition of whiteness, which held dissent in check, shaped Dallas politics for more than 130 years afterward.

The legal division of Texas into completely separate white and black boxes purportedly meant that all white people were created equal. The poorest white Texans were at least not black slaves and could claim higher social status than their servile neighbors. It was just that some white Texans were more equal than others.[2] Dallas' wealthiest pioneer Anglo families saw no contradiction in creating a community in which a few families rapidly accumulated great wealth while simultaneously praising the principles of democracy. Men such as Frank M. Cockrell, son of the city's first business magnates, Alexander and Sarah Cockrell, divorced the concept of aristocracy from anything so crass as monetary wealth. Dallas, Frank Cockrell insisted, developed as a racial aristocracy, with a white ruling class atop a permanent black underclass.

From the perspective of the 1930s, Cockrell admired the culture of 1850s Dallas, where "[t]here were among the women the refined, cultured and accomplished. Socially all on an equality. Merit the only distinction." Cockrell, however, emphasized another distinction: "the adaptability and self-government of the Anglo-Saxon race, characteristic of the Southern people," which made the average pioneer in early Dallas "a very superior immigrant."[3] Cockrell's words carried a particular sting in the 1930s after many non–Anglo-Saxons from Europe made America their home and faced mixed assessments of their whiteness by their contemporaries. Early on, elites like Cockrell portrayed Anglo-Saxons as the sole creators of civilization, a vital first element of the city's Origin Myth. The Anglo-Saxon majority participated, at least theoretically, in what sociologist Howard Winant calls a *herrenvolk* democracy, a nominally free society in which political participation depends on skin color or ethnicity.[4]

William H. Wharton, pleading with Americans to support the 1835–1836 Texas Revolution, declared that God would prevent Texas from becoming "a howling wilderness, trod only by savages, or that it should be permanently benighted by the ignorance and superstition, the anarchy and rapine of Mexican misrule . . . the wilderness of Texas has been redeemed by Anglo-American blood and enterprise."[5] The founders of Anglo Texas envisioned a race-based society in which Indians would be driven out, blacks exploited as slaves, and Mexicans reduced to the role of surplus labor. The state's white leadership shuddered at the thought of miscegenation. "[A]malgamation of the white with the black race, inevitably leads to disease, decline and death," Galveston State Representative and later Dallas mayor John Henry Brown warned in 1857.[6] The Constitution of the Texas Republic adopted in 1836 specifically denied citizenship to "Africans, the descendents of Africans, and Indians."[7] Interracial sex, particularly if it involved slaves, threatened this racial order. In 1837 the Texas Congress criminalized marriage between persons of European ancestry and African ancestry, even free blacks.[8] The law denied black consorts' claims to white lovers' estates and reduced mulatto children to illegitimacy.[9]

Hoping to discourage miscegenation, the Texas Legislature in August 1856 defined the children of mixed-race unions as persons "of color." By law, anyone with at least "one eighth African blood" would be excluded from whiteness and defined as a slave.[10] Such mixed-race persons immediately suffered the same social and political disabilities as African Americans. Both slave and free African Americans could suffer the death penalty, according to a December 1837 state law, not just for murder but also for insurrection or inciting insurrection, assaulting a free white person, attempting to rape a white woman, burglary, and arson.[11]

By drawing a sharp legal line between the races, elites hoped that they secured a greater degree of white unity. This simple white-black hierarchy, however, failed to maintain social order. Conflict boiled to the surface, stoked by a short money supply and inadequate law enforcement. Frontier violence between debtors and debt holders soon threatened the power structure in fledgling towns like Dallas. In 1841 Dallas was born when a Kentucky investment group headed by W. S. Peters won an empresario grant from the Republic of Texas. His Texas Land and Emigration Company received more than ten million acres from the Republic, a tract including all of future Dallas County except for a ten-mile strip on the eastern border. In return for the vast acreage, the company would encourage Anglo settlement by surveying the land, assisting in housing construction, and promoting immigration.[12] Peters could scarcely have picked a worse time economically to start the colony. "Times were bad [in 1841]," wrote Seymour V. Connor, an historian of the Peters Colony. "The public treasury [of the Republic of Texas] was empty and private pocketbooks were nearly so."[13]

Though the settlement grew from the 1840s through 1860, unpredictable weather aggravated chronic economic insecurity, keeping Dallas-area farmers on the edge of disaster. Dallas averages about thirty inches of precipitation a year, much of which falls in late April through May and in early autumn. But residents frequently experience long dry seasons, such as a drought from 1857 to 1859. Historian and Baptist minister B. F. Riley describes the thirsty year 1857 in Texas as hope-sapping, with "water ceasing from the streams, then from the springs, and finally from the wells. Animals . . . died in great numbers . . . The earth was so dry and scorched that crops were a total failure."[14] In addition to harsh weather, the lack of a rail connection particularly hurt the wheat-growing farmers who emigrated from free states and formed the backbone of Dallas' early economy. "[W]heat growers of Dallas county have but a poor market for their staple, on account of their inland location," a traveler noted in a letter printed in the *Dallas Herald*. Affordable real estate also became scarce, with "no vacant lands, and no places to rent or sell at prices which emigrants are disposed to give."[15]

Even as some Dallas farmers feared they would be unable to provide for the basic necessities of life, wealth and power in the state concentrated in the hands of a small slaveholding elite during the 1850s. Those holding real estate worth less than $250 represented about 45 percent of the 1850 population, yet they held only 1.1 percent of the available real estate. Ten years later, the same class declined to only 37 percent of the population, but their share of the state's total real estate holdings fell more dramatically to 0.2 percent. The rich grew richer. In 1850 the wealthiest Texans, the 3.2 percent holding $10,000 or more in real property, owned 43 percent of the real property. A decade later, that class had grown to 6.3 percent of the population. Their share of the state's real property swelled to 60 percent. Accounting for all forms of wealth—real estate, personal property, and slaves—by 1860 the richest 2 percent of the state population held almost one-third of the state's riches.[16] Nonslaveholding white farmers, the largest population group in the North Central Texas region that included Dallas, possessed total wealth of one-third less than the professional class and less than half what their neighbors engaged in commerce owned.[17]

In 1860, Dallas County had 8,775 residents, including 2,888 white adults and 1,074 slaves. Among the white adults, 23.5 percent were born in free states (Connecticut, Illinois, Indiana, Iowa, Maine, Massachusetts, Michigan, New Hampshire, New Jersey, New York, Ohio, Pennsylvania, Rhode Island, and Vermont). Another 28.5 percent were born in slave states that stayed in the Union during the Civil War (Delaware, Kentucky, Maryland, and Missouri). About 33.5 percent of Dallas County adults were born in the Upper South (North Carolina, South Carolina, Tennessee, and Virginia). Finally, 8.4 percent were born in the Deep South and the Southwest (Alabama, Arkansas, Louisiana, and Mississippi). Another 6 percent of adults were born in other countries, and one resident was listed as having been born in the Cherokee Nation.

Approximately 60 percent of white Dallas County residents in 1860 were farmers, mostly with humble holdings and no slaves. Another 23 percent were small producers, merchants, and craftsmen, such as saddle makers, grocers, blacksmiths, and millers, and professionals, such as lawyers, physicians, and teachers. The remaining 17 percent of the working population consisted of wage laborers, such as farmworkers, handymen, well diggers, stage drivers, teamsters, and hostlers. Breaking down the county's 1860 population into nine "wealth categories,"[18] one finds that almost 47 percent of the county's working population belonged to the poorest brackets. Only about 8 percent belonged to the top three wealth categories.[19]

Differences in wealth often broke along regional lines. Birth in foreign nations or in free states corresponded more strongly with lower economic status than birth in states of the Upper South. Nearly half of white residents born overseas or in free states occupied the lowest three income categories. Only 4.5 percent of foreign-born Dallas County white residents and 3.5 percent born in non-slave states belonged in the upper three wealth brackets, while almost 11.5 percent of Dallas residents born in the Upper South belonged to the highest economic classes.[20]

Tennessee native G. M. Record was typical of Dallas County's economic elite, holding $16,850 in real estate and $23,650 in personal assets.[21] George Wheeler of New York represented the typical free-state white immigrant. The thirty-year-old miller possessed only $885 in personal assets.[22] About 21.5 percent of residents from free states worked in such low-prestige wage-earning occupations as farm laborer. Those of Upper South origin were the least likely to be salary-dependent workers (with about 13.6 percent of the subgroup belonging to that class).[23] Leading citizens of the county like Sarah H. Cockrell and William B. Miller came almost exclusively from Upper South border states such as Kentucky and Virginia. With the exception of John W. Swindells, a New York native who published the *Dallas Herald*, most free-state immigrants were shut out of powerful positions in Dallas society.[24] White immigrants to Dallas from the Lower South states such as Alabama, Georgia, Louisiana, and Mississippi were the poorest, with slightly more than half of that subgroup belonging to the three lowest income categories.[25]

In antebellum Dallas County, economic conflict would often be expressed as interregional warfare. Nearly all Dallas residents were directly involved in the means of production or belonged to the managerial or professional classes. Fewer than one-fifth were wage-dependent workers. Nevertheless, the 1860 Census reveals that the county aristocracy largely derived from the Upper South, while the foreign-born, free-state, and Lower South immigrants served as the mudsill of the county's white society. After the Civil War, immigrants to Dallas from the Lower South, generally poorer than their Upper South peers, would be identified by elites as violence-prone "white trash" whose racial status declined as the twentieth century approached. From the ashes of the 1850s and 1860s, a postwar racial order arose in which some whites—poorer and seen as more dissent-prone—became "off-white" and would occupy an uneasy racial middle ground.

Economic insecurity led the earliest Dallasites to embrace violence as a means of survival, belying the city's modern image as an orderly business empire conquering the savage frontier. The so-called Hedgcoxe War broke out in 1852 over conflicting land claims made by white residents and the Texas Emigration and Land Company (TELC), W. S. Peters' investment group. Inhabitants with uncertain title to land feared they would be uprooted, and they organized resistance against Peters Colony agent Henry Oliver Hedgcoxe.[26] In July 1852 a mob of Dallas County citizens ransacked Hedgcoxe's office and home in McKinney, thirty-two miles north of Dallas, as Hedgcoxe hid in a cornfield with all the company records he could grab.[27] Back in Dallas a spontaneous carnival broke out to celebrate the returning ragtag army. The crowd carried William Myres, an alleged Peters Colony spy, on a sharpened rail.[28]

Many Dallas residents found themselves sinking into debt in the 1850s. With the example of mob violence in the Hedgcoxe War before them, the debt-ridden found firearms to be handy tools in renegotiating loans given by wealthier neighbors. The culture of violence that Dallas leaders created claimed the life of Alexander Cockrell, considered Dallas' "first capitalist," who built his riches on the failures of the town's founder, John Neely Bryan. In 1841 Bryan staked a claim on a bluff above the Trinity River, a strategic crossing that today would be the foot of Main Street at the Triple Underpass, thus beginning permanent Anglo settlement in the area that became Dallas. In the late 1840s and early 1850s, Bryan launched numerous unsuccessful money-making schemes—acting as the town's first lawyer; selling powder, lead, whiskey, and tobacco out of his cabin; and serving as unofficial postmaster.[29] By the late 1840s, Bryan sank into depression and alcohol abuse and unloaded his remaining Dallas property as well as his right to operate a ferry across the Trinity.[30]

These properties ended up in the hands of Alexander Cockrell. An illiterate Kentuckian, Cockrell first came to Texas in 1845 as a slave catcher before he made a small fortune hauling freight between Texas and Louisiana. For $7,000, Cockrell bought most of what remained of Bryan's holdings in Dallas, including his ferry concession. Selling Bryan's old lots, Cockrell and his wife, Sarah, who served as her uneducated husband's bookkeeper, opened a brick business, a sawmill, and a lumberyard and planned to build a bridge spanning the Trinity that would replace the slow ferry service. Most Dallas residents did not experience such breathtaking financial success. Some, like carpenter Andrew Moore, owed Cockrell money. In 1855 Moore apparently purchased between $100 and $200 of lumber from Cockrell's mill but never paid back the debt. Cockrell successfully sued Moore for the amount in late 1857. Moore won election as Dallas marshal on April 1, 1858. Two days later, Moore arrested Cockrell, possibly for disturbing the peace. Cockrell was released, and the two men encountered each other again that evening, both armed with revolvers and double-barrel shotguns. Moore, while arresting Cockrell, fatally shot the town's most successful businessman eight times in the lower abdomen. Cockrell died after lingering for an hour and a half, and Moore was quickly arrested for murder.[31] The bloody death of Dallas' chief wheeler-dealer provoked little sorrow. Moore faced trial for murder. Rather than outrage, the subsequent "not guilty" verdict provoked "an irrepressible outburst of applause in the court-room, which was caught up in the streets and made the welkin [sky] ring with demonstrations of satisfaction," according to a contemporary *Dallas Herald* account.[32]

The celebration after the verdict suggests a deep social rift in early Dallas, with Moore's supporters representing an army of the discontent. Indebted whites perhaps saw the inequalities in their society and refused to accept them as natural, celebrating when men of wealth and power such as Cockrell fell. No starker symbol of antebellum inequality existed than slavery. Texas slavery dramatically expanded from the time of Dallas' founding to the start of the Civil War, the slave population growing proportionately faster than the white population. One estimate suggests that slaves made up 13 percent of the Texas population at the Republic's birth in 1836. By 1861, the year the Civil War began, white Texans owned 169,166 slaves, 30.2 percent of the state's 1860 population.[33] In 1848 only 106 slaves lived in Peters Colony, which included parts of present-day Dallas, Tarrant, Collin, Denton, and Ellis Counties. By 1860 Dallas County alone held 1,074 slaves as opposed to 7,591 whites.[34]

As fast as slavery expanded in Texas, some wanted it to grow more quickly. John Henry Brown served as chairman of the state House Committee on Slaves and Slavery. In December 1857 Brown proposed a joint resolution calling for resumption of the African slave trade that had been prohibited by the U.S. Constitution since 1808. Brown argued that the Negro was "indisputably adapted by nature, to the condition of servitude" and, rescued from the savagery and disease of Africa by the white man, enjoyed "a degree of health unequalled" by slaves anywhere else in the world. As long as Texas had black slaves, Brown argued, even the "laboring masses" would not occupy the bottom rung of Texas society.[35] Brown's proposal proved too extreme for his legislative colleagues. The Committee on Slaves and Slavery rejected his resolution.[36]

However desperately elite Texans may have thought they needed slaves, they also feared them. In 1856 perhaps as many as four hundred slaves in Colorado County in South Central Texas plotted to kill whites and battle their way to Mexico. According to some sources, authorities hanged or whipped to death five slaves.[37] White Dallas recoiled in horror in 1852 when a slave woman, Jane Elkins, murdered her master. A widower "by the name of Wisdom" in nearby Farmers Branch hired a "negro woman by the name of Jane . . . to keep house for him and take care of his children." Whether suffering a sudden burst of psychosis, finding herself unable to bear the indignities of slavery any longer, or becoming enraged at an act of physical or sexual abuse, Jane killed the sleeping Wisdom "by splitting his head open with an ax." Jane left the children unharmed. Convicted of murder, she became the first person hanged for homicide in Dallas County.[38] Four years later, a slave named Isaac killed his master, Hastings Dial, ten miles northeast of Dallas, when Dial tried to punish him for being "annoying." Unwilling to endure a beating, Isaac gave Dial "two angry violent blows on the head" with a stick and then stabbed his master in the heart. A posse pursued the ax-carrying Isaac, who was determined not to surrender. Dr. William H. Dial, the deceased's brother, ended the standoff by fatally shooting the slave.[39]

Such acts of resistance resulted in an increasingly repressive slave code. Fearing that free blacks incited slaves to violence and rebellion, lawmakers passed legislation in February 1840 making it illegal for free blacks to immigrate to Texas.[40] Seventeen years later, some wanted to deport resident free blacks. "[A] free negro population is a curse to any people," John Henry Brown warned in a state House committee hearing in 1857. Free blacks and mixed-blood persons had been allowed to remain in Texas, Brown said, due to white "humanity and generosity," but suspected rebellions had proven the policy a mistake.[41] The 1860 Census reveals that Dallas County successfully excluded free blacks from living there. "Free negroes were frowned upon; they created trouble among the slaves," Frank M. Cockrell later recalled.[42]

Elites held onto slavery as the only path to wealth, yet in embracing human bondage they also exposed themselves to revolt at the hands of wrathful slaves and their free black allies. Meanwhile, in the critical decade of the 1850s, pro-slavery elites could not even guarantee the loyalty of the entire white population should Civil War erupt between North and South. By 1860, 23.5 percent of the adult white population in Dallas had migrated from free states. Many Southerners, particularly in the Upper South, and in mountainous regions with few slaveholders such as eastern Tennessee or western Virginia, rejected the extremism of radical elites, so-called fire eaters who demanded immediate secession from the Union if the supposedly abolitionist Republican Party captured the White House or Congress. In the 1860 Census, 34.5 percent of Dallas residents came from Southern states of shaky pro-Confederacy sentiment like Tennessee or slave states like Kentucky and Missouri that stayed in the Union during the Civil War or from foreign nations that had already abolished slavery. Only 42 percent of Dallas' population came from the Deep South states such as Mississippi and Alabama most passionately committed to slavery.[43]

At a time of volatility over land titles and debt, the expansion of slavery in the 1850s underscored the iron link between wealth, slaveholding, and political power. Slaveholders constituted the most grossly overrepresented constituency in Texas politics from the city to the statewide level. In 1850 only about 30 percent of Texans owned slaves, yet these slaveowners represented 58 percent of office holders. The year before the Civil War, the proportion of slaveowners dropped to 27 percent of the population, but they held 68 percent of the state's political posts.[44] Yet, instances of white rebellion such the Alexander Cockrell murder and examples of black defiance such as the Elkins case added to anxieties already stoked by national debates over slavery and secession. The slaveholding class in Dallas grew insecure as the 1850s closed despite their increasing political dominance.

Leaders became more frantic to convince lower-income Texans that in spite of all outward appearances, the only divisions that mattered were the struggles between blacks and whites on one side and the conflict between the North and the South on the other. The attempt to force consensus on slavery, and then on secession, only opened deeper economic and cultural fissures in the white community and hastened the collapse of the old social order.

As the fateful year of 1860 opened, Charles R. Pryor, a part-time doctor who became editor of the *Dallas Herald* (the city's only weekly newspaper) in 1859, worried that the town of 581 whites and 97 blacks could not long remain at peace. Throughout January 1860 the physician and his associate, publisher John W. Swindells, printed lurid dispatches on the evil work of abolitionist fanatics who might incite Texas slaves to butcher whites. Pryor accused Republicans opposed to slavery as having racial miscegenation and slave rebellion as their hidden agenda, a belief increasingly held by the newspaper's readership. One letter, signed "Caucasian" and printed in the *Herald* on January 18, 1860, warned that the triumph of the Republicans would cause the world to take "a step backwards for 500 years . . . Mongrelism, as seen in Mexico and Central America, will become . . . characteristic . . . This destructive, abhorrent, damnable, intermixture of the races, is ever slowly going on at the North—white women marrying black negro men and *vice versa*."[45]

Fires and rumors of fires raged across the state in July and August. Pryor blamed the fires on local abolitionists, thereby aggravating an already volatile atmosphere encouraging harassment, intimidation, and violations of civil liberties against political dissidents. Pryor's readers might think that if there was not an abolitionist hiding under every bed, there was at least one dangerous anti-slavery agent in each county. With Pryor's help, the 1860 fires stoked the Texas slaveholding class' already deep fears and rushed the state into the Confederate camp at the beginning of the Civil War.

Pryor's anxiety boiled in 1859 when, during public meetings held August 12 and 13, Solomon McKinney and Parson Blount,[46] two Dallas County residents described as Iowa natives, faced accusations that they advocated "free soil sentiments and abolition doctrines." A mob gave McKinney, a minister, his "walking papers" and told him to leave Texas for daring to "tell Southern men how to manage their servants." Authorities confined McKinney in the county jail to await expulsion. Parson Blount made the mistake of defending McKinney during the public meetings. Blount requested a place in the jail for himself, fearing he would be in danger. The *Herald* darkly threatened Blount. "[U]ntil he came, all was peace and quiet, harmony and good will," the newspaper said. ". . . He has offended a generous community, who will not soon forgive him; hence, he had better consult his own safety and *leave*." When Blount and McKinney mysteriously disappeared from jail, the *Herald* suggested that this happened through the aid of "the Prince of Darkness" or perhaps "the assistance of outside pressure."[47]

In a county with a more than 94 percent literacy rate among whites ages fifteen and older, Pryor's inflammatory warnings about abolitionist conspiracies reached a widespread audience.[48] All year long, Pryor had anticipated a racial conflagration prompted by Northern outsiders. Pryor's predicted holocaust finally arrived on July 8, 1860, when a fire consumed almost all of downtown Dallas. The fire began that hot Sunday between 1:00 and 2:00 P.M. in a rubbish heap outside the W. W. Peak and Brothers drugstore. Temperatures reached 105 degrees that afternoon, and a high southwest wind fed the blaze, which in just five minutes engulfed the store. The flames, fueled partly by chemicals stored at the drugstore, spread fast as "the fire caught most of us in our siesta," Charles Pryor wrote in a letter to the *Houston Telegraph*. "We barely escaped with our lives—some like myself, without clothes, boots, shoes, or anything else." The fire reduced dry goods stores, groceries, law offices, inns, the three-story St. Nicholas Hotel, and the offices of the *Dallas Herald* to ashes. Officials calculated the loss at $400,000, with a mere $10,000 of that insured.[49] Some of the richest and most powerful people in Dallas, among them General John Good, attorney Warren Stone, publisher John Swindells, and Alexander Cockrell's widow, Sarah, lost their fortunes in the fire.[50] Volunteer firefighters diverted the inferno from the courthouse, although "the heat was so great that the curtains on the inside of the windows caught fire through the glass." When the fire burned itself out, Dallas smoldered, a smoking ruin.[51]

On the day after the downtown fire, a home burned down a mile and a half from town, inspiring gossip about a conspiracy. Men "with inflamed minds, swearing vengeance," gathered at the courthouse, insisting that Dallas had been targeted by arsonists.[52] District Judge Nat M. Burford left court proceedings in Waxahachie to preside over an inquisition held on the fire. A fifty-two-man Committee of Vigilance formed, and their suspicion quickly settled on slaves and their reputed abolitionist accomplices. If the committee kept any records, including the suspects' alleged confessions, these documents have apparently disappeared. The chief source of information on the investigation is a series of letters Charles Pryor wrote to newspapers across Texas, including the politically allied *State Gazette* in Austin.[53]

Pryor's letters instigated a statewide panic about a slave revolt inspired by abolitionist outsiders. These letters told the same story: black rebels plotted to set fires across the state, murder white leaders, and poison wells. At a time when prolonged drought made water a much-protected commodity, the rumor that slaves planned to poison water supplies must have inspired particular terror. The slave rebels, Pryor told readers, intended to commit horrors on "certain ladies . . . selected as the victims of these misguided monsters."[54] On July 28 the Austin *State Gazette* carried Pryor's letter proclaiming the Dallas fire as the opening gambit in a statewide revolution. Abolition preachers "expelled from the country last year" had hatched a scheme to "devastate with fire and assassination" the "whole of Northern Texas." Slave rebels hoped to destroy military targets such as stores of gunpowder, lead, and grain to "[reduce] this . . . country to a state of utter helplessness." The revolution in each county was "under the supervision of a white man, who controls the action of the negroes in that district . . . Many of our most prominent citizens were to be assassinated . . . Arms have been discovered in the possession of the negroes, and the whole plot revealed, for a general insurrection and civil war at the August election."[55]

Blount and McKinney, expelled from Dallas the previous summer, now emerged as masterminds of the revolt. "Bl[o]unt and McKinney, the abolition preachers, were expected here at the head of the large force at that time," Pryor wrote to the *State Gazette*. "We are expecting the worst, and do not know what an hour may bring forth."[56]

The Committee of Vigilance secretly interrogated nearly one hundred slaves, using torture to extract confessions. The inquisition dragged on for fifteen days as eight suspects languished in jail. The brutalized witnesses implicated all but three of the county's 1,074 slaves.[57] By Texas law, all 1,071 suspects faced the death penalty for insurrection and arson, representing not only a massacre unprecedented in Texas but also a potential financial loss of about $820,000 to slaveowners.[58]

Whipped slaves told the committee what its members already believed, that a slave revolution had begun. "One of the negroes whipped became very sick afterward and thinking that he was going to die, he made a confession to his old mistress, telling her all about the plot," a community leader told the *Dallas Morning News* in 1892.[59] The committee already had settled upon three suspects—Patrick Jennings, Sam Smith, and another slave called Cato—as the plot's ringleaders. Jennings, brought to Texas by his owner Dr. Roy B. Scott from their native Virginia, belonged at the time of the fire to George W. Guess, a prominent thirty-one-year-old Dallas attorney.[60] "Old Pat continued to be an agitator in Texas as he had been in Virginia," Dr. Scott's son, Samuel, recalled in 1922.[61] Rachel Overton, the widow of Aaron Overton, a successful farmer in the county, owned "Old Cato," a slave highly regarded by the family. The Overtons owned the first mill in the county, which they entrusted Cato to run. Cato "made all decisions regarding priority" at the mill "and many a fee of 25 or 50 cents bestowed on Cato would greatly facilitate your turn," recalled J. O. Cructhfield.[62] Pryor describes the third suspect, Sam Smith, as a slave preacher "who had imbibed most of his villainous principles from two abolitionist preachers," Blount and McKinney.[63] Smith possibly belonged to rich and powerful W. B. Miller. A fourth slave, also owned by Miller, would be identified as a suspected ringleader as well.[64]

The three slaves found themselves targeted because they in some way offended racial etiquette: Jennings perhaps because of an abrasive personality; Cato because he commanded a position of authority at the Overton mill; and Smith because of his highly visible and threatening role as a slave preacher. Slave preachers figured prominently in previous suspected and realized revolts, led by Gabriel Prosser (1800), Denmark Vesey (1822), and Nat Turner (1831). Texas slaveholders often prohibited their servants from holding services, fearing that religious gatherings merely masked meetings where charismatic preachers hatched rebellion.[65] The committee, in any case, carefully selected its victims to teach slaves the value of subservience.

The panic, however, opened a rift between large and small slaveholders. As soon as Burford entered the courthouse, a man cornered him and declared, "Now, we must vote to hang them three negroes, but it won't do to hang too many. We can't afford it. After we get the three let's call up some rich man's negro and make a fight to save him. If we save the rich man's negro the meeting will not then turn around and vote to hang the poor man's negro."[66] Judge Burford apparently became so disturbed by the proceedings that he abruptly left the meeting after only forty-five minutes. Shortly after his departure, the committee voted to execute Jennings, Smith, and Cato. As already agreed upon, a fourth slave belonging to W. B. Miller stood accused of being a ringleader as well. "Sure enough a fight was made to save him and succeeded, but Miller said the negro shouldn't stay in the county, and he afterward sent him away," Burford said. The committee further decided to whip every slave in the county.[67] With all sides satisfied, the committee announced its decision on July 23 to the agitated mob outside. Jennings, Smith, and Cato faced hanging the next day. Shortly thereafter, "we whipped every negro in the county one by one," a source later told the *Dallas Morning News*.[68] One witness, David Carey Nance, recalled slaves being rounded by "like cattle" and whipped "without mercy." Some slaves were almost beaten to death. The sight of the mass floggings, Nance later said, "made his blood run cold."[69]

All whites of free-state origin now became targets of suspicion. "At that time there was considerable wagon immigration to this country from the north, and the idea somehow gained currency that those Northern people were coming down here and supplying the negroes with firearms and ammunitions," a member of the vigilance committee later said. "People actually held up the wagons and searched them as they entered the town, but nothing was ever found to confirm these suspicions."[70]

On July 24, officials led the three purported ringleaders from the jail to the bank of the Trinity River near the site where the Commerce Street Bridge later spanned the waterway. A gallows, in close view of an "immense concourse of citizens and negroes," awaited the accused rebels.[71] Jennings remained calm and "betrayed no remorse or feeling whatever in view of his approaching doom." Displaying "unparalleled *nonchalance*," he made no final words and died with a "chew of tobacco in his mouth."[72] If the committee meant to terrify the assembled slaves in the audience, they accomplished their mission. The executioner apparently made a mistake tying the noose around Jennings' neck. The slave's neck did not break as intended. Jennings slowly strangled, "dying very hard," as he swung from the scaffolding.[73]

The hangings heralded a season of violence in Texas. Fires causing an estimated one million dollars in damages were reported in fourteen North and Central Texas counties. The accompanying hysteria lasted eight weeks.[74] Paranoia gained momentum as the August statewide elections approached when "the Bailey Letter" was supposedly found near Fort Worth. Reportedly written by William H. Bailey to the Reverend Anthony Bewley, the only Texas elder of the anti-slavery Methodist Episcopal Church, the letter purportedly outlined in great detail an unfolding abolitionist scheme to set fires across the state and murder slaveowners.[75]

The "hellish document," reportedly uncovered by a "most reliable and undoubted source," was sent to the *Belton Democrat,* edited by John Henry Brown (at that time retired as a fire-eater state legislator and yet to become mayor of Dallas). Brown advised slaveowners to "whip no abolitionist, drive off no abolitionist — *hang them,* or let them alone."[76] In response to the circulation of the Bailey Letter, local assemblies called for opening mail to check for subversive literature, compiling "black lists" of Republicans and abolitionists to be hanged, and monitoring suspected traitors for anti-slavery activities.[77] Texas became a killing field where historian Alwyn Barr has estimated that mobs executed eighty slaves and thirty-seven suspected white abolitionists as a result of what the *New Orleans Daily Picayune* labeled "the Texas Troubles."[78] As historian Wendell G. Addington suggested, pro-slavery Texans believed it was better to "hang ninety-nine innocent men than to let one guilty one pass."[79] One Mississippi newspaper editor sardonically described Texas slaves as "dancing to the music of the cracking of the necks of the Abolitionists." This music, the *Austin State Gazette* predicted, would last until the final abolitionist was "elevated on his platform."[80]

By late September much of the fear and passion that stirred over the summer had burned out, and even some ardent fire eaters began to doubt whether a plot ever existed. The *New Orleans Daily Picayune* held as dim a view of "Black Republicans" as the *Dallas Herald,* yet on September 8 the *Picayune* editor concluded that "not half of what has been confessed seems to have been born out by later facts . . . wells thought to have been poisoned . . . [were] untainted by any deleterious substance."[81] The fact that many of the slave suspects possessed guns, a violation of Texas law, was neither unusual nor sinister but reflected common frontier practice.[82] There is reason to suspect that "the Texas troubles" were a series of accidents exploited by pro-secessionists to intimidate their opposition. Many fires reported in the press never took place. For instance, the burning of trash behind the Brenham courthouse sparked a panic there, while a newspaper editor in Weatherford expressed his surprise at reading in another city's newspaper a false report that Weatherford had been set ablaze.[83] Many of the fires that did occur happened in a time of drought that would facilitate accidental fires.

One might question the authenticity of the Bailey Letter, suddenly produced by a newspaper editor who was one of the fiercest fire-eater voices. Why one plotter wrote a letter to a co-conspirator not to convey new information but to review details of capital crimes already under way is hard to fathom. If the 1860 rebellion was authentic, it must rank as the strangest in history. One would have to believe that slaves and abolitionists feverishly worked to set fires simultaneously across the state and then passively waited to be arrested. During the chaos of the 1860 fires, no slaves attempted to seize forts or ammunition stores. No slaves killed or injured whites. No slaves took hostages. No slaves poisoned wells or fired shots in anger. If there was a second phase to this rebellion beyond setting fires, no participant seems to have reached that page in the playbook.[84]

Rather than uncover a conspiracy, the Committee of Vigilance in Dallas most likely ruthlessly exploited a tragedy to pursue a political agenda. The statements of an unnamed member of the committee in a July 1892 *Dallas Morning News* retrospective on the blaze cast doubt on the proceedings. Requesting anonymity and telling the reporter that he voted against the convictions of the three slaves, he claimed that the Dallas fire was a simple accident. "When the town was burned it was a hot day — so hot that matches ignited from the heat of the sun," the committee member said. "Wallace Peak had just finished a new two-story frame building and in the upper story that day a number of men were lounging and smoking." Near the Peak drugstore, he said, were "a lot of boxes filled with shavings, and I think a cigar stump or a match was thrown into one of the boxes, and from that the fire started . . . somebody had to hang; and the three negroes went."[85]

White leaders probably reasoned that mass whippings and hangings would discourage treasonous thoughts should Texas secede from the Union and a Northern army of emancipation march toward the Red River. The suppression of abolitionists also imposed a degree of political conformity during the secession crisis. A virtual civil war ravaged Texas months before the first shots were fired at Fort Sumter, a war won this time by the South. Dallas leaders clearly hoped the sense of danger created by the summer fires would bridge the village's deep social chasms. Elites scheduled a unity barbecue October 3 that would "successfully rally every patriot, regardless of being . . . an Oppositionist, or a Democrat."[86] Hope that oppression could force harmony on the community, however, proved to be in vain. In spite of a summer of intimidation and violence, Dallas fire eaters such as Pryor never completely silenced dissent.

Following Abraham Lincoln's victory in the November presidential race, Texas scheduled a secession referendum on February 23, 1861. Historians usually interpret Dallas County's 75 percent "yes" vote for secession as a solid endorsement of the Confederate cause. However, Texas laws allowed anti-secession voters to be easily intimidated, which makes the number of "no" votes remarkable. Under the 1860 state code, election clerks recorded the name and an assigned number for each voter when he showed up at the ballot box. When the voter turned in his completed ballot, an election manager wrote the voter's assigned number on the back of the ticket. It would be easy to check the number on the voter list against the number on the back of the ballot to determine how a person voted. The law prohibited the election manager or clerk from opening the ballot, but in a county obsessed with treason, it is hard to believe that some secession opponents would not have been frightened into staying at home election day or into voting "yes." Considering the lack of ballot security and the fact that the election came just seven months after the fire and the ensuing violence against suspected abolitionists, the 25 percent anti-secession vote in Dallas County suggests a deep reserve of white resentment against elite policies on the eve of the Civil War.[87] Neighboring Collin County voted against secession, as did most counties north of Dallas. At least 40 percent of the voters in nearby Wise, Denton, Hunt, and Van Zandt counties also voted "no." Far North Central Texas represented the most anti-secessionist region of the state outside the "German Belt" in Central Texas.[88]

Even though most Texans supported the Confederate cause, East and North Central Texas became centers of the anti-secession opposition, with nearly three thousand deserters making the woods and brush of northern Texas home. One historian lists Dallas County, along with neighboring Wood, Van Zandt, Henderson, Denton, Cooke, Grayson, and Jefferson counties, as the South's "Deserter Country." Union sympathizers, called "Jayhawkers," roamed the nearby Big Thicket country of East Texas during the Civil War and fought pitched battles against various home guards.[89] Determined to crush wartime opposition, a Confederate militia swept through Cooke County and neighboring communities and arrested more than two hundred people on the morning of October 1, 1862. After trials by a kanga-roo court, at least forty suspects were executed in Gainesville. Confederate sympathizers there shot two others as they tried to escape.[90] Dallas Confeder-ates joined the bloodletting. A pro-Confederate gang hanged a "Mr. Record" in 1862 "for being a Union man a deliberate cold blooded murder without a mitigating excuse," according to a later U.S. Army report. "Not satisfied with hanging till dead they shot him all to pieces."[91]

The fire and subsequent violence against suspected abolitionists and anti-secessionists suggests how insecure Dallas elites had become about their grip on power as the Civil War began. Traditional elites would again be in charge of the city by the end of the 1860s. Worried that the 1860 fire represented a dangerous revolutionary precedent, Dallas leaders tried to dampen its mem-ory. Decades after the Civil War, Dallas leaders filled the city with memorials commemorating the Confederacy's "Lost Cause." Yet, no memorials mark the prolonged civil war that raged between secessionists and suspected Union-ists from before the fires of 1860 until Confederate General Robert E. Lee's 1865 surrender. Remembering that past could only raise disturbing questions about Dallas' founders.[92]

Late-twentieth-century Dallas proved the power of forgetfulness. Com-merce Street forms a bridge between a downtown dominated by white-owned businesses and, as it crossed Stemmons Freeway, a poorer and mostly African American South Dallas. The city formerly designated a triangle of grassy land between Stemmons and the Southern Pacific railroad tracks as Dealey Annex, named after the family of the powerful publisher of the *Dallas Morning News,* George B. Dealey.[93] In 1991, under pressure from a citizens' group, the city park board renamed the grassy patch of freeway easement "Martyrs Park" in reluctant tribute not only to the assassinated President John Kennedy but also to Samuel Smith, Patrick Jennings, and Cato.[94]

Yet, even eight years after the park board approved a new name for Dealey Annex, no marker proclaimed the rare undeveloped Dallas turf as Martyrs Park and no sign explained the significance of the location or the site's am-biguous name.[95] To reach Martyrs Park, one had to pass under a bridge fol-lowing a pathway smelling of urine. Rather than explanatory plaques, a visi-tor encountered the empty liquor bottles, abandoned shopping carts, and unoccupied bedding that marked the spot as a homeless village. Longtime theology professor Dr. William Farmer once taught a continuing education course on the 1860 fire at Southern Methodist University before moving on to the University of Dallas. He found it predictable that the leadership of the city could not squarely face the city's past. "Dallas is unlike Chicago—it doesn't know about its fire," Farmer said. ". . . It's like a family going through a trauma but suppressing the memory. The past is forgotten, but essential to coming to health is recalling."[96]

The city landscape, littered with statues honoring the Confederate dead, suggested that Dallas had been the southwestern heart of Dixie. A fog surrounds a past marked by clashes between rich and poor and between secessionists and unionists so that in the twentieth century it seemed as if Dallas had been a nest of Johnny Rebs who unquestioningly followed their leaders to the battlefield. After the Civil War, few recalled the dissenters, black or white, who challenged the Dallas establishment, making sustained resistance in the future more difficult to imagine. Dallas elites failed to suffocate opposition through violence before the Civil War, but by the postbellum period, they had learned an important lesson. The long, difficult project of manufacturing consent had begun.

To maintain its legitimacy, Dallas' ruling bloc could not acknowledge past political division. A combination of economic, political, ethnic, and regional tensions, heightened by sensationalist journalism and fear over outside events like the John Brown raid, formed the combustible elements when a match or cigar butt was thrown atop dry kindling one hot summer day in Dallas. The violence unleashed by the Texas troubles eventually proved so embarrassing to one radical pro-secessionist that he devoted only one sentence to the incident when he published his *History of Dallas County, Texas from 1837 to 1887* almost three decades after the 1860 fire. As editor of the *Belton Democrat*, John Henry Brown had published the infamous Bailey Letter. He moved to Dallas in the early 1870s and became mayor in 1885. An amateur historian, Brown published his chronicle of Dallas County in 1887. He barely mentioned the Texas troubles, preferring more comfortable topics. "To recount the more recent events preceding the war, the destructive fire of July, 1860 . . . would be to open a question, the discussion of which should be left to a later day—farther removed from the acrimonies of the war and of the actors in those scenes," he wrote.[97] In the next paragraph, after barely alluding to the divisions in 1860s Dallas, Brown painted a picture of sweet consensus in the following years. "When the sectional controversy assumed the character of war, there were probably not twenty bona fide citizens of Dallas County who were not truly and sincerely Southern in feeling and sentiment," he wrote.[98] This myth of unity rested on a foundation of terror instigated by men such as Brown. The "Southernness" of Dallas could be measured by the length of a hangman's rope.

TWO

TRUE TO DIXIE AND TO MOSES

Yankees, White Trash, Jews, and the Lost Cause

The 1861 Texas secession convention adopted a resolution explaining its reasons for joining the Confederacy. The convention proclaimed that the state's government had been established "exclusively for the white race." Blacks, the convention said, "were rightfully held and regarded as an inferior and dependent race" and could be tolerated in Texas only if they remained slaves. All white males, meanwhile, were "entitled to equal civil and political rights."[1] After four years of Civil War, some state leaders no longer held so certainly to that proposition. Some elites preferred a small number of politically reliable, educated blacks over "inferior" whites.

Before the Civil War, John H. Reagan won election as U.S. congressman from East Texas, including Dallas County. At best an ambivalent Confederate, Reagan seemed to come down firmly on both sides of the secession issue. In 1859 Reagan backed a pro-secession gubernatorial candidate against Unionist Sam Houston while simultaneously campaigning for re-election to Congress as a pro-Union moderate. Reagan served as the Confederate postmaster during the war. After the Confederacy's defeat, he urged other Texans to accept limited reforms demanded by the federal government if that was necessary to keep the pre-war power structure mostly intact.[2] In August 1865, while in a Union military prison at Fort Warren near Boston Harbor, Reagan predicted that Congress would not allow former Confederate state governments to be re-established unless some former slaves were granted suffrage. In an open letter to the people of Texas, Reagan called for "fixing an intellectual and moral, and, if thought advisable, a property test, for the admission of all persons to the exercise of the elective franchise, without reference to race or color."[3] He insisted that requirements such as a literacy test would block most freedmen from voting. The tiny number of blacks earning the franchise, he argued, would pose no threat to white supremacy. He assured his readers that no white men would be disenfranchised.

Failure to grant freedmen minimum voting rights would result not only in continued military occupation but even a "war between the races." Granting the freedmen "their reasonable and necessary rights," however, would "prevent them from becoming an element of political agitation, and strife, and danger."[4] Returning to Palestine, 106 miles southeast of Dallas, after a twenty-two-month prison stay, Reagan found himself disowned by the state's political community. Perhaps many doubted his assurances that no whites would lose the vote due to new "intellectual and moral" tests. Reagan seemed to believe that some whites were inferior intellectually to certain blacks, an ideological break from the entirely race-based biologic republic Texans sought during the Civil War. Dallas' antebellum black-white color spectrum was adding a new shade—the gray mass of conditional whites not thought competent or loyal enough to gain full admittance into the master race.

This chapter examines how discourse concerning inferior whites began in Dallas just after the Civil War as elites used violence, laws, and even theology to crush lower-class mobilization. In antebellum Texas, black skin marked an individual for lifelong servitude, and even the most humble whites occupied a higher rung on the social ladder. In return for poor whites' support of slavery, elites paid lip service to white equality. Elites warned that without black slavery, poor whites might be required to perform the hardest, lowest-status physical labor. This threat, elites hoped, would guarantee lower-class white assent to both slavery and the political dominance of slaveowners. After the Civil War, elites could no longer unite whites around the defense of slavery. Starting during Reconstruction, a new ruling bloc formed that included wealthy white Southerners, their Northern counterparts, and a growing Dallas middle class that disliked the social disorder characterizing the city's politics since the 1850s. This clique maintained power through the early 1900s, assaulting the idea of democracy and suggesting that the white masses were as ill-equipped for citizenship as politically empowered black men.

Immediately after the war, men like John H. Reagan fantasized about the eventual disappearance of African Americans and their replacement by a permanent white underclass. "The negroes will, it is hoped, gradually diffuse themselves . . . many of them will probably go to Mexico, and other countries, in search of social equality, and few or none of their race will be added to their numbers by accessions from other countries," Reagan wrote. Those migrating blacks, Reagan suggested, would be replaced by "the steady and rapid influx of great numbers of the white races, from other countries."[5]

The new white immigrants replacing black slaves were often seen as drudges filling a labor void. The *Dallas Herald* protested against a proposal by some political leaders to replace emancipated slaves with Chinese laborers. "We want neither niggers nor Mongolians—we want white men," a *Herald* editorial declared.[6] The new immigrants, city leaders conceded, would include inferior whites. "The social caldron keeps boiling, however," the *Dallas Herald* said, "and the refuse in the way of the floating population is skimmed off by time, and the congenial elements naturally begin to assimilate."[7] Even as the *Herald* predicted the disappearance of inferior whites, it still conceded an inevitable division in the ruling racial community: "it will not be long before the lines are drawn here, as they are elsewhere, between the educated, refined, well-bred people, and the course, vulgar, illiterate, [and] under-bred, whether either be rich or poor."[8] Just a decade after the Civil War, elites divided the white population into the well-bred and the under-bred, a demarcation with increasingly racial overtones.

The racial desirability of some whites became a central issue in post–Civil War Texas politics. Whatever Reagan told his audience, the former congressman would have been happy if his plans disenfranchised some whites. Reagan complained that "our system of popular government" had been carried to "a vicious extreme" and that "the frequency . . . of popular elections" and "the great number of offices filled by the popular vote" had stirred "an unnatural and injurious public excitement . . . [with] no compensating benefit."[9] Reagan wanted to limit the political influence of lesser white voters. In fact, some former slaves might be worthier of the franchise, he suggested in a letter to Texas Governor J. W. Throckmorton in October 1866. Any intelligence test required of potential voters that "would only affect the negroes, and would allow whites of a less degree of intelligence . . . to vote, would do no good towards securing the great ends we desire to attain."[10]

Reagan's postwar views won few adherents. Following his release from Fort Warren, he received "abuse and ridicule" across Texas.[11] Under President Andrew Johnson's lenient 1865 plan of Reconstruction, former Confederate states could, after ratification of new state constitutions that abolished slavery, elect new governors and legislatures. Once the new governments approved the 13th Amendment to the U.S. Constitution prohibiting slavery, those states could re-enter the union. Texas' 1866 constitutional convention met the president's minimum requirements but ignored Reagan's advice and refused to grant freedmen even limited suffrage.[12] Even without Reagan's threatening ideas, the white working class sensed their social standing had declined because of emancipation. The race war Reagan feared became a reality, instigated by white status anxiety rather than black empowerment. After the Civil War, gangs of ex-Confederate soldiers and "other economically dispossessed elements" roamed North Central and East Texas, terrorizing just-freed slaves, Yankees, and their Southern allies.[13] The death rate for blacks from 1865 to 1868 was 3.5 percent higher than in modern-day Dallas, Houston, or New

York City.[14] Between 1865 and 1868, whites murdered about 1 percent of black males between the ages of 15 and 49, according to historian Barry Crouch.[15]

Union General Joseph B. Kiddoo in August 1866 observed that a "class of men who never owned slaves who have been their competitors in labor to some extent and consequently been their lifelong enemies" had been outraged by emancipation and committed the bulk of anti-black violence.[16] J. W. Swindells, editor of the *Dallas Herald*, happily fanned the flames of racial tension. In 1868, the *Herald* warned that a race-based revolution was brewing, one in which white men, "the lovers of their race, the *natural men* of America," would raise a "loud roar of Democracy" that would reestablish prosperity and absolute power for the white majority.[17]

Violence against Texas freedmen would be just one factor provoking the U.S. Congress to take over Reconstruction policy from President Johnson. Just as John H. Reagan predicted, Radical Republicans in Washington reacted unhappily to Texas' failure to grant black suffrage. The state's rejection of the Fourteenth Amendment, which granted citizenship to African American men, pushed the Republican majority in Congress over the edge. Congress refused to seat the Texas delegation and passed its First Reconstruction Act in March 1867. The law placed Texas under army command and declared that governments elected under Johnson's Reconstruction terms were provisional and subject to removal.[18]

The Congress required Texas to hold another constitutional convention before it could rejoin the Union, with the delegates elected by all male citizens age twenty-one and over, regardless of race, color, or "condition of previous servitude." The state of Texas, the *Dallas Herald* warned, was to be "Africanized." Swindells declared, "It has been a few brief months since the struggle first began in this State for black supremacy. Since then it has made fearful progress."[19] To protest what they saw as an illegitimate electoral process, a large number of Confederate-sympathizing whites still on the voter rolls participated in a boycott, promoted by conservative newspapers like the *Dallas Herald*, of an election to determine whether Texas should write a new state constitution. This strategy unintentionally gave African Americans and pro-Union whites a magnified voice at the ballot box. Dallas County approved holding a convention to write a new state charter by a vote of 521 to 243. Texas approved a new state constitution granting black male suffrage in December 1869, with Dallas approving the new constitution by a vote of 826–47.[20] Unrepentant Confederates then organized to "defeat the negro supremacy sought to be imposed upon them by the new constitution."[21]

The federal government sent military agents to Texas in part to protect the new civil liberties of freedmen and their white allies. Congress created the

Bureau of Refugees, Freedmen, and Abandoned Lands in March 1865. The agency's duties eventually included administering justice in criminal cases involving recently emancipated slaves, regulating freedmen's work contracts, and providing for the former slaves' education.[22] Bureau agents often became the thin blue line shielding freedmen from violent deaths.

One agent, a Chicago native and Union Army veteran, William H. Horton, found the cruelty of some Dallas residents beyond comprehension. On May 10, 1867, Horton arrived to assume his new post as sub-assistant commissioner for the Dallas bureau.[23] Horton discovered that the town's best and brightest embraced common hooligans in order to reassert white supremacy. On August 14, 1867, Corporal Williams, executing an arrest warrant, shot W. R. A. Vivion, an English immigrant who "tho only 22 years of age & quite intelligent had become a fearful terror to the people living near him." Before the shooting, Vivion acquired a reputation for extraordinary brutality in a town already famed for its violence. "One day feeling especially bloodthirsty he swore he would kill a nigger," Horton wrote his superior, Lieutenant J. T. Kirkman. "The first man or person he met was a Freedman. He shot him through the top of the head . . . He made a white boy 12 years of age dance until exhaustion brought him to the ground. Meeting three Freedwomen one day he made them pray get down on their knees & pull grass and eat it."[24] Vivion obviously bullied whites as well as blacks. His harassment of former slaves, however, plus his arrest warrant from the Freedmen's Bureau, made him a hero to unrepentant Confederates. Dallas residents hid Vivion and warned Army officers that they would "resist them to the death" if the bluecoats attempted an arrest. An army corporal found Vivion hiding in the home of J. M. Alderman, one of Dallas' leading citizens. Vivion died in the ensuing shootout. The bloody end to Vivion's short, ugly life failed to stop white harassment and intimidation. Shortly after the incident, "the freedpeople were fired into several times while holding [church] services. No one [was] injured . . . [but] all [were] badly frightened and scattered in many directions," Horton wrote.[25] In 1868 Horton predicted that if Army occupation of Dallas ended, freed slaves "would be slaughtered like dogs & robbed when the troops withdraw."[26]

Unreconstructed Confederates such as John J. Good campaigned to remove Horton from the Freedmen's Bureau in Dallas, alleging that Horton demanded a bribe from Daniel Murry, the heir of a former slaveholding family accused of murdering freedwoman Ann Bell.[27] Horton, fearing assassination, had already requested a transfer from Dallas and was reassigned to Bastrop, near Austin, in Central Texas.[28] The Army may have been eager to placate hostile locals. After receiving numerous affidavits charging Horton with corruption, the Freedmen's Bureau dispatched Lieutenant Charles A. Vernon to Dallas to investigate the allegations. Following the inquiry, Texas Army commander General Joseph J. Reynolds removed Horton from his duties for accepting bribes. Horton responded with outrage and despair, threatening to "blow my brains out . . . The humiliation is too great to bear."[29]

Horton's departure marked the effective end of the Freedmen's Bureau in Dallas and a low point for white opposition to the city's traditional leadership. Later city historians tried to portray these dissidents as recently arrived "carpetbaggers," outsiders who exploited political and economic chaos to win public office and make a quick buck. Carpetbagger Unionists, according to the myth, won office either by buying votes outright from easily corrupted blacks or by promising land in compensation for former slaves' unpaid years of labor.[30] In truth, Reconstruction Dallas was dominated by men who had immigrated to the city before the Civil War and therefore could not have anticipated the postwar chaos or expected black enfranchisement.[31] Unlike mythical carpetbaggers, these Reconstruction leaders had established deep roots in the city. A. Bledsoe, an immigrant from Kentucky, had been an outspoken Unionist in Dallas County before the Civil War.[32] The Reconstruction-era mayor, Ben Long, arrived in 1855 as a Swiss immigrant, part of the anti-slavery, utopian socialist La Reunion colony near Dallas. Appointed as mayor by Horton during Reconstruction, Long would win the office once again, after the withdrawal of federal troops, in an 1872 popular election.[33] A. J. Gouffe, a French immigrant, arrived in Dallas in the 1850s and held stock in the Dallas Iron Bridge Company.[34] Rather than exploitative drifters with little long-term interest in the city's success, these prosperous middle-class men remained entwined in the city's power structure after Reconstruction ended, though perhaps as a contrary minority.

Many Unionists, however, found themselves in danger at the end of Reconstruction. Thirty-one signed a petition in June 1867 begging the federal government to post a full Army company in Dallas for their protection. "There is still a disposition to oppress and intimidate & many a good Union man is afraid to come out openly even at this late date publicly to avow his opinions," the petition said.[35] Horton's successor, George F. Eben, was murdered on April 8, 1868, in nearby Kaufman County before he reached the Dallas town limits. A suspect was arrested, but more than three years later he still had not been tried. The Army appointed William A. Bledsoe, son of A. Bledsoe, as the chief agent for the bureau, but he was so frightened that he rarely visited Dallas. Lieutenant Henry Norton followed Bledsoe's brief tenure, serving from July until late October. Afterward, freedmen and Unionists lacked any protection.[36]

Dallas elites tolerated violence as long as the postwar economy expanded. Before the war, elites predicted that abolition and black suffrage would destroy civilization. Instead, the period after the South's defeat marked the village's most dramatic economic growth to that point, with taxable property increasing in value 324 percent between 1865 and 1876. Reconstruction proved less than revolutionary. Of the wealthiest 5 percent of Dallasites at the end of the Civil War in 1865, half remained in that class 15 years later and one-quarter had moved from the area. Southern-born families wealthy before the war, such as the Caruths, the Cockrells, and the W. B. Miller clan, remained economic elites.[37]

The Reconstruction era marked not an expansion of black civil rights but the wildest fulfillment of white capitalist dreams. The Dallas leadership class in the late nineteenth century consisted of unstable coalitions of small business owners, bankers, industrial leaders, and newspaper publishers. Before the war, these ruling elites' fond hope had been the construction of a railroad line connecting Dallas to major trade centers.[38] In 1870 Houston and Texas Central Railroad surveyors proposed a transcontinental line terminating in California that would miss Dallas by eight miles. A five-member committee secured a route through Dallas by promising the H&TC board 115 acres of county land, a free right-of-way through the city, and $5,000 in cash. With the railroad came the construction of telegraph lines that connected Dallas to the rest of the world.[39] The railroad, the telegraphs, and a new iron Trinity River Toll Bridge dramatically altered the Dallas landscape. In fewer than two years after the railroad's arrival, more than 1,600 new structures were erected in Dallas, including 33 boarding houses for itinerant single men eager to find work in a boomtown.[40]

The railroad brought more than prosperity to Dallas elites. The 1870s economic boom forever changed the town's racial, ethnic, and political landscape. Population expansion accounted for much of the economic growth of the 1860s and 1870s, most of the new population arriving with the new rail lines in 1872 and 1873. By 1870 the population had jumped 54 percent from the previous decade, and 13,314 people called Dallas County home. By 1880, the county's population exploded to 33,448. At the end of the nineteenth century, the town had transformed from a trading outpost to the second-largest city in the state. Population growth generated enough economic activity to offset the effects of an 1873 depression that devastated much of the country.[41] Immediately after the war, immigrants fled the economic havoc of defeated Deep South states. The percentage of white adult Dallas County residents born in Union states dropped from 52 percent before the war to 42 percent in the immediate postbellum period before the 1870s.[42] The population arriving after the railroad's construction, however, had a decidedly more Northern identity. Phil Lindsley, in his 1909 history of Dallas County, noted that of the more than 1.2 million people immigrating to Texas from 1872 to 1876, "fully one-half of these came from what is generally termed 'the North.'" Demographics changed so dramatically, Lindsley observed, that by 1880 five of the Dallas' eight aldermen were Northerners.[43]

These immigrants added an unprecedented ethnic and religious diversity to Dallas. Shortly after the Civil War, a visitor noted, "In Dallas all along Main Street, the shops are closed for Rosh Hashanah. A stranger going by and seeing the shop door closed, remarked that if the Jews ever left the city, nothing would any longer deserve the observer's notice."[44] Jewish merchants like E. M. Kahn and Alexander and Philip Sanger joined the immigrant rush of the 1870s.[45] The Sangers were part of a much larger German colony in Dallas that appeared with arrival of the railroad and dotted the city with beer halls, breweries, and bakeries. The Germans published their own newspapers, held "Saengerfests," or musical festivals, and established separate Lutheran and Methodist Episcopal churches. By the 1890s, a village once almost entirely Protestant now counted more than 5,000 Catholics in its total population of 38,000, and the city's first synagogue, Temple Emanu-El, claimed 125 members.[46]

Increased immigration became a key component of elite plans for Dallas' future, a dream threatened by a continued atmosphere of violence. The perception of Dallas as dangerous threatened the spectacular economic growth. The *Herald*, which applauded "Southern lawlessness" (meaning lynching) as an effective tool of racial control,[47] in an editorial ten days earlier called for harsh penalties against mob action. Texas had become, the *Herald* said, "the refuge of a horde of escaped villains from the older states." Continued anarchy would end economic and cultural progress, the *Herald* warned. Specifically, the Herald demanded an end to "lawlessness under the cloak of conservation of the peace" such as "'vigilance committees' and lynch law."[48] The *Herald*, almost completely silent during the racial violence of the 1860s and 1870s, now described lynch law as "one of the most despicable of crimes" and condemned politicians who embraced it.[49]

The *Herald* celebrated the intensified pace of court-sanctioned capital punishment in the late 1870s and hoped it would be applied to those guilty of mob violence. Writing of upcoming hangings in Gonzales and Denton, Texas, the paper cheered. "This looks as if we are to have law and order again. The next important step is to hang the lynchers as fast as possible."[50] A newspaper long devoted to rabid sectionalism became a mouthpiece for regional reconciliation, recoiling at attempts by some state politicians to inject North-South antagonism into the 1878 gubernatorial race. The paper insisted there was a deep harmony between residents of "northern, southern [and] . . . foreign origin" that politics could not tear asunder. "The people of northern Texas are too thoroughly united, know and respect each other too well to be set together by the ears by any such campaign trick as this," a *Herald* editorial said.[51]

With Benjamin Harrison's ascension to the presidency in 1877, the North surrendered any active role in protecting black civil rights in the South. Across the former Confederacy, elites attempted to cool regional hostilities to attract Northern investment. Atlanta regional propagandists preceded Texas elites in this regard. Atlanta served as the birthplace of the "New South," a public relations concoction of Southern businessmen, journalists, and politicians eager to whitewash the region's tortured past and to convince the rest of the world that the former Confederacy was a safe place to invest. Henry Grady, editor of the *Atlanta Constitution,* served as chief mouthpiece for the new order. A former correspondent for Northern newspapers, the Southern-born Grady tirelessly promoted industrialization and agricultural diversity as a means of breaking the region's economic dependency on the North. He also supported what he considered racial cooperation, ending racial violence and encouraging black economic advancement as long as it occurred within the context of segregation. Praising Northern Civil War heroes like Abraham Lincoln and William Sherman before Northern audiences, Grady insisted that the South had nothing to apologize for regarding its past but still thanked God for ending slavery. Because of this divine intervention, Grady argued, "the American Union was saved from the wreck of war." Such an approach, historian Edward L. Ayers argued, allowed Grady to "have it both ways, to be proudly Southern and yet partake of the new [Northern-funded] industrial bounty." Men like Grady made possible the explosive growth of cities like Atlanta, Dallas, and Houston in the late nineteenth century.[52]

In recalling the troubled past, Southern elites focused on the common experience of Civil War battlefield valor and shared "Anglo-Saxonism." They settled on a plastic racial formulation that partially ignored regional or religious identity. Whiteness would be defined as, first, the absence of blackness, and, second, the absence of a specific culture and identity. Jews, lighter-skinned Mexicans, and others could win at least partial white status by surrendering their specific languages and cultures in return for an amorphous "Americanism." The shapelessness of white identity made its possession more uncertain, while the consequence of losing it remained terrible. As historian David Roediger wrote, "Whiteness describes . . . the absence of culture. It is the empty and therefore the terrifying attempt to build an identity based on what one isn't and on whom one can hold back."[53] If whiteness meant the absence of culture, however, it couldn't be tied specifically to a Southern regional identity. To construct whiteness, regional elites at first had to redefine Southernness.

In post–Civil War Dallas, the city developed an elaborate Lost Cause mythology, abundantly commemorating the city's noble Confederate past. Such memorials and observances suggested that white Southerners were a uniquely virtuous people in a sinful world marked, like the Old Testament Hebrews, for testing by God.[54] Dallas hosted a Confederate veterans reunion in 1892 that drew between 20,000 and 30,000 people.[55] In 1897 the Daughters of the Confederacy unveiled a massive Confederate monument at City Park in a solemn ceremony attended by the widow of wartime hero Stonewall Jackson and the daughter of Confederate President Jefferson Davis.[56] The presence of so many Northerners in the city, however, uniquely shaped the Lost Cause mythology in Dallas. A local chapter of the Grand Army of the Republic, a Northern Civil War veterans organization, formed in 1885 with 250 members and grew in seven years to 2,000 members statewide, most of whom lived in the East and North Central sections of the state. These former Union soldiers made their large presence felt at the city's war commemorations.[57] Paradoxically, the Lost Cause civil religion promoted regional reconciliation across the South. Lost Cause observances, Dallas elites carefully pointed out, were made "in no spirit of sectionalism."[58] A "good and fraternal feeling" existed between the "old soldiers of the late war," one observer claimed.[59] Confederate veterans invited their Union peers to participate in the 1897 unveiling of the Confederate Memorial, a ceremony in which "Texas flags and tattered, worn Confederate flags, and the flag of 'Old Glory,' waved together in patriotic harmony," as Phil Lindsley noted.[60]

Union and Confederate veterans shared a heritage of bravery, Union veteran Col. W. D. Wylie told the assembled crowd at the city's 1887 Memorial Day observance. "To-day we have no North, no South, no East, no West, but one common country, one common object, i.e. the paying tribute to our heroic dead," Wylie said.[61] In Dallas, Civil War commemorations honored not only Southern icons like Robert E. Lee, but Northern heroes as well. "I rejoice that a reunited people speak of [Northern Civil War President Abraham] Lincoln in words of blessing," Colonel W. L. Crawford, a Confederate veteran, said at an 1890 Memorial Day gathering. ". . . As we look to Lincoln let us remember every kind and generous act he did—that greatest of great men."[62] Echoing the sentiments of Henry Grady, men like Crawford argued that the North had acted as an instrument of divine will and saved the South from the onus of slavery. Although Southern slavery had been benign and uplifting for blacks, the mythology insisted, it had been a terrible financial and emotional burden on Southern whites. By abolishing slavery, the North allowed for the development of a Southern white working class and a more perfect and complete racial separation. "Slavery abolished, I rejoice with you in these things," Crawford, a former soldier from Texas, said at the 1890 rally. ". . . [W]e are thankful that [from the war] . . . came . . . a higher salvation—a better promise than the man who participated in it ever dreamed of."[63] The Lost Cause cult maintained that the tragedy of the Civil War was that Anglo-Saxons had butchered each other over the slavery issue, a slaughter instigated by abolitionist fanatics portrayed as cynical, alien outsiders exploiting the kindness some whites felt toward slaves. Northerners and Southerners now knew they could live in harmony if only Northerners conceded the wisdom of Southern policies regarding the "Negro problem."

Events in Dallas reflected a larger trend across the new urban South. The explosive economic growth of some Southern cities in the late nineteenth century and early twentieth century seemed to confirm the wisdom of the Lost Cause priesthood. Easing regional tensions opened the way for the federal government to dig a ship channel through Galveston Bay and Buffalo Bayou, a project that culminated in the 1914 opening of the Houston Ship Channel. Houston became one of the top three deep-water ports in the United States, which tied the city fast to the world economy, especially as Texas rose as a major oil supplier. By the early twentieth century Houston was on its way to becoming one of the world's wealthiest cities. As would happen in Dallas, even as its economy became more complex, Houston and the Texas coast became a magnet for Northern capital and for immigrants from the Deep South and Europe. Poles, Sicilians, Jews, and "white trash" added complexity to Houston's hierarchy. As the economy expanded, class conflict intensified and Anglo workers asserted racial privilege over their off-white competitors.[64]

In their enthusiasm to remake Atlanta as the capital of the New South, residents there leveled the four hundred antebellum homes and buildings left behind by General William Tecumseh Sherman's torch-bearing troops at the end of the Civil War. The city would eventually strike some as so unlike Dixie that one Southern writer, John Shelton Reed, commented, "Every time I look at Atlanta, I see what a quarter million Confederate soldiers died to prevent." Atlanta was a key railway junction before the war, and after it, Atlantans ruthlessly plowed over the Confederate past to transform the city into a Southern metropolis. By the beginning of the twentieth century, Atlanta was the intersection of eleven key railroads, a distribution center between the Tennessee Valley and the East Coast, a regional banking center, and home to at least one soon-to-be international business, the Coca-Cola Company. As in Dallas, the new architecture in Atlanta seemed completely cut from its geographic moorings. Atlanta elites, like their Dallas peers, tirelessly erased evidence of past racial conflict, promoting their overgrown town as a city "too busy to hate."[65] This urban makeover drew both Northern immigrants and Northern money to the "Gateway City." Industrialization and population growth narrowed the poverty gap between North and South. In 1900 per capita income in the South was half of the national average. At the start of World War II four decades later, Southern per capita income had climbed to two-thirds the national average.[66]

African Americans found themselves the chief victims of this North-South reconciliation. Northern and Southern whites shared a racial identity and the common interest of keeping blacks in their place, the Lost Cause priesthood proclaimed. Speaking in Texas to a mixed crowd of Northern and Southern war veterans, W. L. Crawford declared, "We are no longer Federals and Confederates. We are the mightiest race of people into whose hands the God of the inevitable ever gave control of the destinies of nation or men, wrung from the Anglo-Saxon, Norman and Celts—a people born to rule wherever they may be domiciled . . . We are to-day the superior of the earth."[67]

As a man born north of the Mason-Dixon line who fought in the Confederate Army and then served as pastor at a church associated with a mostly Northern membership, no prominent Dallas figure better embodies elite efforts to forge a common Northern and Southern whiteness than the Reverend Cyrus Ingerson Scofield. A man of shaky theological credentials, Scofield nevertheless emerged as the city's most important cultural innovator. Scofield not only paved the way to regional reconciliation in Dallas: with his multimillion-selling *Scofield Reference Bible,* he transformed relations between fundamentalist Christians and Jews throughout the United States while providing a reactionary counterbalance to the Populist and Progressive movements dominating political debates in the late 1800s and early 1900s.[68]

Born about fifty miles southwest of Detroit, Michigan, on August 19, 1843, Scofield moved to live near two older sisters and a brother-in-law in Lebanon, Tennessee, thirty miles east of Nashville, in early 1861.[69] At the outbreak of the Civil War, the seventeen-year-old joined the Seventh Tennessee Infantry Regiment for a one-year hitch, entering and leaving the Confederate Army as a private.[70] After the war, Scofield married Leontine Cerre, the youngest daughter of a prominent French Catholic family in St. Louis. He earned a law license, and his in-laws helped him land employment in a Kansas firm headed by John J. Ingalls, later elected to the U.S. Senate. Riding Ingalls' coattails, Scofield won two one-year terms to the Kansas state legislature and, through Ingalls' patronage, earned appointment as a U.S. district attorney in 1873. Scandal plagued Scofield, and he resigned as district attorney in December 1873 after only six months on the job. Kansas newspapers charged that Scofield accepted bribes from railroads, stole political contributions meant for Ingalls, and secured bank promissory notes by forging signatures.[71]

His wife, Leontine, filed for divorce.[72] Scofield said he soon thereafter converted to Christianity under the influence of James Brooks, a believer in a dispensationalist theology that emphasized the prophetic nature of the Bible and taught that a literal Second Coming of Christ loomed in the immediate future. Scofield won a post as acting YMCA secretary in St. Louis before being invited to serve as pastor of the struggling First Congregational Church in Dallas in October 1882.[73] Though Scofield received only spotty theological training,[74] he became one of the most influential preachers in the nineteenth and twentieth centuries.

The Congregationalist Church was a tiny flock that rode into Dallas with the post-railroad 1870s immigration wave. Eleven of the seventeen original members claimed Northern origin. The Dallas Congregationalists first organized in 1876 but suffered from a serious public relations problem as their denomination was associated with the famous Northern pre-war abolitionist Henry Ward Beecher.[75] Even though Scofield was not yet ordained, the Congregationalists enthusiastically gave the Confederate veteran a chance at the pulpit.[76] As word of his wartime record spread, Scofield acquired social standing.[77] He pleaded for North-South reconciliation, and on one Memorial Day in Dallas, a Confederate veterans group and the Grand Army of the Republic separately invited him to speak. Scofield addressed both groups simultaneously and received an enthusiastic response.[78]

His Confederate credentials established, Scofield built a growing church and won followers through door-to-door evangelism. Always conscious of image, Scofield further enhanced his status by claiming the title "Dr. Scofield, D.D. [doctor of divinity]" in the early 1890s, although there is no record of an advanced degree from any college of university at his church's archives.[79] Scofield drew one of the most powerful families in Dallas, the Dealeys, to his congregation. In 1885 the A. H. Belo Corporation, owners of the *Galveston News,* opened the *Dallas Morning News.* The *Morning News* quickly bought and absorbed the *Dallas Herald* and became the dominant newspaper in the city.[80] The *News'* business manager, George Bannerman Dealey, identified himself as a Presbyterian most of his life, but other Dealeys, including his father (also named George), filled the pews of the First Congregational Church and served as officers and fund-raisers.[81] Scofield's persuasiveness, plus his friendship with wealthy members, spurred the church's growth. Membership grew from 16 resident members in 1882, his first year as pastor, to 465 twelve years later.[82]

Scofield grounded his theology in "pre-millennial dispensationalism," the core of which is that "the course of history, and the sequence of events that will herald the end of the world, are foretold in the Bible."[83] The scriptures, Scofield said, divide time into seven "dispensations" marked by some change in God's method of dealing with mankind. For instance, under the "Man Innocent" dispensation during which Adam and Eve lived in Edenic bliss, they failed to follow the commandment to "abstain from the fruit of the tree of knowledge of good and evil" and were expelled from paradise. "Each of the Dispensations may be regarded as a new test of the natural man, and each ends in judgment—marking his utter failure," Scofield wrote.[84]

The modern age, Scofield argued, represents the "Church Age," the sixth and penultimate stage of history. The Christian church, evangelizing since Jesus' return to heaven nearly 2,000 years earlier, has failed to save the human race from sin. End-time events would begin when Jesus "raptures" his church, whisking the saved into the clouds so they might escape the horrors of the coming "Tribulation." Jews would return to Palestine to establish a modern state of Israel, Scofield predicted. The Gentile nations of the earth would unite under an Antichrist, a world dictator determined to defeat God's plan for salvation by destroying the Jews. Under the reign of the Antichrist, Scofield promised, millions will die and the earth will suffer vast ecological devastation. The Antichrist's armies will gather in the Middle East to complete the annihilation of the Jewish nation, but before this happens, 144,000 surviving Jews will convert to Christianity. Jesus and his raptured followers will miraculously return to save these converts and destroy the "princes of the Earth" in a final battle of Armageddon. Christ will then begin an earthly reign of 1,000 years, followed by a final Judgment Day and the creation of a new heaven and earth.[85]

In Dallas, anxieties generated by social dislocation made Scofieldism particularly attractive. Dispensationalism neatly divided the world into those aligned with Christ and those in thrall to the Antichrist.[86] This Manichean viewpoint heightened a sense of identity for Scofield's flock just at a time when the chronic fears wrought by industrialism—unemployment, inflation and recession—aggravated anxieties and alienation. In spite of Scofield's theological conservatism, his sermons reflected the terrors of the industrial age. "Business is organized on a vast scale; the unit counts for nothing—the mass for everything," he observed in one sermon. "The hours of the day are not enough for toil, business burns up the nights as well. God's rest day is ruthlessly appropriated; men are worn out, burnt out rather, and left behind without thought or mercy."[87] Scofieldism spread as it offered both empathy for the working class and support for elite values.

Scofield built largely on the work of predecessors such as early-nineteenth-century theologian John Darby, but he was dispensationalism's most successful popularizer. His influence extended far beyond Dallas and the South, reshaping Protestant fundamentalism, its relationship to progressive political reform, and its attitude toward Jews. His dispensationalist reading of prophecy reached a broad audience through his masterwork, the *Scofield Reference Bible*. Published in 1909, the Scofield Bible supplemented the King James translation with explanatory footnotes and suggested cross-references for related verses. Although annotated English-language Bibles date back to the seventeenth century, no version of the Bible so completely entwined the editor's doctrinal interpretations with the biblical text, a technique that made Scofield's theological pronouncements appear as part and parcel of Holy Writ. Scofield's Bible, which replaced archaic phrases with more modern English, became one of the twentieth century's most popular versions and saved its publisher, Oxford University Press, from bankruptcy during the Great Depression of the 1930s.[88]

The Scofield Bible may have exceeded 10 million copies sold before the release of a revision in 1967. The revision sold another 2.5 million copies by 1990. A religion scholar characterized the Scofield Bible as "perhaps the most important single document in all fundamentalist literature." Middle-class Baptist and Presbyterian congregations became, as historian Paul Boyer puts it, "bastions of pre-millennialism." In many fundamentalist Protestant congregations, ministers found themselves measured by a Scofield yardstick and found their careers threatened if they ventured too far from this new orthodoxy.[89] The Dallas Theological Seminary became a center of dispensationalist teaching, with graduate Hal Lindsey writing the nonfiction best-seller of the 1970s, the Scofield-inspired *The Late Great Planet Earth*, which registered 28 million in sales by 1990.[90]

Scofield saw the march of history not as a tale of progress but as a long slide into faithlessness and degeneration. History would end "not as some would have us believe, by the gradual process of evolution, lifting the race higher and higher . . . but in sudden and awful ruin."[91] Preaching in an age of middle-class Progressivism, Scofield urged his followers to place no faith in politics. "The true mission of the church is not the reformation of society," he declared. "What Christ did not do, the Apostles did not do. Not one of them was a reformer."[92] To put faith in political activism was to lack faith in God. "When Christ was on earth all the social problems—slavery, intemperance, prostitution, unequal distribution of wealth, oppression of the weak by the strong—were at their worst," Scofield argued. "To cure them He put into the world one message—the gospel, one means—regeneration, one agency—

the Holy Spirit in the church."[93] Genuine, permanent reform could come only with the establishment of Christ's kingdom on earth. All else was satanic delusion. Scofield compared human civilization to the *Titanic*, the famed vessel that sank in the North Atlantic in 1912: "we're all on a doomed ship; but that God and his mercy had brought a life boat alongside that would hold us all."[94]

Scofieldism served the political and racial status quo admirably. As an industrial order rose in Dallas, Scofieldism blunted class conflict, urging the poor to wait for justice in the sweet by-and-by. At a time when Dallas-ites feared the political mobilization of dissenters, working-class whites, and blacks, Scofield offered a theology that was implicitly antidemocratic. The Antichrist, Scofield argued, would achieve power through his persuasive guile by deceiving the masses into supporting his rule. Democracy and a free but morally corrupt press would become vehicles through which the Antichrist would reign.[95] In contrast, dispensationalists celebrate Christ's millennium rule as "absolute in its authority and power."[96] In his *Scofield Reference Bible*, the Dallas minister referred sarcastically to "popular will, fickle and easily moulded."[97] Constitutional liberties, in any case, could not free anyone from the slavery of sin.

Scofieldism's rejection of political activism also signaled a rejection of the social experimentation of the Reconstruction era. In terms of racial ideol-ogy, Scofield largely reflected conventional white attitudes. Men, he said, were born into an "invisible net" created in part by "race predisposition [and] . . . race habit."[98] The *Scofield Reference Bible* implied that blacks were the descendents of Noah's son Ham, who was cursed after the flood for disre-specting his father. From Ham, Scofield wrote, descended an "inferior and servile posterity."[99] Black subordination was a fulfillment of Ham's curse, an interpretation Scofield echoed.[100] Scofield laughed at the efforts of whites like Massachusetts Senator Charles Sumner, a pre-war abolitionist, who made an "annual attempt to enact a law to abolish the distinction made by God Almighty between black and white."[101] Black social inferiority was the will of God, Scofield apparently believed.

If Scofield reinforced white attitudes toward African Americans, his big-gest innovation came with his views on Jews. Here the conservative Scofield was truly revolutionary. Scofield worked to replace traditional Christian anti-Semitism with an aggressive philo-Semitism. Scofield's worldview gave mod-ern Jews a pivotal role in God's plan of salvation and even conceded Jews a path to salvation outside of Christianity. In so doing, Scofield paved a way for Jews to achieve conditional whiteness. This innovation came when immi-gration made Jews more visible within Dallas' population, with many leaders such as the Sangers and the Marcus family playing integral roles as part of the city's rising merchant class. These Jewish "Merchant Princes," as author Leon Harris describes them, brought to Dallas a global view of trade that would further expand the city's economy. Dallas' new Jewish merchant class soon became too valuable to keep on the fringes. Dallas leaders wrestled with long-standing Gentile fears of Jews to find a way to enfold them in the banner of whiteness.[102]

By the late nineteenth century and early twentieth century, Jewish white-ness emerged as one of the central racial controversies in the North. The rela-tively small number of African Americans north of the Mason-Dixon line and the Northern political surrender on Reconstruction meant that, for a time, black-white relations receded in importance to Northern white elites. Jews, however, represented part of a mass wave of Southern and Eastern European immigrants whose language, religion, and culture represented a challenge to Anglo Protestant hegemony. Ivy League professors, New England political patricians like Henry Cabot Lodge, and much of the Northern press declared that Jews, accused as carriers of the socialist virus while also ironically blamed for lowering Gentile wages, were intellectually inferior, had congenitally un-trustworthy characters and were inherently incapable of upholding demo-cratic institutions. Though the verdict among Northern Anglo elites was by no means unanimous, many declared Jews members of a distinct "Oriental" race incapable of assimilation. Jews received much less focus in the South, not only because fewer Jews lived there but also because the implementa-tion of Jim Crow laws seemingly divided the region into two clearly marked categories—black and white. In the South, unlike the North, no population seemed evident between the white/black polarities. Many Southern Jews de-cided that, given the onerous liabilities of blackness, no sane alternative to claiming a white identity existed. Many Jews achieved probationary whiteness by serving in the Confederate Army or by practicing or defending segrega-tion. Most Southern Jews who disapproved of anti-black racism kept quiet. Not all Southern Jews played this game, and some vocally supported Afri-can American civil rights. In any case, whether they were collaborators with or opponents to their Southern Gentile peers on racial issues, Jews even-tually would face questions about their whiteness in the South as growing Jewish immigration became entwined with the controversy over Southern industrialization.[103]

By the time European Jews first encountered Anglo Gentiles in Texas, Christians there had constructed a split image of the Jewish community. The "good Jews" of the Old Testament who brought the Ten Commandments to the world vied for prominence in Christian imagination with the "bad

Jews" who crucified Jesus and grubbed for money.[104] In an 1853 edition, the *Austin State Gazette* reprinted an editorial from the *Congressional Journal* that asked how Jews survived in a hostile world. Amid their sufferings, the editorial warned, Jews became an invincible force. "In money power the Jews hold in their hands the destiny of kingdoms and empires, whose governments become bankrupt and their sovereigns turn beggars at a Hebrew's nod," the writer commented. Texas anti-Semites mixed the fear of alleged Jewish power with awe at what appeared to be the divine favor Jews enjoyed. Jews, the editorial concluded, were a "race so indomitable, so imperishable" that they "must have been raised up and preserved for some grand purpose."[105]

Dallas Jews stood on a precipice, not sure if their Gentile neighbors saw them as the monotheistic Old Testament heroes slaying Philistines or the mythical Christ-killers. From the time the first Jewish resident, dry goods warehouse owner Alexander Simon, settled in Dallas in the 1850s, the city's Jewish residents presented themselves as the "good Jews" of the Bible. Jewish immigrants freely used the term "Hebrew" to evoke memories of heroic Old Testament patriarchs in naming their civic organizations, such as the Dallas Hebrew Benevolent Association, founded in 1872, or the Young Men's Hebrew Association, an answer to the Young Men's Christian Organization, formed in 1879.[106] Dallas Jews embraced cultural assimilation to win acceptance. German Jews like the Sangers adopted the more Westernized Reform movement of Judaism, which bridged considerable distance between the two cultures.[107] Classical Reform Judaism defines Jews as members of a common religion, not of a race or nationality, thus mitigating separatism. At Dallas' Congregation Emanu-El, Reform Jews followed Southern Protestant patterns of religious practice. The temple resembled a church, services incorporated English, and the term "minister" was used interchangeably with "rabbi." Such religious assimilation characterized American Judaism from the time of the American Revolution. American Jews rarely spoke Hebrew, and as a result, across North America services often strikingly resembled Protestant gatherings. Dallas only represents an extreme.[108]

However assimilated, Dallas Jews did not seek invisibility but made their mark as joiners. At the start of the 1870s, all seventeen of the city's Jewish males enrolled as volunteer firefighters.[109] When yellow fever struck the area along the Texas-Louisiana state line in 1873, the city's growing Jewish community raised $1,000 to help the epidemic's victims in Shreveport, Louisiana. "They open their purses and give to the extent of their means, never inquiring whether their contributions are destined for the relief of Jew or Gentile," the *Dallas Herald* marveled.[110] Dallas Jews were rewarded for their civic-mindedness by winning a broad level of acceptance. Although Jews constituted less than 5 percent of the city's population, five Jews, all from the merchant class, were elected aldermen between 1873 and 1905.[111]

Jewish weddings in Dallas became front-page news, with Gentile writers bubbling with adjectives to capture the elegant flavor. The *Dallas Daily Herald* described a reception for Dallas merchant E. M. Kahn and his bride as "one of the grandest and most brilliant" society events with "nothing undone to make it a magnificent success," the hall "brilliantly lighted," and "the whole scene conspiring to render an effect as beautiful and charming as fairy land."[112] Wealthy nineteenth-century Jewish society mirrored the fantasy cosmopolitan future desired for Dallas by Gentile elites. The "good Jew" of Dallas— always loyal, generous, and supportive of the local leadership's policies and priorities—would be welcome as long as he conformed to narrow, stereotyped expectations. Jews were accepted, not as part of the Anglo-Saxon ruling bloc, but only as closely related cousins of the master race.

Jews assimilated not only culturally but also politically. It did not hurt the Sanger family that brothers Isaac, Lehman, and Philip had served in the Confederate Army.[113] Yet, even while some supported the South in its defense of slavery, Jews remained oddities to the Christian community, a comic people separated by anachronistic custom. T. R. Burnett in his poem "Story of a Ham," distributed at the 1888 State Fair in Dallas, depicted a fictional "single lonely Jew," Jacob Joses, as "true to Dixie and to Moses." In spite of being "full of zeal" and "always true" to the Confederate colors, "Jewy Jake" remains an outsider who "maintains his Jewish fashions/And will not eat all kinds of rations." After getting lost, a hungry Jake happens upon a smokehouse. "And through a handy crack e-spying,/A luscious ham he saw there lying," Burnett, fascinated by Jewish difference, continues in his clumsy verse. Jake the Jew nearly succumbs to unfaithfulness, almost violating his dietary code. "He tried to think of Moses' law/But had a cramping in his craw: O ham, thou almost (mouth a twisten')/ Persuadest me to be a Christian!"[114] Jake's observance of Old Testament edict marks him as impractical and superstitious, an outsider not quite white in spite of his wearing the Confederate gray.

Many Christians thought that only those who accepted Jesus as the son of God would reach heaven. Jewish rejection of Christ's messianic role left these ancient promoters of monotheism as heathen outsiders. Here, Cyrus Scofield played his most important role in helping Jews acquire higher racial status. Scofield, like other Christians, saw Jews as separate from the white community but felt this made them a "little nation which has ever had the strongest marks of race distinction and race peculiarity."[115] This segregation, he argued, resulted from a divinely inspired unique Jewish role in history. "Their history alone is told in Old Testament narrative and prophecy—other peoples being mentioned only as they touch the Jew," Scofield wrote.[116] Jews acted as "a trouble to the Gentile, yet witnessing to them; cast out by them, but miraculously preserved."[117] Anti-Semitism, to Scofield, was a sin and the prelude to divine retribution. "When [God] . . . comes back, it is first of all for their [Jews'] deliverance; then, for the judgment of the Gentiles according to their treatment of Israel," Scofield said. "I tell you, dear friends, it is a very serious thing to mistreat a Jew . . . Wherever a Jew goes he is a blessing or a curse, just according to the way he is received."[118]

Scofield directly challenged conservative Christianity's claim to represent the only path to salvation. Scofield claimed that Jews held a unique compact with God and could reach heaven without acceptance of Jesus as savior, a revolutionary doctrine for a Christian fundamentalist.[119] He also suggested Jews would play a pivotal role in the end-time. The conversion of 144,000 Jews before the Battle of Armageddon would be a miraculous sign of God's power, a necessary precursor to the Second Coming.[120] Ultimately, the fate of heaven and earth depended on Jews. Yet, for all his philo-Semitism, Scofield dehumanized Jews as completely as did anti-Semites. Individual Jews—whether of mixed heritage, secular, atheist, non-observing, Reform, Orthodox, or converted to Christianity—all collapse into a single identity and shared fate. The world's future depends on their "national conversion," meaning that there is no place for the Jewish religion in the indefinite future. As historian Paul Boyer notes, "at the heart of dispensationalism lies the assumption that Jews are essentially and eternally *different*. The view of 'the Jew' is not necessarily hostile, but he is always *separate*."[121]

In Scofield's prophetic scenario, the segregation between Christians and Jews remains through eternity. After the creation of a new heaven and earth, Christians go to heaven to be with Jesus, Scofield said. Jews rule the New Earth for eternity. God's promise to Abraham in the Book of Genesis that his descendants, as numerous as the stars, would inherit Palestine, was interpreted by Scofield to be a literal, eternal divine pledge.[122] "Israel's distinction, glory and destiny, will always be earthly," Scofield wrote. After this dispensation, "there will of necessity be a division."[123] Scofield attributed to Jews the central role in the human drama, but that assignment meant that Jews ultimately could not be part of the larger human family.

Scofield had departed from the First Congregational Church by the time of his death in Douglaston, Long Island, New York, on July 24, 1921. In spite of his relocation to the North, three memorial services were held for Scofield in Dallas on November 27, 1921. "[T]he thought comes to me that he was greater than we realized," George Dealey said at one service. The day after the memorial services, the Sanger Brothers department store, owned by one of

Dallas' most established and successful Jewish families, ran a full-page advertisement promoting sales of twelve models and styles of the Scofield Bible.[124] On May 16, 1923, the elders of the First Congregational Church in Dallas voted to change the congregation's name to Scofield Memorial Church, a name that remains to this day.[125]

Scofield changed the way many Protestants read the Bible, yet no one commented upon his transformation of Dallas race relations at his memorial services. Scofield burst upon post–Civil War Dallas at a time of explosive changes in the city's racial ideology. Jews achieved whiteness to a degree impossible for later groups on the racial margins. The uncertainty of whiteness, however, would prove to be a dilemma. In the late nineteenth and early twentieth centuries, the Jewish "merchant princes" played major roles in erecting the city's emerging capitalist order. In so doing, they entered into conflict with other Jews who helped lead the city's nascent labor movement, often promoting an anti-capitalist, socialist ideology. Even as Jews gained partial whiteness, the pressures of capitalism meant that working-class Gentiles would increasingly lose theirs, a reversal of fortune that by the 1920s would help fuel the rise of the Ku Klux Klan. At the same time, working-class Gentile whites and Jews would both soon learn that whiteness gained can become whiteness lost. To some Dallas Gentile elites, Jewish workers would remain Semitic aliens, carrying the non–Anglo-Saxon toxin of socialism. Jewish elites would find themselves suspected as disloyal by the Gentiles and attacked by leftists within their community. Scofield had argued for the separateness of Jews after the millennium, but the city's Jewish community would remain outsiders in this world. For Dallas Jews, separate would not mean equal.

THREE

THE GREAT WHITE PLAGUE

Whiteness, Culture, and the Unmaking of the Dallas Working Class

While Cyrus Scofield contemplated Jews' role in the cosmic struggle between God and Satan, Philip Sanger considered the proper relationship between workers and capitalists in the here and now. The *Dallas Daily Times-Herald* heaped praise on Sanger and his wife after a lawn party for employees of the Sanger Harris department store, a soiree metaphorically reflecting elite views of Dallas' class structure. "The merchant princes of Texas," the newspaper said, should be honored for their "solicitude . . . for the advancement and protection of the rights of those in their employ." Even while praising the sumptuousness of the Sanger's "Night in Venice" party, the newspaper declared that the gala demonstrated that the idea of "republican equality and democratic simplicity are not mere empty sentiments for dress parade, but glorious principles that are part and parcel" of the Sangers' beliefs.[1]

The *Daily Times-Herald* saw no contradiction in an event of "republican equality" being hosted by a "merchant prince." Industrial-age elites sought to conceal emerging class conflict with egalitarian rhetoric. If the Sangers' lawn party represented republican values, however, an implied hierarchy separated the wealthy host from the indulged guests. With all their *noblesse oblige,* even the Sangers could not long maintain the illusion that Dallas lived in "democratic simplicity."

Back in the 1870s, Alexander Sanger wistfully insisted, "there were no classes," but by the next decade he admitted that class lines had hardened as elite neighborhoods like The Cedars formed, isolated from the noise and bustle of working-class Dallas.[2] Alexander Sanger may have missed Dallas' supposedly classless past, but his family and their peers came to see hierarchy as a social good. For all their republican-democratic rhetoric, the wealthy were determined to maintain class supremacy. Philip Sanger proposed using the educational system to create a compliant labor pool. In an 1897 speech to the Commercial Club Directory he called for ending the teaching of "dead languages" at public schools. Working-class children needed a new "industrial" school curriculum that would provide "a little more education of the muscle in fashioning constantly needful things . . . a little more drift of the intellectual along the industrial, and a little less foolish yearning after political prominence."[3] Public schools should create an obedient working class equipped only with "useful" knowledge and certainly should not encourage plebeians to demand shared power with self-ordained elites.

From the late 1880s to the 1930s, the Dallas working class refused to conform to Sanger's dream of an apolitical proletariat. Until the early 1920s, labor—through the Populist, Socialist, and trade union movements—convinced much of the city's middle class that workplace fairness was consistent with American values. This worker–middle class nexus proved powerful. Politicians friendly to labor won elections, while strikes forced employers to make concessions regarding wages and the length of the workday. Elites then mounted a counteroffensive, manipulating popular culture to delegitimize democracy and racialize white workers. Elites, fearing that the rising political consciousness of white workers presaged the rule of racial undermen, altered election laws to diminish working-class influence. Through institutions such as the public schools, elites discouraged mass participation in politics. In these years, Dallasites were taught that being white meant conformity to the ideas of capitalism and rule by elites, concepts presented as hallmarks of civilization.

Dallas emerged as a major city in the late nineteenth and early twentieth centuries. Powered by the railroads, the population zoomed from 38,067 in 1890 to 260,475 by the start of the Great Depression in the 1930s. From the late nineteenth century to the late twentieth century, Dallas ranked second to Houston in population among Texas cities. The largely agricultural frontier town evolved into a metropolitan banking, manufacturing, and trade center of increasing ethnic and religious diversity. Around the turn of the twentieth century, Dallas bankers, early industrialists, and retailers, with their allies in the city's press, had at their disposal a vastly improved communications network with which to extend their ideological influence over the state. Yet these elites failed to coalesce politically.[4] Relative elite disunity allowed for greater influence on the part of an emerging Populist-Labor coalition.

The seeds of Dallas working-class radicalism had been sown in the agricultural misery of late nineteenth century. Rural refugees who suffered from a farm depression that raged since the 1870s made up much of Dallas County's new population. Hammered by a tight money supply, falling cotton prices aggravated by overproduction, and high interest rates charged by creditors, farmers in the Dallas area found that they worked harder only to sink deeper in debt. Desperate, many of these farmers, "poverty-stricken men, women and little children," fled to Dallas and other cities in search of a better life but instead found "petty money wages, almost nothing an hour, and no limit to the hours," as Dallas Socialist George Clifton Edwards wrote in his personal notes. These rural refugees found hope in the reform agenda of the Populist movement and the Socialist Party, which demanded higher wages, an eight-hour workday, an end to child labor, and the right of workers to organize unions. Led largely by middle-class, well-educated men and women, the Populist and Socialist movements tapped into agrarian and working-class culture in building their movements, "holding 'Encampments' which were more like Methodist camp meetings" where socialist ideology was discussed, Edwards recalled.[5] Carl Brannin, another Dallas radical, also mixed religion and politics, rejecting the elitist, apolitical dispensationalist gospel and arguing that the church should "give people a vision and a desire for the kingdom of heaven on earth, where justice between mankind will prevail and where unemployment, crime, disease and unrighteous acts will be unknown."[6]

This message fell on fertile ground. Following the arrival of the railroads in the 1870s, many Dallas County landowners saw the value of their real estate explode and became rich overnight. The inflation of land values, however, hurt debt-ridden tenant farmers, who outnumbered owners 2,295 to 1,975 by 1900.[7] About 61 percent of Dallas County residents, whether rural or urban, rented their homes. Salary-dependent industrial workers, who now numbered almost 9 percent of the population, struggled to make their average yearly salary of $493 stretch.[8] The boom-and-bust economy from the 1870s to the 1930s deepened the county's class divide. Radicalized by hardship, farmers formed the Texas People's Party, better known as the Populists, in the 1890s. Populists adopted a bold political program in 1886 in Cleburne, Texas, fifty miles southwest of Dallas. The "Cleburne Demands" called for a vast expansion of the nation's money supply and for the government to provide direct credit to farmers as a way to cut out greedy middlemen.[9]

In Dallas, the Populist movement included not just farmers but also urban workers, middle-class reformers, and marginalized black trade unionists. By 1900 a larger constituency existed for such a movement, as the city featured a significantly more complex class system than existed in the mid-nineteenth century. In 1860 more than 60 percent of Dallas County residents were farmers, and another 23 percent were classed as artisans or professionals. By 1900 an increasingly modern urban working class peopled the city. About one-third of Dallas' 18,393 wage earners were employed in what the U.S. Census Bureau called "domestic and personal service," including barbers, bartenders, janitors, day laborers, nurses, policemen, and firefighters. Another third worked in "trade and transportation," a census category dominated by teamsters, sales clerks, and railroad employees. Skilled workers—the masons, carpenters, plumbers, and mechanics who made up the city's labor elites—comprised less than 25 percent of the population. In the four decades between 1860 and 1900, Dallas transformed from a rural society in which most residents were small-scale independent producers who owned their own farms or specialized in crafts such as blacksmithing to a salary-dependent, service-oriented economy.[10]

Although the Populists kept their movement segregated, the fact that white members collaborated with parallel black Populist organizations led Texas Democrats to charge the People's Party with undermining white supremacy. By the 1890s, because of violence, intimidation, and the charge that it advocated "race mixing," the Populist movement collapsed.[11] Nevertheless, a Dallas Labor-Populist alliance elected union painter Patrick H. Golden as the county's state representative in 1892, butcher Max Hahn to the Dallas City Council from 1898 to 1900, and union musician John W. Parks to the Texas state legislature from 1912 to 1918.[12]

Dallas Populism and Socialism won substantial middle-class support largely because these movements reflected the concerns of their bourgeois leaders. Edwards, the son of a lawyer, received a Harvard education and briefly studied to become a minister. Carl Brannin, Edwards' frequent ally, grew up in Cisco, Texas, 150 miles west of Dallas, the son of a horse and cattle rancher who acted as an agent for Eastern landowners. These relatively privileged men empathized with the poor and the working class. Edwards lived in the cotton-mill district in South Dallas and saw firsthand the horrors of child labor: "some of these hovels here in Dallas, managed by the mill, are almost inconceivably crowded, wretched, and filthy . . . when the mill does not run at night, the children hurry home at six-thirty, gobble down their food, and then take to the streets, seeking the electric light and saloon corner as a relief after the monotony of the mill and the misery of their home."[13]

Populism, however, proved less committed to fundamental economic change than to a milder agenda of capitalist reform. Texas Populists viewed politics as thoroughly corrupted by monied interests, but they still clung to the hope that real change could be realized through the ballot. Populists proceeded as though grassroots movements, without directly addressing racism, could pressure elites into creating a more equitable society. Under pseudo-Populists like Texas governor Jim Hogg, the state Democratic Party absorbed the People's Party by the end of the 1890s, and Populism virtually disappeared as a political alternative for farmers and workers. "Texans had responded to the Populist agitation rather warmly but the Populists were not very far from the Democrats in principle . . . and the movement faded more quickly than it arose," Edwards said.[14]

In their eagerness to rally the powerful middle class under the Labor banner, even the Socialists created a movement so broadly based that it could not resolve its inner conflicts. Dallas Socialists defined the working class not just as wage earners but also as the "class who have but little land and [few capital assets] — the small traders and small farmers," according to a 1908 editorial in *The Laborer*, the city's Socialist newspaper. The labor movement hoped to mobilize wage earners, small merchants, and farmers in a common front against the "ruling minority" of capitalists who were growing steadily more "useless and parasitic."[15] This parasitic class, according to George Edwards, consisted of those few who earned their incomes by owning rather than working. Opposed to this group were not only wage workers but an exploited army composed "of professional men, of high salaried employees, [and] of little business men." Edwards saw this ambiguously defined middle class as suffering a "pitiable plight" as they found themselves "ground between the capitalists above, who constantly try to 'freeze them out' and the workers below who are far more powerful against the small employer than against the big corporation."[16] As this comment suggests, Edwards knew that the Dallas middle class might not always see its interests as inherently linked to a restless proletariat. Middle managers might see a more attractive immediate payoff in controlling labor costs by holding down wages than in the uncertain gamble of entering the class struggle. Such an unstable coalition may have been necessary in a struggle against Dallas' powerful oligarchy. Yet for all their efforts, labor leaders won — at best — lukewarm acceptance from newspaper publishers, ministers, and other professionals.

Middle-class supporters, declaring that workers were not "slaves to be driven by the company," were vital in the success of an 1898 strike by the Amalgamated Association of Street Railway Employees. The Dallas Consolidated Railway Company gave workers a 2.5 percent raise and agreed to arbitrate future contract disputes through the courts. Much of the middle class supported Socialist and Populist candidates. Yet, the middle class abandoned unionists during the unsuccessful three-month 1919 strike of Texas Power & Light linemen, who demanded a closed shop, higher wages, and an eight-hour workday. Middle-class support for the strike collapsed when a June 1919 clash between strikers and replacement workers resulted in the death of a company security guard.[17]

Internal pressures fragmented the labor movement even as normally fractious elites achieved unprecedented unity in the early 1920s through the auspices of the Open Shop Association. The association arose in response to a limited strike by typographers demanding a forty-four-hour work week. Led by W. S. Mosher (whose family played a major part in building Scofield Memorial Church), the Open Shop Association portrayed unions as run by alien outsiders destroying a worker's freedom to follow "his line of employment either in or out of a labor union, just as he saw fit."[18] Such pamphlets aimed at a middle-class audience increasingly uneasy over expanding unionism. The association exploited, in a distorted way, middle-class emphasis on "fair play" by portraying unionists as organized thugs who denied non-union workers freedom of choice.

The open shop campaign aided the formation of a new ruling bloc involving wealthy elites and Dallas' middle-class professionals, including ministers and educators. For the first time since the 1880s, membership in Dallas' principal unions declined.[19] An alliance of wealthy and upper-middle-class reformers then altered the law to undermine working-class voters. A 1902 state law, opposed by a broad coalition of unions, Populists, and people of color, imposed a poll tax that reduced voting by blacks, Hispanics, and poor whites. Texas' 1903 election law allowed major political parties to determine who could vote in their primaries, regardless of the voting rights guaranteed by the Fourteenth and Fifteenth Amendments to the U.S. Constitution. The state Democratic Party followed up this law by establishing a whites-only primary system. Since the collapse of the state Republican Party in the 1870s and the Populists in the 1890s, the Democrats held a virtual monopoly on elective office. The new Democratic rules meant that African Americans in Texas would have no voice in determining who would win statewide office. Although a series of Supreme Court decisions starting in 1927 undermined the white primary, this legislation had a chilling effect on black political participation.[20]

The new state election laws did allow African Americans to vote in municipal elections, but Dallas elites saw to it that the political strength of blacks and poor whites would be diluted. At the turn of the century the Dallas City Council was organized on the ward system, meaning that council members were elected on a neighborhood basis. Middle-class "progressive" reformers charged that ward politics served as engines of corruption. According to the reformers, ward politicians were concerned only with the parochial concerns of their neighborhoods, not with the good of the city as a whole. Supporters of the ward system, largely members of the working class, countered that neighborhood-based politics made city aldermen more responsive to the needs of ordinary citizens. Elites and middle-class progressives united behind a campaign to institute a "commission" form of government. The mayor and four commissioners, responsible for finance and revenue, waterworks and sewers, streets and public property, and fire and police, would be chosen in citywide elections, a system, as one alderman charged, that would allow "banks and the *Dallas News* . . . to dominate all the wards." The commission proposal passed in an April 3, 1906, referendum by 2,183 to 401, an impressive margin rendered less significant by the fact that more than 55 percent of eligible voters did not cast ballots in the election.[21]

Elites and their middle-class progressive partners cloaked their campaign against ward government in the discourse of public service. Yet the new commission consisted of "five men who all represented the commercial elite of Dallas," in the words of historian Patricia Gower. "At-large elections of commissioners watered down the voice of individual neighborhoods and enabled commissioners to prioritize services to downtown and upper and middle class neighborhoods." White poor and working-class neighborhoods as well as black communities for years would lack basic services such as modern plumbing, electricity, and trash collection.[22]

Following the elimination of the ward system, commercial elites controlled Dallas to a degree not achieved by their peers in most other emerging Southern metropolises. Only Houston rivaled Dallas in the cohesiveness of its power brokers in this period. Houston, like Dallas, adopted a new charter in 1904 under which city aldermen were elected at large. The city of Houston, however, had evolved with no zoning laws, resulting in haphazard housing patterns that diffused working-class voters throughout the city and thus diminished the potency of the labor vote even before the charter revisions. Atlanta's ward system, on the other hand, survived well past World War II, frequently dividing Atlanta's moderate business elites into opposing political camps. This division gave progressive groups such as the Commission on Interracial Cooperation a visibility and influence such organizations would not enjoy in the more tightly controlled Dallas environment.[23]

With the Dallas commercial elite firmly in charge of their city, neighborhoods increasingly segregated not just racially but also by economic class. African Americans concentrated along the city's floodplains, particularly in a section of North Dallas near the Houston & Texas Central Railroad bordered by Ross Avenue, Haskell Avenue, and Pearl Street. Elites amended the city charter in 1907 to impose racial segregation in schools, churches, and public amusement venues. In 1916, by a referendum vote of 7,613 to 4,693, Dallas became the first city in Texas to allow racial housing segregation by law. The law created three categories of neighborhoods—white, black, and open. Neighborhoods already exclusively occupied by one race would be closed to the other. Open blocks, made up of poor and working-class families, were already integrated and would remain so. The Texas Supreme Court invalidated the ordinance in 1917, but in 1921 the Dallas City Council passed a new law by which residents of a neighborhood could request that their block be designated as white, black, or open. Once a designation was made, only a written request by three-fourths of the residents in that block could change the neighborhood's racial assignment. In 1927 and 1929, whites enforced segregation by bombing and burning the homes of blacks moving into marginal all-white neighborhoods. Dallas set a pattern for the rest of the state, although segregation was a more difficult task in Houston, where the lack of zoning laws meant that blacks and whites had lived in close proximity since the end of the Civil War.[24]

Dallas' prosperous residents, meanwhile, retreated into protected enclaves on Ross Avenue and The Cedars, an affluent neighborhood south of downtown "enclosed by a natural thicket of cedar tress that blocked out much of the noise and confusion of the city."[25] Landscape architect Wilbur David Cook developed Highland Park in 1907 as a refuge from an increasingly diverse city. Completely surrounded by Dallas, Highland Park incorporated as a separate town in 1913 and bitterly resisted attempts at annexation by its urban neighbor. Highland Park became the residence of "the executives of big businesses, utility companies and bankers" who founded the mini-city as a congenial tax dodge. Residents protected "from the depredations of the minorities" avoided higher city taxes while Dallas provided them with water at much lower cost even as rates climbed for city residents.[26] The city limits of in-burbs like Highland Park and University Park, with their own school systems and police departments, became moats and the residents eagerly raised the drawbridges to keep away frightening African Americans, Mexican Americans and white radicals.

As law professor Ian F. Haney López argues, segregation made concrete the racial and, by extension, class differences asserted by elite ideology. In other words, through their control of urban planning, elites limited city services in black, brown, and poor white neighborhoods. Such neighborhoods became crowded because segregation law limited housing options for people of color and because low wages limited the housing available to impoverished whites. The near-monopoly of the wealthy on political power also guaranteed that unhealthy developments like dumps and liquor stores were located predominantly within impoverished, disenfranchised communities. The resulting crowding, poor maintenance, and filth provided proof in the elite mind of the inferiority of the poor and colored masses.[27] This was true across the United States, and Dallas certainly was no exception.

The process of class segregation accelerated in the 1920s as the white working class concentrated in the southern end of East Dallas while a middle-class community formed near Baylor Hospital. By 1925, 60 percent of elites lived in Highland Park or North Dallas and 25 percent along tony Swiss Avenue in East Dallas. Only 14 percent still lived in South Dallas, with the remaining 1 percent holding out in the strongly blue-collar Oak Cliff community.[28] Elites sought these hiding places as the city increasingly represented a cesspool of racial pollution and they increasingly racialized its off-white, working-class, Euro-American residents. Neighborhood names like Deep Ellum reflect the ongoing cultural blending of early-twentieth-century Dallas. Then a vibrant center of jazz and blues, Deep Ellum is a small area on Elm Street east of the old Houston & Texas Central railroad track, a mile from the Texas School Book Depository Building, in downtown Dallas. "Deep" referred to its distance from the center of town. "Ellum" represents a "phonetic spelling for a colloquial pronunciation of Elm [Street] by African Americans or Eastern European Jews, or both," according to authors Alan Govenar and Jay Brakesfield. Dense with pawnshops, clothing outlets, whorehouses, and bars in the 1920s, Deep Ellum was a national music center that drew such blues legends as Blind Lemon Jefferson and Leadbelly.[29]

Deep Ellum became "the gathering place of blacks from all over the country, for Mexicans fleeing oppression in Mexico, for Jews who established businesses and poor whites looking for 'action,'" recalled Robert Prince, a local historian from the nearby State-Thomas district.[30] The result was cultural miscegenation. "The black music played in Deep Ellum was . . . a force in the development of Western swing," Govenar and Brakesfield wrote. "Deep Ellum, then, was a crossroads, a nexus, where peoples and cultures could interact and influence each other in relative freedom."[31] Deep Ellum attracted both nonwhites and probationary whites. "Deep Ellum was a Babel," reporter Lee Ballard wrote of the old district. "Itzhack Abramson [a Yiddish-speaking shopkeeper] learned enough English to carry on business . . . Greek brothers ran a café. Mexican men stood on street corners at sundown with their charcoal-fire buckets of hot tamales. A banjo-playing Indian called Two Pennies went from door to door making music. And, as a backdrop to everything, there was the near-Gullah dialect of that generation's black population. Standard English was rarely heard."[32]

Elites saw such multicultural neighborhoods as signs of cultural deterioration and the declining power of "true" whites in an increasingly "colored" city. Among their number was Dallas attorney Lewis Meriwether Dabney, a Virginia transplant and son of a University of Texas at Austin philosophy professor. Dabney opened his Dallas law practice in 1888 and soon befriended some of the most powerful men in the city.[33] Dabney urged other Dallas leaders to restrict immigration and eliminate the right to vote to all but the most "qualified" white men. Dabney's comments came in the context of mass German and Jewish immigration into Dallas in the late nineteenth century, the arrival of Mexican Americans in large number between 1910 and 1930, and the development of a growing Sicilian community in the first three decades of the twentieth century. He blamed the growth of those communities on Anglo-Saxons who created such a comfortable civilization that now even the racial dregs of the world thrived. "As society has advanced from the primitive to the semi-civilized . . . its functioning has been biologically adverse to the best strains and favorable to the worst," Dabney said in an address to Dallas' influential Critic Club in December 1922.[34]

Dabney feared the rise not just of the "African Hottentot" in places like Deep Ellum but also white racial deterioration.[35] American cities had filled with inferior whites such as "mongrelized Asiatics, Greeks, Levantines, Southern Italians, and sweepings of the Balkans, of Poland and of Russia," Dabney complained.[36] In letters written during World War I, Dabney mourned that "stalwart, clean-cut" Anglo-Saxon men faced death in Europe to "preserve liberty and happiness for the swarms of maggots of the human kind I see wriggling in the vile heaps we call our cities."[37] Dabney told one friend that he did not, for the most part, regret the South losing the Civil War except that "as the negroes put it, 'the bottom rail got on top.'" The real tragedy of the Confederacy's defeat more than a half-century earlier was "the emerging of these 'half-strainers' from the bottom to the top. These the war liberated much more than it did the Africans. This is the day of the poor white in the South."[38]

Like African Americans and Mexican Americans, the white working class was seen as carrying racially impure blood and was thus incapable of civilization. Along with blacks and Mexican Americans, white workers were treated as disease carriers in a physical and political sense. Zoning laws and housing patterns separated all three groups from white elites who sought to quarantine race mixing and political radicalism. To fully understand how far elites had come to circumscribe Anglo working-class whiteness, it is necessary to compare the racialization of African Americans and Mexican Americans in the nineteenth and early twentieth centuries with that of their Anglo working-class peers.

Elites dehumanized African Americans since the days of slavery, customarily suggesting that blacks represented either an inferior brand of humanity or even a separate species. In *The Texas Almanac for 1857*, published by the *Galveston News* (parent company of the *Dallas Morning News*), a statistical table casually lumped together Texas "Negroes, Horses and Cattle in 1850 & 1855." Author Charles Carroll in his 1900 book *The Negro a Beast* argued that African Americans were soulless apes. America's first cinema epic, the immensely popular 1915 D. W. Griffith film *The Birth of a Nation*, portrayed African Americans as near-simians bent on the rape of white women. Griffith's film spurred the rebirth of the Ku Klux Klan in the 1920s and reinforced anti-black sentiment North and South.[39]

Whites more subtly dehumanized blacks by suggesting they were incapable of creating civilization, defined by Dallas Anglos as the creation of a technological, capitalist society conforming to Euro-American norms. A 1927 textbook approved by the Dallas School Board explained to world history students in white high schools why blacks, browns, and Native Americans remained invisible in the historical pageant: "No account is given of the black races of Africa and Australia, of the brown races of southeastern Asia and the Pacific islands, or of the red races of America; because the elements of culture among these people have rarely influenced modern civilization."[40] Blacks were "dark of skin . . . [and] even darker of mind, for the light of civilization had not yet reached them." Dallas textbooks casually grouped native Africans with other violent, mindless forces of nature. Africa, one textbook claimed, was a land of "cannibals and strange wild beasts of the forests."[41] Dallas Anglos had an obligation—the "White Man's Burden"—to take nonwhites under their wing and allow them the privilege of life under white civilization, another textbook declared. "The European white man has taught, and if need be, has compelled his yellow and black and brown brothers to adopt the ways of the European," a high school textbook of the 1930s declared. ". . . Truly it is a burden, and a heavy one, to lead hundreds of millions of strangers into the paths of European civilization and progress."[42] Clearly, nonwhites could only be wards, not leaders or creators of civilization, which remained the exclusive gift of Anglos.

White Dallas elites also associated African Americans with contamination. A white doctor at a Dallas health conference in 1915 accused black servants of infecting their employers with dangerous diseases like tuberculosis.[43] This threat rationalized the promulgation of Jim Crow housing laws in Dallas the next year, even though blacks continued to be welcomed into wealthy white homes as servants. Some reformers, however, insisted that blacks must live in cleaner ghettoes. In 1927 Justin F. Kimball, a former Dallas school superintendent and professor of education at Southern Methodist University, urged the city to provide better housing for blacks because these workers could transmit "the seeds of diphtheria, scarlet fever, tuberculosis and other dreadful diseases" to their white employers.[44]

White Dallas also long associated Mexicans with barbarism and contagion. A *Dallas Daily Herald* reporter in the 1870s squirmed with disgust as he described a government train that arrived from Fort Griffin driven by "Mexicans, tawny, scowling, lurid of eye and racy with dirt."[45] Not only were Mexicans disease carriers, but early Dallas historians like John Henry Brown and Philip Lindsley emphasized that Mexicans were a "mixed-race people" whose white, Spanish heritage had been corrupted through centuries of miscegenation with Indians and blacks.[46]

Many Anglo Texans held to the so-called one-drop theory that any individual with any degree of black heritage should also be defined as black. This, combined with an Indian heritage widely seen as degraded and inferior, generally meant that Texas Anglos defined Mexicans as nonwhite. Traveling in Texas in the mid-nineteenth century, Frederick Law Olmsted noted that Anglos saw their Mexican neighbors at best as "improved and Christianized Indians." Many Anglos, Olmsted observed, saw Mexicans as indistinguishable from blacks. "There are thousands in respectable positions [in Mexico] whose color and physiognomy would subject them, in Texas, to be sold by the sheriff as negro-estrays who cannot be allowed at large without detriment to the commonwealth," he wrote.[47] Furthermore, the Tejano's darker skin revolted whites, according to historian Arnoldo de León, because "to whites, dark colors connoted filth and therefore Mexicans were a dirty, putrid people, existing in squalor."[48]

Lingering bitterness over Mexican atrocities in the Texas Revolution intensified Anglo questions about Mexican racial character. Dallas schoolchildren were taught that Mexicans at the Battle of the Alamo slaughtered Anglo soldiers after they had surrendered and that a similar atrocity happened in Goliad, where four hundred Anglo prisoners of war were shot and their bodies stripped and burned. Anglo atrocities against Mexicans, meanwhile, vanished from the public memory.[49] From the fall of 1926 until June 1927, the *Dallas Morning News* printed a cartoon series, "Texas History Movies," which depicted events in Texas from colonial times until the end of Reconstruction. History teachers used the comic strip in their Texas history classes across the state. Dallas schools approved the distribution of "Texas History Movies" in booklet form to elementary students in November 1932.[50] According to "Texas History Movies," one Anglo soldier was worth several of his Mexican peers. One strip depicts an Alamo defender rejoicing when thirty-two soldiers arrive from Gonzales to reinforce the Anglo troops. "We've got 188 men now," the soldier declares. "That's enough for 4,000 Mexicans."[51] Even Mexico's undeniable victory in that battle morphs into defeat. Mexican victory at the Alamo, according to myth, resulted from Latin ruthlessness, while the ultimate Anglo victory in the Texas Revolution, the Battle of San Jacinto, is credited partly to Mexican ineptitude. Thus Mexicans lose whatever the actual battle results. Children reading "Texas History Movies" learned that Mexican dictator Santa Anna's army suffered 500 casualties, while all 181 Alamo "defenders" perished. "Several versions of the Texas creation myth state with pride the number of Mexicans killed versus the number of Texans killed," anthropologist Holly Beachley Brear wrote. "This juxtaposing of the war dead creates a scoring technique which allows the Texans to 'win' both at the Alamo and at San Jacinto."[52]

Anglos saw Mexicans as outside of whiteness and their culture only worthy of extirpation. A federal district court determined in the 1897 *In re Rodriguez* case that a "full-blooded Mexican" could legally obtain American citizenship but admitted that according to the "strict" scientific standards of anthropology he could not be considered white.[53] The Texas Legislature in 1918 passed an English-only law that banned any school employee from using Spanish on school grounds and made it a criminal offense to teach in any language other than English. Viewed as the amalgamated by-product of inferior races and depicted as cowardly, dishonest, and violent, Mexicans encountered a cold welcome in Dallas even as the railroads and other industries recruited them as a source of cheap labor. The first permanent Mexican population in Dallas County arrived around 1900, most of whom picked cotton or served as railroad laborers. The first sizable wave of Mexicans and Mexican Americans migrated to Dallas in the 1920s. Immigrants escaped the violence and economic chaos of the Mexican Revolution from 1910–1920 or sought greater opportunities than existed in poverty-stricken South Texas. By 1930 approximately 6,000 native Mexicans and Mexican Americans settled in Dallas. Mexican Americans comprised 2.3 percent of the city's population, most of them crowded into the "Little Mexico" barrio along McKinney Avenue. About 75 percent of these new arrivals worked as laborers and had received between fourth- and sixth-grade educations.[54]

Lighter-complexioned, wealthier Mexicans, so-called *gente de razón*, had an easier time winning acceptance as white. In Dallas only a small portion— 1.6 percent—of the city's Mexican population belonged in the "professional" class.[55] Most Mexicans in Dallas and elsewhere in Texas occupied a social position at times indistinguishable from that of blacks.[56] Their status as some of the lowest-paid workers in the county, their Catholic religion, and the fact that most of the county's Mexican population primarily spoke Spanish made it easier for Anglo elites to view Mexicans as unassimilated aliens.[57]

"Most of the Mexicans who live in Dallas are not American citizens, do not speak English, do not expect to remain in Dallas or the United States long, and are unaccustomed to our conditions of life and housing," wrote one-time Dallas school superintendent Justin Kimball in the 1920s. "They will accept conditions of housing to which no other people in our city or state will submit . . . Every such congested, overcrowded, unhealthful center [like Little Mexico] is like a canker or eating sore on our fair city. The rest of our city can no more live and grow and prosper with such a condition, than our body can be well when it has an angry, bleeding inflamed sore on some part of it."[58] Unless Mexican "slums" were cleared, Kimball warned, "The rest of the [city] . . . will be injured in health and strength."[59] Poor Mexicans would continue to be associated with disease and uncleanliness in the following decades. In 1938 the press noted that the Little Mexico barrio ranked first among all Dallas neighborhoods in deaths from tuberculosis and pellagra.[60]

Anglos tried desperately to erect an antiseptic wall between the races. "Pancho" Medrano, a Dallas labor leader, was born in Little Mexico in 1920. Medrano recalled seeing metal rails built around Pike Park to keep Mexican Americans and African Americans out and that "no restaurant would let us in. I can remember during the hot summers having to go with my mother and brothers to a café. None of us had shoes, and we had to stay outside while they brought us some food and drinks. Then, we just sat out on the concrete, which burned our feet and bottoms, and ate our meals there."[61]

Anglos avoided even indirect contact with "unclean" Mexicans. Through the effort of Mexican consul Adolfo Dominguez, Mexican American children in 1938 won the right to swim at the Pike Park pool, but only from 7 to 9 A.M. "At 15 minutes before nine, they would tell us to get out of the pool," Medrano remembered. "They would empty out the water from the pool and make us clean the pool before putting in new water for the white kids who would use the pool the rest of the day. They would also make us pick up trash in the park and check us real closely for body sores and lice."[62]

Like blacks and Mexican Americans, white workers found they were associated with filth and disease, an indication that lower-income Anglos lost racial status in this period. An unsigned appeal to the city's literary club in 1909 and to the United Charities Organization in 1910 addressed the issue of tuberculosis and other epidemics in Dallas' poor neighborhoods. The poor—white, black, and brown—lived in an environment of "poverty, dirt, and more or less degradation . . . Poverty, untidiness and filth abound, the bath tub a mile away."[63] The appeal called for improved housing standards and holding rents to no more than 20 percent of poor workers' salaries. The authors described this as simple self-interest. Poverty and disease carried explosive political implications. "Out of this environment, it can easily be seen, naturally arise the spirit of unrest, of discontentment, of immorality and criminality, and the frightful expense produced by these results must finally be paid by some one else."[64] The report called the tuberculosis raging in such slums "the

Great White Plague," but this could have referred to the residents as much to the disease devastating them.[65]

Just as whites had earlier grouped slaves with livestock, men like Dabney dehumanized white immigrants from southern and eastern Europe as "maggots." In early-twentieth-century America, eugenics served to support the racial demotion of the white working class. The eugenics movement, which sought to improve the human race by preventing the "breeding" of the genetically inferior and promoting reproduction among the superior, argued that southern and eastern Europeans represented distinctly different racial groups than northern Europeans. By measuring skulls, eugenicists believed that they not only "scientifically" proved that whites had larger brains than blacks but that northern Europeans had larger brain cases than Spaniards, Italians, Greeks, Russians, and Jews. They then incorrectly assumed that brain size correlated to intelligence rather than to body size. Relying on the same dubious, inconsistent measuring techniques, eugenicists also determined that successful people had larger brain cases than the poor and working class. Eugenicists deeply influenced American public policy, inspiring laws allowing state officials to legally sterilize alleged mental defectives in California and the Deep South (laws later imitated by the Nazi regime in Germany) and culminating in the 1924 U.S. Origin Act aimed at ending immigration from southern and eastern Europe.[66]

Dallas elites hoped they could improve the city's stock by encouraging the biologically promising to breed and the genetically dysfunctional not to reproduce. In 1914 a "Better Baby Contest" proved one of the most popular events at the Texas State Fair in Dallas. A committee of doctors measured the skulls and other traits of the five hundred entrants, with fifteen dollars given to the parents of the "best" child, any class, and five dollars for the best twins and best triplets.[67] The winning children in such contests, as historians have noted, were chosen in a similar way that prize "cattle, chickens and pigs" received blue ribbons elsewhere on the fairgrounds.[68]

To the shock of one Dallas newspaper writer, the 1914 contest contradicted expectations of male supremacy. The winner, a girl named Grace Gulden, was picked by a committee described as "coldly scientific and putting sentiment behind them." The "embryo suffragette—no disparagement—had just a teeny, weeny bit the better of the boys," a *Dallas Daily Times-Herald* story reported, speculating the girl might one day be "presidentress of the United States." While a "perfect" girl barely edged out two equally flawless boys, purportedly objective science reconfirmed Dallas' racial and class ideology for a large, fascinated audience. Winners were white, flaxen-haired, and often, like the Cranfill twins, the scions of elite families. Hoping to evangelize the Dallas crowds to the gospel of better breeding, A. Caswell Ellis of the University of Texas flattered the crowd, declaring that "Texas babies are better babies than the babies of any other state" before he "lightly touched on eugenics."[69]

The chief lesson of eugenics was that the dysgenic white threatened the biologic republic as much as the enfranchised black. This fear reverberated throughout America in the first three decades of the twentieth century. Like John H. Reagan before them, leading American eugenicists like Madison Grant feared the voting power of poor whites as much as they did extending the franchise to other races. The advance of democracy, Grant argued, led to "the transfer of power from the higher to the lower races, from the intellectual to the plebian class," with the universal franchise resulting in the political triumph of the mediocre.[70] In America, he warned, "we have nearly succeeded in destroying the privilege of birth; that is, the intellectual and moral advantage a man of good stock brings into the world with him."[71] Such tendencies forecast doom for the United States, Grant predicted, because "true aristocracy or a true republic is government by the wisest and the best, always a small minority in any population." The United States replaced "true aristocracy" with mobocracy, leaving civilization in the hands of the incompetent. In the first years of the twentieth century, an Alabama doctor warned of the threat posed by so-called white trash and proposed at a state medical convention a final solution to prevent a racial apocalypse. Genetically inferior poor whites, he said, "ought not to be allowed to get married, and men who persist in [degenerate behavior] ought to be confined in reformatory institutions, or have their testicles removed, so that it would be impossible for them to propagate."[72]

Dallas men like Justin Kimball also worried about the influence of a lower-class electorate who might be unfit for full citizenship. "Ignorant or corruptible citizens can always be counted on to vote, although they usually vote wrong," he wrote.[73] Dallas intellectual Lewis Dabney echoed Grant's sentiments about the dangers of mass politics. "The trouble about a democracy is that things are settled by voting and ninety-five percent of the voters, not having the sense of an ant or squirrel in the summer, but having the vote, will ravage the stores of those who have laid up a few nuts when they could," he wrote. "Like any other maddened baboon they will tear the whole fabric of civilization to pieces," he complained, thoroughly mixing his zoological metaphor.[74] Dabney regretted the rising power of the poor white and prophesied the collapse of American civilization if those inferiors attained too much influence. Democracy, he warned, "by its very nature rejects the best and seeks the worst and is stumbling down into the mire."[75]

Dabney, in his December 1922 speech to the Critic Club, desired for the

United States an elitist republic directed by the "superior man . . . the torch bearer of the race" with the active support of the "mediocre man," Dabney's term for those of average ability. Mediocre man, Dabney said, "accepts the work of genius, and performs the interminable and complex tasks necessary to construction and preservation of what the superior man devises." Mediocre man would agree to the dominance of superior man, Dabney predicted, because of the physical comforts created by ingenious elites.[76] Unfortunately, Dabney claimed, the advance of culture and civilization allowed inferiors to prosper. The "African Hottentot," the "American Indian," and the "Mongrel inhabitants of South and Central America" either were biologically incapable of civilization or could achieve it at only the lowest level, he said.[77] But "superior man" and "mediocre man" had a foe to fear within the white community as well. Both should unite to prevent the rise of the "under man, the congenital savage, incapable of civilization, hating it, and desirous of reverting to the primitive, under the unchangeable biological law of his being."[78]

Dabney made it clear who he thought these undermen were. Southern and eastern Europeans, particularly Jews, haunted Dabney's imagination. Dabney worried that inferior whites had been tainted with a socialist ideology "poisoning the rising generation with doctrines all right for Russian Jews but not to be tolerated by any free Anglo-Saxon soul."[79] Dabney told his Dallas audience in 1922 that the rise of the undermen could be prevented by encouraging "superior men and women" to increase their families; promoting birth control among the lower classes and sterilizing "criminals, lunatics, idiots, defectives and degenerates"; and ending "promiscuous immigration."[80]

By the 1920s elites launched their first concerted effort to transform the minds of mediocre men and undermen. Elites sought to manufacture consent to aristocratic rule. Working-class children were taught that reformers generated social chaos. Rule by the wealthy inevitably yielded progress if the process was not halted by foolish dissent. The children of the white lower classes were encouraged to surrender hopes for political power. Subtly, they were compensated for their disenfranchisement with the psychological comforts of white supremacy.

Textbooks praised the undemocratic nature of the American Revolution and the U.S. Constitution. American "mobs" lobbying for group rights could threaten the delicate fabric of society, textbooks said, so checks on popular will were put in place. Dallas' American history texts carefully contrasted representative republics with "radical" democracies. "[A] pure democracy demands that the people and their representatives must place the good of the whole above their individual interests," according to *The Record of America,* published in 1935 and adopted by the Dallas School Board four years later.

"Unhappily, however, it is hard for most human beings to put the good of the whole against their personal gain . . . one of the most marked tendencies of our later democracy has been to form groups to bring pressure on Congress to gain something for themselves without considering the rest of the people."[81]

The wisdom of the Constitution, according to the authors of *The Record of America,* lay in its protection of elite rule against the shortsighted demands of the unpropertied. The Founding Fathers, the Dallas text said, "had little faith in the ability of people as a whole to maintain self-control and wisdom in government. They had no confidence in the man without property . . . a man who had failed to [accumulate property] . . . would be regarded as shiftless, lazy, or incompetent, and not deserving a voice in the government of others." With this view, the Founding Fathers wrote the Constitution "to retain power in the hands of those who were least radical, and to set obstacles in the way of radical mob action."[82] Thus the disenfranchising of Lewis Dabney's undermen represented American values in their purist form.

Twentieth-century elites found in the Reconstruction Era a useful past justifying aristocratic rule in the 1920s and 1930s. In Dallas school textbooks, Reconstruction became a metaphor for the dangers of democracy run amuck and the threat political reform posed to social stability. The "negro rule" of Reconstruction had been a nightmare of corruption, greed, and race mixing, students were taught. Textbooks implied this was the peril of social change launched by reformers. Granting political power to poor whites could result in similar anarchy. In Dallas textbooks, abolitionists were just precursors of later troublemakers like the Populists or socialists, who divided the white community and risked the advent of "negro supremacy." The alleged failures of Reconstruction revealed the dangers of rule by undermen.[83]

Politics posed a threat to progress, working-class children were taught. The division of true whites into different political camps might lead to the supremacy of immigrants, laborites, Catholics, and Jews, just as the conflict between North and South had allowed Negro supremacy. Here was the ultimate danger of democracy. As historian Ivan Hannaford argues in *Race: The History of an Idea in the West,* racist discourse is ultimately apolitical. In ancient times one was defined as an insider or an outsider by one's relationship to the state, whether or not one was a citizen of a political realm.[84] As racial ideology developed in the West, insider status came to be less linked to one's civil status than to one's color. Biology trumped politics. Genuine leaders, Dabney argued, are bred, not elected. They arise naturally, and their triumph can only be frustrated by an ill-informed democratic mob. Non-elites were encouraged to surrender foolish notions of achieving political influence. In this, Dallas' racial ideology of the 1920s and 1930s reinforced the apolitical theology of Cyrus Scofield, which suggested that faith in democratic processes marked one as a sinner. As compensation for political disempowerment, however, Dallas workers could receive the wages of whiteness. Even as their political voices were muted, subordinate whites were encouraged to uphold their racial superiority to blacks and darker-skinned, poorer Mexicans. Unlike the political-racial formulation offered by John H. Reagan in the 1860s, in the newest incarnation of whiteness even the best-educated, most accomplished black individual occupied an inferior status to a white of the meanest circumstances.

Even suspect immigrants could hope for a degree of whiteness if they disappeared into the undifferentiated, vaguely Caucasian mass. On October 27, 1925, the Dallas School Board approved a textbook for "foreigners," the *Reader and Guide for New Americans*.[85] Foreign-born children and adults attending special Dallas English courses were told to leave their native languages and cultures behind. Upon acquisition of Anglo-Saxon culture, even immigrants would assume a place in the racial hierarchy above blacks and mixed-race Mexicans.

The United States, as one poem in the *Reader and Guide* insisted, is specifically a European-American society. Immigrants could become "American," the code word for "white," if they surrendered any specific ethnic identity. The poem "Just American" depicts an encounter between a citizen and a recent immigrant aspiring to full white status. The narrator asks "whence he came/What was once his nation's name . . . And what of you? Are you Pole or Russian Jew?" The immigrant replies, "What I was is naught to me/In this land of Liberty;/In my soul as man to man/I am just American."[86] Dallas schools invited newly minted Euro-Americans to join the white man's club. Part of the price of admission was anti-black racism. The *Reader and Guide for New Americans* used racist stories about a stereotypical black character named Rastus to teach English.[87] The process of Americanization in Dallas thus involved trading a specific culture for an identity based on both the absence of blackness and contempt for people of color. To have a class or ethnic identity meant to belong to an identifiable constituency, a group that could achieve self-consciousness and forge unity over and against powerful white elites. Whiteness primarily functioned to diffuse such mobilization.

Whiteness reaped a harvest of alienation, with lower-class Anglos, Mexicans, Jews, and blacks each fighting a lonely battle for limited political influence and status. The white working class traded political enfranchisement for the flattery of white supremacy. Even if white elites faced serious challenges in the past by anti-secessionists, Reconstruction-era Republicans, Populists, and socialists, the successful diffusion of whiteness in Dallas' popular culture made resistance by non-elites a far more difficult proposition after the 1920s.

Many Mexican Americans wanted to pursue the path trod by European immigrants, shunning linguistic and cultural tradition as a means of escaping the onus of an assumed Indian and black heritage. As writer Walter T. Watson observed in the late 1930s, younger Mexicans in Dallas felt pressure to reject the traditional ways of their parents. "Hurried through the English language when they do attend school, regimented in American patriotisms and historical episodes, told to forget Spanish, forbidden on occasion to speak their own language on the playground, these and other second-generation scholastics lose respect for their old-country-oriented parents; the parents in turn, find difficulty in digesting the ridicule and attacks which their children wittingly and unwittingly levy against the Mexican customs and traditions they revere," Watson wrote. "I don't like being a Mexican," one child told Watson. "I want to be an American." Dallas children of Mexicans even shunned their religious heritage on racial grounds. "I don't like the Catholic Church . . . all the Mexicans go there," another child said.[88]

From the 1920s on, the pursuit of whiteness would result in little actual power for the white working class, Jews, or Mexicans but only frustrated the coalition-building power of the city's disinherited and guaranteed continued misery for much of the city's black population. From the 1920s to the 1960s each of these groups pursued solitary strategies of accommodation and confrontation with city elites, each approach ending in symbolic racial promotion but often little tangible gain. With poverty and violent oppression the cost of a nonwhite identity, whiteness became too great a temptation even for those with little hopes of fully attaining it.

FOUR

CONSEQUENCES OF POWERLESSNESS

Whiteness as Class Politics

Words can kill. For decades North Central Texas elites told poorer whites that African Americans represented near-beasts who desired nothing more than to rape Anglo-Saxon women and to overthrow their racial superiors. Such myths helped block a potential alliance between blacks and poor and working-class whites, but elites also feared civil disorder as unhealthy for business. The elite agenda became tangled in its own contradictions. In the first three decades of the twentieth century, mobs agitated by perceived lost racial status turned lynchings into routine public spectacles statewide.

On March 3, 1910, Dallas authorities arrested a sixty-eight-year-old African American man, Allen Brooks, for raping a three-year-old white child. Brooks had been found in a barn with a blood-smeared Mary Ethel Huvens, the missing child of a wealthy white family.[1] Brooks insisted on his innocence but never got a chance to present his defense. Before his indictment was even read in court, Brooks' court-appointed attorney George Clifton Edwards said, "a crowd of people . . . pushed . . . towards the Jury room after the Negro." The judge pleaded with the mob to let the court do its job, but a vigilante screamed, "To [hell] with the courts; they defeat justice."[2] Pushing past more than seventy officers, the lynchers grabbed Brooks, who weighed a diminutive 110 pounds, tying a noose around his neck and pitching the other end of the rope out the window to the waiting throng below. The outside crowd then yanked Brooks through the window. Brooks fell two floors to the ground, where those gathered "jumped on the negro with their feet and kicked him and stamped him" until his face was "crushed into a pulp." The mob then tied the rope still dangling around Brooks' neck to an automobile, "dragging the poor creature as if he were a sack of potatoes." Hoisting the lifeless Brooks on a telephone pole and leaving it dangling, whites cut swatches of clothing off his body as grisly souvenirs.[3] After Brooks' lynching, a grand jury failed to return a single indictment when law enforcement officials insisted that they had recognized no one in the courtroom swarm.[4]

Historian Grace Elizabeth Hale points out that some fellow historians often portray lynching as an atavistic response to the alienation engendered by the modern world. Hale instead argues that lynching sprang directly from the market economy. The rise of a small black middle class in the South that had access to consumer products poor whites could only dream of shook the foundations of the Southern social order. Blacks and whites, she writes, may have had to shop at separate stores, and African Americans may have been required to stand at the back of the line, but the marketplace turned whites and blacks into consumers of the same products. Many Southern merchants were more concerned with the green of a customer's cash than the color of his skin. Jim Crow and lynching spread partly because of these phenomena. Due to other nineteenth- and twentieth-century innovations like the telegraph, the radio, and the national press, lynchings also could become instantaneous national public spectacles reaffirming white supremacy even as market forces called racial hierarchies into question.[5]

As noted earlier, Dallas elites, alarmed at labor unrest between the 1890s to the 1930s, responded by diluting the electoral strength of white workers. The elite class that would solidify in the 1930s — a clique of real estate magnates, downtown department store owners, bankers, manufacturers, insurance company executives, and owners of utilities and media outlets — already began to take shape. They derived further support from elements of the middle class, such as club women who supported social reform as a means of mitigating the harshness of urban life and staving off working-class discontent. This elite/middle-class axis attempted to psychologically compensate disenfranchised whites with the ideology of white supremacy. Abstract racial superiority, however, did little to pay the bills. White workers felt their economic standing was sacrificed to the interest of racial and regional aliens — blacks, Mexicans, Northerners, and others. Mob violence represented one response of "native" whites to their declining status.

The Ku Klux Klan rose in Dallas in the 1920s, presenting itself as a defender of white workers' privileges. White supremacy thus became a self-destructive expression of working-class discontent. As in the nineteenth century, elites provided the match that lit burning crosses across Texas and then wondered how the fire started. By the 1920s, Dallas completed its transformation from a rural center to a major metropolis peopled largely by a wage-dependent proletariat. In 1920, the city had 158,970 residents, and fewer than 1 percent of them worked in agriculture. About 75 percent of the city's workforce age ten or older were wage earners, those who did not own their own farms or businesses and were not artisans or independent professionals such as doctors or lawyers. This broadly defined working class, which included municipal employees such as policemen, firefighters, and teachers, unskilled and semiskilled laborers, clerks, and servants, proved receptive to the Ku Klux Klan message.[6]

The Klan served not just as a platform for working-class fear and resentment against blacks and to a lesser degree Jews and Catholics but also as a vehicle for anti-elite sentiment. Many elites and members of the middle class initially applauded the Klan's opposition to what were seen as symptoms of lower-class rebellion such as socialism. Some Klansmen, however, insisted that elites make good on a perceived promise of white supremacy—that whites of all economic classes would be treated with the respect due racially superior Anglo-Saxons. Even though many of the powerful, including many Dallas elected officials, had donned the hood, elites increasingly perceived the Klan as a gaggle of uncouth undermen. An expression of white supremacy, the Klan ironically became another excuse for the racialization of poor whites.

In Texas, violence became the most obvious expression of racist discontent. From 1882, the first year such statistics were kept, until 1930, lynch mobs murdered 492 Texans including 143 whites and 349 blacks. Texans ranked behind only the Deep South states of Mississippi and Georgia in this bloody tally.[7] Graphic newspaper accounts of lynchings drove home for blacks and other potential victims the "consequences of powerlessness," as historian Jacquelyn Dowd Hall suggests.[8]

Texas lynching rose just before and during the 1920s partly as a reaction to the women's suffrage campaign, which represented one more challenge to elite rule. Black men achieved at least the legal right to vote in the 1860s, while farmers and working-class whites had expressed their political independence with the rise of the Populist, Socialist, and trade union movements. Now the Dallas leadership faced one more unpredictable electorate in the form of enfranchised women. Historian Jacquelyn Hall notes that most lynchings did not result from charges of rape but often happened when blacks were too successful or insufficiently obsequious to whites. Southern society, however, was not only racist but also patriarchal. Since slavery, white men had insisted upon access to black women as a prize for waging a successful racial war. The notion of voluntary sex between black men and white women conjured up, in Hall's words, "an image of black over white, of a world turned upside down." Lynching, Hall argues, functioned as a means of both sexual and racial suppression.[9]

The desire of the wealthy for commercial orderliness clashed directly with the need to thwart challenges posed by white women and African Americans to the established white male hierarchy. In the U.S. House of Representatives, Dallas Congressman Hatton W. Sumners argued that a 1922 lynching resulted from "all this preaching of social equality" between whites and blacks and that violence was a natural response by white men to the black rape of white women. "When the call comes from the woman, crying out from the depth of her outraged chastity, there comes to a man a call that reaches back to the days when he was a savage in a cave . . . The impulse is to kill, to kill as a wild beast would be killed."[10] In Sumners' formation, "manhood" could be measured by willingness to violently defend not just weak women threatened by black assault but the principle of white supremacy as well. The fact that white mob violence prevented black men from conversely protecting black women served as a symbolic emasculation of African American males.

White women in Southern rape folklore appeared as weak victims, thus confirming notions of contrasting male strength and vigor. Portraying women as victims of rape symbolically enfeebled the threatening "modern woman" and also denied her a voluntary role in her own sexuality, Hall suggests. The myth of the black rapist provided a rationale for white male supremacy. "The lynch mob in pursuit of the black rapist represented the trade-off implicit in the code of chivalry: for the right of the Southern lady to protection presupposed her obligation to obey," Hall writes.[11] The new political power of women, including the ratification of the women's suffrage amendment over strenuous objections from Texas males in 1920, terrified men already emasculated by market forces and inspired repeated lynchings.[12]

The myth of the black rapist provided a powerful counter-discourse to early-twentieth-century feminism, effectively frightening women across the South and leaving many feeling they needed male protection. Historian Edward Ayers quotes one woman in a 1952 interview who grew up in the middle Tennessee countryside and recalled that women were taught to sew, not cook, "because we were never allowed to enter the kitchen. There was a prohibition because the Negro men on the place that didn't have families were fed in the kitchen." The woman told her interviewer that her peers in the mid-twentieth century couldn't remember and "maybe couldn't understand the horror that had grown up of any contact with a Negro man."[13]

Negrophobic images of the black man as ravishing beast suffused the language of even counter-hegemonic movements such as Texas feminism to the extent that the state's suffragists hitched themselves to the cause of white supremacy. Texans advocating extending the vote to women distributed a leaflet published by the Congressional Union for Woman Suffrage, "Will the Federal Suffrage Amendment Complicate the Race Problem?" Some suffrage critics charged that an amendment granting women voting rights imperiled white supremacy because black women would be given the ballot. Many Texas suffragists countered that the addition of white women to the voter rolls more than made up for that risk. "In all of the fifteen Southern States, except Mississippi and South Carolina, THE WHITE WOMEN GREATLY OUTNUMBER THE NEGRO WOMEN," the Congressional Union leaflet declared. "In nine of these states, THE WHITE WOMEN OUTNUMBER THE TOTAL NEGRO POPULATION. There are in the Southern States 2,017,286 MORE WHITE WOMEN THAN NEGRO MEN AND WOMEN PUT TOGETHER." In effect, women's suffrage would double the white vote. The leaflet pointed out that black men, ostensibly possessing the vote, had already been denied the ballot due to duplicitous registration requirements. The same could be done to deny black women suffrage, the leaflet implied. With the addition of white women's ballots, female political equality would solidify, not dilute, racial inequality.[14]

Blacks in early-twentieth-century Texas inspired not just fear but also a patronizing envy. If their alleged absence of civilization marked African Americans as inferior it also, in the white mind, summoned an image of freedom from what psychoanalyst Sigmund Freud in the early twentieth century called "civilization's discontents." Western civilization meant a greater degree of physical comfort and convenience, but modern industrial society also brought depersonalization, a sense of lost power, an oppressive sense of economic vulnerability, and intense class conflict. Freud may have spoken for many of his contemporaries in Dallas when he suggested that "what we call our civilization is largely responsible for our misery, and . . . we should be much happier if we gave it up and returned to primitive conditions."[15]

In contrast, whites imagined that their black neighbors, in spite of grinding poverty, lived in infantile, carefree joy. The combination of contempt and envy many in white Dallas felt toward blacks transcended class boundaries. Even some elites desired escape from the pressure of modern existence into the presumed simplicity of black life. Evelyn Miller Pierce Crowell was the granddaughter of one of the city's wealthiest and most powerful early citizens, William Brown Miller, whose 1850s-era Millermore Mansion represents one of the town's few classic antebellum plantation homes and now serves as the heart of Old City Park. Evelyn Crowell's 1931 novel, *Hilltop*, depicted slaves as happy savages, guilt-free about their sensuality. *Hilltop* relates the experiences of Amy, a young girl who befriends Oz, the beau of Lucindy, a family slave. Oz was "the biggest and blackest negro in Polk County" (Miller's stand-in for early Dallas County) with the "reputation of being able to pick more cotton than any two darkies." Amy marvels at his muscular chest, which bulges in his "white piqué vest—the one which had once been stained with the blood of a man Oz stabbed." She sits, her eyes round with wonder, as Oz entertains her with B'rer Rabbit stories. Eventually sent to bed, Amy makes Oz promise to yodel the song "Turpentine" as he walks home. "There was something strange and elemental in the wordless song," Crowell writes. "It made the house-bound people of Polk stir restlessly on their pillows. It thrilled and excited Amy, left shivering pleasantly in the darkness after the last echo had died away."[16]

Frightened neither by Oz' exotic blackness nor the memory of his violence (the blood-stained vest), Amy felt only an erotic attraction to his presence. *Hilltop* suggests that even the wealthy desired a simpler life, closer to nature and free of the demands of the industrial order. Elite women like Crowell chafed at the sexual restrictions placed on them by the ideology of whiteness, which reduced women to the sexual prizes white men earned through their sacrifices in building civilization. Crowell, through her character Amy, shivered at Oz's animal magnetism and the thought of flaunting the city's racial and sexual boundaries by living a sensuous life completely outside the cold boundaries of whiteness.

Through black minstrelsy, an entertainment staple for organizations ranging from the Ku Klux Klan to the Elks and Masons through the 1960s, middle-class Anglos also shared a fantasy of shedding their white skins and its assumed burdens. White Victorian culture, while awash in mawkish sentimentality, emphasized severe emotional restraint for men in their personal relationships. As Victorianism crumbled in the industrial conflicts of the early twentieth century, Anglos looked to nonwhite models for an alternative cultural response. Music stores like J. P. Crouch in McKinney, Texas, thirty-two miles north of Dallas, sold music sheets with titles like "Looney Coons," "Coon Time Rag," "Ma Dandy Soldier Coon," and the minstrelsy-flavored "My Georgia Lady Love." Black-faced "coon" songs allowed middle-class white Dallasites gathered around a piano an opportunity to fantasize about simpler lives marked by boiling passions and unrestrained by the discipline of Western civilization. The free-spirited, syncopated rhythms of "Looney Coons" and the "Coon Time Rag" suggest the elation with which Anglo audiences fled from the emotional pressure of whiteness in a hypercompetitive, capitalist city.[17]

The imaginary world created by minstrelsy served as a rebuke to the cold, tightly controlled industrial order white men had created. The imagined pleasures of blackness thus became the genie white men desperately fought to return to the bottle. As they used lynching to subordinate blacks, working-class white men used the club of chivalry to beat unruly women back into their subordinate place. Elite and lower-income men made maleness synonymous with whiteness. By the 1920s white men in Dallas flocked to the standard of the Ku Klux Klan in their battle to maintain racial and sexual hegemony. The Klan soon took over the city, making Dallas the epicenter of a national KKK revival. The Klan, however, suffered serious inner conflict. Led largely by middle-class professionals locked out of Dallas decision making, the Klan attracted a considerable lower-income following. Klan leaders tried to win elite acceptance by echoing upper-class racial and gender ideology. The movement, however, splintered along class lines and could not form a stable ruling bloc.

The Ku Klux Klan loudly announced its presence on April 1, 1921. With a *Dallas Daily Times-Herald* reporter as a witness, a group of Klansmen drove to a desolate road six miles south of town and tormented Alex Johnson, an elevator operator from the Adolphus Hotel who allegedly had sex with a white woman. Klansmen abducted Johnson, threatened to hang him, and then burned "KKK" on his forehead with acid. The Klan dumped their bloody, shirtless victim in front of the Adolphus, scene of the alleged affair.[18]

The original Ku Klux Klan largely faded from the scene by the early 1870s, partly as a result of federal pressure. Original Grand Wizard Nathan Bedford Forrest distanced himself from the group by 1869, perhaps to placate Republican investors for his railroad enterprises.[19] William J. Simmons, a habitual joiner of fraternities, launched the revived Ku Klux Klan on Thanksgiving eve 1915 with a ceremonial cross-burning at Stone Mountain in Georgia. The new Klan added to the anti-black, anti-federal government message of its predecessor a new gospel preaching against the decadence of modern cities and warning of the dangers of immigration and of Jewish and Catholic plots to undermine Anglo-Saxon society. Fortunately for Simmons, he got a significant publicity boost with the release the same year of the pro-Klan film epic *The Birth of a Nation*. Simmons tapped into the Southern anti-Semitism stirred by the 1913 murder of Mary Phagan near Atlanta and the lynching two years later of a Jewish pencil factory superintendent, Leo Frank. Many of the disturbing undercurrents lurking beneath the Frank lynching arose in the later Klan harassment and violence against Jews in Dallas. The modern industrial order provided as much fuel to the Klan fire as did traditional Southern bigotry.

The Frank lynching marked not just suspicions about Jewish whiteness in the South but also resentment over Northern economic invasion of the South. The Phagan family, squeezed off their farm by dropping cotton prices, perfectly symbolized the New South jointly created by Northern capitalists and Southern boosters like Henry Grady. Mary Phagan, a thirteen-year-old at the time of her murder, worked ten hours a day for twelve cents an hour at the pencil factory to supplement her family's paltry wages.[20] Despite questionable evidence, Frank was convicted on the eyewitness testimony of a black man, James Conley, whose testimony would not have even been allowed had Frank's whiteness not been so widely questioned. Georgia demagogue and former Populist politician Tom Watson, in his newspaper, depicted Frank and his fellow Jews as an alien and depraved nonwhite race.[21] Disturbed by a lack of substantial, convincing evidence against Frank, the outgoing governor of Georgia, John Slaton, commuted his sentence to a life term, but a mob took the law into its own hands, seizing Frank from prison and hanging him on August 16, 1915.[22]

In the end, however, the trial and Frank's subsequent murder were as much about the disorder and fear bred by capitalism as about anti-Semitism or anti-black racism. "Frank represented the penetration of the South by the industrial revolution in a new and frightening way," writes historian Joel Williamson. "He was a rich Jew, managing a factory mostly owned by his New York uncle. Little Mary Phagan was Southern, white, and an innocent virgin. She was born in the country and killed in the city, in a Yankee-owned factory, fighting to preserve her purity against a bestial Jew. Such was the menace to the South at large, and the South turned its anger away from blacks and toward those alien forces that seemed most frightening to its essential virtue."[23]

By late November of that year, a group of two dozen men who called themselves the Knights of Mary Phagan announced the rebirth of the Ku Klux Klan with a cross-burning at Stone Mountain. The ceremony was cleverly timed just before the Atlanta premiere of *The Birth of a Nation*.[24] The new Klan skillfully blended xenophobia, antifeminism, and distress at the disrupting effects of industrial capitalism with traditional negrophobia, a popular message that made the revived movement, unlike its Southern-based Reconstruction-era counterpart, a powerful national force.[25] By the mid-1920s, the organization had a likely membership of three million. The Klan played a dominating role in Northern states like Indiana. In Texas, the KKK helped one of its members, Earle B. Mayfield, win election as a U.S. senator.[26]

In books, speeches, and public school curricula, elites had questioned the working-class white man's capacity for "civilization." Klansmen "proved" their whiteness by presenting themselves as defenders of traditional values, even if such a defense required vigilante violence. Presbyterian minister C. H. Storey made clear in a May 1922 address in Corsicana, fifty-five miles southeast of Dallas, that reasserting male supremacy represented a major objective of the KKK. "The coming of the automobile, the licentious screen . . . have multiplied many times the evil snares for womanhood in the land. The so-called double standard of society has been a great protection to American womanhood. It has been loosened, and men now . . . make remarks about women as they pass that in the last generation would have been treated as the most reprehensible."[27] Storey presented the Klan as a defender of women against sexist catcalls, but it is clear he was equally worried about women expressing the freedom allowed by the automobile and encouraged by sexually oriented movies.

At first, Dallas elites rushed to be counted as defenders of traditional virtue, and the Klan craved the respectability that came from an A-list membership. So eager was the Dallas Klan to sign up business elites that a KKK delegation paid a visit to Edward Titche, the owner of the Titche-Goettinger department store and asked him to join their organization. The merchant explained that, while he appreciated their time, he was unable to join because he was Jewish. "Too bad," one Klansman said, "you would have made a wonderful kleagle (recruiter)."[28] Generally, the Klan's recruitment proved more successful, with the organization dominating 1920s Dallas politics. With approximately 13,000 members, Dallas boasted the nation's largest Klan chapter. Hiram Wesley Evans, a downtown dentist and thirty-second-degree Mason, served as exalted cyclops for Dallas Klan No. 66. In 1922 Evans led a palace coup that overthrew Simmons as leader of the national Klan headquartered in Atlanta. Along with Evans, attorneys, city bureaucrats, elected officials, physicians, and ministers formed the Dallas Klan's leadership corps. The group's membership roster resembled a list of the city's who's who.[29]

By 1922 the Dallas Klan's Executive Committee included the city police commissioner, while the Klan's Steering Committee of One Hundred included a *Dallas Daily Times-Herald* reporter, four Dallas Power & Light Co. officials, the Ford Motor Company's local superintendent, the Democratic Party chairman, and the county tax assessor. Robert L. Thornton, president of the Dallas County State Bank (who served as Dallas mayor from 1953 to 1961) joined the Klan, as did Police Chief Elmo Straight. Klan sympathizers included Mayor Louis Blaylock and Congressman Hatton Sumners. Future notables who joined the Dallas Klan in the 1920s included Jesse E. Curry, police chief when President John Kennedy was assassinated in 1963, and Captain Will Fritz, head of the police homicide division when nightclub owner Jack Ruby murdered accused Kennedy assassin Lee Harvey Oswald.[30]

Boycott threats forced some small businessmen to join the Klan. Large businesses in Dallas avoided Klan embargoes by encouraging their employees to join. Even Jewish-owned businesses avoided Klan sanction through this means.[31] The Klan made every effort to appear as just another benevolent civic organization, opening Hope Cottage, a home for foundling children, and sponsoring a special Klan Day at the 1923 State Fair of Texas that 151,192 people attended.[32] Far more commonly, the Klan revealed itself as a terrorist enforcer of race and gender norms. The Trinity River bottoms echoed with the crack of the lash as the Dallas Klan enthusiastically bullwhipped accused sex offenders, Prohibition violators, and African Americans ignoring their assigned place in society. The Klan flogged sixty-eight victims at its favorite whipping post near the river, a setting that provided the desired eerie effect. "The flitting of a myriad fireflies in the damp weeds of the humid bottom made the scene a weird one," the *Dallas Daily Times-Herald* reported after one Klan whipping. "The hoot of owls and croaking of frogs on the river bank drowned the victim's groans."[33]

Misogyny ranked a near-equal with racism in the Dallas Klan's value system. Recalling the attack on Alex Johnson, an ex-Klansman noted in the 1940s, "They got mad when I wouldn't take part but I told them it was the woman who should be whipped. She was just a whore and he was getting business for her."[34] The defense of whiteness required not just keeping African Americans in their place but regulating the sexual behavior of unruly white women. "Whores" became a target as surely as any "nonwhite" group such as blacks or Jews, while defending "pure" women—always portrayed in Klan iconography as nonsexual, passive, and dependent on men for protection—became a leading rationale for Klan violence.

The Klan's presumed Puritanism won support from many mainstream Protestants, such as Dr. C. C. Selecman of Dallas' First Methodist Church (who would soon be president of Southern Methodist University) and the pastors of Westminister Presbyterian and the First Presbyterian Church.[35] However, with a series of well-publicized beatings and kidnappings, fissures formed in ruling circles. Elites outside the Klan worried that the KKK represented white working-class resentment of the ruling business oligarchy.

English immigrant George Bannerman Dealey became president of the *Dallas Morning News* in 1919 and, like the leadership of the newspaper to this day, spoke for a white, prosperous, and extremely conservative constituency of bankers and real estate oligarchs. For Dealey, the Klan represented trouble because violence and disorder discouraged outside business investment. More subtly, Dealey expressed concern over the class origins of many Klansmen. The *Morning News* consistently portrayed Klansmen as backward and unsophisticated and described the goals of the KKK as irrational and irrelevant. "White supremacy is not imperiled," a *Morning News* editorial of 1921 said. "Vice is not rampant . . . And if freedom is endangered, it is by the redivivus of mob spirit in the disguising garb of the Ku Klux Klan."[36]

The reference to "mob spirit" hints at some elites' concern that Klan control might pass from the sheriffs, police chiefs, and politicians to non-elites pursuing an unpredictable agenda. In cities like Dallas, the Klan usually launched membership drives by recruiting first from the leading citizens of the community, lending the group instant prestige. Next, organizers enrolled middle-class members. Then, to keep fees from new enlistments flowing up the organizational chart, the Klan made its pitch to the poorest strata of society. Each Klan chapter thus represented a cross-section of the community. The tensions within the Dallas Klan echoed those in Dallas society at large.[37]

For its non-elite members, the Klan provided a working-class cultural alternative to that offered by the earlier Populist and Socialist movements. Music like "Ku Klux Kismet," with its tonal suggestions of mysterious, supernatural power, gave Klan listeners a fantasy escape from political and economic impotence. The Klan, mindful of its constituency, staged dramatic initiations featuring cross-burnings, barbecue picnics, lemonade socials, special screenings of *The Birth of a Nation,* and, on one occasion, a blackface minstrel show to raise funds for Hope Cottage.[38] If elite whites considered themselves Anglo-Saxons and heirs of a lofty cultural tradition and saw white workers as inhabiting racial twilight, Klan leaders in Dallas tried to forge a new white brotherhood that transcended class boundaries.

Once a hobby of the rich and powerful, the Invisible Empire was portrayed by the *Dallas Morning News* as falling into the hands of grubby, middle-class schemers and working-class hoodlums. In spite of a national record of breaking strikes and disrupting labor unions,[39] the Dallas Klan recruited labor support. The Dallas Klan "declared war on Bolshevism, Socialism, Syndalcism and I.W.W. Ism,"[40] yet the *Dallas Morning News* saw the Klan as representing working-class revolt. "According to the tale of the street, the Klan is made up, in the cities at least, mostly of men whose impulse in politics is radical," an August 1922 editorial declared.[41] Many readers saw the *Morning News* as opposed to both the Klan and unions, thus strengthening the association for Dallasites between the KKK and the working class. F. L. Sherrill, a traveling agent for the *Dallas Morning News,* wrote a February 1922 memo to the management complaining of a growing perception that the *Morning News* was "against the oil business, The Unions [and] The K.K.K." Sherrill thought the newspaper should make clear that it "is not against the unions. Only a small percent of people belong to unions and they are two sides to questions. *News* is not against the K.K.K. but against its methods that it goes about to accomplish a purpose that all are interested in."[42] Even as the Klan harassed unions, the battle between the *Morning News* and the KKK embodied for some a struggle between rich and poor.

In Texas, the ranks of the labor unions and the Klan largely overlapped. In the 1922 Democratic Senate primary, Klan-backed candidate Earle Mayfield presented himself in his campaign literature as a friend of organized labor. Like the Klan itself, Mayfield suggested he could bridge the class gap tearing at Texas society. "HE IS the candidate of the Farmer. He is the candidate of the Business Man. He is the candidate of the Manufacturer and Jobber. He is a Union Man," one campaign leaflet declared.[43] Mayfield's opponent Jim Ferguson, an impeached former governor who tangled with the Klan on Prohibition, attributed his defeat in Dallas County and other cities to the Klan's ability to induce "a great majority of the labor union voters to quit me and vote for Mayfield."[44]

Labor activists communicated with their constituents through the Klan. On March 30, 1923, the Dallas Klan newspaper, *The Texas 100 Per Cent American,* published a petition signed by "representative members of the various crafts of Organized Labor in the City of Dallas." The petition called for an end to the immigration of Mexican laborers into the city and their employment in the city's streets and bridge department. "Illiterate, inefficient, incompetent Mexicans and aliens have for the past two years been given employment, to the exclusion of white, American citizens of our community, many of whom have had to walk the streets of Dallas jobless while their wives and children suffered for food and clothing." Signers of the petition charged that "efficient, white, American laboring men" could not "exist on the wage scale set by the present Street and Bridge Commissioner" and urged workers to block the commissioner's reelection.[45]

In this appeal, gender and race mutually reinforced white supremacy. The ability of white men to earn enough money to allow their women to stay at home caring for children and managing the household supposedly marked the dividing line between superior Anglo-Saxons and inferior blacks, browns, and southern and eastern European immigrants. Furthermore, cases where poverty forced non-Anglo and poorer women to work supposedly proved not only how unfeminine nonwhite and off-white women were but also the degree to which their husbands lacked masculinity. Hence, unions made earning "white men's wages" a priority for its membership, a cause the Klan claimed to support.[46]

Hiram Evans, the energetic head of the Dallas Klan, certainly tried to present the group as a friend of the city's workers. An Alabama native and son of a judge, Evans settled in Dallas shortly after the turn of the century and established a dental practice across the street from the downtown Neiman-Marcus department store.[47] Aware that his prestige in Dallas rested on his alliance with business elites, Evans tried to walk a tightrope, appealing directly to workers' grievances but blaming workplace trouble on blacks and immigrants rather than the city's merchant oligarchs. Believing in capitalism, the Klan could only blame people of color for the low wages and the poor working conditions of its Anglo union members. This message carried a particular resonance as the number of Dallas residents with foreign parentage expanded 51 percent between 1910 and 1920. The city's growing immigrant population "darkened" in that period, deriving increasingly from the eastern and southern European and Latin American origins. In 1900 fewer than 16 percent of immigrants living in Dallas came from eastern and southern Europe, Latin America, and Asia. By 1920, 54.4 percent of immigrants came from these regions, the largest group arriving from Mexico.[48]

At a time when Dallas unions splintered along racial and ethnic lines and divided between skilled and unskilled workers, the Klan presented itself as the white, working-class alternative to what it described as Jewish-inspired bolshevism. Contrary to the evidence, a Klan newspaper in Dallas, *The Texas 100 Per Cent American,* insisted that the Klan was not "an open shop organization."[49] A cartoon appearing in the newspaper, renamed *The Texas Kourier* in 1924, shows a sheeted and hooded Klansman as the conductor of an orchestra that included "Industry," "Agriculture," "Labor," "Capital," the "Legislature," and the "Judiciary." The Klansman leads all in a musical piece labeled "Patriotism." "Now, Perhaps, We'll Get Some Harmony," the caption reads. By uniting producers against Jews, blacks, and Catholics, the Klan could succeed where the Populists, Socialists, and labor unions failed.[50]

In his appeals to the working class, Evans damned corporate greed. With their insistence on incessant toil, Hiram Evans said during his Klan Day speech at the 1923 State Fair, capitalists had even profaned the Christian Sabbath. "The command from on high was to work, work, work, work, work, work."[51] Wealthy elites, Evans claimed, had instituted slavery to fill their insatiable demands for labor, thus racially polluting the nation with Africans, but even that was not enough. "There followed logically, inevitably, the more modern and monstrous cheap labor idea," he said. ". . . Humanity has become a commodity. For mercenary motives, our importers of it want the most inferior grade . . . Do our overlords of industry realize what they are doing to America?"[52] As in other communities, the Klan in Dallas often blurred the boundary between reactionary and progressive politics. Whatever place the Klan occupied in Dallas' political spectrum, however, its rhetoric sounded red to Dallas elites.[53]

Like its Reconstruction-era ancestor, the 1920s Klan proved to be murderous and ruthless. The purported elite class origins of the original Klan covered all its sins, however, while the working-class origins of some 1920s Klansmen made their crimes symptoms of public disorder.[54] Associated with Confederate officers like Nathan Forrest, the old Klan appeared in the elite Anglo mind as an association of gentlemen defending refined ladies from underclass depredations. To elites, the new, more vulgar Klan lacked such elán. "It [the first Klan] had been organized to protect the women and children because this proclamation of freedom for the slaves had come out [and] . . . they wanted to . . . protect the home front," Carrie Kearney recalled in a 1974 interview. Kearney lived in East Dallas during the 1920s with her sister and her father, Martin McNulty Crane, who had served as the lieutenant governor of Texas from 1892 to 1894 and state attorney general from 1894 to 1898. "They said that [the Klan] had nothing to do with religious prejudice or racial fears," Kearney continued. Kearney's father led the Dallas County Citizens League, the chief anti-Klan organization in 1920s Dallas.[55]

By contrast, Klan opponents saw the modern Klan as a fraudulent copy whose existence defamed the legendary Klan of Reconstruction. White men were expected to uphold gender norms by protecting passive white women. In this role, the old mythical Klan ostensibly proved itself the defenders of Anglo-Saxon tradition. According to the Dallas County Citizens League, the record of the new Klan's "treatment of women in Texas and elsewhere constitutes one of the blackest pages of its black history." The Citizens League, in its pamphlet "The Case Against the Ku Klux Klan," cited a June 16, 1922, incident in Shelby County, 173 miles southeast of Dallas near the Louisiana border, as an example of the new Klan's unmanliness. Klansmen there seized a woman from the hotel where she worked, stripped her naked, tarred and feathered her, and then abandoned her. Multiple incidents like this made the new Klan "a travesty upon the name of the original organization . . . of the Reconstruction period," the pamphlet declared.[56]

The Dallas Klan also generated backlash from some elites as it defined immigrants from southern and eastern Europe and Mexico, as well as Jews and Catholics, as nonwhite. In this, they merely echoed views widely held by some of Dallas' powerful citizens. J. C. McNealus, Dallas' state senator from 1911 to 1921, developed a pro-labor reputation. Even this relatively progressive elite, however, called for the deportation of the "filthy" Greek, "Dago and Slav" who crowded "Americans" from jobs, even "dethroning the American negro from his shoe-shining stand."[57] This view drew opposition from some elites who profited particularly from exploitation of Mexican labor in agriculture and industry. Klan leaders also faced some resistance from rank-and-file members for whom anti-Semitism held little attraction.

Hiram Evans shared the fears of many wealthy, powerful Dallasites that the immigrants pouring into the city represented racial degeneration. "In the beginning of the national life . . . our policy was rightly that of the open door,"

Evans said in his 1923 Klan Day speech at the State Fair. ". . . Those who would might come. Millions did come—the best the earth had to offer—Huguenot and Cavalier and Puritan . . . Then, suddenly, the character of our immigration changed . . . There was a fundamental inferiority of racial and national strains. The Anglo-Saxon, the Scandinavian, and the Teuton began to recede, with an overwhelming preponderance of peoples like the Slav, the Latin, and the Greek."[58] Only Anglo-Saxons could truly respect the rule of law, Evans declared. "From the British Isles and Scandinavia and Germany and Holland and Switzerland have come people born to that divinely essential attitude," Evans said in his Fair Park speech. "Let more of them come. They are our kinsmen in tradition and ideals. But generations, or centuries, cannot school the Latin, the Greek, the Balkan and the Slav to that fundamental conception."[59] Evans asserted that Americanism meant a "Nordic" heritage and that southern and eastern Europeans lacked the divinely inspired gift of republicanism. In a debate published in 1924, Evans held that such immigrants were as "utterly and eternally hopeless from the American point of view" as any black person.[60] Elites in the early twentieth century hit upon a largely class-based definition of whiteness. To Evans, regardless of wealth or poverty, one could be white if one descended from northern Europe, believed in Protestant Christianity, and opposed Marxism. Evans also makes clear the connection many Dallasites made between white racial identity and support for American-style democracy.

Evans ranked two groups, Jews and Catholics, as particular threats. Klan anti-Catholicism tapped into a deep well of Dallas culture. Like Jews, Catholics represented a religious group from multiple national origins that had integrated into the city's power structure but nevertheless faced racial demotion in the early twentieth century. Also like Jews, Catholics faced accusations of participating in a vast conspiracy to control the world. Dallas served as a hotbed of anti-Catholicism, giving wide support to the anti-Catholic, anti-immigrant Know Nothing Party during the 1850s.[61] Nineteenth-century Texas anti-Catholic rhetoric echoed anti-Semitic accusations. "Imagine our Senate and cabinet composed of a majority of Catholics . . . and our glorious republic would be metamorphosed into a Catholic hierarchy," declared the *Texas State Times,* a Know-Nothing newspaper. "The inquisition, the crucifix, the torture, the faggot and torch would be reared in the forum of Justice . . . our rivers blush with the blood of protestants. The Catholics . . . openly call themselves anti-democratic, anti-republican . . . and they hold fast their allegiance to a foreign potentate."[62]

The allegedly anti-democratic, anti-republican nature of Catholicism contrasted in the minds of Dallas elites with the innate republicanism of

Anglo-Saxons, although light-skinned Catholics could still win positions of authority in Dallas after the Civil War. Anti-Catholicism, however, was commonplace among Southern Baptists, a growing Protestant sect within Dallas. In 1874 the town of Jefferson, Texas, hosted the Southern Baptist Convention. Railroad companies provided members of the convention free passes. When the entourage reached Dallas, the mayor and other leading citizens arranged a reception for the Baptist delegates at the city's opera house. One Georgian, Dr. J. H. DeVotie, spoke for many delegates when he contrasted the "soul-liberty" Baptists supposedly represented as opposed to "the propagation of the religion of Romanism by the sword and faggot." DeVotie and his fellow delegates discovered to their embarrassment that Dallas' mayor was Catholic.[63]

In spite of DeVotie's apologies, his statement reflected a strong current in Dallas Protestantism that was only reinforced by Cyrus Scofield's dispensationalism. Perhaps embittered by his divorce from his Catholic first wife, Scofield, in his reference Bible, identifies Catholicism with paganism and the corrupt, one-world religion he predicted the Antichrist would create in the final days. "Romanism weds Christian doctrine to pagan ceremonies," Scofield wrote in one footnote. The future world dominance of "apostate" Catholicism's false doctrines were prophetically symbolized by the "Whore of Babylon" mentioned in the seventeenth chapter of Revelation.[64] Thus, in the Scofieldian view, Catholicism was both alien and demonic.

Like Scofield, the Klan also identified the Vatican with the "Great Scarlet Woman" of Revelation. In this interpretation of the Apocalypse, Scofield and the Klan alike argued that the Vatican would be the vehicle through which the Antichrist would impose false Christianity on the world in the final days.[65] Furthermore, by insistently referring to Catholic doctrine as "Romanism," mainstream Protestants like Scofield and DeVotie as well as the Klan characterized the Catholic Church as innately foreign, linking the institution with southern European racial decadence. Catholics inherently represented the antithesis of Anglo-Saxon democracy, Hiram Evans declared in one pamphlet. "Catholicism is built . . . upon the monarchial idea of the individual as subject instead of citizen. The doctrine of democracy in its every relation to humanity is exactly the reverse."[66] Because Catholics were opposed to democracy, Klan leader Colonel Joe Camp of Georgia implied to those assembled at a Klan rally in nearby Corsicana, they could not by definition be Anglo-Saxon and therefore represented something less than white. "The germ of the principles of the Ku Klux Klan is as old as the Magna Charta of England," he told the assembled Klansmen:

This government is an Anglo-Saxon achievement . . . This Anglo-Saxon influence, statesmanship and leadership is being undermined by alien blood. The Catholics are organized and have been for centuries, and we cannot join them if we wanted to, and thank God we do not want to. The Jews are organized and we could not join them, if we wanted to, and thank God we do not want to. The Negroes are organized and we could not join them if we wanted to, and thank God we don't want to . . . we have permitted the Trojan horse to enter our gates. The slum of the Old World, illiterate treacherous and envious, have flooded into this country to be the tools and weapons of designing men, unscrupulous demagogues, and crooked politicians.[67]

In a few short sentences, a national Klan leader characterized Catholics and Jews as having "alien blood." Like other racial inferiors, Catholics and Jews were totalitarian by nature, he argued. Camp grouped Catholics and Jews with African Americans, casting them outside the community of white folks. The Klan movement, with its substantial working-class support, threatened to racialize Catholics and to loosen the Jewish community's tentative grips on the levers of commercial power that whiteness bestowed.

The relationship of the Catholic Church to African Americans raised further Protestant suspicions. The Dallas Roman Catholic diocese, established in 1890, opened a black parish, St. Peter the Apostle, in Dallas' Freedman's Town near the modern State-Thomas historic district in 1905 with a dozen African Americans as members. A school for African American children, the Sisters' Academy, opened three years later at the request of Mary and Valentine Jordan. The Jordans, Baptist former slaves impressed by the Dallas Ursuline Sisters' teaching methods, grew frustrated with poorly funded black public schools and saw greater educational opportunity at the Catholic school, later named St. Peter's Academy. Immersed, however, in nonhierarchical, highly expressive Protestant faiths, African American children attending the academy and their parents rarely responded to Catholicism's more austere theology. Only three of St. Peter's original forty students were Catholic, and for decades white priests expressed frustration at their inability to win converts.[68] In a November 1924 canonical report, Father John T. Neifert noted that St. Peter's had not much difficulty in maintaining religious orthodoxy where "one or both parents are Catholics, but most of our converts have been children with (non)Catholic parents and it is difficult to make their family continue to make them attend church."[69]

Over the decades, tensions built between those African Americans who did convert and a church some blacks saw as one more white-dominated institution.[70] In spite of future conflict, in the 1920s the Catholic Church seemed one of the most open establishments to African Americans, prompting the Klan to charge that the church promoted miscegenation. The Klan accused the church of forcing "white women to confess their sins and even the thoughts of their hearts to bachelor Negro Buck Priests." The church's purpose in installing black priests, the Klan claimed, was for "the purpose of marshalling the Negroes to help kill out white Americanism."[71] To accomplish this, the "negroes are being Catholicized all over the South, and are being made to believe they are on a social plane, equal and, no doubt, superior to the WHITE PROTESTANT peoples of the earth."[72] Evans and other Dallas Klan leaders sought to make Protestantism and whiteness synonymous.

The large migration of mostly Catholic Mexican refugees fleeing revolutionary violence south of the border after 1910 only underscored the alien image of the Dallas Church. The Roman Catholic diocese founded Our Lady of Guadalupe Parish, the first in the city for Mexicans, in 1913. By the late 1920s, the city had two more Mexican parishes.[73] As previously noted, Mexicans in the Anglo mind were born of the sexual union of southern Europeans with Indians and blacks. Many Anglos believed Mexicans represented the worst traits of all three groups. Some Klan members saw the stance of the Catholic Church toward Mexican immigrants as race treason.

In the decade following the outbreak of the Mexican Revolution in 1910, the Daughters of Charity order of nuns brought food, medicine, and clothing to Mexican refugees huddled on the city's outskirts. In the 1920s another wave of Mexican immigrants found themselves stranded in the city by unscrupulous labor contractors who failed to secure promised jobs in Northern states. Nuns working in a warehouse across the street from Our Lady of Guadalupe ran a school featuring religion and English classes, operated a free medical clinic, and in 1925 opened a kindergarten that provided children with free breakfasts. A high school for Mexican girls soon followed. Large Mexican American communities formed along Eagle Ford Road, now known as Singelton Boulevard, and in "El Cemento Chico." The "Cement City" community in West Dallas housed impoverished whites and immigrant workers employed at the Lone Star Cement Plant. Carmelite priests seeking to alleviate poor working conditions acted as intermediaries for Mexican workers employed at Texas Power and Light and a brick factory in nearby Malakoff.[74] The Catholic diocese's attempts to make life for immigrants more bearable further heightened Klan suspicions.

To Dallas Klan leaders, the fear caused by the alien Catholic menace eclipsed even anti-Semitic paranoia. The Vatican schemed for world dominion, Klan leaders insisted, and Jews served as unwitting pawns. "The Catholic has all to gain, and nothing to lose, by tying the Jew on to his kite's tail for a short while until he gets tired of using him and ditches him," warned a Klan editorial entitled "Can It Be Possible the Sharp Jew Is Being Hoodwinked?" The Catholic Church "is determined to exterpate [sic] all (Jews and Gentiles alike) who fail or refuse to bow to the will of the Pope."[75]

By the 1920s Jews were a small but highly visible part of the Dallas community, numbering approximately 8,000 of the city's 135,000 residents.[76] Some elites had embraced successful Jews such as the Sangers as part of the commercial elite, but Jews had little direct political power in the city. Some elites like Lewis Dabney condemned Jews as dangerous aliens. Perhaps tapping into public fears generated by the Frank case, the Dallas Klan publicly warned Jewish men to not date Gentile women. The Dallas Klan targeted a Jewish picture framer, Austrian immigrant Phillip J. Rothblum, for a whipping in February 1922 and warned him to leave town by 6 P.M. the next day. A nine-year resident of Dallas, Rothblum sold his home and business at a loss.[77]

If some Gentile Dallasites saw Jews as Christ killers, many still saw modern Jews as the heirs of the Old Testament Hebrews. Gentiles influenced by Scofield believed Jews would play a key role in provoking the second coming of Christ. The Klan answered such reluctant anti-Semites by embracing British Israelism, an eccentric theology developed in England in the nineteenth century. British Israelism taught that white "Aryans" descended from the ten "lost tribes of Israel" who disappeared from the Old Testament after their dispersal by the Assyrian Empire in 609 B.C.E.[78] Adherents of British Israelism believed that Jews, while descending from the Israelite tribe of Judah, became racially tainted by mixing with inferior Middle Eastern pagans. The ten lost tribes of Israel, meanwhile, had migrated to northern and central Europe and founded the most powerful empires in the modern world, including Great Britain and the United States. The white Western world's wealth and power in the twentieth century served as fulfillment of God's promise to the Old Testament patriarchs. "Aryans," including whites of northern European descent in Dallas, and not Jews were the chosen people of Bible, divinely granted racial superiority to subdue the planet. A Klansman could now maintain his anti-Semitism and at the same time revere a Bible cleansed of its Jewish taint.[79] The Texas 100 Per Cent American told its readers that "the Anglo Saxons are the ten tribes of Israel." The Klan would lead the God-chosen Anglo-Saxons in a battle of Armageddon against dark-skinned undermen.[80]

By the 1920s, however, Catholics and Jews represented religious, not racial, groups to many if not most Dallasites. Gentiles largely refused to abandon traditional Christian theology and embrace British Israelism. Even Dallas whites agreeing with the Klan on male supremacy and the suppression of vice rejected what was seen as the Klan's hostility to religious freedom. When the Klan responded to the *Dallas Morning News'* editorial campaign against the organization by spreading rumors that the paper was run by Catholics, the newspaper circulation lost 3,000 subscribers. Some readers, however, took offense at the Klan's efforts. "[A]lthough, my sympathies are with the Ku Klux Klan, in their efforts to do good, at-the-same-time, I will never join them in a fight on the Catholics and the Jews," one reader, S. Webb, wrote the *Morning News* in 1922.[81] Even some rank-and-file Klansmen rejected the leadership's anti-Semitism and anti-Catholicism. "A Colonel Simmons had a dream of reorganizing the Ku Klux Klan along the lines of the old Klan," a former Klansman recalled in the late 1940s. "But promoters got ahold of the organization and decided the old ideas were not good enough. They started the anti-Jew and anti-Catholic ideas even though the Klansmen swore to the memory of General [Nathan Bedford] Forrest who had been head of the Knights of Columbus . . . I could see no reason for opposing the Jews as I have never been anti-religionist and I became disgusted when the Klan started jumping on Catholics. I can't see telling anyone what religion they must believe in."[82]

Responses of the Jewish community to the Klan varied, with Rabbi David Lefkowitz of Temple Emanu-El mounting a highly public campaign against the Klan. The most important Jewish merchants in the city, Alex Sanger, Charles Sanger, Herbert Marcus, Leon Harris, and Arthur Kramer, lent substantial support to the anti-Klan Dallas Citizens League. The Jewish-owned Schepps Bakery, however, paid the KKK membership dues for fifty employees. Julius Schepps later said he did this to monitor Klan activity, with his employees serving as a source of inside information. One Jewish firm bought $400 worth of advertising in the Klan's *Texas 100 Per Cent American* newspaper, perhaps to avoid a crippling business boycott. The Young Men's Hebrew Association helped raise funds for the Klan's Hope Cottage, with Alex Sanger appearing alongside Grand Titan Z. E. Marvin at its opening ceremonies. Three Jews—Charles Sanger, Harry Sigel, and Lawrence Kahn—sat on the board of Klansman R. L. Thornton's Dallas County State Bank, a firm that advertised as a "KKK Business Firm 100%."[83] Such Jewish collaboration with the Klan led Jim Ferguson, the previously impeached Texas governor and anti-Klan leader who was himself an anti-Semite, to charge that a conspiracy existed in which "the Ku Klux are to get the big offices and the Big Jews are to get the big business."[84]

Southern Jews often sharply split from their Northern peers on civil rights for African Americans. Northern Jews, many of them recent immigrants from eastern Europe, where they had suffered harsh persecution at the hands of the Russian czar, participated in and actively supported groups like the National Association for the Advancement of Colored People (NAACP). Southern Jewish communities felt more vulnerable. "Southern Jews," as author Mark Bauman notes, "were aware that in times of crisis, they served as convenient scapegoats." Some Southern Jews actively embraced Southern racism. Others opposed black oppression on strictly moral grounds but did not believe in racial equality. Another segment of the Jewish population supported black civil rights and opposed white supremacist ideology, but most in this faction preferred to work behind the scenes for fear of making their community a target of violence. Relatively few Southern Jews actively campaigned against Jim Crow or lynching. Where this did happen, generally a Northern-born rabbi not emotionally tied to the racial order in Dixie led the resistance. Such would be the case in Dallas. Most Southern Jews, however, resented the civil rights activism of Northern Jews who would not be around to suffer the consequences of Southern Gentile backlash.[85]

Dallas Jews probably felt outnumbered by potentially hostile Gentile neighbors, while internal ethnic divisions further weakened resistance to the Klan. A sharp line divided Jews of western European and German origin—many of whom had immigrated before the twentieth century—and later immigrants of eastern European heritage. German Jews were more integrated into the Dallas economic power structure, more assimilationist in philosophy, and more Reform in theology. Eastern European Jews were less prosperous and more likely to be union activists. "Intermarriage" to the Jewish community less often referred to the union of Jews and Gentiles and more often to marriage between German and eastern European Jews. One Jewish woman recalled her father's anger when she dated a Russian tailor's son, whom he saw as a social inferior. "If you plant potatoes, you don't get apples," he said.[86] Divisions within the community probably made insecure Jews less likely to confront the Klan.

Privately, this accommodation strategy distressed Rabbi Lefkowitz. Lefkowitz, born in Austria-Hungary in 1875, lost his father at an early age and grew up in the Hebrew Orphan Asylum in New York City, where teachers fired his interest in the Hebrew language, Jewish history, and the Talmud. Lefkowitz entered rabbinical studies at the liberal Hebrew Union College in Cincinnati and was appointed rabbi by a Dayton, Ohio, congregation upon graduation, a position he held for twenty years. Lefkowitz then accepted the leadership of Dallas' Temple Emanu-El in 1920.[87] Lefkowitz' experiences inspired a commitment to social justice and a faith in the ultimate goodness of American society. Evil could be defeated, or at least mitigated, by living an exemplary life and through moral, rational persuasion. Lefkowitz' response to the Klan was passionate but gentle.

Answering a friend concerned about Alex Sanger's appearance at the opening of Hope Cottage, Lefkowitz emphasized the need to keep the small Jewish community unified. "I can't answer your question concerning brother Alex Sanger sitting on the platform at the Hope Cottage dedication," Lefkowitz wrote. ". . . [D]on't get too blue about it and don't let the Klan situation worry you too much. It is bad enough, to be sure, but we mustn't let it reduce our own power by worrying us and making us sick. We need the best we have to fight it to a finish." [88] In a 1934 letter to a Christian minister, Lefkowitz recalled that a Klan member ran in an election for the principle office in the Scottish Rite. The non-Klan opponent won by one vote. Lefkowitz was asked to address fellow Masons following the election. Reminding the audience of sacrifices made by Jewish servicemen and clergy during World War I, Lefkowitz asked his audience if those Jewish men should be considered "100% American." Regarding the Klan, Lefkowitz asked, "what would Christ do?" The response from Gentiles, Lefkowitz said, was instant. "The end of my address was marked by applause of Klansmen as well as non-Klansmen . . . Masonry was on its way to kicking the Klan members totally out of its membership," Lefkowitz said.[89] Working around the reticence of fellow Jews and not confronting the Klan's anti-black racism, Lefkowitz relied on Gentile iconography in persuading Christians to reject the KKK.

Both Jewish and Gentile opponents of the Klan portrayed it as a mob movement rooted in the lower classes. By attacking the Klan as the madness of the dysfunctional lower classes, Jews, Gentile liberals, and elites could prevent middle-class men like Hiram Evans and Z. E. Marvin from forming a new Dallas ruling bloc. The Little Theater of Dallas openly critiqued the hypocrisies of white racism during the height of Klan activism in the 1920s, winning national recognition and drawing enthusiastic crowds in the process. The theater's attacks on racial violence, however, supported class hierarchy. Many participants in the Little Theater were targets of Klan hostility. Prominent Jews such as Eli Sanger and Louis Lipsitz served on the board of directors, while the Little Theater's acting troupe included newspaper writer John Rosenfield.[90] The irrational, unpredictable poor white served as the primary bête noir in the imagination of the Little Theater company. Alarmed by its potential radicalism, elites such as those who ran the Little Theater now indirectly condemned the 1920s Klan for causing public disorder.

In its debut 1923–1924 season, the Little Theater portrayed poor "white trash" as the authors of injustice, violence, and racial discord. The theater

staged *Judge Lynch,* a one-act play written by *Dallas Daily Times-Herald* entertainment editor John William Rogers Jr., concerning an innocent black man
unjustly hanged by a mob after being accused of committing murder during
the theft of a watch. As the play opens, two major characters, Mrs. Joplin and
Ella, discuss the shocking death of a hot-tempered man called Squire Tatum,
who was fatally struck on the head with an ax handle. The black suspect (referred to only as "the Jacks nigger") is described as "a hard-workin' hand, and
perlite and respectful as a body could want. Kinder timid-like too." Ella and
Mrs. Joplin have a hard time picturing the black man committing the crime
yet decide that he must be guilty because he has already been judged and sentenced by the local mob. "It does look like niggers would learn, but I reckon
they wouldn't be niggers if they did," Mrs. Joplin says.[91]

A mysterious white stranger arrives who seems unduly curious about the
Tatum murder. The stranger nervously asks if the killer has been caught. In
a most unheroic description of lynch law, Ed, a witness to the lynching, says
the mob struck the suspect as a man taunted him, screaming, "Confess you
black baboon, or we'll burn you alive." The lynch mob begins to chant, "Burn
him—build a fire." It looks like the black victim will be immolated when a
member of the mob makes a "generous" offer: "If he'll confess we'll only hang
him. If he don't—Well, boys, we'll give him a minute to make up his mind
how he's going to die before we start gathering the wood."[92] Facing the prospect of being burned at the stake, the accused man breaks down and makes
a confession. The stranger, who has been listening with rapt attention, gasps
with shock, "He's confessed!"[93] Mrs. Joplin reacts with a shrug of the shoulders to this rite of human sacrifice and gives an ironic lecture on the difference
between white civilization and African primitiveness:

> Something that belongs to the wilderness—that ain't got no place in a white
> man's land, and never will. Niggers has got used to Christian clothes, they
> don't put rings in their noses no more, and some of them's ironed most of
> the kink out of their hair. But they ain't never got rid of that other thing
> . . . Mostly it's asleep now, but you can never tell when it's going to wake
> up—when it's going to lie waiting for you like one of those African animals
> they has in cages at the circus would . . . That's why no white woman dares
> go down a lonely road, or cross a field after dark.[94]

The description of the lynching leaves the stranger agitated. Squire Tatum
had a foul temper, the stranger insists, and maybe "got what was coming to
him."[95] After the others leave the stranger alone on stage, he reaches into his

pocket and drops an object onto the wood pile that turns out to be Squire Tatum's watch. "That nigger was here this afternoon," Ella says upon discovering the watch. "I told you Ed ought not to leave us alone."[96]

Judge Lynch was both a critical and popular success, winning a prize in a national competition. Performed at the Majestic Theater, *Judge Lynch* drew more than 23,000 to ten sell-out performances.[97] Strikingly, this one-act script directly challenged many of the mythologies upon which white supremacy was based. Whites hypocritically proclaim their moral superiority to "niggers" while committing the savage murder of an innocent black man. The characters' bigotry blinded them to the guilt of a white stranger. The play also represented a more subtle discourse on class. With their substandard English, Ella, Mrs. Joplin, and Ed are coded as poor white trash, the undermen responsible for racial violence. Lynch law, Rogers asserts, springs from ignorance, not raw power politics. As a Dallas journalist, Rogers undoubtedly knew that among the Klan, the chief instigators of racial violence in his time, numbered policemen, lawyers, and even a one-time editor of his own newspaper among its members. Yet white trash are portrayed as truly "something that belongs to the wilderness—that ain't got no place in a white man's land, and never will."

Elite attacks on the Klan only enhanced its popularity with the working class. The anti-Klan Dallas County Citizens League, made up of men like former state attorney general Martin M. Crane and merchant Alex Sanger, proved ineffective. Four days after the formation of Citizens League, 2,342 new members enrolled in the Klan at a mass meeting. The Citizens Association, dominated by bankers and real estate interests, opposed the Klan in the 1923 municipal elections, pledging to rule Dallas "without regard to color, race, religious or other affiliations." The Klan-backed slate won the April 3 election in a landslide, capturing every race, the first shutout of the Citizens Association municipal slate since its formation eighteen years earlier. The Klan-backed mayoral candidate, Louis Blaylock, won more than 73 percent of the vote.[98]

The fall of the Klan in Dallas, however, came swiftly following the victory of Miriam "Ma" Ferguson, wife of the previously impeached governor James Ferguson, in the 1924 Democratic gubernatorial primary over pro-Klan candidate Felix D. Robertson.[99] The *Morning News'* reluctant support of Ferguson notwithstanding, Robertson carried Dallas County two-to-one in the primary but lost to Ferguson in the statewide runoff.[100] Yet the Klan no longer appeared as politically omnipotent as it had just a few months earlier. "After Robertson was beaten the prominent men left the Klan," a former member later recalled.[101] Klan leadership became primarily a realm of "low-level, white collar workers and civil servants, who kept the secret organization alive."[102]

The Klan was devastated in 1925 when one of its national leaders, David Stephenson, was convicted of second-degree murder and sentenced to life imprisonment for the abduction and sexual assault of a secretary who later committed suicide. In the wake of this scandal, state membership declined from a peak of 97,000 to 18,000 in 1926. Dallas membership dropped from 13,000 to 1,200 that same year. The KKK remained marginalized, playing an insignificant role when the final crisis over legal segregation in Dallas arrived in the 1960s.[103]

Nevertheless, the 1920s Klan profoundly shaped Dallas' racial beliefs for decades to come. Jews, to some degree, discovered common interests with African Americans, and many future leaders such as Rabbi Levi Olan bravely battled the city's racial conventions, but the community never completely abandoned accommodation. The Klan and the ongoing phenomenon of racial violence politicized many Texas women who saw an intimate relationship between racial and gender oppression. In 1924 Dallasite Jessie Daniel Ames, the college-educated, widowed wife of an Army surgeon, became the director of the Texas council of the Atlanta-based Commission on Interracial Cooperation. In 1929 she moved to Atlanta to become director of the CIC's Women's Committee.[104]

While there, she founded the CIC-financed Association of Southern Women for the Prevention of Lynching. Ames fought to shatter the sexual and racial mythologies reinforcing lynch law. "Lynching . . . far from offering a shield against sexual assault, served as a weapon of both racial and sexual terror, planting fear in women's minds and dependency in their hearts," historian Jacquelyn Hall notes, summarizing Ames' critique of lynching. "It thrusts them into the role of personal property or sexual objects, ever threatened by black men's lust, ever in need of white men's protection."[105] Not consigned to the margins like earlier Socialists and Populists, Lefkowitz, Ames, and progressives like them believed in capitalism and American democracy. Insinuating themselves into elite circles, they believed that changing Dallas was a matter of appealing to reason and hoping that consensus for reform would follow. Dallas liberals in the 1950s and 1960s would follow the Ames and Lefkowitz model of implementing incremental changes on the margins but never directly critiquing the role capitalism played in generating racial and gender oppression.

Already by the 1930s Dallas was more complex and more diverse than much of the South, making the battles for human justice more difficult to pick and victories harder to calculate. African Americans could not help but notice that the disappearance of the Klan did not bring a freer or more just racial climate. Dallas racism and extremism simply no longer drew the national press or generated sensationalistic headlines. By the late 1930s the phenomenon of lynching had virtually disappeared. A quieter regime of racial violence reigned, one not under the glare of the burning cross. Dallas elites had used lynching as a form of institutional violence to control dissent before the Civil War and during Reconstruction and to suppress black assertion in the early twentieth century. This proved a risky strategy, as violence often spun out of control and passed from elite to lower-class hands. The Jim Crow system that fully developed in Dallas after the 1920s represented a more subtle and effective form of establishment dominance. Lynching had oppressed both black men and white women. Segregation served a similar function, representing a symbolic form of establishment violence. The draconian edicts of all-white juries, the ramshackle condition of Jim Crow schools, and the inferior or nonexistent medical care offered to sick blacks undercut African American resistance and underscored to Anglo workers, Jews, Catholics, and Mexicans the dangers of losing whiteness. In the coming decades, segregation became lynching by other means.

FIVE

WATER FORCE

Resisting White Supremacy under Jim Crow

One tree native to North Texas, the bois d'arc, seems impervious. Finely grained with a yellowish interior that grays as it ages, the stump of a bois d'arc twists in such a way that one sees flow and motion in the wood fiber. When Dallas residents started using the bois d'arc as a building material, they found it was almost impossible to cut or shape with hand tools, but this durability was the tree's chief attraction. Use bois d'arc to build a fence, and one hundred years later the wire will have rotted away from rust and age but the wood remains, rock solid and resistant to weather, insects, and the ravages of time. So hard was bois d'arc wood that it became the favored material to pave Dallas streets in the late nineteenth century.[1]

The endurance of the bois d'arc inspired admiration. A similar perseverance in Dallas' African American community drew rage. Under slavery, white masters attempted to strip blacks of their African culture and religion and replace them with a white supremacist theology that valued subservience more than mercy. A combination of mob violence and the federal government's indifference made a mockery of the political rights embodied in post–Civil War amendments to the U.S. Constitution. After Emancipation, the white city leadership still considered African Americans near-animals. The white working class felt a patronizing envy of blacks' "childlike" simplicity. Yet at best they saw African Americans as job competitors and at worst as dangerous sexual predators. Meanwhile, Jim Crow laws made seeking economic comfort, much less power, for blacks an energy-sapping and often futile struggle. Still, the African American community did not merely survive. It thrived. In the face of persistent hostility, African Americans created a counterculture that valued blackness. Dallas' black leaders held a realistic view of human corruption and violence, but they also believed in the redemptive power of their Christian faith to change hearts.

Later white writers like Jim Schutze portrayed Dallas blacks as accommodationists.[2] Schutze saw the civil rights campaign there as timid compared to the epic battles in places like Birmingham. To understand the Dallas civil rights struggle, however, one must look beyond movement politics. One must appreciate the degree to which twentieth-century black Dallas society was shaped by its African and slave heritage and how this influenced its view of race, activism, and spiritual destiny. African Americans built institutions designed to resist the ideology of whiteness. This chapter will explore the development of those institutions—schools, churches, newspapers, and political organizations—and how they contradicted and obliged the objectives of the white ruling class. Dallas' black leadership believed that institutional reform and participation in America's electoral democracy, rather than directly challenging the economic system, provided the most reasonable path to social justice.[3] African American leaders did not expect white leaders to be empathetic, but they did expect the smartest of the ruling set to be reasonable.

Ironically, by insisting that any person with "one drop" of black blood was a "nigger" and thus forever incapable of acceptance as white, the ruling Anglos created a more cohesive, more unified black community than might have existed otherwise. To discourage miscegenation, ruling Anglos had long insisted that the mixed-raced offspring of black and white couples represented degeneration, the poorly amalgamated hash of both races' worst traits. Centuries of rape and exploitation under slavery, however, left African Americans in a more complex, multiracial world. The term *black* concealed the universe of color that existed among African Americans. Potentially a source of ethnic strife within black Dallas, this spectrum of pigment instead stood as mute testament to white oppression and a shared alienation from mainstream culture. John Mason Brewer, a black teacher in Dallas, expressed this unity in "Apostolic," a 1936 poem in which he gazed at an African American congregation displaying all the hues produced by white supremacy:

> a seething mass of black, brown and yellow beings
> Shouting tunes, mysterious mixtures of Jazz, Religious and
> Jungle melodies
> Swaying of bodies, clapping of hands
> Moaning of voices, unknown-tongue commands.[4]

Perhaps the polyphonous voice of this chorus betrayed future inner black strife. Tensions developed between light-skinned and dark-skinned blacks as the African American community at times mirrored white concerns about the corrupting influence of miscegenation. Yet, though whiteness divided rich and poor, Jew and Gentile, and northern and southern European, it became the impenetrable fortification that intimately bound together the black mass outside its ramparts. Dallas' black population ultimately proved too diverse and too subject to ordinary human frailty to completely withstand the pressures of white supremacy, but the vague outlines emerged of a shared identity that rejected the dehumanization of white culture. If whiteness demanded the corrosive rotting away of individual identity, it left in its wake a weathered but resistant black sense of self.

Life for African Americans in Texas might have been expected to inspire surrender rather than activism. Crime, pressure from the police and the courts, and spontaneous mass violence bore down mercilessly on all of black Dallas. By the mid-1920s, black leadership in Dallas and across Texas had fallen into disarray. A July 1919 riot in Longview, Texas, 124 miles east of Dallas, stemmed from the lynching of a black man who supposedly raped a white woman. A story in the *Chicago Defender* suggested that the lynching victim had actually been involved in a consensual romance with the woman. Longview whites suspected a local black teacher, Samuel Jones, of authoring the article. A mob beat Jones, then went on an arson spree and killed a black man just west of town. After the Longview riot, the state attorney general's office subpoenaed the records of the NAACP's Austin office, allegedly to investigate whether the organization was subversive and properly licensed to conduct business in Texas. NAACP National Secretary John Shillady traveled to Austin to defend the organization and was beaten by local officials, resulting in permanent impairment. Government officials dumped the bloodied Shillady on a train and warned him to not return.[5]

Founded in 1918, the Dallas NAACP chapter suffered under an edict by the Klan-dominated police department in the 1920s that a police officer be present at all meetings. A member of the city's NAACP chapter recalled that the branch president was "afraid to death" to hold meetings, and another member suggested that the local group was "run by cowards." The NAACP national office was forced to reorganize the Dallas branch and install new officers not intimidated by the Klan.[6] By 1926 the most visible lobbying organization for African Americans in Dallas, Booker T. Washington's National Negro Business League, was "drawing, from even its most ardent supporters, criticism for its lack of any directed programs."[7] In November 1926 the Dallas Negro Chamber of Commerce formed to address this problem but suffered from a lack of strong leadership, from paltry financing, and then, in the 1930s, from the Depression.[8] Poor, harassed, and disenfranchised, African Americans might well have submitted to the message of black disability pervading the dominant culture. Instead, black churches, schools, and media provided a foundation for later resistance, battling whiteness head on, though on cultural rather than political terrain.

By the 1930s some older Afro-Texans worried that their community had lost its spiritual center through exposure to a vacuous white society. William M. Adams, a former slave born in San Jacinto County, about fifty-seven miles north of Houston in Southeast Texas, mourned the loss of such ancient spiritual values in modern black Texas. Adams moved to Fort Worth in 1902 and still called the city home when interviewed by a writer for the federal Works Progress Administration (WPA) in the 1930s. Adams claimed healing and prophetic powers. "There are some born under the power of the devil who have the power to put injury and misery on people, and some born under the power of the Lord to do good and overcome the evil power," Adams said. "Now, that produces two forces, like fire and water. The evil forces start the fire, and I have the water force to put the fire out."[9] Adams saw his water force as part of an ancient craft that came directly from God via African culture. "The old folks in them days knew more about the signs that the Lord uses to reveal His laws than the folks of today," Adams said. "It is also true of the colored folks in Africa, their native land. Some of the folks laugh at their beliefs and say its superstition, but I know how the Lord reveals His laws."[10]

Adams believed that the prolonged contact with white society corrupted blacks, the adoption of Western secularism leaving African Americans diminished. To him, the mixing of white and black represented a surrender of the heavenly for the corporeal, the ascendant for the vulgar. Dallas' black community rejected the notion that white meant right. For many African Americans the personal was political. Creating a positive black identity became the most durable form of defiance. This sensibility shaped twentieth-century Afro-Texan Christianity. Secular political concerns were pursued in the context of an African cosmology. Blending African traditions with Christianity, Dallas' black leaders created a universe that was morally self-correcting, one in which justice would be restored and imbalances of power reversed over vast stretches of time. Such a worldview was sufficiently ambiguous to accommodate both activism and strategic political withdrawal. Black leaders recognized the vast array of police power, economic might, and social pressure arrayed against their community. They responded accordingly, seeking the most opportune moment for reform while deeply believing that time, inevitably, was on the black community's side. Rather than accommodation, this approach represented quiet resistance.[11]

African patterns of worship reinforced the notion of Afro-Texans as part of a global family of color. William Moore, a former slave living in Dallas, described prayer in the slave cabins of Mexia, eighty-two miles south of Dallas, to a WPA interviewer. When praying, Moore said, slaves "circled themselves on the floor in the cabin and prayed. They go moaning low and gentle. 'Some

day, some day, some day, this yoke is going to be lifted off of our shoulders.'"[12]
The prayer circle Moore described reflected religious practices with origins in
ancient Central and Western Africa.[13] A form of praying, singing, and dancing called the ring shout was performed in a circle during weddings, funerals,
and other religious rituals throughout West and Central Africa, the ancestral
homeland of most African Americans.[14] These circle ceremonies served as "a
means of achieving union with God."[15] To the Texas descendants of these
Africans, participating in a prayer circle or ring shout reminded Afro-Texans
of a black culture that spanned millennia, a worldview more durable than a
bois d'arc and capable of withstanding temporal white institutions.

Lewis Jones, who was eighty-six at the time his stories were collected by
the WPA, recalled to interviewers at his Fort Worth home the ring shouts
led by a black preacher: "Sometimes they had a jig contest; that when they
put the glass of water on the head and saw who could jig the hardest without
spilling the water . . . Preacher Tom set all of us niggers in the circle and sang
old songs . . . such as: '*I'm in the new Jerusalem, In the year of Jubilee.*'"[16] Undoubtedly, these celebrations provided an escape from daily cares and woes.
The ring shout and dance also represented continued union with a larger pan-
African community and symbolized endurance in the face of current hard-
ships. Those who survived such tests of perseverance, "jigging hard" without
spilling a drop of water, would also survive slavery, lynching, poverty, or segregation to experience paradise in the "new Jerusalem." Afro-Texan culture
taught the community to view the struggle for justice as a battle over the
longue durée. Such a worldview built an inner defense against nihilism in the
face of repeated cruel disappointment.[17]

Such were the sermons taught by the city's pre–World War II civil rights
leaders, many of whom, such as the Reverend Maynard H. Jackson, arose
from the pulpits of the approximately 130 black churches in Dallas.[18] Yet the
black church was not always a source of strength. Many black ministers depended on white patronage to maintain their status and were condemned
as collaborators. "The Negro clergy had enormous power over the African
American population of Dallas," African American author Robert Prince observed. ". . . The city leaders and politicians believed that if they controlled
the ministers then they controlled the community. This was often the case.
Several preachers were accused of selling out."[19]

Whatever the deficiencies of some black ministers, however, the black
church was more than the aggregate talents and character of its clergy. The
black church served as the chief medium of a culture that strengthened generations of children. The world, black children learned, was a dangerous place
that one could only cope with through humor and self-respect. Folktales first

disseminated in slave times continued to impart these lessons well into the twentieth century, thanks in part to the work of John Brewer. Born in Goliad, Texas (north of Corpus Christi), on March 24, 1896, Brewer won appointment as a professor at Samuel Huston (now Huston-Tillotson) College in Austin before making his mark as a Spanish teacher at the all-black Booker T. Washington High School in 1930s Dallas.[20] Brewer published extensive collections of black Texas folktales, customs, slave narratives, spirituals, blues lyrics, and poetry.[21]

Themes of intelligence winning over brute force and of loyalty prevailing over greed pervade Brewer's folktale collections. His heroes do not triumph in the traditional sense; the powerful remain powerful. The tone is not one of resignation, however, but smart realism. Put-upon protagonists stand in disapproving judgment of a materialistic, racist society. In Brewer's tales, sarcasm was often the only dignified weapon left the politically disenfranchised. An example of the sharp-tongued hero is Unkah Sug Miller, a janitor at the Hays County Courthouse in the Central Texas town of San Marcos. One day, according to the tale Brewer collected, a county judge who hates Miller tells the janitor he will lose his job even though he has never missed a day of work in twenty-five years if he can't satisfy a new rule requiring all employees to read and write. Miller is fired. Four years elapse before the judge passes Miller on a San Marcos street. Miller, the judge discovers, now owns a successful forty-acre farm. The judge is amazed at Miller's prosperity and praises Sug who has, "come up in de worl' fas'—'taint no tellin' what you'd of been sho 'nuff, if'n you'd of knowed how to read an' write.'" Sug is unimpressed with the Judge's reaction. "Ah knows zackly what Ah'd of been," Sug says. "Ah'd of still been de janitor at the Hays County Coa'thouse."[22]

Sug knows that white society has set a low upper limit on black prestige—a literate janitor will still only be a janitor to the white world. Blacks like Brewer saw education as a value in itself but did not delude themselves that schooling alone would blunt white racism. Once Miller exits the white world, however, his genius realizes its potential and he becomes a prosperous farmer. Brewer does not defend segregation but informs his black audience that black poverty is the direct result of white oppression.

Dallas' Jim Crow schools gave Brewer a chance to bring the lessons of black folklore directly to the city's African American children. Ironically, segregated schools became the bedrock of community building. While teaching at Booker T. Washington High School, Brewer and his principal, John Leslie Patton, gave history back to their students, exposing them to the achievements of Africans and of African Americans. If the existence of crowded, underfunded, and undersupplied black schools were designed to send a message of black inferiority, Brewer and Patton exploited the opportunity provided by segregation to inspire black self-awareness unmediated by a racist white power structure.

The city's first white public school opened its doors in 1883, and Colored School No. 1 opened the next year.[23] By 1890 black students attended seven elementary schools. The Dallas Colored High School opened in 1892 and was renamed Booker T. Washington High in 1922. In the early twentieth century the black school year lasted only sixty days, compared to one hundred days a year for white students. Black schools had no libraries, and the school district spent $51 annually per white student on facilities compared to only $22 per black student. By the 1930s Booker T. Washington High School held 1,664 students on a campus meant to hold only 600.[24] In spite of Jim Crow–imposed limitations, men like Brewer and Patton saw black schools as political incubators that would prepare young blacks to battle the assumptions of whiteness.

John Leslie Patton taught and served as principal at Booker T. Washington High for thirty-nine years, during which time he developed a course in Negro History that influenced "the development of race pride in the students and his co-workers."[25] Patton attended Dallas' segregated schools as a child before earning a degree at Prairie View College northwest of Houston and pursuing postgraduate education at New York University. Patton returned to Dallas in 1928 to teach at J. P. Starks Elementary for $72.50 a month. Patton quit after a year because he could earn more as a Pullman porter, but his parents insisted he resume his classroom role because he had a duty to his people— "the kind of duty St. Paul felt," as Patton put it.[26] Black students could shape the future, he believed, if they were conscious of their past. "It's difficult for a people to tell where they're going unless they know where they've been," he once explained.[27]

Rising to the position of principal, Patton proclaimed in his Negro History classes that "the Negro has formed an integral part of American civilization."[28] As opposed to curricula at white schools, at Booker T. Washington High the history of Egypt, "the cradle of civilization," was taught as part of "Negro" history.[29] "Africa, the Mother country . . . is often called the Dark Continent; but this is a misnomer, for Africa gave to civilization the smelting of iron, stringed instruments, trial by jury, etc.," Patton's curriculum guide for the course declared.[30] Patton saw it as his goal as a teacher to "awaken a proper social consciousness and pride in the developments and achievements which the Negro has made."[31] He taught his students that every life choice, including picking a career, carried responsibilities to the greater black community. "The Negro today stands in need of an economic emancipation,"

Patton told his students, "but this cannot be accomplished through laws . . . but through the wise occupational choice of every Negro boy and girl."[32]

Dallas' black press carried these messages to an even broader audience. The *Dallas Express,* a black-owned newspaper, played an unusually influential role in a city where by the 1930s African Americans enjoyed a 93 percent literacy rate, 50 percent higher than the rate for blacks in the rest of Texas.[33] The paper emphasized great blacks of the past, recorded contemporary African American achievement, and encouraged political activism. The tone was often angry but ultimately optimistic in conveying the belief that the passage of time would bring progress if blacks insisted on fairness.[34] The *Express* protested against voting restrictions and segregation.[35] This political activism, however, was seasoned with Dallas-style pragmatism. The newspaper did not criticize, for instance, the state's oppression of the NAACP or the savage beating of John Shillady in Austin. While not timid, the *Dallas Express* chose its battles carefully and avoided what it saw as lost causes.[36]

Patton, Brewer, and the staff of the *Dallas Express* knew that young African Americans faced a brutal world. By 1924 African Americans accounted for 15 percent of the city's population and, according to a 1927 report by the Civic Federation of Dallas' Interracial Committee, approximately one-fourth lived in rental housing "unfit for human habitation," with about 66 percent of these units lacking baths, toilets or water.[37] Nevertheless, Patton and his allies had erected mental defenses for their young charges. "The years of public school taught me well," recalled Robert Prince in his memoir, *A History of Dallas from a Different Perspective.* "I became street wise . . . I learned that my black teachers cared for all of us. They taught us survival tactics for black people . . . We were taught that the white man would never give us our rights without a fight . . . This was a good education. Education should teach one to survive in one's own environment. Our environment was hostile."[38]

That hostile environment grew harsher in the Great Depression. Because of an oil boom in East Texas, Dallas fared better than most American cities. Even as cotton prices plummeted, the expansion of nearby oil fields prompted petroleum companies, investors, and independent producers to move their headquarters to Dallas, which transformed from an agricultural center to "the most important oil city in the world." By August 1932, 787 oil-related companies made Dallas their home base, a tenfold increase in a two-year span.[39] Not all Dallas residents, however, shared in the prosperity. Wholesale business fell sharply, from $729 million in 1929 to $48 million ten years later. By 1931, 18,500 unemployed men and women filed for welfare relief at city hall. Male employers could not conceive of a household that depended on female wages. Most companies saw married women's salaries as superfluous and assumed that such employees could fall back on their husband's paychecks. These assumptions remained in place even as male unemployment skyrocketed. This made married females a particularly vulnerable class of workers in Depression-era Dallas as companies fired these women en masse. In 1931, after already reducing the salaries of municipal employees between 5 and 20 percent, the City Council voted to pay heads of families it employed with food. Blacks suffered more than the rest of the population, as they constituted half the city's unemployed. Black-owned businesses virtually disappeared, and by 1937 only one, Excelsior Mutual insurance company, survived.[40]

The harshness of the Depression inspired a degree of interracial cooperation unseen since the days of Populism, but this spirit proved short-lived. In 1934 Carl Brannin led an integrated "sit-in" of between 600 and 700 white and black recipients of federal relief grants at the city hall auditorium to protest proposed cuts in public assistance. Brannin's protest lasted eleven days, but local officials retaliated by cutting off electricity and water at city hall and arresting many of the protestors.[41] "[T]hey cut off the fans and locked the toilets, and they wouldn't allow people who were tired from sitting three days and nights to sleep, and if a person left the building, the police stopped him from returning; so finally we were pushed out by the inability to withstand the pressure they put on us," Brannin said.[42] The interracial cooperation Brannin achieved in the city hall sit-in proved exceptional. The year before, white workers and farmers disrupted a rally of the Workman's Cooperative League in nearby Lancaster, jeering and throwing eggs at those in attendance in reaction to rumors that the league advocated intermarriage between whites and blacks.[43]

Seeing blacks as job competition for white union members, Dallas labor leaders in the Jim Crow era either ignored or were hostile to the needs of the black working class. Walter C. Reilly, a Dallas typographer and officer of the Texas Federation of Labor, recalled that Bill Moran, a power in the state's Bricklayers International Union, insisted "that discrimination was a figment of the Negro's imagination."[44] Black delegates representing segregated locals at statewide labor conventions had to enter and leave the hotels where the meetings were held through back doors and ride "with the garbage on the freight elevators," according to John W. "Preacher" Hays.[45] A president of the Dallas Newspaper Printing Pressmen's Union and at one point vice president of the Texas Federation of Labor, Hays said white members shuddered at the thought of blacks joining their ranks. "Are there ever going to be negro pressmen, preacher?" he said he was asked. When Hays predicted African Americans would eventually participate, members snapped, "You think I'm going take a shower with a black?"[46]

By the 1930s African Americans had more than cultural resources to draw upon. Few individuals would have as direct an impact on the lives of African Americans in Texas as A. Maceo Smith. A native of Texarkana, Smith obtained a master's degree in business administration from New York University in 1928. When he returned to Texarkana to attend his father's funeral, he intended to stay only three weeks. Appalled by segregation, however, he stayed to fight racism in his home state. An insurance man, he moved to Dallas in 1933, resuscitated the Negro Chamber of Commerce, revived the state NAACP, and led the fight to desegregate the University of Texas. Through Smith's Progressive Voters League, Dallas whites grew accustomed to a limited level of black political involvement, a factor that might have made the city in the 1950s and 1960s a less contentious site of the civil rights struggle than many other Southern communities.[47] Smith pursued an incrementalist strategy that forged African American unity while negotiating piecemeal reforms with the white power structure. Smith achieved high visibility in his effort to win funding for a Hall of Negro Life exhibit at the Texas Centennial Exposition.

Like Patton and Brewer, Smith believed that recapturing history from racist mythology was essential to black Dallas' political growth, even if the exhibit was part of a segregated fair. "Some felt it was another Jim Crow thing," Smith recalled in the late 1970s. "But those of us that sponsored this felt that . . . you've got to start somewhere, you can't start on an integrated pattern." Smith and his allies gathered photos depicting Negro life in Texas and testified before a joint state legislative committee in Austin to request a $100,000 grant for an exhibition hall and expenses. Smith was warmly received and won the appropriation.[48]

Smith, however, quickly encountered the limits of cooperation with the white city fathers. In spite of Jim Crow laws, Texas had failed to completely disenfranchise African Americans in municipal elections. In 1923 the state legislature barred African Americans from voting in Democratic primaries. In a one-party state, this law was tantamount to the complete removal of black voting rights. In 1927 El Paso dentist Lawrence A. Nixon, with the support of the NAACP, won a unanimous decision in *Nixon v. Herndon* when the U.S. Supreme Court ruled that Texas election laws denied African Americans their Fourteenth Amendment rights. The legislature passed a new law that allowed rather than required political parties to deny blacks the right to vote in primaries. In 1932 Nixon and the NAACP challenged this legislative dodge and won another favorable Supreme Court decision in *Nixon v. Condon*. This time, the legislature passed a law allowing the Democratic Party to declare itself a "voluntary organization" that could freely choose its membership and qualifications without reference to state law, in full knowledge that the Democratic Party would keep its voter rolls lily white. The Supreme Court upheld this approach in the 1935 *Grovey v. Townsend* case. The Democratic Party barred African Americans voters from its primaries until 1944, when the court reversed itself in *Smith v. Allwright,* thus finally killing the white primary.[49]

Even before *Smith v. Allwright,* African Americans could vote in nonpartisan municipal, school board, and general elections. To vote, however, blacks had to pay a poll tax, and by 1928 fewer than one-third of the potential 10,000 black voters in Dallas were registered. As Negro Chamber of Commerce Executive Secretary in 1933, Smith helped form the Progressive Citizens League, which organized a poll tax payment campaign in black neighborhoods and filed an unsuccessful lawsuit against the all-white Dallas County Democratic primary.[50]

When Texas legislator Sarah T. Hughes was appointed in 1935 by Governor James Allred to preside over the state's Fourteenth District Court, a vacancy was created. This required a nonpartisan special election. The founder and former president of the Dallas NAACP chapter, African American attorney Ammon S. Wells, entered as one of sixty candidates for the state House seat. In spite of Klan threats against black voters, Wells finished sixth, drawing 1,001 votes in a race in which the winner polled only 1,860.[51] Smith and the Reverend Maynard Jackson enlisted as Wells' campaign managers, which displeased Dallas' white elites. "Key leaders . . . called us in and said, 'Now, you boys want, you know, Negro participation [in the Centennial]. Now, if you pull this black guy out of the race, you see, you'll get your money . . . We declined . . . and we lost our Texas money for the Centennial."[52]

When the state legislature approved a $3 million appropriation for the centennial in April 1935, the bill provided no funding for the Negro hall. Some whites, however, believed black support of the fair was crucial in the economically uncertain days of the Depression. Smith won the backing of a white oilman, Walter D. Cline of nearby Wichita Falls, to gain federal money for the Negro exhibit. In return for Cline's support, African Americans launched a campaign to sell $50,000 worth of Centennial Central Corporation bonds as a "show of good faith." With evidence of black enthusiasm for the fair, Cline persuaded Fred Florence and R. L. Thornton to support the campaign for a

Hall of Negro Life. The U.S. Congress approved a $3 million appropriation package for the fair, and an advisory committee recommended that a total of $100,000 of that amount be set aside for the Negro exhibition.[53]

The appropriation came only ninety days before the centennial festivities commenced in 1936. A 10,000-square-foot hall was built, officially opening on Juneteenth (the celebration of the day the Union Army first informed Texas slaves of the Emancipation Proclamation on June 19, 1865). On opening day, Secretary of Commerce Daniel C. Roper singled out the black exhibit for praise. "No people in all history can show greater progress in their achievement in seventy-three years than can the American Negro," Roper said in an opening ceremony. "This is traceable to their patient, loyal, patriotic attitude toward their country and to their gifts of soul and song."[54] This is precisely the essentializing message Smith, Patton, and others hoped the hall would convey, but it would have to compete with the master narrative of white supremacy enveloping the Centennial Exposition.[55]

The enshrinement of the Confederate Lost Cause begun in late-nineteenth-century Dallas reached its architectural apotheosis during the centennial years. President Franklin D. Roosevelt's unveiling of a massive equestrian statue of Robert E. Lee astride his horse Traveler at the corner of Hall Street and Turtle Creek Boulevard (soon afterward renamed Lee Park) served as a centennial highlight. A statue representing the Confederacy stood in the front of the center portico of the Centennial Building at Fair Park, while murals in the Great Hall of State depicted numerous Confederate officers.[56] Visitors were left with the impression of Dallas as an unambiguously Southern city but a sophisticated one that had achieved progress through elite white leadership supported by broad consensus.

More than erasing Dallas' history of dissent, elites also used the centennial to portray Texas history in stark racial terms. The Anglo defeat of Mexico in the 1830s, visitors were taught, represented a triumph over racial chaos. At the Cavalcade of Texas historical pageant, viewers were told that Texas history marked the planting of civilization on a colored void. "A mighty commonwealth has been robbed out of the vast wilderness of the Southwest," a narrator boomed during the pageant's prologue. Once again, the "wilderness" in Dallas popular culture referred to that part of the world populated by Indians, Mexicans, and other people of color.[57] Blacks became obsequious bit players, and Mexicans turned into invaders in their own country in the Cavalcade of Texas. "Texas pioneer women escape with their faithful slave from the oncoming Mexican army in the Terrible 'Runaway Scrape,'" declared one written description of a scene in the pageant depicting the flight of Anglo refugees during the Texas Revolution. The only float acknowledging African

Americans in the centennial opening day parade portrayed blacks picking cotton.[58]

The centennial echoed what whites learned in their schools and read in their newspapers. Whiteness meant the creation of civilization, defined as the advancement of capitalism. The exposition defined progress as the accumulation of material goods, not as the advancement of social justice. Exhibits trumpeted a mind-numbing array of statistics measuring the forward march of Anglo civilization in Texas, cultural advance demonstrated by beef produced, cotton bails grown, and automobiles purchased. The marginal role of blacks as uncreative, unskilled farm laborers stood in contrast to numerous exhibits demonstrating white inventiveness, such as the display of a primitive microwave oven at the General Motors pavilion. Nothing better illustrates the commodity fetishism of the centennial than the giant cash register that recorded hourly attendance figures.[59] Racial superiority could be thus measured by the spread of consumer products.

Black organizers of the Hall of Negro Life sensed that whiteness defined itself in terms of binary opposition. If whiteness equaled progress, blackness must mean stasis. To portray blacks as a people who had progressed since slavery would directly undermine this view, even if this historical narrative implied that African Americans needed white tutors to achieve civilization. Visitors were hammered by the theme of progress as they entered the hall. At the front door, visitors encountered a sculptured plaster model of a black man "with broken chains from slavery, ignorance, and superstitions falling from his wrists." Pamphlets proudly touted statistics demonstrating declining rates of tuberculosis among blacks and rising literacy rates. A series of murals along the walls of the lobby by the artist Aaron Douglass of New York became the exhibit's most eye-catching and subversive feature. One mural, the "Negro's Gift to America," portrayed blacks as builders of the country, contributing music, art, and religion to American culture. A woman with a baby in her outstretched arms in the center of the painting symbolized "a plea for equal recognition," according to Alonzo J. Aden, a curator at the Hall of Negro Life. "The child is a sort of banner, a pledge of Negro determination to carry on . . . in [a] struggle toward truth and light."[60]

The Hall of Negro Life stood as an island of integration, the one place where whites and blacks peacefully mingled. Otherwise, African Americans faced the usual humiliating hassle of finding restrooms and concessions open to them.[61] The hall drew more than 400,000 people during the course of the exposition, about 60 percent of them white. Whites often found the experience unsettling. "Many of the white people came in expecting to see on display some agricultural products . . . and 'Black Mammy' pictures, as many of them suggested," recalled Jesse O. Thomas, an exhibit organizer. "They were so shocked with what they saw, many of them expressed doubt as to the Negroes' ability to produce the things there on exhibit."[62] Earline Carson, a librarian who staffed the information desk at the hall, remembered the reaction of one white woman from nearby Corsicana, Texas. "She advanced a few feet into the hall and was standing as one transfixed, looking all about her," Carson said later. "All of a sudden she exclaimed . . . 'No! No! Niggers did not do this.'" Other visitors went beyond disbelief and saw a dangerous implication in the exhibit. "Why if you were to give Negroes an equal chance, they would surpass white people," one woman declared.[63]

The *Dallas Morning News* responded to the hall's dangerous message by heaping ridicule on the exhibit and its visitors, passing no opportunity for juvenile insults. "History of Negroes from Jungles to Now . . . Centennial to be Turned Over to Darkies Juneteenth," one headline read.[64] Black critics who saw the exhibit as collaboration with Jim Crow also attacked the hall. In a letter to the *Dallas Express,* Charles H. Bynum, a teacher at Booker T. Washington High, dismissed officials associated with the hall as "Uncle Toms" who rationalized the "gross injustices" suffered by black visitors to the fair.[65] Nevertheless, the Hall of Negro Life proved too dangerous to survive. When officials announced that the Centennial Exposition would continue in 1937 as the Greater Texas and Pan American Exposition, the hall was demolished, the only original permanent structure immediately destroyed.[66]

Nevertheless, Wells' strong electoral showing and A. Maceo Smith's successful lobbying for the Hall of Negro Life imbued Dallas' black community with an enhanced sense of political potency. If men like Bynum ridiculed Smith's incrementalism, more African Americans now believed that patient political activism would yield tangible positive results. In January 1936 Smith created the Progressive Voters League (PVL), an umbrella organization uniting the voter registration and poll tax payment efforts of fifty-two groups. A poll tax drive from October 1936 to January 1937 pushed the number of registered blacks to 7,000.[67]

The poll tax drives created an opportunity for African Americans during an off-year municipal election in 1937. When the *Dallas Journal* reported that approximately 20 percent of the registered voters were black, Smith said there was "quite a bit of excitement . . . We got 5,000 [black registered voters] and then you've got six or eight tickets running for the [city] council election, you know, you've got something."[68] An unusually divided white electorate split into five factions. To the city's professional politicians, it was obvious that a larger-than-usual black electorate united in aims by the PVL would provide the decisive swing vote. The March 27, 1937, *Dallas Express* published the PVL's five-point program, which included mild demands such as the hiring of black police officers, construction of a second black high school, and increased employment opportunities for blacks at city hall. Smith insisted that any slate wanting the PVL endorsement would have to agree to all five demands.[69]

The leaders of these factions each appeared at the PVL office, Smith said. "They may not admit to this . . . but all their candidates [were] up there [and] their managers," Smith said. The PVL would reiterate the five-point program to the representatives of these competing slates. "These were the five and we'd sit down and say, 'Now, gentlemen, what's your position on these? It's either yes or no.' . . . Each of those tickets endorsed that total program." The establishment press endorsed the Citizens Charter Association, but the PVL backed the Forward Dallas Association, which won five of nine council seats. One of its candidates, George Sprague, was chosen mayor. Within months, the Dallas City Council fitfully fulfilled parts of the PVL's five-point program. A second black high school campus, Lincoln High, was built, and the city increased the number of African American employees by 300 percent, although mostly in "traditional" black occupations such as custodial work. Dallas, however, maintained an all-white police force at a time when cities such as Houston and San Antonio had black officers. Smith's incrementalism quickly revealed its limitations.[70]

Smith's efforts in the 1930s set the tone for racial politics in Dallas for the next four decades. They also reflect the typical pattern of African American civil rights campaigns across the urban South. The suspenseful path of the Freedom Riders of the 1950s and 1960s, enduring threats and beatings as they sought to integrate interstate bus travel, drew fascinated, horrified, or angry television news audiences. The suffering of blacks in places like Birmingham, Alabama, where the bombing of a black church by a white supremacist in September 15, 1963, killed four young girls, drew mostly tears and shame. But most civil rights battles in the South in cities like Dallas, Atlanta, and Houston unfolded behind the scenes and were decided by middle-class black men and women and moderate leaders in the white business community. While Anglo businessmen sought to avoid trouble that might disturb profits, African American politicians in Atlanta and Houston, like those in Dallas, used nonpartisan school board and city council races to flex their political muscle. Southern urban black leaders typically negotiated for mild concessions from whites such as the expanded construction of black-only schools, working within the boundaries of segregation while backing lawsuits aimed at ending Jim Crow through judicial fiat.[71]

Although Dallas' African Americans were still shut out of state and national politics, they comprised 20 percent of the municipal electorate, a small proportion but one that nonetheless ensured some limits to Jim Crow politics. Black voting strength in Dallas played a moderating influence in the city, dampening any white impulse toward the massive resistance to desegregation that marked the Civil Rights struggle in the Deep South.[72] Regardless of the PVL's efforts, however, half the eligible black voters did not participate in the electoral process when such a presence theoretically could have made a decisive impact in the 1935 special election. In spite of Ammon Wells' strong showing, the PVL did not field an African American candidate in the 1937 city elections.[73]

On November 23, 1941, Dallas celebrated another centennial. At Fair Park's majestic Hall of State, celebrants commemorated the 100 years that had passed since John Neely Bryan constructed a crude ten-by-twelve-foot earthen-floored cabin on the banks of the Trinity River. Those gathered at Fair Park praised the elements they believed made Dallas great—the land, the white pioneers, and their religious faith. The service heaped loud applause on the city's business oligarchs, "men and women who yet retain the pioneer virtues and faith."[74] Poet Lexie Dean Robertson, however, saw the city as more than the brainchild of its white residents. Robertson's overwrought verse, "Dallas Articulate," highlighted the city's centennial. "You, too, have built Dallas," she declared. "You, tired woman, bending over a hot sudsy tub/You, worried man, with the unpaid bill in your pocket . . . You, black boy, from Deep Elm/And you, girl, from Little Mexico, /You with your pickaxe, your plow, your adding machine . . . Build a dream bigger than Dallas."[75] Robertson's view of Dallas history may have been inclusive but remained laden with racial hierarchy. Sharing a hope for future prosperity, Robertson fantasized that a multihued army could create a "new dream of a city/Uninhibited by race prejudice and animosity."[76] While black and brown people played their part, their roles were subservient. The heart of the Origin Myth is its idealizing of hierarchy. The city worked because it was led by a narrow band of elites at the top. In Robertson's poem, whites were men and women, the city's adults. When she refers to people of color, she uses terms like "boy" and "girl." Blacks and Mexican Americans helped build Dallas by being obedient children.

The Dallas establishment celebrated a fantasy future of brotherhood even as the city bared its old scars of hatred and fear. Whites still measured progress in direct proportion to the spatial, biological, cultural, and material distance northern Europeans placed between themselves and the rest of humanity. History represented the steady march toward a biologically superior tomorrow in which blacks, browns, and other nonwhites would become ever more clever but still inferior imitations of their light-skinned betters. African American leaders in Dallas accepted their own notion of history as progress. Men like Patton, Brewer, and Smith believed that racism and black poverty reflected only poor education. Neither, they thought, was innately part of the city's economic system. Yet as early as 1940, A. Maceo Smith and his allies faced abundant evidence that political reform represented a dead end. Institutions changed incrementally, but hearts did not.

Mason, Brewer, and Patton constructed an image of the African American as a dignified, durable soul belonging to a community bound by mutual obligation to fight for justice. White elites had placed their faith in biology, black elites in democracy. This ideology bound together a diverse black community to a remarkable degree during the first phase of the civil rights movement of the 1930s and 1940s. By the 1940s Smith and his allies in Dallas had already politicized African Americans to a degree other Southern cities would not see until the 1950s. What Smith and others perhaps did not see is that white elites perceived black progress as only relative and that African Americans were still viewed as the pupils, not the teachers, of freedom. This patron-client relation set tight boundaries on the accomplishments of Smith's civil rights campaign in the 1950s and 1960s. Many African Americans clung to the patient hope that with the gradual dismantling of Jim Crow, racism might abate and the antagonistic world they knew would be replaced with what the civil rights movement of the 1950s and 1960s would call the "beloved community." Some leaders became so fired with this vision of future brotherhood, so certain that continued compromise would achieve this result, that they faced accusations of "Uncle Tomism" within their own community.

Statewide, a series of legal victories by the NAACP would cast doubt on the long-term future of Jim Crow. This uncertainty caused deep divisions in Dallas society. A minimal expansion of African American rights continued while traditional elites maintained control. Jews would occupy a particularly ambiguous position, generally supporting African Americans' integration campaigns but sometimes serving as Jim Crow's defenders. Dallas' growing Mexican American population also found itself caught between the polarities of black and white, with statewide organizations like the League of United Latin American Citizens simultaneously fighting anti-Latino segregation while resisting attempts to define Latinos as nonwhites. To win inclusion in the white man's club, some Latinos advocated the separation of blacks from the rest of Dallas society. Elites worried whether a bitter struggle to maintain segregation would produce social instability. Under a deceptively calm surface, Dallas' famed consensus slid into chaos.

Hints of this grim future abounded in the early 1940s. The bad housing situation for blacks only got worse. In spite of the Depression, Dallas enjoyed a reputation as an economic mecca as its population, already at more than a quarter-million, leaped another 13.2 percent during the 1930s. By 1940 the city's 50,407 African Americans (out of a total population of 294,734) found themselves crammed into segregated neighborhoods covering a mere 3.5 square miles, with several thousand more living in alleys and shacks in unincorporated areas outside the city limits. About 80 percent of black homes were deemed substandard. No new housing was being built for blacks, and whites often fiercely resisted the intrusion of African Americans into their neighborhoods.[77] A flashpoint developed in South Dallas. Angry Anglo parents complained that black schoolchildren walked through white neighborhoods on their way to school. The City Council briefly debated a proposed ordinance that would have specified which streets African Americans could walk on. The Reverend John G. Moore of Colonial Baptist Church proposed construction of an eight-foot concrete or brick wall to solidify the border between white and black.[78]

Tensions only increased as African American families began to move into racial hinterlands around Oakland Avenue, Pine Street, and Eugene Street near Oakland Cemetery. An angry mob including "rock-throwing housewives" greeted C. L. Walker and George Johnson as they attempted to move into their new homes in the 3600 block of Howell Street in South Dallas on September 3, 1940. Terrorists ignited dynamite between the homes of two black families on Hatcher Street two days before Christmas 1940. Fires and hangings in effigy greeted other African Americans venturing forth from black neighborhoods. The eighteenth bombing of the terror campaign rocked South Dallas by late November 1941. Those guilty of the bombings were never apprehended. In spite of the PVL's endorsement of the victorious CCA slate in the 1939 election, the City Council never vigorously pursued a police investigation of the bombings. Instead, the council tried to buy back the homes of blacks encroaching on a dangerous racial borderland.[79]

As elites celebrated Dallas' 100th birthday, the bombings had been officially forgotten. Historical consciousness presented danger. Rather than reaching a "dream bigger than Dallas," blacks saw their hopes tragically deferred. The real city was a violent urban nightmare. Dallas' black community was stronger than any specific political agenda, its roots sunk deeply in a soil of faith in the human potential for change. The city's black leadership again relied on bois d'arc-style endurance, bracing for disappointment yet certain the larger black family would survive. Nevertheless, the gushing of the *Dallas Express* in 1938 that for Negroes it was a "privilege to live in Dallas" now rang as a hollow lie.[80]

SIX

WHITE LIKE ME

Mexican Americans, Jews, and the Elusive Politics of Identity

Even as Dallas evolved into a modern city, the Department of Public Health still saw the human population as parceled into cleanly divisible racial segments, using identification cards in the 1940s to loudly announce that Jews did not belong to the white race. Rabbi David Lefkowitz of Dallas' Temple Emanu-El fought to abolish the department's "Hebrew" racial classification. To Lefkowitz, a Reform rabbi, Jews represented a religious group, not a racial category.

In 1942 Lefkowitz protested when the health department included Hebrew as a race along with Anglo-Saxon, South European, Mexican, Negro, and Asiatic on its documents. "The use of the word 'Hebrew,' under any circumstances, except as the designation of the original language of the Bible, is incorrect," Lefkowitz wrote. "The designation 'Jewish' is a proper one for religion . . . You are not, of course, seeking to determine the religion of those to whom you distribute the identification cards, otherwise you would put down Episcopalian, Baptist, Catholic, Methodists, etc. In this group, the word Jewish could well be included, but not in the former."[1]

The unfolding drama of the Nazi Holocaust provided a deadly example to American Jews of the dangers of living in Gentile-majority countries where their neighbors viewed them as not just religious but racial outsiders. If anti-Semitism in early-twentieth-century America rose in part from religious intolerance, the Leo Frank murder case and American immigration policy strongly demonstrated that even in relatively safe America, Jews could be viewed by ruling Anglo-Saxons as racial poison. In the 1920s the U.S. government imposed immigration quotas aimed at limiting the number of Jews and other groups who could enter in a given year, abandoning later would-be Jewish immigrants to the mercies of the Third Reich in the 1930s and 1940s. Lefkowitz and others happily received the news in 1944 that U.S. immigration authorities no longer considered Jews as racially different from northern Europeans, a move that might allow more Jews to enter the United States.

As they celebrated their newfound whiteness, however, many Jews still saw blacks, Asians, and other groups as belonging to separate racial categories. "In our country statistics of Jews must not be collected from the point of view that we are a race or ethnic group, in the manner of the American races, Negroes, Chinese, Indians, etc.," H. S. Linfield, director of the Jewish Statistical Bureau, informed Aline Rutland, secretary for Temple Emanu-El, in a letter dated March 7, 1944. Until recently, "the government continued to regard incoming alien Jews as constituting a separate race. The new order has put an end to this practice."[2]

The black civil rights movement and convulsive demographic changes from the 1940s through the 1960s made the issue of racial identity crucial to Jews and other marginal whites. The black freedom struggle in those three decades and the development of a new class of what historian George Norris Green called "little rich" merchants ignited the most intense period of anti-Semitism in Dallas since the heyday of the Klan.[3] These factors placed additional pressure on Dallas Jews to demonstrate their whiteness, thus troubling the relationship between Jews and African Americans.

A similar pressure shaped the racial and political attitudes of Mexican Americans. For that community, life in the 1950s and 1960s became a race to escape the bottom of the social ladder. Many Mexican Americans, locked in an uncertain civil rights struggle of their own, felt they had nothing to gain by helping the African American community. These Mexican Americans instead battled for a white identity, but this goal proved elusive. Jews and Latinos remained marginalized even as they strained relations with African Americans, ultimately limiting the gains made by black activists.

After Cyrus Scofield, Dallas had come a long way toward accepting Jews as part of the racial ruling class, but many still struggled with the meaning of Jewish identity. As in Scofield's time, philo-Semitism existed side by side with anti-Semitism. Jews like Lefkowitz had changed the Dallas health department's racial classification schemes but not the Gentile perception of the community. Even after the discovery of the Holocaust at the end of World War II, some Gentiles saw Jews as nonwhite and found biblical justification for their exclusion. The Dallas Independent School District created an Old Testament course in 1952. In the course materials, Judaism was depicted as a half-baked religion awaiting Christ's arrival for its completion. "While there are sixty-six books in this one volume [the Bible], they are unified in the person of Christ whose coming was prophesied in the first book of Old Testament," declared a bulletin outlining the course. "As you study the lives of these Hebrew people, you will be conscious of expectancy which existed throughout the Old Testament period and which had its fulfillment in Jesus Christ."[4]

Jews possessed only half a loaf regarding divine truth, according to the course, and they were not even part of the white race. According to the notes for the lesson titled "The Origin of the Races, the Tower of Babel, and the Confusion of Tongues," all mankind descended from the three sons of Noah following a flood that wiped out the rest of humanity. Japheth, according to the lecture, was the father of the Europeans. The Old Testament course then reinforced the Southern white Protestant rationale for African American subordination by claiming all "colored races" were descended from Ham, whose family line was forever cursed by God after the flood, according to Genesis, to be a "servant of servants." According to the DISD, "The children of Shem, inhabiting the land of Arabia, and southeastern Asia, [included] . . . the Hebrews, Arabians, Assyrians and Persians, all of whom speak the Semitic languages." Jews thus yellowed as Asians in the eyes of the DISD.[5] This classification followed soon after an American war with Japan in which U.S. troops at times fought with a genocidal fury unmatched by their peers in Europe. The depiction of Jews as Asians came amid widespread concerns over the "loss" of mainland China to the communists in 1949 and during the 1950–1953 Korean War, whose outcome was uncertain at the time the DISD launched the course. This racial assignment not only symbolically darkened Jews but also threatened to render them part of a dangerous yellow horde in Gentile eyes.[6] Alarmed by recent political convulsions within the city, some Gentiles demanded that Jews come down clearly on one side of the black/white divide.

The issue of Jewish whiteness came to a head just as the black civil rights movement in Texas picked up new momentum during and after World War II. In the 1940s Juanita Craft won appointment as the Dallas NAACP's membership chair. In 1944 she became the first black woman in Dallas County history to vote, and in 1946 the NAACP named her a field organizer. Due to Craft's tireless proselytizing, the Dallas NAACP branch claimed 7,000 members by 1946 as it became the epicenter of the state's civil rights movement. In 1941 blacks served on juries in Dallas County for the first time since the 1890s. In 1943 the NAACP won a lawsuit on behalf of Thelma Paige and the Negro Teachers Alliance of Dallas, achieving gradual equalization of teacher salaries. A. Maceo Smith's efforts to end the white primary system finally paid off with the NAACP prevailing in the 1944 *Smith v. Allwright* decision.[7]

Divisions within the African American community over political priorities, however, sometimes complicated the civil rights struggle. Some African Americans felt ambivalent about a future of integration. A 1947 statewide poll of African Americans showed that a clear majority favored the creation of a separate black university over the integration of the University of Texas. "Some Negroes had, or at least believed that they had, a vested interest in retaining segregation," observed Michael Gillette, an historian of Texas' NAACP. "These were often professionals, such as teachers, who feared that they would lose their jobs to whites if desegregation occurred. Thus . . . there existed, 'many, many Negroes who are deathly afraid of the elimination of segregation.'"[8]

Other African Americans internalized the lessons of black inferiority pounded home daily by segregation and the mainstream culture. Even the *Dallas Express,* a vigorous supporter of political activism and pride in black culture, at times conveyed negative messages about blackness. Advertisements for hair straighteners and skin bleach abounded in the pages of the *Express,* which carried the message that kinky hair and dark skin were unattractive social liabilities. "Enjoy the Light Side of Life with new, improved 'Skin Success' Bleach Cream," one ad beckons. "Now you can enjoy the popularity and admiration that goes with a lighter, fairer complexion."[9]

Black assertion, however, alarmed some marginal whites, such as Jews and darker-skinned or working-class and middle-class Mexican Americans. Fate granted some men like Pete Garcia both a Spanish surname and a light skin. In 1950s Dallas society, the middle-class Garcia rated as a higher grade of human than did his black neighbors, tantalizingly close to the Caucasian status he so desired. Aware that his Mexican ethnicity marked him as an outsider, Garcia sought ethnic promotion. In 1950 and 1951 Garcia was part of a small army that dynamited a South Dallas neighborhood for about eighteen months to preserve the boundary between black and white. The 1950s bombings echoed the 1940 terrorism against socially mobile blacks. Dallas culture taught Garcia to see the world in terms of a zero-sum game. African American gains could only mean loss for Mexican Americans while oppression of his black neighbors provided a quick route to whiteness.

The city's World War II population boom aggravated an already disastrous black housing situation. From 1940 to 1950 Dallas' population grew by about a third, from 294,734 to 434,462. Dallas' black population grew by 30,000 in that time, but private builders constructed only 1,000 new dwellings open to African Americans.[10] White residents protested construction of a proposed 2,000-home tract south of Dallas' city limits set aside for blacks. The City Council promptly refused to supply water to the development, killing the project. A 1950 "Report on Negro Housing Market Data" found 21,568 black households occupying 14,850 housing units. This meant that one of three black families shared crowded housing with other families, and even those substandard structures skyrocketed in price.[11]

By 1948 a nine-square-mile community of 25,000 blacks, Mexican Americans, and poor whites lived on a low flood plain in West Dallas. Created by the earlier construction of levees along the Trinity River, West Dallas consisted of "flimsy shacks, abandoned gravel pits, garbage dumps, open toilets and shallow wells." Fewer than 10 percent of those dwellings had indoor toilets, and only 15 percent had running water. Tenants drank from wells located near human waste disposals. West Dallas accounted for 50 percent of the city's typhus cases, 60 percent of the tuberculosis, and 30 percent of the polio.[12]

Desperation forced relatively prosperous blacks to again venture in the early 1950s into the Exline Park neighborhood, scene of the 1940–1941 bombings. Twelve bombings in the next year and a half targeted homes sold to blacks in formerly all-white neighborhoods in a two-square-mile area of South Dallas. Not expecting white protection, African Americans armed themselves. Juanita Craft noted in a letter to Walter White, the executive director of the NAACP, that bombing stopped on Crozier Street when "the widow Sharpe" ran from her home firing a gun at a speeding getaway car after one explosion.[13] Fearful that violence threatened the city's postwar economic boom, elites could not ignore these bombings as they had the 1940 attacks. A special grand jury that included several prominent Dallasites, such as wholesale liquor distributor Julius Schepps and *Dallas Morning News* managing editor Felix McKnight, investigated the bombings. In an unusual move for 1951 Dallas, the grand jury also numbered three African Americans as members, including NAACP chapter president Bezeleel R. Riley and W. J. Durham, an attorney on the *Sweatt v. Painter* case that led to desegregation of the University of Texas law school.[14]

Dallas police arrested a series of suspects beginning in September 1951. The accused shared a decidedly working-class background and included pants pressers, machinists, and garage mechanics. Two suspects, Claude Thomas Wright and his half-brother, Arthur Eugene Young, told police they had been hired to carry out five bombings by labor leader Charles O. Goff, chairman of the Exline Park Improvement Association. When police arrested Goff, former district attorney and ex-Klansman Maury Hughes bailed him out. Other evidence pointed to Baptist preacher John G. Moore, but no charges were ever filed due to "insufficient corroborating evidence." Yet only one of the suspects was ever put on trial—Pete Garcia, a member of Moore's South Dallas Adjustment League. Garcia was one of two Hispanics indicted in the bombings.

His participation revealed the racial ambiguity of being a Dallas Latino. Even as Mexican American children attended de facto segregated schools and their parents earned inferior wages compared to Anglos, Garcia claimed Caucasian status, painting "For Whites Only" signs and placing them in the yards of families agreeing to not sell their South Dallas homes to black families. Garcia threatened other families at knifepoint to maintain the ban. Dallas newspapers, which had a policy of identifying black and Mexican American crime suspects by race, acknowledged Garcia's whiteness by frequently not mentioning his ethnicity. A chief witness at Garcia's trial testified that she had seen Garcia enter a vacant house moments before an explosion. She recanted her testimony, however. A jury deliberated for twelve hours before acquitting Garcia.[15]

Garcia's compulsion to be seen as white made crude economic sense in 1940s–1960s Dallas. To be classified as nonwhite at that time was to be limited to low-wage jobs and to have few opportunities for economic advancement. By 1960, according to the last U.S. census taken before desegregation officially began in the city, the median annual income in Dallas County was $6,845. For the nonwhite population it was $1,513. Nearly 81 percent of the nonwhite population labored in low-wage occupations such as domestic or farm labor. The burden of racism leaned harder on nonwhite women, who averaged an annual income of $960 as opposed to $2,317 for nonwhite men. Men like Garcia were locked into a system of racial and gender oppression in which whiteness and masculinity were essential for escaping poverty.[16]

Few Mexican Americans in Texas were prosperous enough to enjoy an easy ticket to whiteness. Mexican Americans in Texas routinely faced exclusion from juries and white schools. The Texas oil and railroad industries paid Mexican Americans, like African Americans, lower wages for the same work as Anglos and forced them to use separate drinking fountains, toilets, and bathing facilities. Anglo-Texan school officials and students regarded Mexican American children as racial inferiors. In the early 1930s a Dimmit County school official noted that Anglos perceived Mexican students as "almost as trashy as the Negroes," while a Nueces County official said, "The white child looks on the Mexicans as on the Negro before the [Civil War]. To be cuffed about and used as an inferior people."[17]

As noted earlier, a Texas court ruled that Mexican Americans were legally white, but the court insisted that Mexicans did not fit scientific definitions of whiteness. Nevertheless, Mexicans in Texas lived with de facto school segregation. This was to change when in 1940 the state superintendent of education decreed that "under the laws . . . children of Latin American extraction [are] classified as white and therefore have a right to attend the Anglo-American Schools in the community in which they live."[18]

Regardless of this decision, white schools remained closed to Mexican Americans, and Latino civil rights groups had to rely on the courts to end segregation. A U.S. district court in Austin ruled in a 1948 decision, *Delgado v. Bastrop,* that segregating Mexican American schoolchildren violated the Constitution, but the court allowed the district to establish segregated "first grades" for the purposes of English-language instruction. Exploiting that loophole, Texas school officials expanded that first grade provision to cover at least four grades. The 1957 *Hernández v. Driscoll Consolidated School District* decision overturned such an interpretation of *Delgado,* in effect outlawing the de facto segregation of Mexican American schoolchildren in Texas. The practice survived, however, due to residential segregation and school policies that separated brown and white children on the supposed bases of English-language proficiency and academic ability.[19]

In mid-century Dallas, Mexican Americans attended one of four segregated elementary schools: W. B. Travis, Cumberland Hills, Benito Juarez, and City Park. Crozier Tech was the only high school open to them. Few teachers spoke Spanish, and students were discouraged from speaking in their native language.[20] Few Anglos noticed, since Mexican Americans constituted only the city's second-largest minority group, with numbers far smaller than the African American community. In 1960 the city's Mexican American population numbered about 30,000. By 1970 the Latino population had grown to only about 40,000, or about 8 percent of the total. Blacks made up 24.9 percent of the total population the same year.[21]

Their small numbers and their relative invisibility compared to African Americans affected the Mexican American community in paradoxical ways. On the one hand, a lower profile combined with Anglo racism meant that Dallas leaders showed little interest in the needs of the community. On the other hand, Mexican Americans appeared as less of a threat than African Americans, and consequently middle-class Mexican Americans, at least, enjoyed a better opportunity to win acceptance as part of the white community. Some Mexican Americans believed their community should keep quiet and not follow the black political example. As one Mexican American in the 1970s put it, "The gringos are getting meaner all the time. They're scared of the Blacks . . . I think those Chicanos are crazy to go marching around, waving those signs. They're just making people mad at Mexicans. And the madder they get, the worse it's going to be for us."[22] In other words, Latinos and Latinas would be better off invisible than hated.

This worry about Anglo backlash acted as a dead weight on 1950s and 1960s Mexican American politics. A large, heterogeneous population in the state as a whole, Mexican Americans in Texas more than doubled in population from 1930 to 1960, from 695,000 to 1.4 million.[23] Individual Mexican Americans identified themselves in complex and often contradictory ways. The identity members chose often shaped their relationship to the African American community. An analogous ideology to whiteness runs deeply through Mexican history. During the long dictatorship of Porfirio Díaz, from

1876 to 1910, Mexican elites promulgated a faith in European supremacy over Indians. Díaz pursued an immigration policy intended to whiten Mexico by encouraging northern Europeans to settle in the nation. In postrevolutionary Mexico at the beginning of the 1920s, in spite of a contrary official ideology hailing the nation's Indian past, those who successfully claimed identity as belonging to *la raza blanca* (the white race) continued to occupy the highest social status, followed by mixed-race *mestizos,* with *indios* dwelling at the social bottom. Mexican immigrants, already immersed in whiteness ideology, thus often absorbed similar racist sentiments north of the border regarding blacks that they had once projected toward indigenous people.[24]

Like Pete Garcia, many of Texas' Mexican American leaders sought to have the Anglo community accept Latin Americans as a white ethnic group rather than as a separate race, and in doing so they stressed their separation from the black civil rights campaign. A generational shift in part accounts for this attitude. As historian Guadalupe San Miguel Jr. notes in a study of the school integration movement in Houston's Mexican American community, the community's immigrant generation, those born in Mexico who arrived in Texas in the early twentieth century, still saw themselves as Mexicans. They still desired to return to their homeland when economic and political conditions made that possible. This "Mexicanist" generation held ambivalent views at best concerning what they hoped was their temporary American home, an attitude hardened by frequent encounters with Anglo racism and discrimination. Not invested emotionally in American society, Mexicanists avoided long-term struggle for social justice and preferred to work for pragmatic, immediate reforms within the system. They wanted Mexican American schools to receive equal funding and equipment as Anglo schools, for instance, but they did not seek assimilation into the American mainstream. If they identified themselves racially, many considered themselves Indians. Few would have declared a white identity.[25]

The Mexicanist generation's children lived in a different world. Born in America, they planned to stay in the United States and therefore had a long-term interest in how they were racially defined by Anglos. Clearly, status could be measured proportionally by distance from blackness. Many agreed with a Mexican American South Texas cotton picker who commented in the early 1930s, "It does not look right to see Mexicans and Negroes together. Their color is different. They are black and we are white."[26]

The Mexican American generation wanted opportunity and acceptance by their neighbors and often was willing to assimilate Anglo attitudes toward African Americans to achieve this. Meanwhile, the horrors of the Holocaust and the rapid decline of southern and eastern European immigration after

1924 led to abandonment of the idea of different white "races" by most in the American academic and political communities.[27] Where once stood races there now existed ethnicities, and many Mexican American leaders saw an opportunity in this semantic shift. They did not want to abandon their cultural heritage; they just wanted to be accepted as white ethnics like Polish or Italian Americans.

From 1930 to 1960, San Miguel argues, Houston's Mexican American leadership sought to integrate schools for their children, to open more opportunities for such children to attend college, and to promote political activism within the community. Such leaders, conscious of their precarious position in the region's hierarchy and fearful of an Anglo backlash, sought to avoid anything smacking of radicalism. "The goal of members of the Mexican American Generation thus was to support moderate social change that would improve, not replace, the existing social order," San Miguel writes.[28]

This ideology shaped the League of United Latin American Citizens (LULAC), founded in 1929 in Corpus Christi, Texas. LULAC drew its membership from "small business owners and merchants, small landowners, skilled workers, artisans, [and] professionals."[29] English was declared LULAC's official language.[30] LULAC's racial politics can be deciphered by its name. By labeling themselves "Latin American," the middle-class group emphasized the community's European origins and American citizenship.[31] Some LULAC chapters expressed their white identity by erecting a color line between the membership and blacks. One LULAC council expelled a member for marrying a "Negress," and members socially shunned the interracial couple. A member of the council bitterly complained that "An American mob would lynch him. But we are not given the same opportunity to form a mob and come clean."[32]

For many Mexican Americans in Dallas, surrendering any separate cultural identity provided the quickest route to the American mainstream rather than absorbing gringo racism. "I just don't believe in teaching the children Spanish," one resident of a Dallas barrio told anthropologist Shirley Achor in the early 1970s. "They'd be better off if they never spoke it at all . . . You know it's true—even a Spanish accent can hurt a person in life."[33]

Such accommodation marked not just LULAC members but also Dallas Latinos who joined the American GI Forum (AGIF) after World War II. Dr. Hector Garcia helped form AGIF in Corpus Christi and became its first chairman in 1948. The organization received national attention in 1949 when it protested a Three Rivers, Texas, funeral home's decision to bar a chapel funeral for Private Felix Longoria, who had been killed years earlier in World War II. In 1954 several prominent Dallas Mexican Americans, including Pancho Medrano (who unlike many of his peers in the group actively participated in black civil rights campaigns) and Joe Landin, founded the Dallas chapter of the GI Forum. AGIF investigated job discrimination and police brutality while lobbying the Dallas school district for improved funding for Mexican American schools.[34]

The American GI Forum, however, held a similar stance to LULAC vis-à-vis racial identity and the black civil rights movement. To both organizations, Mexican Americans were white and African Americans would have to fight their own battles. "LULAC has been the lone spokesman on Civil Rights for over a quarter of a century," the group's president, Paul Andow, sniffed in a 1963 policy statement just three days before Martin Luther King Jr. and other black civil rights leaders held their famous March on Washington.

> We have not sought solutions to problems by marching to Washington, sit-in's or picketing or other outward manifestations . . . We believe that a man should not receive a position of trust or other emoluments simply because he belongs to a particular ethnic group—we believe that an individual must earn and merit this position.[35]

LULAC leaders like Andow clearly worried that too close an alliance with black civil rights leaders like Martin Luther King and endorsement of their tactics would imperil the position of Latinos and Latinas in a white supremacist society. Andow further implied that blacks succeeding in the wake of the civil rights movement did not deserve their good fortune. Meanwhile, LULAC sought a white identity for its members, campaigning against racial designations on government forms that classified Latinos as Mexicans. The term Mexican referred to a nationality, not a race, LULAC insisted, and Latinos were as white as any Anglo-Saxon. Jacob I. Rodriguez of LULAC bristled at the Mexican label. "There's no sense of shame in being, or being called, a Mexican—*IF YOU ARE A CITIZEN OF MEXICO!*" Rodriguez wrote in a 1963 letter to the *San Antonio Express*. "There's just no reason why we—*as U.S. Citizens*—should be called what we are not."[36]

Dr. Hector Garcia of the American GI Forum also fought a long battle to get state institutions to stop classifying Latinos as nonwhites. Garcia protested to Homer Garrison, director of the Texas Department of Public Safety, that state troopers should stop making the notation "Mex" in the blank space on traffic reports calling for racial designations. "Is the Department aware that there is no such thing as a Mexican race, no more than an American race?" Garcia asked Garrison in a letter dated April 17, 1950.[37] Hector Garcia celebrated the decision of the Department of Welfare to classify Mexican

Americans as "Race—White, Nationality—Americans."[38] Like his LULAC counterparts, Garcia sought to distinguish his group from African American civil rights organizations. On March 9, 1954, an American GI Forum local secretary in Crystal City, Texas, Gerald Saldaña, requested that Garcia send a brief history of the organization. Saldaña asked if the forum was a "Latin counterpart" of the NAACP. Garcia was adamant that no comparison should be made between the two groups. "We are not a civil rights organization," he wrote. ". . . Personally, I hate the word . . . [Definitely] we are not to be considered at all as a counterpart (Latin) of the NAACP."[39]

One American GI Forum supporter, Manuel Avila Jr., was alarmed when Ed Idar Jr., the forum's executive secretary, published an article in the group's newsletter depicting the AGIF and the NAACP allying in the struggle against school desegregation. In 1956 Avila wrote:

> I only hope this does not hurt our cause but I can already hear the Anglos saying 'those nigger lovers' . . . Anybody reading [your newsletter] can only come to the conclusion we are ready to fight the Negro's battles, and God only knows we have a big problem ourselves and aren't that strong to defend someone else . . . sooner or later we are going to have to say which side of the fence we're on, are we white or not . . . Let's face it first we have to establish we are white then be on the 'white side' and then we'll become "*Americans*" otherwise never.[40]

An impulse toward whiteness thus runs through the history of mainstream, middle-class Latino political organizations such as LULAC and the American GI Forum. However, some Mexican Americans like Pete Garcia moved beyond mere accommodation to violent support of segregation. Garcia was not alone in seeing virulent anti-black racism as a means to achieve whiteness. P. R. Ochoa concluded that the enemy of Dallas' Mexican American community was not the Anglo power structure but the state's politically disenfranchised African Americans. Part of being white, in Ochoa's view, was holding white supremacist beliefs.

Ochoa in the late 1960s served as a Nueces County Republican Party precinct chairman. In the 1950s and early 1960s, however, he ran a variety of businesses—a publishing company, a "commercial academy," an auto parts store, a real estate firm, and a variety store—out of his Dallas office on Singleton Boulevard near Norwich Street.[41] He was also the publisher and only identifiable writer for a chain of Texas newspapers—the *Dallas Americano* and related editions in San Antonio, Corpus Christi, and Kingsville. Ochoa signed his front-page column "Pedro el Gringo" and represented the assimilationist approach in its extreme. Ochoa urged his Mexican American readers to use the terms "Americano," "Spaniol," or "Texano" when referring to themselves because "Latin, Mexican and European are foreigners."[42] Ochoa, who fancied himself the head of the "Spaniol Organization of White People," went much further in promoting white racial identity for Mexican Americans. Integration meant slavery for "Spaniol" Texans, Ochoa argued. He regularly printed slogans in bold type on the pages of his six-page weekly such as *conserve su raza blanca* (preserve your white race) and *segregacion es libertad* (segregation is liberty).[43]

Like Pete Garcia, Ochoa also saw Dallas society in terms of a zero-sum game. "The modern and first-class Negro public school located at Dallas, west housing project, it is far better and has more commodities than many public schools for Spaniol pupils and English speaking pupils at the valley near the border," he complained in an editorial of August 6, 1958. "Under what article of the Constitution, we should base our complaint?"[44] In a Spanish-language editorial he accuses groups like the AGIF, LULAC, and the NAACP as engaging in a conspiracy to destroy Texanos. "The American GI Forum, LULAC, the NAACP, congresses and other nigger groups have repeatedly professed to be integrationists to push up the equality, intelligence and superiority of the black race," he writes.[45]

Anti-black racism by no means proved any more universal in the Mexican American community than it did among Texas Anglos. Following the U.S. Supreme Court's 1954 decision mandating school desegregation in *Brown v. Board of Education*, Texas Governor Allan Shivers placed three nonbinding referenda—preserving school segregation, strengthening laws against interracial marriage, and supporting "local" rule against federal interference—on a statewide Democratic primary ballot. These measures passed by a four-to-one margin statewide, but in twelve counties with significant Mexican American populations the ballots were approved by less than 60 percent. Democrats in three heavily Mexican American counties—Bexar, Kleberg, and Uvalde—refused to put the measures on the ballot, while voters in Webb County beat the proposals by an eight-to-one margin. In a state where Mexican Americans became targets of segregation, such opposition might reflect self-interest, but it might also reflect a smaller degree of racist sentiment in the Mexican American community as compared to the Anglo community.[46]

There is less ambiguity in the career of the state's most visible Mexican American politician, Henry B. Gonzalez of San Antonio. As a member of the San Antonio City Council in 1956, Gonzalez promoted measures that abolished all of the city's segregation ordinances. As a state senator in 1957, Gonzalez filibustered for twenty hours to block legislative proposals that would have impeded implementation of *Brown v. Board of Education* in Texas. In his lengthy oration, Gonzalez drew comparisons between his own experiences with segregation as a Mexican American and the freedom struggles of African Americans. "Is Texas liberty only for Anglo-Saxons?" he asked. The next year Gonzalez won the NAACP's Man of the Year award. Even with his visible support of black civil rights groups, Mexican American voters enthusiastically continued to vote for Gonzalez. He was elected to the U.S. Congress in 1961.[47]

While anti-racist discourse could be heard in the Mexican American community, the desire of groups like LULAC and AGIF to keep the NAACP at a distance provided a counterweight, reflecting a fear that such an alliance would complicate Latino efforts for equality. In some cases the embracing of a white identity also revealed deep currents of white supremacy among Mexican Americans. Ochoa and 1950 bomber Pete Garcia were middle-class men who saw their social status as dependent upon the isolation of blacks. The ideological differences between LULAC and AGIF on one hand and Ochoa and Garcia on the other reflect politically dominant sentiments in the community that ranged from indifference to African American rights to outright negrophobia.

If relations in Dallas between blacks and Mexican Americans were at times hostile, divisions between blacks and two other marginalized groups, Jews and Anglo Catholics, were distant but friendlier. Catholics and Jews found themselves attacked by the same public figures that ranked among the city's most vocal negrophobes. Many Protestants suspected the whiteness of Catholics because of the high number of Mexican Americans and other nonwhites in the church, the church's highly visible provision of private education to blacks, and the foreignness of its Vatican leadership. Like Jews, Catholics represented an ethnically and linguistically varied religion on the verge of racialization by the Protestant majority.

Federal defense spending in Southern metropolitan areas during World War II and continuing through four decades of Cold War brought a migration of highly skilled workers of unprecedented ethnic, linguistic, cultural, and religious diversity.[48] Fundamentalist Protestants, fearing a loss of cultural hegemony in the region, expressed this anxiety by striking at a familiar target, the Catholic Church.

Catholics represented one of the fastest-growing demographic groups in Texas at mid-century, numbering from just over 600,000 in 1930 to more than 1.3 million in 1960. By the time John Kennedy was inaugurated as the first Roman Catholic president of the United States in 1961, the Catholic Church represented the largest denomination in the state.[49] One of the most vociferous spokesmen for Dallas anti-Catholicism in the 1950s and 1960s was the Reverend W. A. Criswell, pastor of the First Baptist Church in Dallas, which in the latter half of the twentieth century became the largest Southern Baptist congregation in the world. Eventually receiving considerable financial backing from oil billionaire H. L. Hunt, Criswell became one of the pulpit's most visible defenders of segregation. In addressing the Baptist Conference on Evangelism in Columbia, South Carolina, Criswell demanded separation not just of the races, but of religions as well. Invoking images of filth and dirt frequently used in depictions of African Americans and Mexican Americans, Criswell called integration the work of "outsiders" (by implication Jews) in "their dirty shirts" who, if they weren't stopped, would "get in your family." Christians, he said, must resist this religious miscegenation, and he urged denominations to "stick to their own kind." At the same time, Criswell attacked the "spurious doctrine" of the "universal Fatherhood of God and brotherhood of man." Criswell was by no means a lonely extremist among Southern fundamentalists. In 1959 one group of Atlanta evangelicals described integration as "Satanic, unconstitutional, and one of the main objectives of the Communist Party." Yet Criswell's vitriol still stood out in an age of widespread demagoguery and garnered national headlines.[50]

Criswell's attacks undoubtedly stemmed in part from the Catholic Church's general support of the civil rights movement. Many Catholic liberals openly supported the NAACP and criticized the prevailing racial order. "Why cannot Dallas, progressive in every other way, be a leader during this critical time?" Sister Mary Ignatius asked the *Dallas Morning News* in a letter from the suburb of Irving. "If, without putting up any signs, we simply served graciously every customer who came to a lunch counter—just as we sell merchandise to anyone who patronizes a store—there would be no need for demonstrations. Perhaps then we could read portions of the Declaration and Constitution without blushing, stammering and rationalizing."[51] NAACP activist Craft recalled that some of the first whites in Dallas to support the NAACP were leaders of the Catholic Church. "Most of them had served all over the world," she said. They "had been to Rome and different places, and they didn't have the racial prejudice."[52]

Liberal Jews also backed the NAACP. About 9,000 Jews lived in Dallas in 1939–1940, comprising about 3 percent of the city's total population. By the early 1950s the Jewish population had increased by about half. Before World War II the Jewish community inclined strongly toward assimilation to aid their attainment of whiteness. After the war, notes historian Marilynn Wood Hill, "a large migration of Jews from eastern and midwestern metropolitan centers came to Dallas [who] . . . were more traditional in religion, more conscious of their Jewishness, and more desirous of Jewish grouping and ingathering." International events also reinforced a need for a more distinct Jewish identity. "The atrocities of Hitler . . . and the establishment of the state of Israel [in 1948], all helped draw the Jews closer together in a common bond," Hill writes.[53] The formation of a more distinct group identity confirmed for anti-Semites the stereotype of Jews as clannish, emotionally disconnected from the larger community, and therefore disloyal.

Because of their higher economic standing than most Latinos, Jews did not see blacks as job competitors or rivals for the spoils of desegregation. Consequently, Jews often supported the civil rights movement in Dallas and condemned economic injustice. However, like Mexican Americans, Jews never completely escaped the pressures of whiteness. Rather than a warm alliance, Dallas blacks and Jews often maintained a chilly distance. Demographic changes in North Central Texas after World War II profoundly shaped Dallas anti-Semitism, the position of Jews in the city's racial hierarchy, and the relationship of Jews to African Americans. The defense industry employed 55,000 people in the city during the war years as Dallas became a major manufacturing center for B-24 bombers and P-51 Mustangs and the new home of firms like North American Aviation, which relocated from Inglewood, California, in 1940. Detroit-based General Motors constructed a $35 million assembly plant in Arlington, nineteen miles west of Dallas, in 1953. Once tied to cotton, then to Texas oil, Dallas became a national center for the electronics industry.[54] Each of these corporate moves brought highly trained, technically skilled workers to the area who had no cultural or political ties to the Confederacy, Jim Crow, or Dixiecrat politics. Ironically, demographic changes weakened the city's commitment to Jim Crow at the same time it fostered the growth of the far right wing.[55]

Dallas' leadership clique, the Dallas Citizens Council (DCC) was not designed to absorb the more socially ambitious of the city's more affluent newcomers. The DCC had only consolidated its political power in the mid-1930s during the city's successful campaign to host the state's centennial celebration in 1936. Led by banker and former Klansman R. L. Thornton, this effort resulted in the formation the next year of the Dallas Citizens Council. This group, through its closely aligned and overlapping Citizens Charter Association (CCA), would dominate city politics until the late 1960s and allowed elites unprecedented hegemony in political affairs.

In 1930 elites completed their campaign of de-democratization in city politics by successfully amending the city charter, replacing the commission form of government with a council-manager form. The new city charter, which provided for a nine-member council including three at-large seats, was approved by a two-to-one margin citywide, but only 26 percent of Dallas' alienated voters bothered to cast ballots. Most opposition to the new city charter came from working-class neighborhoods in south and southeast Dallas.[56]

By the mid-1930s those who had supported the charter amendments formed the core constituency for Dallas' bid to host the 1936 Texas Centennial celebration. In this campaign, Thornton and fellow banker Fred Florence led a new, relatively homogeneous leadership clique. Florence was Jewish and yet was accepted as part of Dallas' inner circle. As another Jewish leader, Stanley Marcus, put it, a Jew could be heard in Dallas if he had a certain amount of "muscle," meaning that he held an executive position in an important business. However, as historian Patricia Hill points out, this leadership group consisted mostly of Gentile men in their forties and fifties who served as the chief executive officers of leading businesses. The leaders of the Dallas centennial movement saw the fair as a prime opportunity to sell the city to the rest of the world as an attractive site for business investment.[57]

Florence and Dallas Mayor Charles E. Turner submitted a $10 million bid to the Texas Centennial Commission, including a promised $3.5 million in city bonds.[58] The city's substantial financial promises earned Dallas the right to host the centennial instead of the less organized delegations from San Antonio and Houston in spite of the vastly more substantive historical claims of those cities. More than 6.3 million visitors attended the centennial festivities at Dallas' Fair Park from June 6 to November 30, 1936, including President Franklin D. Roosevelt, but the fair still lost money. Nevertheless, success in amending the city charter and hosting the centennial led Thornton, Florence, and their allies to institutionalize the Dallas Citizens Council.[59]

Bankers, insurance company executives, publishers, and the managers and owners of utility companies made up almost the entire membership of the all-white, all-male Citizens Council.[60] By the early 1940s more than half the membership did not even live in Dallas proper but called the exclusive downtown enclaves of Highland Park and University Park home.[61] Journalists, educators, and ministers found themselves excluded from the organization. The narrow social base of the Citizens Council smoothed the path to consensus but also promoted self-delusion. This new leadership clique, Patricia Hill notes, avoided issues "that engendered even minor disagreement . . . The apparent consensus gave the illusion of a small group of men who could do whatever they wanted to in Dallas." Citizens Council support became so essential to any Dallas politician that once a candidate received the clique's blessing he could win office without making a single campaign speech or holding one rally.[62] After two successful anti-union campaigns in the 1930s, elites completely constructed a political apparatus that quietly divided Gentiles, Jews, blacks, and Mexican Americans, a subtle structure that dampened dissent and aborted cross-racial alliances.

After the U.S. Supreme Court struck down the National Industrial Recovery Act (NIRA) codes that set minimum wage and maximum working hours standards, Dallas manufacturers of work clothes and overalls immediately rolled back wages to pre-NIRA levels. Dressmakers feared their employers would do the same. Dallas garment workers, making an average of $9.50 a week, earned 40 to 70 percent less than their counterparts in the North. About 100 Dallas dressmakers decided to unionize. The International Ladies Garment Workers Union (ILGWU) dispatched Meyer Perlstein from New York to organize union locals. Perlstein arrived in November 1934 and within four months signed on 400 of approximately 1,000 dressmakers in the city. The city's dress manufacturers refused to recognize the ILGWU and fired workers suspected of union activism. A strike began in February 1935. Strikers faced a hostile press, with the *Morning News* implying Perlstein was a communist. The newspaper quoted a strikebreaker who responded to union hecklers by taunting, "I might be yellow, but I'm not red."[63]

The garment workers strike re-Semitized union activists in some Gentile minds. About one-third of the union membership was Jewish, as was their most visible spokesman. The *Dallas Morning News* referred to Perlstein, who had been a U.S. citizen for twenty years, as a "Russian-born Jew" in its headlines. This label aimed at painting the ILGWU organizer as foreign, Bolshevik, and nonwhite in the eyes of the public. E. G. Wadle, owner of a factory targeted by strikers, at first refused to answer during a hearing of the Industrial Commission of Texas whether there was any "objection" to Perlstein "because of his being of Jewish blood." Wadle later denied that Perlstein's Judaism was ever discussed.[64] In his testimony before the committee, Perlstein claimed his place alongside Old and New Testament monotheists and Gentile heroes revered in the Protestant tradition. "I am proud of the name 'agitator,'" he said. "I will go further, if there was anyone that ever did help anyone they were called dangerous agitators. Abraham Lincoln was called an agitator; Moses was called an agitator; Christ was called an agitator, and so were many others."[65] Perlstein insisted that unionism represented the patriotic alternative to Marxism. "The only chance communists have is among unorganized workers, where people are not given the freedom to organize, where they are not given an opportunity to develop their opportunities," he said. "It is those people that fall for propaganda of this type."[66]

Dress manufacturers never lacked for strikebreakers, many of whom were poor Gentile émigrés from rural Texas who sought escape from rural poverty. Factories stayed open and filled orders. Dallas elites successfully depicted the strike as alien subversion. With their strike fund depleted, ILGWU workers voted to end the walkout. Elites soon embarked on a final anti-union offensive to ensure their hegemony. In 1937 Ford Motor Company officials, hearing rumors that the Congress of Industrial Organizations (CIO) hoped to organize workers at its Dallas assembly plant, hired a brigade of more than twenty company thugs to terrorize union activists. Using blackjacks, whips, and lengths of rubber hose, this private police force kidnapped more than fifty people, crippled a dozen, blinded one man, and killed another during an anti-union campaign in the summer and fall of 1937. Despite findings in 1940 by the National Labor Relations Board (NLRB) that Ford had been guilty of "indiscriminate ruthlessness and organized gangsterism," the elite-organized thuggery had achieved its purpose of stalling United Auto Workers (UAW) organizing."[67] After the failure of the garment workers and Ford strikes, many in the white working class concluded that political activism garnered little material benefit. Demoralized, labor played a declining role in Dallas politics after the late 1930s.

The working class, mired in self-destructive racism, rendered itself largely irrelevant to the Dallas power structure by the end of World War II. Dallas elites, however, faced a new challenge directly related to the economic transformations wrought by the war. Right-wing men chafed at rule by old patriarchs with long roots in the city and feared they would be pushed aside by aggressive minorities. The newly rich and the ambitious middle class joined in their suspicions of the DCC clique and its collaboration with an increasingly "socialist" government in Washington, D.C.[68] The emerging Dallas New Right saw the U.S. Supreme Court as locked in a conspiracy with the NAACP and the Communist Party, "all dedicated to the overthrow of 'normal' race relations."[69] The social changes represented by the civil rights movement, critic Theodore White writes, most threatened the South's "little rich" —the "prosperous car dealers, the contractors, the bottling concessionaires, the little oil men, the real estate men"—who made up a significant part of Dallas' increasingly complex society.[70]

Dallas held no monopoly on right-wing panic in Texas. For a time in the 1950s, obsession with alleged communist conspiracies competed with the negrophobia generated by the Supreme Court's *Brown v. Board of Education* decision in 1954 as the central issue in Texas politics. Many white Texans saw the rise of the post–World War II civil rights movement and communist subversion as intimately linked. This anxiety emanated not just from the right-wing fringe but from the state's mainstream press, such as the *Dallas Morning News,* the *Houston Post,* and the *Houston Chronicle,* as well as political leaders from 1950s Governor Allan Shivers down.[71]

Local school boards fanned much of the Red Scare. Houston, like Dallas, experienced tumultuous, explosive growth—stimulated in part by World War II and Cold War defense spending—and attracted a new, diverse population from all over the country and even the world. Houston's population more than doubled in two decades, from 300,000 in 1930 to 726,000 in 1950. The strain on infrastructure and the cultural upheaval generated by so many newcomers settling in what was once an overgrown provincial town generated what Theodore White described as the "Anguish of Modernization." These concerns found voice in one writer to the *Houston Post* who bitterly complained of the city's new "metropolitan café society who condone immorality, drunkenness, plural marriage, divorce and worse among themselves." The letter writer, fretful that he and his fundamentalist Protestant ilk had lost control of the emerging metropolis, believed these social changes had to be a result of a communist conspiracy.[72] This message resonated, particularly among Houston's "white, upper-middle class Republicans and conservative Democrats who attracted allies among the city's previously politically inactive professional and white collar workers," who made up the bulk of the city's Red Scare extremists, according to historian Don Carleton.[73]

Flocking to hard-right organizations like the Minute Women, such anti-communist zealots opposing "integration, New Deal Reforms, and progressive education" took over the Houston school board. Once there, they forced the resignation of George W. Ebey, the deputy superintendent, because while in California and Oregon he had openly backed the New Deal and expressed support for black civil rights. School officials fired one math teacher in Houston because he mentioned in a teacher's lounge that he backed liberal Democratic presidential candidate Adlai Stevenson. The school board yanked books out of the school library if they had something nice to say about the United Nations and delayed the teaching of world history and geography until tenth grade for fear of even mentioning Karl Marx, the Russian Revolution, and the Soviet Union to younger children. Such actions took place all over the state, including Dallas, where the city's Museum of Fine Arts and the public library were forced to ban exhibits of left-leaning artists such as Pablo Picasso and Diego Rivera.[74]

Many of the affluent in Dallas perceived a federal government profoundly transformed by the Great Depression and World War II and a city dramatically changed by immigration. They did not like what they saw. Historian George Norris Green observes that "in Dallas, the Conservative Establishment itself came under fire from the right and failed to truly meet the challenge." The DCC, always hunting for federal dollars to feed Dallas' economic expansion, was seen as collaborating with big government and, because of its quiet, backroom deal making with the black community, was viewed as insufficiently hostile to desegregation.[75]

Hoping to counter the communist menace, a Dallas school board less flamboyantly conservative than its counterpart in Houston approved the creation of the course "The Principles of American Freedom in Contrast to the Tyranny of Communism" in 1961. The school district purchased 15,000 copies of FBI Director J. Edgar Hoover's *Masters of Deceit: The Story of Communism in America and How to Fight It* as the textbook.[76] Hoover argued that communists thoroughly infested the black civil rights movement.[77]

Much of the right-wing politics centered on the public schools, the integration issue, and the allegedly subversive curriculum taught at campuses. Women in cities like Dallas and Houston still found that they were largely shut out of political power, but education was accepted as a woman's proper domain, even by ultraconservatives. Many of the most visible New Right activists, therefore, were women, but the financing and directing of the movement still largely came from men. Many of the new rich behind the Texas Red Scare were oilmen who were generally political outsiders whose influence did not match their wealth. In Dallas their business orientation was global and therefore not Dallas-centric enough to win inclusion in the Citizens Council. Many of these men, such as H. L. Hunt and Clint Murchison along with their Fort Worth peer Sid Richardson, became financiers of the far right in the mid-twentieth century.[78] Murchison, whose son in 1960 founded the Dallas Cowboys National Football League franchise, became one of the largest financial contributors to red-baiting Senator Joe McCarthy of Wisconsin.[79]

Hunt underwrote the tax-exempt Facts Forum organization, which published pamphlets like "We Must Abolish the United Nations" and "Hitler Was a Liberal" and privately sponsoring an ultraconservative news commentary show called "LIFELINE" that was hosted by Dan Smoot and broadcast on more than 80 television and 150 radio stations across the country.[80] Echoing traditional elite hatred of the universal franchise, a belief outlined in his novel *Alpaca,* Hunt once raged at Smoot after the former FBI man said in a "LIFELINE" broadcast that democracy was "a political outgrowth of the teachings of Jesus Christ." Hunt corrected Smoot, deriding democracy as the handiwork of the devil and a "phony liberal form of watered down communism."[81]

To the far right, every social justice reform represented a step toward the socialism and miscegenation plotted by conspiratorial Jews. "THE PRESIDENT OF NAACP . . . IS NOT A NEGRO, BUT A MEMBER OF THIS MINORITY NON-CHRISTIAN GROUP BY THE NAME OF A. SPRINGARN," one anti-Semitic flier proclaimed in all capital letters. The flier, distributed in Dallas in the 1950s by Texas Christians for Freedom, quoted a "Rabbi Rabinovich" outlining a sinister Jewish plot to eliminate the white race. "We will openly reveal our identity with the races of Asia and Africa," the flier quoted Rabinovich as predicting. "I can state with assurance that the last generation of white children is now being born. [We] . . . will . . . forbid the whites to mate with whites. The white women must cohabit with members of the dark races, the white men with the black women. Thus the white race will disappear, for mixing the dark with the white means the end of the white man, and our most dangerous enemy will become only a memory."[82]

The themes of the Jew as nonwhite racial alien, as instigator of communism, as tireless conspirator and determined race mixer, all came together in the work of John Owen Beaty, longtime chairman of the English department at Southern Methodist University in Dallas. First appointed to the SMU faculty in 1919, the West Virginia native served as chief of the Historical Section in the War Department's Military Intelligence Service during World War II. By the time he returned to SMU, he had become embittered by what he saw as the Jewish domination of culture.[83]

His 1951 opus, *The Iron Curtain over America,* warned that Jews threatened American democracy. Because of its British Israelism, the 1920s Dallas Klan had acknowledged a distant kinship with modern-day Jews, though the early Klansmen believed Jews had become hopelessly corrupted through race mixing and rejection of Jesus Christ as savior. Beaty went further in his anti-Semitism, denying that the eastern European Jews who represented the bulk of the American Jewish population descended from the biblical Israelites. Most Jews, he claimed, descended from Khazars, a "belligerent tribe" of "mixed stock, with Mongol and Turkic affinities" who, while living between the Ural Mountains and the Caspian Sea, converted en masse to Judaism in the eighth or ninth century C.E.[84] "The blood of Abraham, Isaac, and Jacob flows not at all (or to a sporadic degree . . .) in the veins of the Jews who have come to America from Eastern Europe," Beaty wrote.[85] Beaty's denial of modern American Jews' Hebrew origins was not original. Anti-Semitic eugenicist Lothrop Stoddard made a similar claim three decades earlier.[86] Beaty's work, however, far exceeded Stoddard's in its populism and its paranoia. Beaty's Khazars are ever ambitious for power and influence and experience almost super-human success. Unable to assimilate in eastern Europe because of their arrogance, he alleged, Khazars eventually provoked the 1917 Bolshevik Revolution. "The Marxian program of drastic controls, so repugnant to the free western mind, was no obstacle to the acceptance of Marxism by many Khazar Jews, for the Babylonian Talmud under which they lived had taught them to accept authoritarian dictation on everything from their immorality to their trade practices," Beaty wrote.[87]

Further, Khazar Jews immigrated to the United States in mass numbers after World War I and took over the Democratic Party, thus leading to the crypto-socialism and racial liberalism of the Roosevelt era.[88] Jews then provoked World War II, he claimed. "*Our alien-dominated government fought the war for the annihilation of Germany, the historic bulwark of Christian Europe,*" Beaty cried in italics.[89] Just six years after American troops had liberated concentration camps in western Germany, Beaty denied the Holocaust happened, labeling the Shoah a fraud launched to justify the slaughter of Aryans and, after 1948, to blackmail the West into political and financial support of Israel.[90] Khazars stood on the verge of world domination. To save America, Beaty argued, Christians must develop "some method of preventing our unassimilable mass of aliens and alien-minded people from exercising" political and cultural power "out of all proportion" to their numbers.[91]

Beaty's message reached a broad audience as his book went through nine printings by 1953. He went beyond familiar anti-Semitic themes. With his Holocaust denial and claims that Jews were sinister Asians not descended from the monotheistic heroes of the Old Testament, Beaty laid out the major doctrines that would dominate the racist far-right wing in the late twentieth century. Beaty particularly influenced the Christian Identity movement that included groups like Aryan Nations, which splintered from other believers in British Israelism in the late twentieth century by insisting that Jews were the literal descendents of Satan and that only western and northern Europeans were legitimate heirs of ancient Israel. A half-century later, Identity Web sites still sell copies of *Iron Curtain over America* and cite it as an authoritative academic justification for anti-Semitism.[92]

More ominous for the Dallas Jewish community than Beaty's fringe ranting was the tepid response mainstream city leaders gave his outbursts. SMU President Umphrey Lee had ignored letters complaining of Beaty's anti-Semitism dating back to 1947.[93] The Public Affairs Luncheon Club, a women's organization, adopted a unanimous resolution backing Beaty and requesting that SMU investigate the faculty's philosophy and values.[94] In spite of his notoriety, Beaty continued teaching at SMU until his retirement in 1957.[95]

Doubts about Jewish whiteness persisted after Beaty. In the 1950s and 1960s several country clubs excluded Jews. The Dallas Junior League remained closed to Jews, as did several SMU sororities and fraternities. Just as the Dallas press emphasized Meyer Perlstein's Russian Jewish origins during the garment workers' strike of the 1930s, Dallas newspapers in 1963 pointedly referred to Jack Ruby, the murderer of President John Kennedy's assassin Lee Harvey Oswald, by the more Semitic-sounding "Jacob Rubenstein." This happened even though Ruby long before legally changed his name.[96] Though many Jews like Fred Florence and Stanley Marcus achieved economic prominence by the 1950s and 1960s, there were no Jews at the top executive level of the major insurance companies at the time, and few Jews held executive positions at banks. The most successful Jews ran the city's department stores, such as Sanger-Harris, Titche-Goettinger, Neiman-Marcus, and E. M. Khan, where they found themselves, uncomfortably, on the front battle lines over Jim Crow.[97]

Many Jewish leaders, like Rabbi Levi Olan, felt that a shared history of oppression made Jewish support of African American civil rights a moral imperative. Born in 1903 near Kiev, the future rabbi grew up in Rochester, New York, in a Yiddish-speaking family. Graduating in six years from Hebrew Union College in Cincinnati, Olan accepted a position as rabbi in Worcester, Massachusetts, in 1929. He remained there until 1949, when he was invited to lead Dallas' Temple Emanu-El congregation.[98]

Dallas Jews had pursued whiteness to the point of losing their identity. Upon his 1949 arrival, Olan found that the temple's entire service was in English with the exception of one Hebrew prayer. Congregation songs were led by a quartet and organist who were, in Olan's words, "all goyim." The synagogue largely abandoned celebrating bar mitzvahs to mark the passage of thirteen-year-old boys in the congregation into manhood, in favor of the more Christian-sounding "confirmation" ceremony marking graduation from religious school. Rabbi Olan saw his major assignment as halting assimilationist extremism. "In Dallas the job was to make Jews out of goyim," he joked. Olan instigated changes at the temple including a repertoire of Hebrew liturgical music for services. "We are being taken over by the third wave of immigration," one temple member of German descent complained, pointedly attacking Olan's eastern European heritage. Olan countered that he was merely trying to reawaken consciousness of Jewish culture and history.[99]

Olan recalled the cold reception he received when he turned his attention to black civil rights. Like his Dallas predecessor David Lefkowitz, and like many of his contemporaries such as Rabbi Jacob Rothschild of Atlanta and Charles Mantinband of Hattiesburg, Mississippi, he became one more Northern-born religious leader trying to prod a sometimes reluctant Southern congregation to more boldly support African American civil rights. Many Southern Jews took up the cause reluctantly well into the civil rights era. A 1961 poll showed that while 97 percent of Northern Jews approved the *Brown v. Board of Education* Supreme Court decision that mandated desegregation of public school systems, 40 percent of Southern Jews considered the decision "unfortunate." A majority of Southern Jews said desegregation was moving too quickly. If Southern Jews proved friendlier to black civil rights than their Gentile neighbors, this seemed too timid to Northern immigrants like Olan.[100]

"When I came down to Texas, I had a program on the air," Olan recalled in a 1983 interview. ". . . [O]ne of my first sermons [was] . . . because I saw these . . . toilets which had signs 'for whites only' and that got me. So I preached a sermon on the radio on the race issue. My phone rang that afternoon. Someone says to me, 'Go back where you came from.' "[101] Olan did not back down on what he considered a basic moral principle. "Segregation is immoral," he preached in blunt language.[102] Because of his support of black political aims, Olan suffered through bomb threats, hate mail, and eggs hurled at Temple Emanu-El and his home. Even as tension rose over Dallas school desegregation, the rabbi delivered a guest sermon at Good Street Baptist Church, an African American congregation.[103] Many Jews applauded Olan and became benefactors of African American institutions such as Bishop College. Olan, Julius Schepps, Jacob Kravitz, and Sam Bloom all played key roles in a publicity campaign aimed at persuading Dallas to react calmly when school desegregation began in 1961.[104]

Most Jews, however, were not as bold as Olan. Some preferred to work within the limits of Jim Crow to improve the lives of African Americans. More typical was Jerome Crossman, an attorney and president of the Ryan Consolidated Petroleum Company. In the early 1950s Crossman campaigned to find a nonprofit corporation that would buy land and extend utilities for a segregated, middle-class black housing development to relieve the South Dallas tensions that resulted in the 1950–1951 bombings. His efforts culminated in the creation of Hamilton Park, a modest subdivision located at Forest Lane, one hundred yards east of Central Expressway and more than ten miles from downtown on the far north fringes of the city. Crossman, as historian William H. Wilson notes, was guided by his Reform Judaism to be "very concerned about the welfare of all mankind, regardless of race, color, or creed." Crossman believed that through incremental changes race relations would improve. "Crossman was an optimist, but no visionary," Wilson writes. "He did not foresee a desegregated society . . . nor was he a racial liberal attempting to move towards that goal . . . He would labor for racial justice within the boundaries set by enlightened whites such as himself."[105]

Many Jews sensed their tenuous acceptance within Dallas and feared going too far in their racial liberalism. In the mid-1950s, Anthony Jones, an African

American professor of international relations and government at Bishop College, studied Judaism under Levi Olan and applied for membership in the congregation. Fearing a violent Gentile backlash, not everyone in the congregation welcomed Jones. "There were some problems, some I must say opposition," said Irving Goldberg, president of Temple Emanu-El at the time. "And there was genuine fear because at that time synagogues all over the country were being bombed."[106]

With so many Jews owning and/or operating downtown department stores, it was inevitable that some Jews would not only work within the limits of Jim Crow laws but also actively enforce them. This was true across Texas, including Houston, where the Jewish community often perceived that they had landed in the racial crossfire between right-wing anti-Semites and civil rights protestors targeting Jewish-owned stores that practiced segregation. Many Jews followed the lead of Rabbi Judah Schachtel, who rarely spoke out against discrimination but who preferred to work behind the scenes to end discrimination. Schachtel "kept his rhetoric low-key, convinced that his friendships with African American pastors and their congregations demonstrated far more than words," author Hollace Weiner notes.[107]

This strategy collapsed when students at Texas Southern University (TSU, established for blacks by the Texas Legislature in 1947) led sit-ins in February 1960 at Weingarten's supermarket located near the campus. The TSU students carefully chose their target. One of the wealthiest families in Houston, the Weingartens depended heavily on black clientele at their stores. "It was a rather familiar statement on the part of many individuals that Joe Weingarten is getting rich off us," said Dr. D. B. Jones, TSU's dean of students. A sit-in would be particularly embarrassing to Joseph Weingarten, the family patriarch, who enjoyed a reputation as a liberal and who had just received a reward from the B'nai B'rith service organization for his community service and humanitarian efforts in the city. Students alerted the media and marched, singing patriotic songs, to the Weingarten's lunch counter. The protests continued for days and spread to other locations. Embarrassed by the press attention, Weingarten tried to diffuse the situation by closing the lunch counter. "We weren't anxious to be the spearhead in this movement," Jack Weingarten later recalled, saying that his family's biggest wish was to get out of the spotlight. The Weingarten lunch counter remained closed by mid-March of that year and the sit-ins ceased, but black customers continued to boycott the grocery store. Rabbi Schachtel served on the forty-one-member Citizens' Relations Committee that achieved a two-week halt to the protests. Further waves of sit-ins finally prompted the desegregation of downtown Houston lunch counters by the end of 1960, even as the local press virtually ignored the historic arrival of integration at downtown lunch counters and department stores.[108]

A similar process unfolded in Dallas, where downtown stores refused to allow black patrons to try on clothes.[109] Other stores excluded blacks altogether. Many African Americans, impatient with the petty humiliations they endured as customers at prominent stores such as Sanger's or Titche-Goetinger's, staged protests. In 1953 the Citizens' Committee to Abolish Discrimination against Negro Women in Dallas Department Stores set up shop at the Excelsior Life Building on Flora Street. W. J. Durham, chairman of the committee, circulated a letter reporting on his efforts. Durham had persuaded Morton Sanger, manager of the E. M. Kahn store, to contact other store managers and operators who were "discriminating against Negro women in the sale of merchandise and the services connected with the sale of merchandise." Stanley Marcus of the Neiman-Marcus store said that he was "leaving on a trip, but he would study the matter and see what could be done about it." Marcus, by reputation one of the city's leading liberals, apparently took his time. The store maintained segregation for another eight years, banning blacks from sitting next to white customers at the dining facility or using the same bathrooms until 1961. Representatives of other stores, Durham wrote, said that " 'they would not meet with the members of [the] committee and discuss the matter,' that their business was their private business and they would operate it in such manner as they desired." Morton Sanger was reported to have said that "such action on the part of the other operators left the management of the Kahn store to choose between two classes of business—white trade and trade from Negro citizens. Therefore, I can do nothing about the racial discrimination policy in force at the Kahn store."[110]

The racism of Dallas' larger white community provided moral cover for individual merchants. No store could safely desegregate unless every store did. "The department stores' position is crystal clear; namely, that such stores will continue to insult Negro women . . . and if Negro men continue to trade at such stores, they will and must do so in the face of the fact that their women will continually be insulted and mistreated," Durham wrote.[111]

Resentments between blacks and Jews developed because of the very different place the two groups occupied on the city's racial hierarchy. Blacks saw their health, safety, and survival at stake in the civil rights struggle. Discrimination aimed at Jews consisted largely of exclusion from country clubs or from the upper limits of the corporate hierarchy. Such complaints might have seemed trivial to African Americans, who may not have been fully sensitive to the impact that the rise of the Klan in Dallas during the 1920s, the

Nazi Holocaust, and other instances of Gentile violence had on the Jewish community's sense of security.

Juanita Craft attributed the strain that existed between blacks and Jews in Dallas to the distance that marked all white-black relations in the South. "They [Jews] accept us, you know, as far as meetings and things of that sort, if you meet them, but they don't put themselves to any trouble to meet us, and we don't put ourselves to any trouble to meet them," she said. Craft said part of the problem was a cultural gulf between the two groups. "You know, a lot of this stuff has developed because of the ignorance of our people," Craft said. "When I was a child coming up, I thought of a Jew as something that was different from everything else. 'He's going to Jew you down.' . . . He's going to be dishonest with you and things of that sort—a stigma that was very unfair." [112]

Some blacks echoed traditional Gentile anti-Semitism, but more often they saw Jews as simply part of an undifferentiated white majority. This perspective was summed up years later, in August 1993, by John Wiley Price, the controversial Dallas county commissioner, who met with a crowd of more than seventy at the North Dallas Jewish Community Center. "Most African-Americans don't know enough to be anti-Semitic," Price told the crowd. "We don't know the difference between Anglos and Jewish people." [113] What Price did not know was that the erasure of that difference between Anglos and Jewish people was the result of about a century of difficult and not entirely successful Jewish effort. Full whiteness for both Jews and Mexican Americans remained a slippery objective. [114]

A tantalizing chance existed for marginal whites to ally politically with blacks in the 1950s and 1960s. The indifference and, at times, hostility of the Mexican American political leadership to African Americans and the compromised humanitarianism of Jewish leaders like Jerome Crossman toward the civil rights cause frustrated any possible victory for Dallas' progressive forces. The distance between these groups arising just after World War II guaranteed that the city's freedom movement in the 1960s enjoyed little visibility and mostly symbolic success. The conflicts between blacks, Mexican Americans, and Jews laid the groundwork for the internecine strife that would characterize much of Dallas politics after desegregation.

As the 1960s progressed, elites were forced to abandon Jim Crow. Elites' actions, however, were based largely on their fear of an enraged, politicized lower class. Even as they sought to incorporate conservative African Americans into the ruling structure, elites continued to see the Anglo working class as uncivilized barbarians, outside the norms of whiteness, threatening to destroy a wealthy metropolis. Elites sought to accommodate these groups with symbolic democracy. Discourse about the dangers of democracy gave way to praise of America's heritage of freedom. This rhetorical shift occurred even as the Dallas Citizens Council lost its absolute control of city hall. The city's Democrats divided into Dixiecrat and liberal wings, as some conservatives, dismayed by the civil rights agenda of the national Democratic Party, set aside political traditions dating back to the Civil War and found the Republican Party an increasingly congenial home for white supremacist politics. The weakening of the Democratic Party undermined support for Jim Crow laws. This prevented the city from adopting harsh measures to preserve the racial *ancien regime*. Softer measures were called for to keep African Americans' demands in check. White Texans should politically reward loyal, subservient blacks and conservative Mexican Americans, elites would believe, in order to thwart the political aspirations of more radical blacks and their white allies.

Rather than ruling for the city as a whole, elites had smashed Dallas into atomized parts. This alienation protected elites from the rebellion they feared. This was far from the "beloved community" that black leaders like John Leslie Patton and Juanita Craft had dreamed of when they began their struggle in the 1930s and 1940s. This outcome was not so obvious at the dawn of the 1960s. For many African Americans, the civil rights era seemed the time of the possible in which liberals could imagine without embarrassment a future of racial fairness. Charles Graggs, an African American writer for the *Dallas Express* whose letters to the editor flooded the *Dallas Morning News* in the postwar years, had not yet lost hope for a better tomorrow. "During the first years of my writing letters to the *News,* pleading for justice and equality, most of the letters, post cards and phone calls I received in reply were ugly and bitter," he wrote ten months before the assassination of President John F. Kennedy in downtown Dallas. "But such responses gradually dwindled until today most of the comment is friendly and cordial. This shows Dallas is throwing off its old idol of hate and segregation, a fact which makes me rejoice." Graggs' celebration proved tragically premature.[115]

SEVEN

A BLIGHT AND A SIN

Segregation, the Kennedy Assassination,
and the Wreckage of Whiteness

By 1960 Dallas blacks and whites lived on the same planet but in different worlds. The black civil rights leadership looked to tomorrow, believing that "The South Is Changed and Can Never Turn Back," as a March 14, 1959, banner headline in the *Dallas Express* proclaimed.[1] If Dallas blacks looked forward to a more equitable future, elites mourned a past they believed had blossomed under the unchallenged rule of wealthy Southern whites. Even as waves of non-Southern immigrants altered the region's politics and culture, Dallas' leadership continued to cloak the city in Confederate gray. A list of Dallas elementary schools in the mid-twentieth century read like a rebel army muster roll. Jefferson Davis, president of the Confederate States of America, generals Robert E. Lee, Stonewall Jackson, and John B. Hood, Confederate postmaster and local politico John H. Reagan, General (and later Dallas Mayor) William Cabell and local banker and Confederate officer William Henry Gaston all had campuses named in their honor. Thomas Jefferson High School, named after the slaveholding president, called its teams the Rebels and adopted the Confederate battle flag as its symbol.[2]

Southernness marked the local architecture as never before. One might have expected North Central Texas voices to drip honey, but by the 1960s Dallas increasingly spoke with a different accent. The post–World War II flood of immigrants to Texas from outside Dixie began as a trickle. In 1950 just under 11.3 percent of Texas residents had been born outside the South. By 1960 that number increased to almost 11.7 percent.[3] This slow prelude to a demographic revolution dramatically accelerated in the last third of the twentieth century. The proportion of native-born Texans living in the state dropped from 71 percent in 1970 to 65 percent in 1994. Unlike the past, when most newcomers to Texas came from the South, most of the immigrants in the last third of the twentieth century previously lived in the Midwest.[4] A human tidal wave altered not just the Texas landscape but also the entire region.

"The South has been Americanized," historian John Boles noted of the postwar immigration boom that turned Dixie into part of the so-called Sunbelt, a neo-region that stretched amoebae-like from the Carolina coast westward to California.[5] The rise of the Sunbelt signified the increasing political and economic power of the South and West and the precipitous decline of a unionized North. Dallas became a port of entry for Rustbelt refugees who brought a more industrial, more high-tech economy and created a less provincial culture. "In 1861 everyone considered Texas a part of the South; a century later its regional identification was debatable," Boles noted.[6] In the postwar years, Texans began electing Republicans to the governor's office and the Senate, legalized liquor by the drink, and repealed the state's blue laws, which outlawed the sale of certain retail items on Sunday. These changes marked the crumbling of traditional Southern elite hegemony. "We're becoming more of national state than a Southern state," one Texan observed upon the blue laws' demise.[7]

Dallas' elites had mythologized the Southern past beyond recognition. They no longer remembered the 1860 fire, the intra-white conflict during Reconstruction, or the conflicts between capitalists and Populists, Socialists, and unionists at the turn of the century. The political turmoil wracking Dallas in the 1960s and 1970s seemed a new thing, shaking elite confidence. Dallas elites in the 1960s and 1970s were paralyzed by their view of the past and unable, for two decades, to fully accommodate new political realities. Elites feared mounting an Alamo-like defense of Jim Crow, worrying that this would dry up the flow of Yankee investment dollars fueling Dallas' economic expansion. Yet they also dreaded a rebellion of lower-class whites should they appear to accommodate the federal government's integrationist demands. Divided, elites passively allowed desegregation in Dallas, opening city hall, the county courthouse, and the local congressional delegation to people of color. Elites, however, retained control by default as blacks and Mexican Americans battled with increasing ferocity.

Old and new racial ideologies existed side by side. Some elites still believed that the line between black and white represented the division between the civilized and uncivilized. One *Dallas Morning News* editorial warned of the dire consequences that the civil rights movement posed for Dallas. "When one million Negroes in Harlem, Chicago and Philadelphia can have more influence in elections—and in Washington's crucial decisions—than all the states from Texas to the Carolinas, then the South has a tremendous danger to face," the editorial cautioned.[8]

When blacks assumed power, the newspaper insisted, civilization fell to jungle rule. Civil war and ethnic cleansing in newly decolonized Africa became a recurring motif of the *Dallas Morning News'* overseas coverage. Jungle stereotypes of blacks with large lips and bones through their noses abounded in advertising and editorial cartoons. One Bill McClanahan cartoon, "Somebody's Going To Get It," depicted factions in the Congo civil war of the early 1960s as cannibals sharpening knives over boiling pots as they hungrily eyed each other. "It is quite true that the people of the Congo are primitive children of the jungle and that many of them are the children or grandchildren of practicing cannibals," wrote columnist Lynn Landrum in 1961. "That has a bearing, of course, on whether we ought to insist that they adopt our form of representative government and conduct their affairs of state as we do at Austin or at Washington."[9] As such, neither Landrum nor his paper could endorse any political party that embraced black political rights. This estranged Dallas elites from a Democratic Party that since the 1930s, they charged, provided "the impetus for racial equality, integration and social mixing."[10]

Regardless of the *Morning News'* hostility toward civil rights, however, some Dallas whites saw America as locked in a bitter ideological war with the Soviet Union for hearts and minds in Africa and Asia. Harry Truman, John Kennedy, Lyndon Johnson, and other liberal Democratic presidents in the mid-twentieth century worried about the impact of Southern racism on America's image during the Cold War. Many Americans suspected the stability of newly independent states in Africa and Asia and felt that they had to convince the gullible, easily manipulated people of the developing world that the United States offered the best model for new nations. With the Soviet Union presenting itself as not just anti-imperialist but anti-racist, according to historian Joel Williamson, the United States found itself in a difficult position. "The United States, offering itself as both the modern exemplar and the champion of democracy, was faced with the problem of wooing the non-white people of the Third World into the anti-Communist camp while racism ran riot at home," Williamson wrote.[11]

Many Southerners shared this fear that the cumulative injustices of American society might provide ammunition for a communist enemy spreading subversive doctrines at home and in the decolonized world.[12] Douglas McKibben, who lived in an apartment in a lower-middle-class white Dallas neighborhood with a median income of $4,574, felt a combination of moral outrage and Cold War fear over the city's racial politics. "As a grammar and high school student in a segregated community in West Texas, I never questioned whether or not Negroes had any rights. Likely I thought of them not at all," he admitted in a 1959 letter to the *Dallas Morning News*. "As a college student in a large integrated community, I never questioned the rights of Negroes, Orientals and others to attend the same school . . . The actions of the Arkansas and Virginia Governors [to block school integration] are indefensible. [Soviet leader] Nikita [Khrushchev] himself could not have caused greater racial discord and disrespect for our country." Mrs. J. Roland Smith, the wife of a draftsman living in a middle-class white neighborhood with a median income of $8,348, echoed McKibben's worries. Smith could not stomach the violent hostility to black student James Meredith's enrollment at the University of Mississippi. "The shooting into the Meredith home in Mississippi was a disgrace to America," she said. ". . . When an American can't go to the college he chooses, he might wonder what we are fighting for."[13]

In May 1958, more than 300 white Dallas-area ministers joined 115 black ministers in issuing a statement condemning segregation as "a blight and sin." "We are requesting only simple justice," the joint statement read. ". . . We ask for nothing that a recognition of the dignity of man does not prescribe."[14] Unlike Anglo Dallasites of an earlier generation, Robert P. Douglass, pastor of the Preston Hollow Presbyterian Church in Dallas, saw neither racism nor racial separation as part of the natural order. In a February 1961 sermon, Douglass declared, "The Christian gospel gave people the idea that no man is second class in the sight of God . . . We adults, both white and Negro, are too deeply ingrained with Jim Crow. But we must let the change come, particularly in the schools. Young people who do not come into the world with our prejudices have a chance to solve these problems if we adults don't force our prejudices upon them."[15]

Texas experienced no campaign of massive resistance with explosive riots accompanying school integration as happened in nearby New Orleans or in the neighboring state of Arkansas. Growing Northern immigration to the state, increasing sophistication in the Texas economy, and stronger ties of cities like Dallas and Houston to the national and global economies all diluted loyalty to de jure segregation as a Southern way of life. As Houston historian William Henry Kellar points out, many school districts in North and West Texas that had a small number of black students implemented *Brown* almost immediately. The El Paso school board approved a desegregation plan by a six-to-one majority within months of the 1954 Supreme Court decision, and San Antonio, Corpus Christi, and Eagle Mountain quickly announced plans to implement *Brown*. Texas school districts with the largest numbers of African American students, such as Dallas, Fort Worth, Houston, and Galveston, dragged their feet in complying with the court decision, but such battles were usually coolly legalistic, not marked by the glandular outbursts accompanying desegregation in the Deep South. Fewer Texas whites defended Jim Crow as passionately as did their peers in Mississippi, but few openly embraced desegregation either. Doing so, many Texas liberals worried, would invite harassment, accusations of communism, or worse. "Most Southern whites who opposed racial discrimination remained fearfully silent," William Kellar writes. Too many churches and universities failed to offer moral leadership on the civil rights issue, Kellar argues, and this dampened public acceptance of desegregation.[16]

The most courageous white support for desegregation in Texas often came from younger voters, with the Dallas County Young Democratic Club testing the limits of white supremacy. State Attorney General John Ben Shepperd tried to abolish the Texas chapter of the NAACP by arguing that the group met the legal definition of "doing business" in Texas and therefore had to remit previously unpaid franchise taxes as well as make its membership list public. Such a move would have exposed supporters to harassment and potential violence. The state and the NAACP settled out of court, with Texas agreeing not to challenge the organization's nonprofit status and the NAACP agreeing to pay the state franchise tax. The NAACP's decision to settle prompted resentment among black supporters across the state. NAACP membership declined from 16,866 in 1956 to 7,785 at the end of 1957.[17] In this hyper-charged atmosphere, Doyle King, president of the Dallas County Young Democratic Club, proclaimed in 1956 his opposition to the state's harassment of the NAACP. King's remarks outraged Lynn Landrum of the *Morning News*, who predicted a backlash against the Democratic Party in Dallas County during Dwight Eisenhower's reelection campaign for the presidency.[18]

Racial liberals gained strength in the Democratic Party as segregationists bolted for the city's growing Republican movement. In 1954 Dallas County allocated its only congressional seat to right-wing Republican Bruce Alger, who proved that the GOP could learn from Southern Democrats how to play racial politics. Alger ran his debut congressional campaign as a political outsider, opposing the establishment-backed Wallace Savage, a former mayor. Alger shocked the city by carrying nearly 53 percent of the vote to become the first-ever Republican congressman from Dallas County and the only Republican member of the Texas delegation to the House of Representatives since the 1930s.[19]

Savage alienated several key constituencies and fought off a challenge from liberal Leslie Hacker in the Democratic party primary by venomously assailing New Deal and pro-Truman Fair Deal Democrats and the NAACP. Roy Evans, president of the United Auto Workers local in Dallas, supported Alger because working for a two-party system was preferable to liberals to being "co-opted constantly by the ruling conservative Democrats."[20] The Republican carried a majority in black precincts, where voters were alienated by Savage's attacks on the civil rights movement.[21]

To whatever degree race was in the background in his first campaign, in later years Alger fought as ardently as any Dixiecrat to defend Jim Crow. Alger's challenger during his first reelection campaign in 1956, Dallas District Attorney Henry Wade, stooped to invoking the Civil War to attack the first-term Republican. "Republicans are running on a platform of peace," Wade said in a September debate. "They forget they were born of the most devastating war in our history—the Civil War." Wade attacked Alger for being insufficiently committed to segregation. "He (Alger) said anyone who thought the Supreme Court segregation ruling was unconstitutional was 'whistling Dixie,'" Wade continued. "Dixie is a grand old tune—a tune both my grandfathers marched to in war. And you'll find Henry Wade 'whistling Dixie' whenever the Supreme Court or anyone else in Washington tries to take away State's rights or local self government."[22] Wade's attacks forced Alger to establish his segregationist credentials. Alger told an audience of Young Republicans at the Baker Hotel in Dallas that he had been informed by "responsible Negro leaders" that they aspired to "equality of education rather than enforced association" in spite of the pretensions of the NAACP.[23] Wade represented the most serious challenge to Alger's tenure until his ultimate defeat in 1964, but the Republican still prevailed.[24]

Stung by Wade's attacks, Alger pursued increasingly white supremacist themes.[25] Alger, however, represented a subtle but significant shift in the national dialogue on race. A Southern peer in the Congress, Democratic Representative John Bell Williams of Mississippi, unequivocally declared in a July 5, 1956, speech on the House floor that "mentally, the Negro is inferior to the white . . . the arrest and even deterioration in mental development is no doubt very largely due to the fact that after puberty sexual matters take first place in the Negroes' life and thoughts."[26] Mindful of his more sophisticated urban audience, Alger refashioned such racist rhetoric with great nuance. He marshaled FBI crime statistics, for instance, to imply that there was a black propensity to commit crimes against whites.[27] But rather than dwell on the mythological black propensity for violence and rape, Alger disguised his racist appeals as opposition to a tyrannical federal government's growing power.

Alger avoided directly proclaiming black inferiority, scrupulously emphasizing that he was against *forced* integration, implying that he would support desegregation of the voluntary sort. "I will observe that I do not believe the Negroes want to go to white schools," he scribbled in notes for a 1950s speech titled "Segregation," and further, "under no circumstances should any child be compelled to be taught by a teacher of the opposite race, against his will. Nor should [there be forced] integration of [the] diseased with the healthy, nor morons with normals, nor criminals with [the] virtuous, nor [should] filthy with clean children ever be permitted under any circumstances."[28] Alger cloaked his defense of segregation as a defense of black rights, at the same time sending a less explicit pitch than John Bell Williams to racists by implying that blacks belonged to the same category of social defectives as morons, criminals, the diseased, and the filthy. Disguising racism as a dispassionate plea for less government, Alger presaged much of "the Southern Strategy" approach taken by the GOP beginning in the late 1960s, long after Alger's departure from Congress.[29]

Alger's approach caused even the die-hard Dixiecrats at the *Morning News* to reassess their attitude toward the GOP. In January 1960 Alger won praise from the *Morning News* for being the only congressman to "get on his feet and salute Robert E. Lee on his birthday." After noting that Alger had fought for "states' rights," the *Morning News* pointedly asked, "Where were the Democrats — so-called party of the South? Courting the support of Eleanor Roosevelt and the NAACP?" A *Morning News* editorial in the 1950s almost gasped at the transformation of the two major parties: "it once would have been a phenomenon for a Republican to stand for states' rights or segregation of the races, but it is no longer so. In recent years the Republican party [has done] more to defend states' rights than the Democratic party."[30]

Alger polarized white Dallas in the early 1960s. In 1962 violence erupted at the University of Mississippi when James Meredith, an African American, attempted to register. Alger backed the state of Mississippi's at-times violent resistance to integration and opposed using the National Guard to integrate the university, earning him support in a December 1962 letter from Jimmy G. Robinson of the blue-collar suburb of Garland just north of Dallas. "Congressman Alger, for the first time in my life on November 6, I went to the polls and voted for a Republican only one and that was you," Robinson wrote. ". . . Prior to the Oct. invasion of Mississippi I took democrats for granted that they were for the south and its southern people. Mr. Alger then I studied the beliefs of my former party & decided that in order for me to vote for the right people I would have to vote Republican just once anyhow." Robinson, a merchant, would be arrested and fined in 1963 for burning a cross on the lawn of a Jewish refugee from Germany who had been giving lectures at Dallas civic clubs about the similarities between the German Nazi Party and far-right-wing groups in America. Robinson's reaction to Alger's segregationist posturing was by no means universal. Segregation deeply offended many new Dallas immigrants. "I have only recently moved into Dallas," Carol Marie Hurd wrote in a September 27, 1962, letter to Alger. "However, I would like you to know that I am deeply disturbed and concerned about the welfare of James Meredith and of all the American negroes . . . It is difficult for me to realize this great scene can yet be carried on in our great country of opportunity and equality."[31]

As these letters suggest, Dallas slouched toward desegregation because no clique was powerful enough to lead the city in a more decisive, dramatic direction. Neither massive resistance nor a true redistribution of economic and racial power was a realistic option.[32] The Dallas Citizens Council, meanwhile, tried to contain the demands of the civil rights movement by working through the Committee of 14, made of seven whites and seven blacks. The black members of the committee were drawn from an older generation of African American leaders such as A. Maceo Smith and W. J. Durham who had long negotiated for incremental change. At the urging of the relatively conservative committee, several stores such as Woolworth's and Walgreen's agreed in the spring of 1960 to integrate their lunch counters. The days were past, however, when Dallas elites could choose which black leaders they would negotiate with, and sit-ins led by blacks outside the traditional power circle broke out all over the city, beginning in October 1960.[33] The protests deepened a generational divide in black Dallas. Reverend E. C. Estell, whose Dallas Community Committee supported the work of the Committee of 14, blasted the sit-ins in a November 1960 speech decrying the picketers as ignorant. The African American political world was as badly divided as its white counterpart.[34]

Regardless, in the spring of 1960 a group of fifty-eight white and two black SMU theology students sat in at the University Drug Store across the street from the campus. When they refused to leave the lunch counter, owner C. R. Bright hired a fumigation service that pumped insecticide inside the store. Most of the students remained seated, covering their faces with handkerchiefs. The day after the SMU students were gassed, W. J. Durham publicly admitted that negotiations carried on by the Committee of 14 had broken down. Protestors targeted the downtown Titche-Goettinger department store, and two hundred angry students returned to the University Drug Store for a five-hour protest. By May 1961 the spiral of demonstrations threatened Dallas' national image. The general manager of Detroit's Metropolitan Opera Company announced that it would no longer play to segregated audiences, specifically mentioning Dallas and Atlanta as cities notified of the new policy.[35] Facing the threat of business boycotts, the Committee of 14 engineered limited desegregation in downtown Dallas. On July 26, 1961, the Committee of 14 took 159 black patrons to forty-nine downtown restaurants and lunch counters, where they were served without incident.[36]

Even as they backtracked from rigid segregation, elites feared the rise of an order-shattering white mob — those racially marginal whites who lynched, whipped, and shot when they faced social demotion. By the late 1950s Dallas

School Superintendent W. T. White prepared for the trouble he expected would follow school desegregation. In May 1957 the board released the results of a questionnaire distributed to Dallas school faculty. Even faculty members more or less favorable to at least gradual integration (about 43 percent of the total) feared "that the troublemakers among students would be those who are already troublemakers or who would be troublemakers in any situation, and they would probably come from the 'underprivileged' of both races."[37] In November 1960 the federal Fifth Circuit Court of Appeals ordered the Dallas Independent School District to implement desegregation the following school year.[38] Elites immediately worked to stop any potential rioting and civil disturbance such as had wracked Little Rock and New Orleans when school desegregation was ordered there.

Key to this effort was a film, *Dallas at the Crossroads,* produced by public relations expert and Temple Emanu-El member Sam Bloom. The film, shown at dozens of work sites, before civic organizations, and on one Dallas television station, argued that violent reaction to school desegregation would psychologically harm children and convince the world that the city was an unsafe place to do business.[39] During the twenty-minute film, Dallas Police Chief Jesse Curry, in full dress uniform, warned, "The police will devote their energy to controlling those few who do not have the judgment or character to obey the law." Curry ominously added, "We know who those few are."[40] Dallas police, meanwhile, prepared for a riot. Emergency station wagons loaded with riot-control equipment waited at strategic points throughout the city.[41] The much-anticipated disorder, however, never came.

On September 6, 1961, the Dallas School Board implemented a so-called stair-step integration plan involving only a grade at time, thus possibly dragging out full integration until the mid-1970s. On the first school day of the 1961–1962 term only eighteen black elementary schoolchildren—attended by an escort of police and school officials—were enrolled at eight previously all-white campuses in the district. Hostile reaction was muted. Officials found a dummy hanging from a flagpole in front of one desegregated school. A nineteen-year-old self-proclaimed segregationist carried a gasoline-saturated cross to Ben Milam Elementary School, one of the integrated campuses, before being arrested. Dr. White promised there would be no additional transfers of black students to white schools until possibly the next year.[42] Dallas supposedly desegregated three grades by 1964. There were 9,400 black students at those grade levels, but only 131 were in desegregated classrooms. The Civil Rights Act of 1964 placed greater pressure on the school system, which classified 67 of 171 campuses as desegregated by 1966. This quickening pace only hastened white flight to the suburbs, however. By decade's end, only 57 of 177 campuses were deemed integrated. By the end of the 1969–1970 school year, 113 campuses were still all white.[43]

In spite of the relatively mild reaction, the threat of backlash from congenitally savage whites continued to be the excuse for keeping Jim Crow writhing in its death throes. Nevertheless, alienation of white elites from the working class increased as the 1960s progressed. No clearer evidence existed of the gap between the city's rulers and the ruled than the Dallas reaction to the presidency of John Kennedy. To the Dallas establishment and its voice, the *Dallas Morning News,* Kennedy represented an ideological nightmare, the personification of federal government policies that redistributed wealth and political influence from the powerful to blacks and the poor. In the 1960 presidential race, Kennedy enjoyed substantial support among lower-income whites. In his race against Vice President Richard Nixon, Kennedy carried 45 percent of the poor white vote in the city during an election that he won with only 49.7 percent of the vote nationally. Kennedy received support from only 23 percent of the Dallas upper class.[44]

As always, elites cast a wary look at the white lower classes for signs of future disorder. Elements of the city's middle and upper classes, however, posed an immediate threat to the public peace. Less than a week before the 1960 presidential elections, a mob assaulted Democratic vice presidential nominee (and Texas Senator) Lyndon Johnson and his wife, Lady Bird, as they left the Adolphus Hotel. The pro-Nixon demonstrators, mostly women followers of Bruce Alger, spat on and shoved Lyndon Johnson and his wife and snatched Lady Bird's gloves and threw them in the gutter as Alger, who had organized the protest, stood nearby with a sign that read "LBJ Sold Out to Yankee Socialists." Embarrassed for the city, one Johnson staffer later unconvincingly blamed the incident on riff-raff from downtown bars and "lower class" restaurants rather than on the well-dressed, upper-middle-class Junior Leaguers who made up most of the crowd.[45]

Once famous as a clean, efficient, well-run city, the rise of the right wing made Dallas appear more like a capital of crackpots, the insanity spreading from the top down. Dallas got more unwanted attention when a reactionary mob including former General Edwin Walker (a Dallas resident who had been fired from the Army by Kennedy for distributing John Birch Society literature to his troops), spat upon United Nations ambassador Adlai Stevenson after he made an October 26, 1963, speech marking United Nations Day to the Dallas Council on World Affairs. Once again, an angry gathering of middle-class, upper-middle-class, and even wealthy men and women rioted, rocking Stevenson's limousine back and forth before the driver finally raced the ambassador to safety.[46]

When the president fatefully visited Dallas on November 22, 1963, the city's class tensions blew apart. On that day the *Dallas Morning News* ran an ad, paid for by a group of wealthy oilmen, that was designed like a wanted poster charging Kennedy with treason. That day, too, massive crowds gathered for the president and showered him and the first lady with affection. The streets along the motorcade routes were lined and triple-lined with a quarter of a million people, Jim Bishop reported in his account of the assassination.[47] Kennedy received a "rip-roaring hell-bent-for-election Western-style welcome."[48] While the "oil men in the mahogany chambers with the deep pile rugs" angrily shut off television coverage of the visit,[49] a wildly enthusiastic throng gave the supposedly too-liberal-for-Dallas president a full-throated welcome. Kennedy "had won the endorsement of the people in spite of their masters," Bishop wrote.[50] Dallas' ruling bloc found it was discredited even before the first angry crack of an assassin's rifle fire echoed through Dealey Plaza.

To an extent that Memphis would not be held accountable for the murder of Martin Luther King Jr. nor Los Angeles for the killing of Robert F. Kennedy, the world blamed Dallas for JFK's assassination.[51] Instead of the civilization builders portrayed by Holland McCombs and other creators of the Origin Myth, Dallas' leaders now seemed small-minded and the source of a climate that made the president's death possible. "In the storm of grief and anger that subsequently swept down upon Dallas, the city was widely characterized as the 'hate capital of the nation,' a place so steeped in violence and political extremism that school children would cheer the President's death," *Fortune* magazine reporter Richard Austin Smith noted. ". . . [T]he business leadership of the city began to be singled out for censure . . . [Elites were] *responsible for the character of Dallas,* and if they had done a better job of leading, the city would not have earned its international reputation for violence and hatred and intolerance."[52] Elites were victims of their own mythology. If Dallas' business rulers were as omnipotent as Holland McCombs had insisted in his portrait of the city's "dydamic" leadership in *Fortune* fifteen years earlier, then they had to bear the bloody responsibility for the actions of a lone, left-leaning nut hiding in a storeroom of a schoolbook depository. They had willed Kennedy's murder just as surely as they had earlier summoned into existence the "city with no reason for being."[53]

Hoping to prevent a public relations meltdown, traditional elites chased the New Right into a political closet. Alger's followers had been implicated in the pre-assassination assaults on Lyndon Johnson and Adlai Stevenson. This association became a liability after November 22, 1963.[54] Elites united behind Mayor Earle Cabell in his bid to unseat Alger in November 1964. The ultraconservative Cabell beat Alger by 44,000 votes out of 200,000 ballots cast.[55] Elites insisted that the lesson from the Alger era was that Dallas should not stray from its traditional, old-rich, male ruling class. Even liberals like author Warren Leslie, a Neiman-Marcus department store executive, contributed to this propaganda. Leslie, in his post-assassination best-seller, *Dallas Public and Private,* blamed the city's right-wing climate of the 1950s and 1960s partly on the community's "shifting class mobility" and on politically active women. "Since problems of insecurity often bring on anger and the desire to lash out, it is not surprising that in emotional matters (and in America, that would certainly include politics) women are often angrier than men," he wrote.[56] In Dallas, status was attached to right-wing politics, which provided competitive incentives for "compulsive right wing women" to outdo their neighbors in extremism. "At manifestations [of the right wing] in Dallas over these years, women have been, on the whole, more obviously numerous, more vocal, more absolute and sometimes more physical than men," Leslie wrote. ". . . In earlier days . . . female fury usually manifested itself in the sex war with men. Since the suffragettes, women have been turning it on ideological concepts . . . Such a [woman's mind] . . . will be politically as organized . . . as it is in other ways. Issues are black and white."[57] No doubt when Leslie wrote these words, he had in mind the women who mobbed Johnson and Stevenson during their Dallas appearances. Texas women for a time did seem to dominate the state's right wing. Segregationist Governor Allan Shivers' efforts to smear opponent Ralph Yarborough as a "red" during the 1954 gubernatorial contest was led by groups like the San Antonio-based Womanpower for Eisenhower. The Minute Women in Houston completely dominated that school district's politics in the mid-1950s, with two members of the group, Dallas Dyer and Bertie Maughmer, winning school board seats and dominating headlines in the local press.[58]

Maughmer neatly fit the stereotype of the compulsive right-wing woman described in Leslie's book. A blue-collar product of a Baptist orphanage rising to prominence in an organization filled with affluent women, Maughmer spent her public career "desperate for recognition and attention," according to historian Don Carleton. Married to a Houston police officer, she frequently spoke on the evils of racial integration before the local White Citizens Council. As parliamentarian for the school board, she succeeded in banning two geography textbooks, *Geography and World Affairs* and *Geography of the World,* from the district because the texts' alleged bias toward the United Nations and "one-worldism."[59]

Dyer and Maughmer led a reign of terror against suspected leftist administrators and teachers in Houston, with teachers harassed even for suspected liberalism. Volatile and given to rambling rants about a creeping communist conspiracy in the United States during televised broadcasts of Houston's school board meetings, Maughmer eventually resigned after being indicted for the attempted murder of her husband in 1960.

Perhaps authors like Leslie found the right-wing impulse in Texas less frightening if they could attribute much of it to female irrationality and childish status envy. For years, Leslie's condescending armchair Freudianism stood as the standard explanation for Dallas culture and politics. If women proved the most visible instigators of a Red Scare in cities like Houston and Dallas in the 1950s and early 1960s, however, that should not minimize the central role men played in the state's political extremism. The leaders and the bankrollers of the right, such as Alger, Walker, H. L. Hunt, and Clint Murchison, were male and had a large male following. Yet elites claimed that the city's right-wing problem resulted from the infusion into county politics of female nouveau riche outsiders not blessed with male calm and rationality. Restoration of traditional conservative male leaders to power would soothe Dallas' troubled waters. Even as traditional racial ideology weakened, elites tried to reinforce the dogma of upper-class male supremacy.

The impact of the Kennedy murder on municipal politics held profound implications. The Dallas Citizens Council and its Citizens Charter Association political arm effectively lost control of city hall by the early 1970s, the death knell coming in 1975 when a federal court ruled that the city's at-large system of electing council members was unconstitutional.[60] This transformation was quiet. But even as white Dallasites congratulated themselves on the city's relative lack of racial disorder, they continued to cast worried looks over their shoulders at their black and brown neighbors. As they lost monopoly control on municipal politics, elites watched with horror the racially charged urban riots in cities like Los Angeles in 1965 and Detroit in 1967. Dallas elites always believed deeply in the city's exceptionalism, but after Kennedy's death this cherished delusion faded. In *Race Relations and the Intergroup Climate in Dallas, Texas*, a 1967 report compiled by the bureaucratically named North Texas Chapter of the National Association of Intergroup Relations Officials, the organization's chairman Robert F. Greenwald noted, "It has been said that Dallas enjoys a healthy climate of racial and ethnic relations. There has been little 'trouble.' Organized protest is rare. Visible signs of unrest are seldom in evidence." In spite of the apparent tranquility, Greenwald felt, at best, a shaky confidence about the city's long-term prognosis. After noting that racial peace and racial justice are not synonymous, Greenwald nervously observed, "*The Reader's Digest* in October, 1964 published an article on 'How Los Angeles Eases Racial Tensions.' It was the story of a city convinced of its own interracial well-being. Los Angeles by then had developed what was thought to be one of the more sophisticated human relations programs in the nation. Then, the following summer—WATTS."[61]

Dallas elites could well be nervous as they looked at other cities still dazzled seven decades later by Henry Grady's late-nineteenth-century vision of a New South. Dallas had shared much with Atlanta, with both cities by the late twentieth century enjoying prominence as banking centers and headquarters for international businesses. Three major players in Dallas' racial history—antilynching crusader Jessie Daniel Ames, Ku Klux Klan leader Hiram Evans, and African American minister Maynard Jackson (whose namesake son would become Atlanta's first black mayor in the 1970s)—played a key role in Atlanta's black-white relations. Both cities, marked by Civil War–era fires, had obliterated most physical reminders of their antebellum pasts and in their boosterism sought to emphasize differences between their communities and the rest of the South. Atlanta and Dallas both had significant Jewish populations whose leadership tenuously claimed acceptance as white. The two cities each had fractured white elites and a political system that for much of the twentieth century blocked African American access to state and national elections but allowed the black community to exercise influence on municipal politics. In both cities, black leaders for most of the twentieth century urged patience, practiced *realpolitik,* and negotiated incremental reforms as the best means to political emancipation. Both civic leaderships had buried their histories of violence and resistance so that Dallas' 1860 fire and Atlanta's 1906 race riot and 1915 Leo Frank lynching seemed grotesque aberrations. Boosters in both cities, while achieving only painfully slow school desegregation and token black political representation by the mid-1960s, bragged that because of their moderate white and black leadership they had escaped the chaos and violence consuming Birmingham, New Orleans, Little Rock, and other Southern cities after World War II.[62]

By the mid-1960s much of Atlanta's carefully woven image had frayed. Mayor William Hartsfield oversaw the minimal and smooth desegregation of Atlanta schools (with Atlanta officials looking to Dallas as a role model). Martin Luther King Jr.'s presence guaranteed that the desegregation of downtown Atlanta would be accomplished nonviolently. Hartsfield and his moderate allies could not completely contain the rage inspired when some whites feared a loss of status or the anger of blacks when minimal reform produced minimal results. In October 1958 a Reform temple was bombed in Atlanta, as was an African American elementary school in 1960. Atlanta's image as a city too busy to hate completely deflated by the time a police shooting inflamed a 1966 revolt in a poor African American neighborhood previously inhabited by middle-class whites who fled to the suburbs. Though the Atlanta uprising proved extremely mild compared to the earlier uprising in Watts, Dallas elites must have been alarmed at the spectacle of unraveling order in such a similar social setting.[63]

The increasing assertiveness of the black political leadership in Dallas intensified such white angst. Newer civil rights groups like the Student Nonviolent Coordinating Committee (SNCC), impatient with the few tangible benefits earned through conservative reform, pushed aside traditional leaders like A. Maceo Smith, who were now viewed as collaborators with white racism. SNCC sought to solve African American problems by buying out white businesses catering primarily to black customers. SNCC aimed its sights at OK Supermarkets, but when the grocery chain refused to sell, members supposedly retaliated with a "bottle-smashing raid" at one store. A jury convicted two members of SNCC of destroying property and gave them the draconian sentence of ten years in prison. The Dallas police and district attorney targeted SNCC, and various members were arrested for felonies, including one member framed on an armed robbery charge. Under such pressure, so-called radical organizations such as SNCC proved short-lived.[64]

African Americans needed allies, but whiteness still held potential partners of the black community in its thrall. Blacks and Mexican Americans in Dallas found themselves more frequently at odds. In the 1970s black leaders pushed for school busing as a means of ensuring equal education opportunities for African American children. This remedy proved unpopular in the Mexican American community, which joined Anglos in resisting mass busing, fearing that "their children would be spread all over Dallas and thus lose contact with each other."[65] Fights broke out between Mexican American and African American boys throughout the 1972 school year, while Anglo administrators did little to stem the violence.[66]

Like African Americans, Mexican Americans were demeaned in newspapers and on television. In the late 1960s Frito-Lay, a corn-chip maker and one of Dallas' largest companies, launched an advertising campaign centered on a character called The Frito Bandito, a Pancho Villa–style caricature dressed in a sombrero, with bandoliers crisscrossing his chest. This fat, swarthy cartoon figure attempted to steal corn chips while twirling his moustache or his *pistolas* as he sang a melody ripped off from *Cielito Lindo,* a ballad from the Mexican Revolution. The Dallas chapter of the National Postal Union fired off an angry resolution to Frito-Lay executives condemning the depiction of Mexicans as "lazy, dirty, thieving and sneaky."[67]

The early 1970s also heralded violent police harassment of Mexican Americans almost simultaneously with a wave of police shootings in the black community, giving both groups a sense of shared danger that intensified following the July 1973 murder of twelve-year-old Santos Rodriguez by Dallas police.[68] Two officers detained the boy and his thirteen-year-old brother following a break-in at a gasoline station. Officer Darrell L. Cain, in the back seat of the squad car, tried to terrify Santos, in the passenger front seat, into a confession. Cain claimed he thought he had emptied his pistol of bullets before he placed the gun against the child's head in a feigned game of Russian roulette. Cain pulled the trigger after a spin of the cylinder, when the .357 Magnum discharged, fatally wounding the child. A check of fingerprints at the crime scene confirmed that neither boy was involved in the break-in. Cain, who fatally shot a fleeing black suspect three years earlier, was arrested, and a judge released him on $5,000 bail.[69]

In the wake of this shooting, rage exploded in the city's black and brown communities. On July 28, more than a thousand protestors marched from Kennedy Plaza to city hall. Marchers set two police motorcycles on fire, smashed windows at city hall, and looted elite downtown department stores in the "closest thing to a race riot in Dallas history," a fulfillment of Robert Greenwald's worst nightmare. Arrests followed, and twenty-three Mexican Americans and thirteen blacks were jailed. A court later found Cain guilty of Rodriguez' murder and sentenced him to five years in prison. He served less than three.[70]

In spite of similar experiences with white authority, many older Mexican Americans rejected common action with blacks and desperately sought assimilation. In Dallas, Mexican cultural nationalism nevertheless inspired leaders of the younger generation of activists such as Pancho Medrano. Medrano early on acquired empathy for the African American cause. In the late 1940s Medrano, who was already active in the United Auto Workers, asked the president of his local why he was having such problems getting a job as a jig builder, a position for which he was well qualified. He was told that he looked "too much like a Negro to be hired." Medrano subsequently became active in *la causa*, diving into the black and Mexican American civil rights campaign in Georgia, Mississippi, and Alabama.[71]

Medrano grew frustrated with the conservative Mexican American leadership. "[W]e tried to get the Mexican Americans to start moving," he recalled later. "Everywhere, wherever we went . . . we tried . . . to stir them to demonstrate or to picket or demand; and nearly all the leadership, especially LULAC's or the American GI Forum . . . would always say, 'No.' . . . Especially the LULAC's; they say, 'We have more pride or education than that. You leave this to the Negroes. They are the ones who do all this—the burning and marching and all that violence. We don't want to do anything with that." Medrano rejected LULAC's embrace of whiteness and had no interest in being a "Latin American." Like many in his generation, Medrano formulated a new racial identity. "We have used the word '*Chicano*' all of our lives, since as far as I remember; whenever we are talking among ourselves, we have always used the word '*Chicano*,'" Medrano said. "Some leaders of these organizations would not want to call themselves '*Chicano*,' saying that *Chicano* was a derogatory word and they would not use it."[72] Medrano saw himself as outside the white world. He was not alone.

The late-1960s youth-oriented American Chicano movement used the language of postrevolution Mexican intellectuals like José Vasconcelos and Manuel Gamio, who in the 1920s praised *mestizaje,* the process of mixture between Indians, the Spanish, and black slaves that had produced Mexico's *la raza cósmica* (the cosmic race). Rather than degeneration, Latin American miscegenation in Vasconcelos' view produced a super race that combined the best traits of the black, brown, and white worlds. *La raza,* Vasconcelos believed, would overthrow the shackles of Anglo racism and colonialism and lead the world politically and culturally.[73]

Vasconcelos' ideas began to circulate among Mexican American college students at campuses such as the University of Texas at Austin in the mid-1960s. As anthropologist José E. Limón points out, because of an increase in financial aid and because of increased recruitment by the university in South Texas, the 1960s marked a period of unprecedented access to higher education for Mexican Americans. Most of these University of Texas students, Limón argues, rose from the lower middle and middle classes. These students turned to radical politics due to three major factors. First, Mexican American students still burned with their own experiences with Anglo racism. Second, these students drew inspiration from their black activist student peers who began to embrace the black nationalist tenets espoused by Malcolm X. Finally, this influx of Mexican American students came at the same time as the rise of the mostly Latino United Farm Workers union, which heavily organized in Texas' Lower Rio Grande Valley. This confluence of events, in the context of student protests against a Vietnam War increasingly seen as a racist crusade against an indigenous liberation movement, led Mexican American students to form an ideology counter to Anglo assumptions about race, class, and the world. In this way the concept of *la raza cósmica,* which embraced rather than disdained miscegenation, which honored Indians rather than animalized them, and which portrayed Mexicans as a super race rather than inferior victims, served admirably.[74]

This 1960s generation of students rejected the assimilationist approach of LULAC and the GI Forum. To them, Anglo culture meant colonialism, racism, and exploitation. As such they rejected "Mexican American" as an identity. They wanted to distance themselves from an American society that had invaded and occupied half of Mexican territory since the 1840s. At the same time, they did not identify themselves as Mexicans and wanted to express their experience as an occupied people. These students adopted as their identity the name *Chicano,* a term that previously referred mostly to poor and uneducated recent Mexican immigrants.[75] In linguistically linking themselves to the poor, Chicanos both rejected what was seen as the materialism and cultural vacuity of the Mexican American generation and politically aligned themselves with the liberation struggles of African Americans, Cubans, the Viet Cong. and other opponents of gringo imperialism.

In spite of all LULAC and AGIF's accommodation, Chicanos could argue, Mexican American children still attended poorly equipped and funded segregated schools. Most Mexican American students still attended classes taught by teachers who could speak only English, and they were routinely designated as slow learners because of their language barrier. Many Texas high school counselors, rather than provide encouragement, attempted to push out Mexican American students deemed as troubled. For all the emphasis made by the Mexican American generation on learning English and flag-waving patriotism, the community never won full acceptance as white nor respect for its culture. The lack of opportunity and fairness after decades of compromise pushed Mexican American groups such as the Brown Berets and the Association of Mexican American Student (AMAS) at the nearby University of Texas at Arlington to promote socialism and reject white identity. Chicanos insisted on "the retention of Mexican cultural traditions—language, ceremonies, songs, family"—as well as their "racial and cultural distinctiveness."[76]

This ideology rejected whiteness, but it substituted Anglo racism with quasi-fascist, *volkish,* Chicano supremacism. Chicanismo clung to the notion that humanity could be divided into distinct racial categories with innate characteristics. In any case, locked in a bitter struggle for food, decent housing, and work, many Mexican Americans had little time to rhapsodize over the earth-shaking destiny of *la raza.* As they attempted to build a movement, many Chicanos found themselves tainted by association with the frequent racism of the older Mexican American generation.

Chicanismo found its fullest expression beginning in the mid-1960s in Houston, where it began as a youth movement. Houston Chicanos, historian Guadalupe San Miguel notes, brought their Mexican and Indian heritage front and center, demanding for instance that Chicano and Mexican history be taught in Houston schools.[77] When the Houston School Board tried to avoid sending Anglo children to desegregated schools by designating

Mexican American children as white and grouping them with black students, Chicano youths found new allies in older, middle-class Mexican Americans who now saw value in a separate racial identity. Both generations began sustained protests against Houston schools—but for different reasons. Chicano youths protested because assignment of Mexican American students to black schools guaranteed poorly funded, poorly equipped educational facilities. Older Mexican Americans often mixed concern about educational opportunity with negrophobia centered on Mexican American children sharing classrooms with backward blacks.[78]

Such attitudes from older Mexican Americans dampened black support for a remarkable two-and-a-half-week strike involving 3,500 students who refused to attend Houston schools in August and September 1970. During the strike, Chicano political leaders organized a network of *huelga* (strike) schools so Mexican American children could continue learning. As a result of the strikes, the district hired more Spanish-speaking, Mexican American teachers, modified the curriculum to provide more positive portrayals of Mexican Americans, and improved conditions at some schools where minority students formed the majority. The Houston School Board, however, never recognized a nonwhite racial status for Mexican Americans, so brown and black children continued to bear the burden of desegregation. While the actions of Houston Chicanos helped shape Mexican American politics across Texas for the next three decades, statewide the movement experienced mixed results, with white flight undermining any educational improvements for Chicano children.[79] Incidents like the 1967 riot on the Texas Southern University campus after the shooting of a police officer and a second uprising on the Houston campus in 1970 after police fatally shot a student only intensified white migration to the suburbs.[80]

White flight also gripped Dallas. The desegregation of public schools, the rage expressed over the Santos Rodriguez shooting, and finally the 1976 arrival of court-mandated school busing convinced some white residents that Lewis Dabney's undermen had take control of the city. White migration to the suburbs ensued, which undermined desegregation efforts and depleted the city schools of desperately needed revenues. By 1973, the city planning department reported that 100,000 Dallas residents had relocated to the suburbs since 1960, most of whom had left after 1968. By 1980 blacks comprised a near-majority of students in Dallas schools—49.2 of all students, compared to whites, who made up 30.4 percent of the total, and Hispanics, who comprised 19.1 percent. Businesses followed the human flood. The Dallas Cowboys football team moved to Irving. Exxon bypassed Dallas in a corporate relocation, settling in Irving as well. J. C. Penney moved from New York to Plano, while

AMR, the parent company of American Airlines, built a new headquarters adjacent to the mostly white suburbs surrounding Dallas–Forth Worth Airport. By 1993 the city tax base had declined for five consecutive years, making higher property taxes necessary to maintain the same levels of municipal services. Dallas and Los Angeles had very different experiences in the 1960s, but the results were the same: the explosion of white suburban enclaves and the impoverishment of increasingly black and Latino city populations.[81]

In spite of federal court decisions outlawing segregation in schools, housing, and employment, the policies of agencies such as the Federal Housing Administration (FHA) subsidized white flight in cities like Dallas. Only 2 percent of the $120 billion of new housing financed by the FHA and Veterans Administration (VA) between 1934 and 1962 went to nonwhite families, and most of that underwrote housing in segregated neighborhoods. Historian George Lipsitz points out that federal highway construction often destroyed black neighborhoods and encouraged the spread of segregated suburbs. Federal and state tax money provided the construction of plumbing lines and sewage facilities in white suburban enclaves, while 60 percent of the housing destroyed by federal urban renewal programs belonged to African Americans, Mexican Americans, and other racially marginalized groups.[82]

Few could have anticipated how separate the black and white worlds would become post–*Brown v. Board of Education*. For black elites, the late twentieth century opened an era of opportunity. In 1966 Dallas County resident Joseph Lockridge, with the full backing of the white business community, became one of the first two African Americans since Reconstruction elected to the Texas legislature. C. A. Galloway broke the color barrier at city hall in 1967 when he was appointed to fill—for two weeks—the unexpired term of a white city council member. In 1969 George Allen, a conservative veteran of the Committee of 14, became the first black elected to the City Council. When Allen retired his seat in 1975, longtime NAACP youth organizer Juanita Craft became the first African American woman to serve. In 1984 John Wiley Price broke the color line at the Dallas County Commission. Ron Kirk, with the backing of white conservatives like former Dallas Cowboys quarterback and Republican activist Roger Staubach and real estate developer Trammel Crow, became the city's first African American mayor in 1995.[83] The Dallas media treated such milestones as proving the wisdom of Dallas' consensus politics. Unlike Birmingham, Los Angeles, and Detroit, there had been little "racial trouble" in Big D. The smooth transition to multiracial government reaffirmed the Origin Myth. Dallas avoided the all-consuming riots wracking other urban centers and experienced relative peace because, to paraphrase Holland McCombs, they damned well wanted it that way.

On the streets, meanwhile, few enjoyed Dallas' simulacra of democracy. More experienced bulldozer apartheid, in which poor neighborhoods were plowed under and replaced by pricey developments out of the economic reach of the former residents. After the ethnic cleansing of formerly black and brown neighborhoods, white migrants flocked back, leaving an army of the dispossessed on the further fringes of the city. The explicit rhetoric of whiteness had virtually disappeared from city politics, the schools, and the media, but it survived in a landscape of sharply divided black and white worlds.

A proposed expansion of Fair Park in the late 1960s, primarily for parking space, required the condemnation of middle-class black-owned homes in a fifty-acre area between Pennsylvania and Fitzhugh Avenues. Planners eventually extended the project and obliterated a large swath of black-owned businesses along Second Avenue so State Highway 352 could be widened.[84]

Nevertheless, a number of new, more assertive activists including Al Lipscomb, whose lawsuit later ended single-member districts in Dallas City Council races, entered politics as a result of the Fair Park controversy. Sporting an Afro in the 1970s and by the 1990s dressed in sashes, African robes, and beaded hats, Lipscomb joined the City Council in 1984. For all his Afrocentric costuming, Lipscomb voted much like his white peers on the council. Convicted in federal court in 2000 of 65 counts of bribery and conspiracy for accepting cash from a taxi company in return for friendly votes, he drew financial support for his political campaigns from conservative white businessmen. Outwardly a rebel, he so served the city's entrenched interests that the head of the hidebound Dallas Citizens Council held a reception for him near the end of his political career.[85]

Less outwardly confrontational black politicians were even more subservient to white business interests. In 1998 Mayor Ron Kirk successfully rallied support for a new $230 million arena for the Dallas Mavericks of the National Basketball Association and the Dallas Stars of the National Hockey League. Kirk's addiction to gigantism continued with his successful campaign for a controversial $246 million flood protection and recreation project along the Trinity River. Critics charged that Kirk's big-ticket projects helped the wealthiest developers while depleting funds for basic city services and neglecting issues such as affordable housing and code enforcement.[86] In spite of the promise that electoral democracy earlier held for the civil rights movement, successful black politicians offered more style than substance and continued to serve the same interests that had been protected by the previously all-white City Council.

Black office holders did little as real estate developers steadily wiped out historically black neighborhoods such as State-Thomas, on the northern and eastern edge of Deep Ellum. State-Thomas once represented the vital cultural and intellectual center of African American life in Dallas.[87] The neighborhood's blend of Victorian cottages and shotgun shacks eventually housed a blend of blacks, Mexican Americans, and whites.[88] After World War II, Jim Crow ordinances crumbled and housing options for African Americans expanded. When black soldiers returned from the war, they abandoned the old shotgun houses of State-Thomas and migrated to neighborhoods newly opened to African Americans in Oak Cliff and South Dallas.[89]

Callous city planning, combined with a series of banking disasters and turmoil in the international oil economy, ultimately did more to pull apart the traditional black neighborhoods than did the wider availability of housing to blacks following the collapse of Jim Crow. While such factors in the 1980s and 1990s dispersed the black community and opened the way to white recolonization of the urban core, the end result was a lifeless city center and enhanced isolation of Dallas' divided racial communities.

In the 1940s the city condemned land along the railroad right of way for Central Expressway's construction, splitting the State-Thomas neighborhood in two. The construction of the Woodall Rodgers Freeway further sliced into State-Thomas. By the mid-1970s a combination of real estate speculators like Lehndorff USA, computer giant Electronic Data Systems, the Southland Corporation, and "assorted trusts and pension funds" paid off most of the remaining residents, leveling homes and leaving vacant lots. Only one grocery store remained, and St. Peter's Catholic Church, the city's first African American parish, closed. By the late 1980s *Dallas Morning News* architecture critic David Dillon wrote, "The neighborhood . . . [looked] like a turn-of-the-century photograph of pre-urban Dallas—empty prairie and a few telephone poles."[90] Following zoning changes in the mid-1980s, predatory developers eyed the neighborhood "with the look of a wolf that has spotted a fresh-cooked Christmas turkey."[91] In the late 1980s a mix of chain restaurants, antique stores, and private clubs arose northwest of State-Thomas. By 1990 Memphis Real Estate and Lehndorff USA erected massive, rapidly filled apartment complexes and condominiums in the area, completing the transformation of State-Thomas from a historically black neighborhood to a middle-class and upper-middle-class white in-burb.[92]

The city facilitated the transformation by spending $20.1 million for infrastructure improvements such as street pavement and the upgrading of water and sewer lines that never occurred when State-Thomas was a black enclave. The placement of a new McKinney Avenue trolley line and a Dallas Area Rapid Transit station completed the yuppification of State-Thomas, turning it into a shopping and tourist haven. "Our company could not have pulled this off without the involvement of the city," a Lehndorff official told the *New York Times*. In 1991 *Morning News* reporter Bill Minutaglio scoffed at the hypocrisy of urban renewal as trumpeted by his own newspaper. "[W]here were the city and private money when the original residents of State-Thomas—the descendents of freed slaves—wanted street signs, sewer systems and newly planted trees around their simple homes?" he asked.[93]

Around the time of school desegregation in the 1960s, 70,000 people lived within a two-mile radius of city hall. By the 1990s that number had dropped to 30,000. The ever-emptying urban center seemingly confirmed dire warnings by men like Lewis Dabney and Justin Kimball of what happened when cities sank in a tide of color. The depopulation of downtown accelerated with the savings and loan crisis of the 1980s. Rising oil prices and banking deregulation by the presidential administration of Ronald Reagan generated a huge pool of surplus capital. Dallas-owned banks and thrifts poured the flood of cash into real estate speculation, with hefty loans dished out to quickly overextended creditors who began a frenzy of constructing office buildings, strip malls, and condos. Some developers took the short ride from real estate speculation to actual fraud, flipping real estate back and forth among coconspirators, often multiple times in a single day, the same parcel selling for more with each transaction. This inflated property values on paper until the circle of investors dumped the flipped land into the hands of greedy but uninitiated investors. Land values topped out even as developers created more retail and office space than the city could absorb. The economic bubble burst, causing real estate prices to collapse. Dallas thrifts and banks fueling the phony boom found themselves buried in loan notes that would never be paid. One after another, the leading Dallas financial institutions such as Vernon Savings and Loan and First Republic tumbled. Dallas lenders fueled a nationwide savings and loan meltdown that eventually cost American taxpayers more than $300 billion.[94]

This crisis hammered the city as oil prices worldwide dropped from $35 a barrel in 1981 to less than $10 a barrel five years later. Once-abundant capital now disappeared. The savings and loan crisis and the oil bust combined to make the city's business district a ghost town. By the late 1980s Dallas had the nation's highest office vacancy rate—more than 35 percent—and the percentage of Dallas residents living at or below the poverty line rose from 14 to 18 percent. Even more whites fled to the suburbs as the city's wealth seemingly evaporated overnight. The percentage of blacks in Dallas' total population climbed from 24.9 percent to almost 30 percent from 1970 to 1990. As whites fled to the suburbs, Dallas property values bottomed out, making the city the hole in the economic doughnut. At the same time the need for social services expanded for an increasingly poor city, Dallas' tax base plummeted from about $51 billion to $43.2 billion.[95] With housing values depressed, developers bought real estate in neighborhoods like State-Thomas at rock-bottom prices and built high-priced housing and shops in hope of bringing back affluent whites.

Part of the process involved selective enforcement of housing codes in which the city overlooked the violations of major real estate developers and focused on poorer homeowners. The city demolished 1,000 homes in Dallas between 1991 and 1994, most of them in poor minority neighborhoods. A *Dallas Morning News* examination of 500 destroyed homes found that 86 percent were in neighborhoods with 70 percent or more minority population. Three-quarters, the *News* reported, were in predominantly black parts of town. The bulldozer blitzkrieg, ordered by the Dallas Urban Rehabilitation Standards Board, "eliminated some substandard housing but also turned some long-time homeowners into renters and reduced the supply of low-income housing." Mattie Nash, who belonged to the thirty-eight-member board, said the program destroyed homes that clearly could have been repaired. "Every week we put demolition orders on houses that could be saved," she said.[96] Agnes Gray, a resident of Vineyard Drive in mostly black West Dallas for more than forty years, stood shocked as the city obliterated her home. "That home meant everything to me," the eighty-one-year-old said, near tears as she stared at what was now a vacant lot. "I just can't understand why they came in and took it from me—a widow woman and a working woman. I feel like I've been robbed."[97]

In the late 1980s only 250 people lived in downtown Dallas proper, all within a single building. As the bulldozers roared through mostly African American neighborhoods, white re-invasion of the core commenced. The number of downtown residents climbed to 13,000 living in high-priced apartments and condos. McKinney Avenue north of downtown became a coven of computer analysts, lawyers, and other professionals, while Deep Ellum, which had declined into a sad collection of empty warehouses, became a chic cluster of lofts, music clubs, and avant-garde art galleries. City developers soon erased State-Thomas from public memory, shrouding its African American past by redubbing the neighborhood Uptown.[98]

As bulldozers uprooted African Americans from their homes, more police shootings reinforced the sense that Dallas was a dangerous place for African Americans to live. In the 1980s the Dallas police killed or wounded an average of twenty-one people a year, with a record of thirty minority suspects in 1983 and twenty-nine in 1986. The majority of the victims throughout the 1980s were black or Hispanic. In the most infamous shootings, officers killed Etta

Collins, a seventy-year-old black woman who had called police to report a burglary at her home on Metropolitan Avenue in South Dallas, and David Horton, an eighty-one-year-old man, at his apartment complex in the same section of town.[99]

In spite of the presence of black elected officials, the Dallas police still saw even elderly African Americans as dangerous enough to shoot on sight. The leaden atmosphere deadened activism and fragmented black resistance. Black neighborhoods were deemed unworthy of redevelopment or improvement and deserving only demolition. The streets had to be purified of their blackness by the cleansing action of urban renewal before whites could again enter the racially polluted space. Much of white Dallas still saw humanity as slowly ascending in grades from blacks on the bottom to darker-skinned Mexican Americans to lighter Latinos to working-class whites and finally to the white middle class and Anglo elites on the top. The very architecture of the city echoed this Great Chain of Being, re-mythologizing elites and dampening further dissent.

After the civil rights struggles of the 1950s, Southernness reeked too much of tear gas and blood and recalled too many images of young black protestors blasted by water cannons. Dallas, in a timeless warp because of its denial of history, now drifted in a spaceless void as well, divorced from its natural setting. As noted earlier, David R. Roediger wrote that whiteness is founded on the denial of identity. In late-twentieth-century Dallas, this involved the erasure of a geographic identity that might have provided non-elites an energizing sense of community.

Dallas Morning News writer David Dillon notes that Dallas is "more Southern than Western, but not decisively so; it has a Lee Park . . . but also bronze longhorns stampeding in front of its convention center."[100] Dallas could fit anywhere and everywhere on the continent and be neither at home nor out of place. Moviemakers have turned Dallas into a geography-free stand-in for dystopia. The skyline and architecture, with equal ease, represented ultraviolent "New Detroit" in *Robocop,* the antiseptic home of a futuristic, patricidal culture dedicated to killing anyone over thirty in *Logan's Run,* and the post-Kennedy, claustrophobic, conspiracy-filled metropolis incongruously plunked in the middle of the Mojave Desert in *The X-Files: Fight the Future.*[101] "This city likes to think of itself as world-class, sophisticated, glitzy," said D. L. Coburn, a local playwright. "Like New York—it's as simple as that. And as a result it has no identity of its own."[102]

Viewed from a distance, the Dallas skyline unites into a futuristic sculpture of high-wattage lights and inscrutable, reflective steel and glass façades that forbid the viewer any glimpse of their inner workings. Once one moves closer, however, the illusory unity of Dallas shatters, fracturing into clashing stylistic splinters as surely as its people broke along racial, ethnic, linguistic, religious, and gender lines. Communal ties have snapped. The days when Dallas oligarchs carefully crafted the city's image for the world have long passed. Outsiders visiting Dallas lost their awe and saw through the public relations. Director Errol Morris captured the loneliness of downtown Dallas as well as anyone in his documentary *The Thin Blue Line.* In his tale of a man railroaded to death row by Dallas police and prosecutors, Morris represents the city as smudge-free windows of look-alike skyscrapers whirling past the viewer to a consciously monotonous Philip Glass score. Each pane represents not just an empty space but a workforce as beaten and anonymous as the worker drones in the Fritz Lang cinema nightmare *Metropolis.* The sense of enclosing isolation that Morris portrays accelerated in real life in the 1980s and 1990s as the number of gated communities—advertised as a "perfect place to live outside the pandemonium of the city"—increased from one, Glen Lakes on Central Expressway, to more than seventy-five, concentrated in white enclaves west and north of downtown.[103]

The dense pack of high-rises assumed totalitarian proportions, dwarfing the individual. "Dallas is a business city, and its skyline says that," Dillon wrote. "It is a city of dueling entrepreneurs, and its skyline says that as well. The vise-grip top of Texas Commerce Tower faces off against the sheer pyramidal lines of Fountain Place . . . The image is not egalitarian, with public and private interests clearly represented, but hierarchical, with capital at the top."[104] Dallas suffered from what New York stage director and critic Harold Clurman once caustically called an "edifice complex," an addiction to monumentality.[105] Absent in Dallas' downtown in the early 1990s were the squares, parks, watering holes, and boulevards, the "connective tissue that pulls a city together."[106] The result left a city that many visitors saw as lifeless and dull. "If New York is the city that never sleeps, Dallas is the city that never fails to give good bank service," the Mexican magazine *Jet Set* quipped.[107] The city's physical structure spoke loudly to whites and blacks alike that in spite of a broader spectrum of color at city hall and on the school board, white businessmen remained solidly in charge.

The Origin Myth continued to shape the city's psychology. In creating Old City Park, Dallas assembled a nineteenth-century pastiche of frontier-era buildings: churches, a bank, a drug store, a hotel, and a log cabin—many of which were imported from other Texas towns—to create a Disneyfied tribute to the city's early days. Less important than the artificiality of the city's "historic core," however, was the tale these buildings tell. Set against a backdrop of skyscrapers, the crude wooden structures of Old City Park, along

with a downtown replica of John Neely Bryan's cabin, embody the city's master narrative of progress, from the frontier to the space age. The cityscape
proclaims, in an echo of Holland McCombs, that the Dallas white business
clique transformed a village into a metropolis. The city, the skyline suggests,
sprang fully realized from the collective skull of the Dallas Citizens Council, unshaped by the surrounding culture. Past conflicts between slaves and
masters, Confederates and Unionists, workers and bosses, Jews and Gentiles,
Mexican Americans and gringos disappeared in the shiny reflected light of
high-rises. The only human drama Dallas freely admitted was the struggle to
wring profits from the prairies. Amnesia made resistance harder to imagine
because of the supposed lack of precedent.

Nevertheless, the ever-present threat of civil disorder haunted Dallas'
dreams of the future. The 1990s began as a horror show for white elites. In
March 1990 John Wiley Price led protests against liquor billboards in minority
neighborhoods and hiring practices at local television stations, getting into
fights resulting in highly publicized arrests for assault and vandalism.[108] Price
sent shivers through white Dallas when, as Dallas searched for a new police
chief, he pledged, "If you try and bring in a good old boy in this system, we're
going to be in the streets. Physically, literally shooting folks."[109]

If elites offered Dallas the simulacra of democracy, politicians like Price
offered the hollow imitation of dissent. No coherent program could be dis-
cerned in Price's scattered demonstrations, and he proved prone to the type
of backroom deal making that provoked him to call Mayor Kirk a "Sambo."
Price and Kirk both ignored the needs of the Cadillac Heights neighborhood,
located along the Trinity River near Cedar Crest Boulevard. A collection of
small frame homes with streets named after a variety of car manufacturers,
Cadillac Heights was 99 percent black and brown in 1999. Two lead smelters
formerly pumped toxins into the community. At century's end, animal rendering plants and the Central Wastewater Treatment Center were located in
the neighborhood, an example of what residents described as institutional
racism by placing black residences disproportionately near unhealthy industrial sites. Cadillac Heights also suffered from regular severe flooding. As the
1990s closed, Cadillac Heights became the latest black community threatened by bulldozer apartheid, this time with the collaboration of the black
"radical" John Wiley Price and his unlikely ally Kirk. Price publicly backed
Kirk's Trinity River Plan, a pricey scheme of lakes, levees, highways, and ar-
chitecturally elaborate "signature bridges." The plan included no funds to
support homeowners wanting to leave their crumbling, flood-prone, and polluted neighborhood to find comparable or better housing elsewhere in the
city. Critics speculated that Price had cut a deal with the University of Texas

Southwestern Medical Center. In exchange for construction of a biotech research center in his district, he would back the Trinity River Plan. "How can a black politician support this?" asked activist Roy Williams. "How come they could not get something to buy these people out? Why did he sacrifice the people in his constituency?"[110]

The leadership of the African American and Mexican American communities seemed more focused on their rage toward each other than on challenging the white power structure, the survival of which seemed ensured by the interracial conflict. Much of the black-brown discord centered on the policies of the Dallas School Board, which now oversaw a minority-majority district. Relations between blacks and Mexican Americans bottomed out with the appointment of Yvonne Gonzalez as superintendent of the Dallas Independent School District in 1997. Gonzalez, later sent to prison for spending district money to buy furniture for her private use, quickly learned to manipulate the racial politics of the board. She had been selected because of an iron alliance between Anglos and Mexican Americans, formed to block the priorities of black members including the hiring of a black superintendent. Nine weeks after her appointment as superintendent, she met with Latino and Latina activists who asked for more focus on the needs of Mexican American students. "I'm Latina," she told the group. ". . . Forty-five percent of my children are Hispanic. And I *will* represent them." Activist Jesse Diaz told Gonzalez that he did not expect her to divert resources from the African American community to the Hispanic community. "There is no way that *can't* happen," she declared. So entrenched had whiteness become in some Mexican American leadership circles that school board policy was designed in terms of a crude racial trade-off—what benefits one group automatically hurt another group. Mexican American progress, Gonzalez insisted, necessarily meant loss to African Americans.[111]

Conflict inspired gloom. Dallas looked at the decayed wreckage of urban America and feared it saw its future. The ideology of whiteness rested on a Manichean worldview in which civilized whites contended with colored savages. If the threat of dark outsiders justified the undemocratic rule of elites, this racial eschatology could inspire only pessimism in an atmosphere of elite political failure. The city's more cynical residents debated whether Dallas would be destroyed by fire—the Watts-style riot Robert Greenwald had feared—or by the icy grip of decay. "From the top of the 73-story Renaissance Center, downtown Detroit looks like Dallas' worst nightmare," a front-page *Morning News* story warned in 1995. "At 6 p.m. on a Monday, the streets are bomb-raid empty. Elevated people-mover trains coast by unoccupied. Pedestrians can be counted on one hand. The looks are deceiving. Detroit's condition is actually worse."[112] Business executive Robert Hoffman worried that Big D might suffer a similar fate. What was once seen as proof of the creativity and determination of Dallas' white founding fathers was now perceived as evidence of vulnerability. Hoffman, former chair of the committee that authored the Dallas Plan, the city's official blueprint for its twenty-first-century development, warned in a terrifying inversion of the Origin Myth that "Dallas did not have a place that created it, like San Francisco's harbor. What created Dallas was economic opportunity and business. But much of our business—what created us—has moved to the suburbs." Reporter Chris Kelly observed, "Because there are so few natural features, such as an ocean, to soothe Dallas' population—let alone attract newcomers—the city may be even more at risk to flight of business and people."[113]

The complex and sometimes sordid politics of color of the 1990s seemed to presage a grim future for even the supposed beneficiaries of whiteness, and much more so for the economically and racially marginalized. But then again, an undercurrent of gloom had always been the unacknowledged twin of the Origin Myth's meglomaniacal optimism. Disbelief in human agency served as a literal article of faith for many in the city who spent their lives anticipating worse than municipal rot. In the last years of the twentieth century, Dallas evangelicals prophesied a coming world war. Some conservative Christian ministers echoed Cyrus Scofield's warning that an Antichrist would arise any minute to conquer the world. Their flocks anticipated the universal collapse of the modern technological infrastructure because of the so-called "Y2K" computer virus and grew certain that the Christian calendar year 2000 heralded the beginning of the Great Tribulation. As the 1990s ended, Dallas army surplus stores reported a rush on hand-cranked radios, MREs (meals ready to eat), power generators, and gas masks from customers anticipating the Y2K computer crash. Many fundamentalists among countless others globally were certain that on January 1, 2000, computers, which used a two-digit system for marking years, would read the abbreviated date 01-01-00 as January 1, 1900. In the resulting confusion, some feared, computer-operated systems for water treatment, emergency medical equipment, traffic control, and other services would self-destruct.[114] Hunkered down in their bunkers, rifles ready and cocked against the onslaught of alien outsiders, these dispensationalist vigilantes created Dallas' ultimate gated community.

Whiteness proved an effective tool for controlling dissent. It was poison to community building. By the mid- to late 1990s, Dallas represented a dispirited collage of mutually antagonistic fragments, a sum much less than its alienated parts. Whiteness, like pre-millennialism, was a theology based on visions of Armageddon. It was not just the desire for the wages of whiteness—improved income, better homes, and healthier lives—that motivated oppressed Jews, Mexican Americans, and white laborers to disdain their black neighbors. If marginalized whites united on any issue, it was to prevent the rule of black undermen, an outcome depicted in the popular culture as a collapse into savagery. The effort spent to prevent this racial apocalypse left little energy for the pursuit of economic justice. In any case, worldly politics were futile. Scofield and other dispensationalists had taught Dallas so. Dallas' denial of history combined with a conservative, future-oriented theology to promote passivity. If Dallas never exploded like Watts, Birmingham, or Detroit, it was not because it enjoyed a more dynamic leadership than those cities but because a self-induced paralysis left the structures of oppression soundly intact. Under the influence of whiteness, Dallas learned to forget the past, regret the present, and dread the future.

AFTERWORD

This work ultimately is a case study on the evolution of white identity in America politics. As noted, the study of whiteness is one of the most rapidly expanding areas of academic research. By the beginning of the twenty-first century, whiteness as an analytical tool reached sufficient respectability to generate a scholarly backlash. A symposium on the value of whiteness scholarship, opened by Eric Arnesen's contentious essay "Whiteness and the Historians' Imagination," occupied most of the fall 2001 issue of *International Labor and Working Class History*. With relentless hostility toward the genre, Arnesen contends that the idea of whiteness is anachronistic, a term projected by some recent American historians on a nineteenth-century context in which the term would be meaningless. Arnesen argues that immigrants were never literally considered non-white by Anglo-Saxon elites and did not at any time think of themselves as such. He charges whiteness scholars with putting words in their subjects' mouths and of relying heavily on dubious psychohistory, putting long-dead subjects on a couch and analyzing their inner, unarticulated worlds of racial identity.

Whiteness literature, he suggests, has little foundation in traditional archival research. Writers in this field, he charges, primarily quote each other as evidence, rendering whiteness as one big circular discourse. Such scholars, he says, also define whiteness too loosely and inconsistently to make the concept a useful category of analysis. See Arnesen, "Whiteness in the Historians' Imagination," *International Labor and Working Class History*, no. 60 (fall 2001): 4–32.

Arnesen's essay too often degenerates into wildly inaccurate ad hominem attacks on historians such as Matthew Frye Jacobson, Neil Foley, and Gunther Peck. Arnesen's accusation that such writers do not ground their arguments in archival research can be easily refuted. One need only scan the extensive bibliographies of works like Matthew Frye Jacobson's *Whiteness of a Different Color*, Neil Foley's *White Scourge*, and Peck's *Reinventing Free Labor: Padrones and Immigrant Workers in the North American West, 1880–1930* to reject the charge.

These three books draw evidence from reams of oral histories, contemporary newspaper accounts, census tracts, published proceedings of government hearings, reports released by government bureaucracies, the published works of contemporary thinkers, and manuscript collections. Even a casual review of sources used by these scholars renders Arnesen's attack a prima facie absurdity.

Arnesen's biases shape his exasperation with whiteness scholarship. His prejudices are revealed in his title, "Whiteness in the Historian's Imagination." To Arnesen, imagination is not insight or innovation but is synonymous with fabrication. As Arnesen himself suggests, he is a hard-core empiricist. To him, discourse analysis of architecture, literature, popular song, and other cultural artifacts represents soft scholarship, acceptable perhaps for English departments but disreputable for historians and other "real" scholars. Arnesen fails to acknowledge the degree to which his treasured archives were collected and organized by people shaped in part by prevailing ideologies of race, class, and gender. Without the technique of discourse analysis, scholars using these materials could only echo the hegemonic ideas enshrined therein.

Arnesen is seemingly also too afraid of literary criticism to think of artists and writers as legitimate historical actors whose works reflect in some degree popular ideas of race, class, and gender. Because he seems wary of any source not explicitly spelled out in an archival manuscript, Arnesen's critique suggests that there should be little or no speculation by historians and social scientists on the evolution and role of ideology in shaping society.

To Arnesen and his ally Barbara Jeanne Fields (see, for example, her essay "Whiteness, Racism and Identity," also in the fall 2001 issue of *International Labor and Working Class History*, 48–56), material conditions are real, but somehow ideas are not. Ideas like race, such critics argue, cannot take on "a life of their own." Apparently Arnesen and Fields assume that ideas only generate directly from interaction with the material world and that ideas can never spawn other concepts several steps removed from the original, concrete source of inspiration. They apparently do not believe that perception matters or substantively affects a person's status in life or that people can build their lives entirely around ideas that may be delusions.

If Arnesen believes that discussions of racial difference within whiteness are only figurative, he leaps back to his obsessively empiricist literalism when he demands to know at what point marginal whites actually bargained for white identity by accepting racism and eschewing class conflict. He refuses historians the privilege of employing metaphor to describe an historical process. He then damns whiteness scholars for failing to prove, through archival materials, of course, the literal advent of the metaphor.

When Arnesen discusses race, he assumes, even though he admits that races are socially constructed, that once the categories of white, black, brown, red, and yellow were created, they received an immediate permanence and impermeability. In Arnesen's world, no group ever moved across or evaded these admittedly artificial boundaries. Arnesen can do this only by ignoring the struggles of the U.S. Census Bureau to find a suitable racial category for Mexican Americans, for instance. Arnesen also ignores the difficulties American courts experienced in fitting Chinese, Japanese, Mexican, and Middle Eastern immigrants on the existing American racial grid, a labor documented amply by Ian F. Haney López.

Meanwhile, if Arnesen takes nineteenth-century Democrats at their word when they describe the Irish as white, he assumes that their contemporaries who referred to the Irish, Jews, Slavs, and others as "races" with innate characteristics differing from whites spoke only figuratively. Arnesen's view seems to be that a pan-white identity formed early on and survived successive waves of immigration to America from Ireland and southern and eastern Europe. Such immigrants, Arnesen suggests, saw themselves as white even as they boarded the boat to the Western Hemisphere. This simple, pan-white European identity would be news on the mother continent, where Europeans still argue whether so-called whites represent a complex web of races. There, conflicts between the neofascist Northern League and Sicilians in Italy, among Serbs and Croatians and Bosnian Muslims in the Balkans, and between various mainstream Europeans and Roma (popularly known as Gypsies) across the continent reflect perceptions of not just religious and cultural differences but racial difference as well. See Marek Kohn, *The Race Gallery: The Return of Racial Science* (London: Vintage, 1996), 188–227, 230–231, 251–252.

If they had their way, Arnesen and Fields would virtually shut down explorations of race. Fields cannot simply disagree with whiteness scholars; she attributes to them malevolent motives. To her, whiteness scholarship implies that the struggle of white workers to achieve higher racial status is somehow equivalent to the black struggle for freedom (see Fields' "Whiteness, Racism, and Identity"). Quite the opposite is true, and when reading Fields' critiques of whiteness, one suspects she is not very familiar with the literature. Historians like Roediger argue that white workers were co-opted by racism and measured their progress in relation to their distance from their black peers. The process is portrayed as tragic, not as a heroic tale of assimilation, as Fields suggests.

Fields sees any prolonged study of race in and of itself as counterproductive. For scholars to continue studying race, Fields argues, is to prolong the life of the concept, which lost real meaning post-slavery (see her essay "Slavery, Race, and Ideology in the United States of America" in *New Left Review* of May–June 1990). Using race as an independent category of analysis, she has maintained, reifies an ideological construct that obscures the "real" class conflict underneath. Thus, the process of analyzing racial construction promotes racism. This is like the argument by Christian conservatives that providing sex education to teenagers that provides alternatives to total abstinence promotes sexual promiscuity.

Arnesen has no more patience with race scholarship. He contends that whiteness studies offer nothing new because everyone in the academy knows that race is contingent and socially constructed. That most certainly is not true, however, of the general public. Life exists outside of academia, and in the world beyond the university most people still think races are real. The process of race formation, in fact, continues with tragic consequences, as seen with the invention by European colonial rulers of Hutu and Tutsi identities in what became Burundi and Rwanda and the subsequent demented bloodbaths that stemmed from those constructs; see Philip Gourevitch, *We Regret to Inform You That Tomorrow We Will Be Killed with Our Families: Stories from Rwanda.* The idea of race proved central in the Balkan and Central African holocausts. The emphasis on racial construction by whiteness scholars has, however, provided an alternative worldview that only now is generating a public debate outside of the academy. Arnesen's unconvincing skepticism of joining politics to scholarship aside, convincing a broader audience that race is a fraud not worth killing for is a noble aim worth fighting for and not inconsistent with good history.

This book is not only a work on whiteness but an attempt to join Dallas history to the larger discussion of Western and Southern history and how scholars define regions. I hope that in the previous pages I have effectively described how Dallas' business leaders, after the collapse of slavery, sought to rescue the city from the weight of the Southern past by creating a mythological past that tied Dallas to the larger national frontier narrative. I would be remiss if I did not mention how important an influence Richard Slotkin's work was on this book. What I uncovered about the Dallas past was in many ways simply a local version of what Slotkin described in his frontier trilogy.

In *Regeneration through Violence: The Mythology of the American Frontier, 1600 to 1860, The Fatal Environment: The Myth of the Frontier in the Age of Industrialization, 1800–1890,* and *Gunfighter Nation: The Myth of the Frontier in Twentieth Century America,* Slotkin suggests that white American elites saw the spread of civilization as the racial mission of Anglo-Saxons. Slotkin focuses on America's frontier mythology, which echoes Dallas' own Origin Myth. The myth of the frontier depicts the descendants of Europeans as united to conquer wild Indians and a hostile environment. This us-versus-them narrative forged consensus among whites torn by class division. In frontier mythology, the high stakes of the war against savagery presented white America with the stark choice between saving civilization and establishing democracy, which Slotkin argues were perceived as mutually exclusive goals. Thus the national frontier myth, like Dallas' Origin Myth, rationalized elite political dominance as necessary for racial survival.

Finally, I add this work to what I have described as the underdeveloped body on literature on Dallas. Although I waxed caustic on the deficiencies of Dallas historiography, I would also be remiss if I did not acknowledge the fine works on Dallas that are available. Though he made no direct reference to Slotkin in his book *The Accommodation*, Jim Schutze coined the term "Origin Myth" and was the first writer to attempt an ideological analysis of the city. Although I attempted to extend upon, revise, and counter much of his work, *The Accommodation* remains groundbreaking and a worthy read.

Unlike most previous works on the subject, Harvey Graff's upcoming work *Dallas, Texas: City at the Crossroads* promises to offer a subtle treatment of power in the city. Other important works critical of Dallas include Jerrold Ladd, *Out of the Madness: From the Projects to a Life of Hope* (New York: Warner Books, 1994); Robert Prince, *A History of Dallas: From a Different Perspective* (Dallas: Sunbelt Media, Nortex Press, 1993); and Roy H. Williams and Kevin J. Shay's *Time Change: An Alternative View of the History of Dallas* (Dallas: To Be Publishing Co., 1991). These authors find encouraging resilience in the African American community, which creatively responded to oppression through a religious and political culture that rejected white racism.

Patricia Evridge Hill in her history of the Dallas labor movement, *Dallas: The Making of a Modern City*, skillfully documents the city's long tradition of political dissent, focusing on Populists, Socialists, and labor leaders. Lawrence Wright's *In the New World: Growing Up with America, 1960–1984* (New York: Alfred A. Knopf, 1988) presents a compelling picture of a Dallas liberal beaten down by the frustrations of resisting the city's racism and class structure before falling into an apolitical resignation.

Alan B. Govenar and Jay F. Brakesfield's *Deep Ellum and Central Track: Where the Black and White Worlds of Dallas Converged* (Denton: University of North Texas Press, 1998) and William H. Wilson's *Hamilton Park: A Planned Black Community in Dallas* (Baltimore: Johns Hopkins University Press, 1998) provide thoughtful, innovative micro-studies focusing on Dallas neighborhoods.

I hope that together these works will focus more attention by historians on what might be considered the capital of "the red states," the states whose electoral college votes went to George W. Bush in the 2000 and 2004 presidential elections. What happened socially and politically in nineteenth- and twentieth-century "Southern" cities like Dallas, Houston, and Atlanta has, by the twenty-first century, already enveloped much of America.

NOTES

PROLOGUE

1. Jim Schutze, *The Accommodation: The Politics of Race in an American City* (Secaucus, N.J.: Citadel Press, 1986).

2. Harvey J. Graff, "How Can You Celebrate a Sesquicentennial If You Have No History? Reflections on Historical Consciousness in the Dallas Area," sesquicentennial essay commissioned by the *Dallas Morning News,* 1986, 6. Computer printout in author's possession.

3. W. Marvin Dulaney, "Whatever Happened to the Civil Rights Movement in Dallas, Texas?" in Dulaney and Kathleen Underwood, eds., *Essays on the American Civil Rights Movement* (College Station: Texas A&M University Press for University of Texas at Arlington, 1993), 66–95.

4. Taylor Branch, *Parting the Waters: America in the King Years, 1954–1963* (New York: Simon and Schuster, 1988); Robert Weisbrot, *Freedom Bound: A History of America's Civil Rights Movement* (New York: W. W. Norton, 1990), 39–40; John Boles, *The South through Time: A History of an American Region* (Englewood Cliffs, N.J.: Prentice Hall, 1995).

5. For most of the past one hundred years, Houston has been the largest city in the eleven-state region of the former Confederacy (which includes Alabama, Arkansas, Florida, Georgia, Louisiana, Mississippi, North Carolina, South Carolina, Tennessee, Texas, and Virginia). In the late 1990s San Antonio surpassed Dallas as the second-largest city. The more broadly defined Dallas metropolitan area (the "metroplex" that also encompasses Fort Worth and smaller towns) is still substantially larger than San Antonio. At the end of the twentieth century, Houston counted 3.70 million in its metropolitan area, Dallas 2.96 million, and San Antonio 1.46 million. See U.S. Bureau of the Census (hereinafter Census Bureau), *Statistical Abstract of the United States: 1998* (Washington, D.C., 1998), 47–49; Kelly Shannon, "San Antonio Hoots and Hollers over News It's Bigger than Big D," *Dallas Morning News,* November 28, 1997, sec. A.

6. "Black Population Change in 14 Central Cities, 1970–1990," *African American Almanac,* 7th ed. (Detroit: Gale Research, 1994), 537.

7. Census Bureau, *Statistical Abstract: 1998,* 44.

8. Dallas has been the regional banking and insurance capital since the Woodrow Wilson administration established a Federal Reserve Bank there in 1913. See A. C. Greene, *Dallas, U.S.A.* (Austin: Texas Monthly Press, 1984), 72. In 1961, Dallas became the first Texas city with a bank holding deposits of more than one billion dollars, and at that time it led the state in bank deposits. See Al Altwegg, "Dallas Holds Banking Title," *Dallas Morning News,* January 7, 1961, sec. 1. Dallas remained dominant in the region economically through the end of the twentieth century. After a recession in the late 1980s and early 1990s, the city re-emerged as an economic colossus in the mid- and late 1990s. See Darwin Payne, *Big D: Triumphs and Troubles of an American Supercity in the 20th Century* (Dallas: Three Forks Press, 1994), 370–372, 381–389, 418–420.

9. For more on Southern political realignment consult two excellent books by Dan T. Carter: *The Politics of Rage: George Wallace, the Origins of the New Conservatism, and the Transformation of American Politics* (Baton Rouge: Louisiana State University Press, 1995) and *From George Wallace to Newt Gingrich: Race in the Conservative Counterrevolution, 1963–1994* (Baton Rouge: Louisiana State University Press, 1996). For a thoughtful analysis of Texas under one-party Democratic rule and the subsequent transition to shared rule by Republican and Democratic conservatives read Chandler Davidson, *Race and Class in Texas Politics* (Princeton, N.J.: Princeton University Press, 1990).

10. Joel Gregory, *Too Great A Temptation: The Seductive Power of America's Super Church* (Fort Worth: Summit Group, 1994), 282–283. For more on the takeover of the Republican Party by Christian conservatives see Sara Diamond, *Roads to Dominion: Right-Wing Movements and Political Power in the United States* (New York: Guilford Press, 1995).

11. For a discussion on the Dallas obsession with image see Paul Weingarten, "Dallas Officials Try to Sell 'Real' City to Its Citizens," *Chicago Tribune,* February 11, 1988, Internet archive, http://www.chicagotribune.com.

12. Patricia Evridge Hill, *Dallas: The Making of a Modern City* (Austin: University of Texas Press, 1996), xvi–xviii.

13. Bryan Woolley, "Dallas History Buffs Look to Legacies," *Dallas Morning News,* March 17, 1999, sec. C.

14. Graff, "How Can You Celebrate," 1, 8. Graff taught one of the first university courses on Dallas history in the metropolitan area. Graff explores the theme of historic consciousness extensively in his upcoming book, *Dallas, Texas: City at the Crossroads.* Graff's work inspired much of this chapter, and I thank him for his kindness and insight.

15. Graff, "How Can You Celebrate," 1–2, 8.

16. For a biographical sketch on Brown consult *New Handbook of Texas,* 1996, s.v. "John Henry Brown."

17. The term "booster" is borrowed from Mike Davis, *City of Quartz: Excavating the Future in Los Angeles* (New York: Vintage Books, 1992).

18. To examine the durability and sophistication of Caddoan culture in the Dallas area see Brenda B. Whorton and William L. Young, "Before John Neely Bryan: An Overview of Prehistoric Dallas County," *Legacies: A History Journal for Dallas and North Central Texas* 3, no. 2 (fall 1991): 4–10.

19. John Henry Brown, *History of Dallas County, Texas: From 1837 to 1887* (Dallas: Milligan, Cornett and Farnham, Printers, 1887), 3–4.

20. For more on the association of whiteness with civilization and people of color with savagery see Matthew Frye Jacobson, *Barbarian Virtues: The United States' Encounters with Foreign Peoples at Home and Abroad, 1876–1917* (New York: Hill and Wang, 2000); and Richard Slotkin's frontier trilogy, *Regeneration through Violence: The Mythology of the American Frontier, 1600–1860* (1973; reprint, Norman: University of Oklahoma Press, 2000); *The Fatal Environment: The Myth of the Frontier in the Age of Industrialization, 1800–1890* (1985; reprint, Norman: University of Oklahoma Press, 1998); and *Gunfighter Nation: The Myth of the Frontier in Twentieth-Century America* (1992; reprint, Norman: University of Oklahoma Press, 1998).

21. Mattie Jacoby Allen, "Cultural Patterns Attained in a Primitive Land," Mattie Jacoby Allen Collection A37.24, p. 1, Dallas Historical Society (hereinafter DHS).

22. Philip Lindsley, *A History of Greater Dallas and Vicinity*, vol. 1 (Chicago: Lewis Publishing Co., 1909), 29.

23. Patricia Evridge Hill, *Dallas*, xvi–xvii; Payne, *Big D*, 160–163; Holland McCombs, "The Dydamic Men of Dallas," *Fortune*, February 1949, 162. The word *dydamic* is a spoonerism coined by R. L. Thornton, mayor of Dallas at the time the article was published. Born in a half-roofed sod dugout in Hamilton County in Central Texas, Thornton gleefully mangled the language, urging his colleagues to toil with "stupenjious" effort. In all quotations from primary sources, I will preserve the original spelling and grammar.

24. Holland McCombs, "Dydamic Men," 98–103, 162–166.

25. *Houston Telegraph and Texas Register*, November 22, 1843, Herbert Gambrell Papers, A7641, DHS.

26. Martin Austin Gauldin, "Texas Journal, 1845," Herbert Gambrell Papers, A3612, DHS.

27. Schutze, *Accommodation*, 52.

28. Warren Leslie, *Dallas Public and Private: Aspects of an American City* (New York: Grossman Publishers, 1964), 85, 228.

29. Richard West, "Censorship or Business Sense? Taylor Drops a Controversial Book," *D: The Magazine of Dallas*, November 1986, 15; Gregory Curtis, "A book's improper burial," *Texas Monthly*, November 1986, 5–6, 242.

30. Schutze, *Accommodation*, 73–74.

31. W. Marvin Dulaney, review of *The Accommodation* by Jim Schutze, *Southwestern Historical Quarterly* 93, no. 3 (January 1990): 419–420. See also Dulaney's "Whatever Happened to the Civil Rights Movement in Dallas, Texas?" Robert Fairbanks' *For the City as a Whole: Planning Politics and the Public Interest in Dallas, Texas, 1900–1965* (Columbus: Ohio State University Press, 1998) essentially blames the politically marginalized— African Americans, Mexican Americans, and labor—for the city's current fragmentation. Fairbanks writes, "Urban politicians today seem much more concerned with promoting programs to address the needs of minorities, neighborhoods, or special interest groups than developing policy for the city as a whole" (3). In Fairbanks' narrative, the fractiousness of

Dallas' late-twentieth-century politics appears small-minded and less idealistic compared to the romantic elites of yesteryear, but he never explains how policies of elites served the "city as a whole" when they rested upon wage inequity, political disenfranchisement, racism, and Jim Crow.

32. Frank Trejo, "Alonzo, Price Are Assailed: Some Hispanics Seek Resignations," *Dallas Morning News,* January 9, 1996, sec. A; Calvin Verrett-Carter, "Parkland's Community-Oriented Healthcare at the Center of Controversy over Minority Personnel," *Dallas Weekly,* December 14–21, 1994, 12.

33. The use of ethnic and racial terms presents major problems for historians. The terms "Latino," "Chicano," "Mexican American," "Latin American," and "Hispanic" all inadequately describe one Dallas population group. The terms "Chicano" and "Mexican American" exclude the many families in the larger "Hispanic" community who originate from Central and South America, the Caribbean, or Spain. The terms "Latin American," "Latino," "Latina," and "Hispanic" (the latter a term coined by the Census Bureau) ignore specific nationalities. Such "pan-Hispano" terms also place excessive emphasis on the Spanish side of the community's heritage, ignoring the Indian past, a focus that reinforces white supremacist thinking. Acknowledging the problems with these categories, this book will generally use the terms "Mexican American," "Latino," "Latina," and "Hispanic" to reflect the politics of the subjects described.

34. Richard Estrada, "When the Political Power Tilts," *Chicago Tribune,* October 1, 1996, Internet archive, http://www.chicagotribune.com.

35. "Only Blacks Were Invited to Dallas Meeting on Race," *Austin American-Statesman,* December 7, 1997, sec. A; Ann Zimmerman, "It's Our Turn To Be Heard," *Dallas Observer,* April 17–23, 1997, 30; the Callejo quote is in Zimmerman.

36. Zimmerman, "It's Our Turn," 31.

37. Ibid.

38. Payne, *Big D,* 406–407.

39. Ibid., 395–417.

40. Ibid., 417.

41. Stephen Jay Gould, *Ever since Darwin: Reflections in Natural History* (New York: W. W. Norton, 1977), 231–242.

42. Howard Winant, *Racial Conditions: Politics, Theory, Comparisons* (Minneapolis: University of Minnesota Press, 1994), 38.

43. The literature on Western racial ideology is too vast to summarize in a footnote, but among the most important works are Barbara Jeanne Fields, "Slavery, Race, and Ideology in the United States of America," *New Left Review* 181 (May–June 1990,) 95–118; Winthrop D. Jordan, *White over Black: American Attitudes towards the Negro, 1550–1812* (New York: W. W. Norton, 1968); Edmund S. Morgan, *American Slavery/American Freedom: The Ordeal of Colonial Virginia* (New York: W. W. Norton, 1975); Michael Omi and Howard Winant, *Racial Formation in the United States from the 1960s to the 1990s* (New York: Routledge, 1994); Alexander Saxton, *The Rise and Fall of the White Republic: Class Politics and Mass Culture in Nineteenth-Century America* (New York: Verso, 1990); and Ronald Takaki, *Iron Cages: Race and Culture in 19th-Century America* (Oxford, England: Oxford

University Press, 1990). Fields' essay provocatively suggests that elites created the idea of race to reconcile the liberal ideas of the U.S. Constitution with black slavery. Fields argues that race lacks explanatory force after Emancipation. Influenced more by Edmund S. Morgan, this author makes no attempt to separate race and class. Race and class are twinned constructs born in the transition of the world economy from mercantilism to capitalism starting in the sixteenth century. Race as an idea survived the Emancipation Proclamation and is used by elites to justify a dual labor market and by the white working class as a justification for demanding superior privileges to their black and brown peers. In this book, race is treated as the language by which class identity and concerns are expressed.

44. Cheryl I. Harris, "Whiteness as Property," *Harvard Law Review* 106, no. 8 (June 1993): 1,713.

45. Census Bureau, *Eighteenth Census, 1960*, vol. 1, *Characteristics of the Population*, part 45, Texas, 374, (Washington, D.C., 1961), 565, 584, 593, 595.

46. David Montejano, *Anglos and Mexicans in the Making of Texas, 1836–1986* (Austin: University of Texas Press, 1987), 315.

47. David R. Roediger, *The Wages of Whiteness: Race and the Making of the American Working Class* (New York: Verso, 1991), and *Towards the Abolition of Whiteness: Essays on Race, Politics, and Working Class History* (New York: Verso, 1994).

48. Neil Foley, *The White Scourge: Mexicans, Blacks, and Poor Whites in Texas Cotton Culture* (Berkeley: University of California Press, 1997). In addition to Roediger and Neil Foley, important recent works in academic research of whiteness include Theodore W. Allen, *The Invention of the White Race*, vol. 1, *Racial Oppression and Social Control* (New York: Verso, 1990); Grace Elizabeth Hale, *Making Whiteness: The Culture of Segregation in the South, 1890–1940* (New York: Pantheon Books, 1998); John Hartigan, *Racial Situations: Class Predicaments of Whiteness in Detroit* (Princeton, N.J.: Princeton University Press, 1999); Matthew Frye Jacobson, *Whiteness of a Different Color: European Immigrants and the Alchemy of Race* (Cambridge, Mass.: Harvard University Press, 1998); and Ian F. Haney López, *White by Law: The Legal Construction of Race* (New York: New York University Press, 1996).

49. Patricia Evridge Hill, *Dallas*, xxvii–xxviii.

50. Carol Estes Thometz, *The Decision-Makers: The Power Structure of Dallas* (Dallas: Southern Methodist University, 1963), 31. For more on wealthy Dallasites who did not enter the Dallas power structure see the discussion on the Dallas right wing in Chapter 6 and the analysis of Congressman Bruce Alger's career in Chapter 7 of this book.

51. This discussion owes much to the work of Marxist theorist Antonio Gramsci and to Stuart Hall's essay "Gramsci's Relevance for the Study of Race and Ethnicity," *Journal of Communication Inquiry* 10, no. 2 (1986). Columbia University began publishing an excellent edition of Gramsci's *Prison Notebooks*, edited by Joseph A. Buttigieg, in the early 1990s. See Antonio Gramsci, *Prison Notebooks*, vol. 1 (New York: Columbia University Press, 1992).

52. For instance, the *Dallas Herald* issue of January 25, 1860, is filled with references to "black Republicans."

53. Boles, *The South through Time*, 459, 467–468; Dana F. White and Timothy J.

Crimmins, "How Atlanta Grew: Cool Heads, Hot Air, and Hard Work," in Andrew Marshall Hamer, ed., *Urban Atlanta: Redefining the Role of the City* (Atlanta: Georgia State University, 1980), 25, 29; David G. McComb, *Houston: A History* (Austin: University of Texas Press, 1981), 114, 143; Joel Williamson, *A Rage for Order: Black-White Relations in the American South since Emancipation* (Oxford, England: Oxford University Press, 1986), 240–244; Alan Dawley, *Struggles for Justice: Social Responsibility and the Liberal State* (Cambridge, Mass.: Harvard University Press, Belknap Press, 1991), 125–126.

54. For an analysis of dispensationalism's importance in American religion see Paul Boyer, *When Time Shall Be No More; Prophecy Belief in Modern American Culture* (Cambridge, Mass.: Harvard University Press, Belknap Press, 1992).

55. Madison Grant, *The Passing of the Great Race or the Racial Basis of European History* (New York: Charles Scribner's Sons, 1923); Lothrop Stoddard, *The Revolt against Civilization: The Menace of the Under Man* (New York: Charles Scribner's Sons, 1922) and *The Rising Tide of Color against White World Supremacy* (New York: Charles Scribner's Sons, 1920).

CHAPTER ONE

1. George P. Rawick, ed., *The American Slave: A Composite Autobiography,* supplement series 2, vol. 2, *Texas Narratives,* part 1 (Westport, Conn.: Greenwood Press, 1979), 103. For more on Texas slavery, a good starting point is Ronnie C. Tyler and Lawrence R. Murphy, eds., *The Slave Narratives of Texas* (Austin: State House Press, 1997). Tyler and Murphy's helpful and concise work is distilled from Rawick's sprawling collection of slave anecdotes. A compelling recent collection of narratives concerning Texas slavery drawn primarily from WPA interviews in Oklahoma in the 1930s is provided in T. Lindsay Baker and Julie P. Baker, eds., *Till Freedom Cried Out: Memories of Texas Slave Life* (College Station: Texas A&M University Press, 1997). A fascinating first-hand account of the negrophobic attitudes of white Texans toward slaves can be found in Frederick Law Olmsted, *A Journey through Texas: Or, a Saddle Trip on the Southwestern Frontier* (1857; reprint, Austin: University of Texas Press, 1978). Pioneering historical works on Texas slavery include Eugene C. Barker, "The Influence of Slavery on the Colonization of Texas," *Mississippi Valley Historical Review* 11 (June 1924), and Lester G. Bugbee, "Slavery in Early Texas," *Political Science Quarterly* 13, part 1 (September 1898): 389–410, and part 2 (December 1898): 648–668. Abigail Curlee's "The History of a Texas Slave Plantation, 1861–63," *Southwestern Historical Quarterly* 26 (October 1922), represents a good early microstudy, even if it is frequently condescending toward its slave subjects. The best and most comprehensive historical treatment of Texas slavery is provided in Randolph B. Campbell, *An Empire for Slavery: The Peculiar Institution in Texas, 1821–1865* (Baton Rouge: Louisiana State University, 1989). Slavery and its aftermath are examined extensively in Alwyn Barr, *Black Texans: A History of African Americans in Texas, 1528–1995* (Norman: University of Oklahoma Press, 1996), while the legacy of slavery is described in Lawrence D. Rice, *The Negro in Texas, 1874–1900,* (Baton Rouge: Louisiana State University Press, 1971). Afro-Texans resisted slavery

in many ways, including running away to Mexico, where slavery had been outlawed. For more on this phenomenon see Rosalie Schwartz, *Across the Rio to Freedom: United States Negroes in Mexico* (El Paso: Texas Western Press, University of Texas at El Paso, 1975). For more on slavery in a Texas urban setting see Susan Jackson, "Slavery in Houston: The 1850s," *Houston Review* 2 (1980); and Carland Elaine Crook, "San Antonio, Texas, 1846–1861" (master's thesis, Rice University, 1964).

2. For more on racial hierarchies within whiteness see Matthew Frye Jacobson, *Whiteness of a Different Color.*

3. Frank M. Cockrell, *History of Early Dallas* (Chicago: Privately published, 1944), 44.

4. For an explanation of *herrenvolk* democracies see Winant, *Racial Conditions.* Antebellum Dallas was not as uniformly Anglo-Saxon as Cockrell liked to pretend. In the mid-1850s about 350 French, Swiss, and Belgian immigrants led by Victor Considerant built a socialist utopian community in the Dallas area. Other immigrants to pre–Civil War Dallas came from Ireland and Poland. For more on antebellum Dallas' ethnic diversity see James Pratt, "Our European Heritage: The Diverse Contributions of La Réunion," *Legacies: A History Journal for Dallas and North Central Texas* 1, no. 2 (fall 1989); and George H. Santerre, *White Cliffs of Dallas: The Story of La Réunion the Old French Colony* (Dallas: Book Craft, 1955).

5. Arnoldo de León, *They Called Them Greasers: Anglo Attitudes Toward Mexicans in Texas, 1821–1900* (Austin: University of Texas Press, 1983), 2–3.

6. John Henry Brown, preamble to his "A Report and Treatise on Slavery and the Slavery Agitation," (Austin: John Marshall and Co., State Printers, 1857), 5, Center for American History, University of Texas at Austin (hereinafter CAH). A contemporary summary of white racist beliefs regarding miscegenation and its deleterious effects can be found in David G. Croly, *Miscegenation: The Theory of the Blending of the Races, Applied to the American White Man and Negro* (New York: H. Dexter, Hamilton and Co., 1864). Two good historical examinations of the subject are Peggy Pascoe, "Miscegenation Law, Court Cases, and Ideologies of 'Race' in Twentieth-Century America," *Journal of American History* 83 (June 1996); and Joel Williamson, *New People: Miscegenation and Mulattoes in the United States* (New York: Free Press, 1980).

7. H. P. N. Gammel, ed., *The Laws of Texas: 1822–1897*, vol. 1 (Austin: Gammel Book Co., 1898), 1079.

8. Mark M. Carroll, "Families, Sex, and the Law in Frontier Texas," (Ph.D. diss., University of Houston, 1996), 180 n. 86.

9. Ibid., 195–196.

10. Gammel, *Laws of Texas*, vol. 4, 1100.

11. Ibid., vol. 1, 1385.

12. *New Handbook of Texas*, 1996, s.v. "Peters Colony." Empresarios were land contractors or agents engaged by the Mexican government to survey the Texas territory and provide settlers in thinly settled areas. Stephen F. Austin was the most famous of these empresarios. Empresario grants continued through the short life of the Texas Republic (1836–1845) and into the early days of statehood.

13. Seymour V. Connor, *The Peters Colony of Texas: A History and Biographical Sketches of the Early Settlers* (Austin: Texas State Historical Association, 1959), 2.

14. George W. Bomar, *Texas Weather* (Austin: University of Texas Press, 1983,) 151, 221, 240; B. F. Riley, *History of the Baptists of Texas: A Concise Narrative of the Baptist Denomination in Texas, from the Earliest Occupation of the Territory to the Close of the Year 1906* (Dallas: Privately published, 1907), 137. Consistent weather data for Dallas are not available before 1874. The Euro-American experience of leaving the more densely populated East and encountering an often forbidding frontier reinforced the notion that the Anglo world represented civilization, while lands inhabited by Mexicans and Indians exemplified both a literal and a cultural wilderness. For more on the interaction of Anglos with the Southwestern environment see three works by Donald W. Meinig: *Imperial Texas: An Interpretive Essay in Cultural Geography* (Austin: University of Texas Press, 1969); *The Shaping of America: A Geographical Perspective on 500 Years of History*, vol. 2, *Continental America, 1800–1867* (New Haven, Conn.: Yale University Press, 1993); and *Southwest: Three Peoples in Geographical Change, 1600–1970* (New York: Oxford University Press, 1971).

15. "News from a Stage Coach," *Dallas Herald*, April 20, 1859, p. 1. The masthead erroneously gives April 13 as the date.

16. Randolph B. Campbell and Richard G. Lowe, *Wealth and Power in Antebellum Texas* (College Station: Texas A&M University Press, 1977), 46.

17. Ibid., 39.

18. Here I follow the model used by Campbell and Lowe in *Wealth and Power* (38) in dividing Dallas County into the following nine wealth categories: persons holding assets of less than $1; between $1 and $249, $250 and $499, $500 and $999, $1,000 and $4,999, $5,000 and $9,999, $10,000 and $19,999, $20,000 and $49,999; and $50,000 and above.

19. Census Bureau, *Eighth Census, 1860,* Dallas County, Texas (Washington, D.C., 1864), vol. 1, manuscript, 294–389. To derive the following economic and regional analysis, the author only considered residents for whom wealth, occupation, and place of birth were provided in the 1860 Census. This left 1,872 residents. Regional categories were defined as follows: those of foreign birth, those born in free states, those born in slave states that stayed in the Union during the Civil War, those born in the Upper South, and those born in the Deep South and the Southwest. One resident was listed as having been born in the Cherokee Nation.

20. Ibid.

21. Ibid., 294.

22. Ibid., 295.

23. Ibid., 294–389.

24. Ibid., 311, 313, 388.

25. Ibid., 294–389.

26. Darwin Payne, *Dallas: An Illustrated History* (Woodland Hills, Calif.: Windsor Publications, 1982), 36.

27. Connor, *Peters Colony,* 142; Claude Elliott, "The Life of James W. Throckmorton," (Ph.D. diss., University of Texas at Austin, 1934), 30–32.

28. "Peter's Colony, Act, of 10th Feb. 1852," *Clarksville (Texas) Northern Standard,* August 7, 1852, p. 4; Connor, *Peters Colony,* 142–143.

29. William Rogers, *The Lusty Texans of Dallas,* (New York: E. P. Dutton and Co., 1960), 47.

30. Ibid., 49.

31. Ibid., 71–76; Monroe F. Cockrell, "A Brief Introduction," in his *Sarah Horton Cockrell in Early Dallas* (Dallas: Privately published, 1944), n.pag.; "Fatal Rencontre," *Dallas Herald,* April 10, 1858; Shirley Seifert, *Destiny in Dallas* (New York: J. B. Lippincott Co., 1958), 18–19; *New Handbook of Texas,* 1996, s.v. "Alexander Cockrell."

32. *Proud Heritage: Pioneer Families of Dallas County* (Dallas: Dallas County Pioneer Association, 1986), 33. Sarah Cockrell would collect two hundred dollars from Moore after a series of lawsuits. She easily filled in for her husband as Dallas' leading entrepreneur, opening the St. Nicholas Hotel the next year. (The hotel was destroyed in a July 1860 fire.) She obtained a charter from the State of Texas for the Dallas Bridge Company, but the Civil War interrupted this dream.

33. Randolph B. Campbell, *Empire for Slavery,* 55–56.

34. Connor, *Peters Colony,* 105; Census Bureau, *Eighth Census, 1860,* 473, 476, 479.

35. Brown, preamble to "A Report and Treatise," 3–4, 6.

36. Brown, "A Report and Treatise," 22.

37. Randolph B. Campbell, *Empire for Slavery,* 184. General treatments on Texas slave rebellions include Wendell G. Addington, "Slave Insurrections in Texas," *Journal of Negro History* 35, no. 4 (October 1950); and Enda Junkins, "Slave Plots, Insurrections, and Acts of Violence in the State of Texas, 1828–1865" (master's thesis, Baylor University, 1969).

38. John H. Cochran, *Dallas County: A Record of Its Pioneers and Progress* (Dallas: Arthur S. Mathis Service Publishing Co., 1928), 54; Addie K. McDermett, questionnaire for Frank M. Cockrell, November 27, 1927, Sarah Horton Cockrell Collection, A4340, Folder A43155, DHS.

39. "A Deplorable Affair," *Dallas Herald,* April 5, 1856, p. 1; Junkins, "Slave Plots," 38.

40. Gammel, *Laws of Texas,* vol. 2, 325.

41. *Official Journal of the House of Representatives of the State of Texas at the Adjourned Session, Seventh Biennial Session* (Austin: John Marshall and Co., State Printers, 1857), 178–179.

42. Frank M. Cockrell, *History of Early Dallas,* 62.

43. Census Bureau, *Eighth Census, 1860,* Dallas County, manuscript, 294–389.

44. Campbell and Lowe, *Wealth and Power,* 115.

45. "The Bible on Slavery," *Dallas Herald,* January 18, 1860, p. 1. For more on Pryor's life and how the pro-slavery physician came to edit the *Dallas Herald* see *New Handbook of Texas,* 1996, s.v. "Charles Pryor"; *Dallas Herald,* April 6, 1859, p. 2; "Death of Judge Latimer," *Dallas Herald,* April 20, 1859, p. 2.

46. Some newspaper stories refer to him as "Parson Blunt."

47. *Dallas Herald,* August 17, 1859, p. 3; "The Climate of Texas," *Dallas Herald,* August 31, 1859, p. 3.

48. Census Bureau, *Eighth Census, 1860*, Dallas County; Census Bureau, *Eighth Census, 1860*, 294–389.

49. The total loss would be $8 million in 2004 dollars, with only $217,000 insured. "The Late Conflagrations," *Austin State Gazette*, July 28, 1860, p. 1; William W. White, "The Texas Slave Insurrection of 1860," *Southwestern Historical Quarterly* 52, no. 3 (January 1949), 259–260; "Terrible Conflagration!! The Town of Dallas in Ashes! Every Store and Hotel Burned! Loss $300,000!!!" *Houston Weekly Telegraph*, July 14, 1860 (an extra edition inserted into the July 17 issue), p. 3; Frank M. Cockrell, *History of Early Dallas*, 70–73; "The Northern Texas Fires," *Houston Weekly Telegraph*, July 26, 1860, p. 1; "Later from Dallas: A Most Diabolical Plot!" *Houston Weekly Telegraph*, July 31, 1860, p. 1; "The Great Fire of 1860 Which Consumed Thirty-two Houses in Dallas," *Dallas Morning News*, December 14, 1890, p. 20. The last source is a reprint of a special edition of the *Dallas Herald* printed as a handbill by the *McKinney (Texas) Messenger* on July 10, 1860.

50. Frank M. Cockrell, *History of Early Dallas*, 73–76; William R. Farmer, "Samuel, Patrick, and Cato: A History of the Dallas Fire of 1860 and Its Tragic Aftermath," n.p., photocopy in author's possession, 17–28. Dr. Farmer provided vital assistance for much of this chapter, pointing out many primary sources and avenues of research. I owe him special thanks.

51. Frank M. Cockrell, *History of Early Dallas*, 74.

52. Ibid., 76.

53. Donald E. Reynolds, *Editors Make War: Southern Newspapers in the Secession Crisis* (Nashville: Vanderbilt University Press, 1966), 97–117.

54. "Later from Dallas," *Houston Weekly Telegraph*.

55. "Late Conflagrations," *Austin State Gazette*, July 28, 1860, p. 1.

56. Ibid.

57. "Red Letter Anniversary of the Burning of Dallas Thirty-Two Years Ago," *Dallas Morning News*, July 10, 1892, p. 12.

58. Gammel, *Laws of Texas*, vol. 4, 1060.

59. "Red Letter Anniversary of the Burning of Dallas Thirty-Two Years Ago," *Dallas Morning News*, July 10, 1892, p. 12.

60. W. S. Adair, "When a Toll Bridge Spanned the Trinity at Commerce Street," *Dallas Morning News*, Sunday magazine, December 31, 1922, p. 6; Census Bureau, *Eighth Census, 1860*, 309; Census Bureau, *Texas Slave Schedules*, 1860, vol. 1, 262.

61. Adair, "When a Toll Bridge Spanned the Trinity."

62. V. K. Carpenter, transcriber, *The State of Texas Federal Population Schedules, Seventh Census of the United States, 1850*, vol. 2, (Huntsville, Ark.: Century Enterprises, 1969), 599; Census Bureau, *Eighth Census, 1860*, 321; "Early Times in Dallas," *Dallas Morning News*, July 21, 1889, 11.

63. "Later from Dallas," *Austin State Gazette*, August 4, 1860, p. 2.

64. The evidence that Miller owned Smith is indirect, based partly on the recollections of Addie K. McDermott, a teenager at the time of the blaze. See the William Miller Family Scrapbook, vol. 1, p. 77, at the Texas/Dallas History and Archive Division, J. Erik Jonsson Central Library, Dallas Public Library (hereinafter DPL). The possibility that

a second slave owned by Miller was accused of involvement in the alleged arson is indicated by Nat Burford's eyewitness account in "Red Letter Anniversary," *Dallas Morning News.*

65. For an example of a slaveowner prohibiting unsupervised religious services see Tyler and Murphy, *Slave Narratives,* 83.

66. "Red Letter Anniversary," *Dallas Morning News.*

67. Ibid.

68. Ibid.

69. B. P. Gallaway, *The Ragged Rebel: A Common Soldier in W. H. Parsons' Texas Cavalry, 1861-1865* (Austin: University of Texas Press, 1988), 10.

70. "Red Letter Anniversary," *Dallas Morning News.*

71. "Later from Dallas," *Austin State Gazette;* Frank M. Cockrell, *History of Early Dallas,* 77.

72. "Later from Dallas," *Austin State Gazette.*

73. "Letter from Dallas," *Houston Weekly Telegraph,* August 7, 1860, p. 2.

74. White, "Texas Slave Insurrection," 269–276; Herbert Aptheker, *American Negro Slave Revolts* (New York: Columbia University Press, 1943), 353–354.

75. White, "Texas Slave Insurrection," 265–267; "Denton Creek," *Austin State Gazette,* August 25, 1860, p. 2.

76. Addington, "Slave Insurrections," 428–429; *New Handbook of Texas,* 1996, s.v. "John Henry Brown."

77. Addington, "Slave Insurrections," 429; White, "Texas Slave Insurrection," 267. Anthony Bewley, the alleged recipient of these letters, was arrested by a posse in Arkansas, brought to Fort Worth, and hanged. He denied his involvement in the expected slave revolt. See Wesley Norton, "The Methodist Episcopal Church and the Civil Disturbances in North Texas in 1859 and 1860," *Southwestern Historical Quarterly* 68, no. 3 (January 1965), 321, 333–335, 338–339; "Texas Abolition Incendiaries," *Austin State Gazette,* September 29, 1860, p. 2; "The Rev. Wm. Buley," *Austin State Gazette,* September 29, 1860, p. 2; and "The Rev. W. Buley," *Austin State Gazette,* October 13, 1860, p. 4.

78. Barr, *Black Texans,* 33; "The Texas Troubles," *New Orleans Daily Picayune,* September 8, 1860, p. 2.

79. Addington, "Slave Insurrections," 425.

80. "Strong Figure of Speech," *Austin State Gazette,* October 6, 1860, p. 3.

81. "Texas Troubles," *New Orleans Daily Picayune.*

82. "Negroes Who Are Free," *Austin State Gazette,* March 8, 1856, p. 2.

83. Reynolds, *Editors Make War,* 108.

84. The secondary literature on the Texas troubles focuses almost exclusively on whether the 1860 fires represented a furtive slave revolt or a series of accidents provoking a panic. Ultimately more important issues, such as the social tensions that provoked such a furious and violent response from pro-slavery Texans, are largely ignored. For a pro-white Southern view blaming abolitionists for the Texas troubles see Joseph Cephas Carroll, *Slave Insurrections in the United States, 1800–1865* (Boston: Chapman and Grimes, 1938), 195–196. For a leftist view of the Texas troubles as an instance of African American

anti-slavery resistance see Aptheker, *American Negro Slave Revolts,* 353–354. Aptheker is so determined to counter the racist portrait of happy Southern slaves that he tends to give every rumor of slave rebellion credence, a serious flaw. More skeptical accounts can be found in Barr, *Black Texans,* 33–34, and White, "Texas Slave Insurrection," 259–285.

85. "Red Letter Anniversary," *Dallas Morning News.*

86. "The Dallas Barbecue," *Austin State Gazette,* September 29, 1860, 2. The quoted passage reflects the original spelling.

87. Payne, *Dallas,* 59; Gammel, *Laws of Texas,* vol. 3, 120, and vol. 4, 1520.

88. Rupert Norval Richardson, Ernest Wallace, and Adrian N. Anderson, *Texas: The Lone Star State,* (Englewood Cliffs, N.J.: Prentice-Hall, 1981), 222–226; *New Handbook of Texas,* 1996, s.v. "Secession"; Ralph A. Wooster and Robert Wooster, "A People at War: East Texans During the Civil War," *East Texas Historical Journal* 28, no. 1 (1990): 4.

89. Wooster and Wooster, "People at War," 4, 10–11. The term "Deserter Country" comes from Ella Lonn, *Desertion during the Civil War* (1928; reprint, Gloucester, Mass.: P. Smith, 1966), 71 and front piece.

90. For the definitive account of these events see Richard B. McCaslin, *Tainted Breeze: The Great Hanging at Gainesville, Texas, 1862* (Baton Rouge: Louisiana State University Press, 1994).

91. W. H. Horton, letter to Lieutenant J. T. Kirkman, July 24, 1867, Roll 6, Records of the Assistant Commissioner for the State of Texas, Bureau of Refugees, Freedmen, and Abandoned Lands, 1865–1869, National Archives. The Freedmen's Bureau archives have been reproduced on thirty-two microfilm reels, which are available at the Texas/Dallas History and Archive Division, J. Erik Jonsson Central Library (DPL). This collection will be referred to hereinafter as Freedmen's Bureau Records.

92. For an eloquent contemplation on the omnipresence of the Confederacy in Southern historical memory see Robert Penn Warren, *The Legacy of the Civil War: Meditations on the Centennial* (New York: Random House, 1961). An intriguing look at how non-historians doubt much of the "official" history they are taught and make often subversive use of the past can be found in Roy Rosenzweig and David Thelen, *The Presence of the Past: Popular Uses of History in American Life* (New York: Columbia University Press, 1998).

93. The tracks were once known as the Missouri-Texas-Kansas, or MKT, line.

94. Larry Powell, "Group preserves memory of Fire of 1860, slave hangings," *Dallas Morning News,* June 20, 1988, sec. A; David Jackson, "Park's name debated: Committee urges honoring 'martyrs,'" *Dallas Morning News,* January 6, 1991, sec. A; and David Jackson, "Board takes up request to rename park; Committee asked to consider honoring Kennedy, lynched slaves," *Dallas Morning News,* January 18, 1991, sec. A.

95. David Jackson, "Park's name debated, *Dallas Morning News.*" The name change took place October 24, 1991. No plaque has been placed at the site, according to a Dallas city official in a personal interview, because city rules require petitioners requesting a name change for an existing park to pay for new signs and markers. The bones of the three executed slaves were unearthed at present-day Martyrs Park when the Texas and Pacific Railway bridge was constructed. See "Among Dallas Pioneers: First Case of Theft in the County and the Punishment," *Dallas Morning News,* July 16, 1892, sec. 1, p. 8.

96. William R. Farmer, interview by the author, Dallas, Texas, January 1999. Dr. Farmer, an acclaimed theologian and a generous help to this writer, died of cancer in 2001.

97. John Henry Brown, *History of Dallas County,* 102.

98. Ibid.

CHAPTER TWO

1. Delegates of the People of Texas, "A Declaration of the causes which impel the State of Texas to secede from the Federal Union" (Dallas: Basye Brothers, n.d), 4, Archives Division, Texas State Library, Austin (hereinafter TSL).

2. For a comprehensive and sympathetic portrait of Reagan see Ben H. Proctor, *Not without Honor: The Life of John H. Reagan* (Austin: University of Texas Press, 1962).

3. John H. Reagan, Letter to the People of Texas, Fort Warren, Boston Harbor, August 11, 1865. Typescript copy, John H. Reagan Collection, Miscellany File 2–23/1079, John H. Reagan Letters, Folder 31, TSL.

4. Ibid.

5. Ibid.

6. *Dallas Herald* quoted in Schutze, *Accommodation,* 44–45.

7. *Dallas Herald,* January 29, 1875, quoted in Philip Lindsley, *History of Greater Dallas,* 97.

8. Ibid.

9. John H. Reagan to People of Texas.

10. John H. Reagan to Governor J. W. Throckmorton, "Necessary measures to Reconstruction," Fort Houston, Palestine, Texas, October 12, 1866, Jefferson Davis Reagan Collection A4674, Folder 10, DHS.

11. Proctor, *Not without Honor,* 181.

12. The best works on Texas Reconstruction include Randolph B. Campbell, *Grass-Roots Reconstruction in Texas, 1865–1880* (Baton Rouge: Louisiana State University Press, 1997); Barry Crouch, *The Freedmen's Bureau and Black Texans* (Austin: University of Texas Press, 1992); Merline Pitre, *Through Many Dangers, Toils, and Snares: The Black Leadership of Texas, 1868–1900* (Austin: Eakin Press, 1985); and James M. Smallwood, *Time of Hope, Time of Despair: Black Texans During Reconstruction* (Port Washington, N.Y.: Kennikat Press, 1981). Campbell's chapter on Dallas was largely derived from a 1992 master's thesis written by University of North Texas student Melinda Diane Connelly Smith, "Congressional Reconstruction in Dallas County, Texas: Was It Radical?" Crouch's work on violence in postwar Texas is particularly innovative and revealing.

13. Barry Crouch, "A Spirit of Lawlessness: White Violence, Texas Blacks, 1865–1868," *Journal of Social History* 18 (winter 1984): 226.

14. Ibid., 226.

15. Ibid., 218–219.

16. Crouch, *Freedmen's Bureau,* 25.

17. Melinda Smith, "Congressional Reconstruction," 118–119.

18. *New Handbook of Texas,* 1996, s.v. "Reconstruction."

19. "Is Texas to become Africanized?" *Dallas Herald,* October 5, 1867, p. 2; Randolph B. Campbell, *Grass-Roots Reconstruction,* 77.

20. Randolph B. Campbell, *Grass-Roots Reconstruction,* 78; Melinda Smith, "Congressional Reconstruction," 156.

21. Lindsley, *History of Greater Dallas,* 79.

22. Crouch, "Spirit of Lawlessness," 219.

23. Thomas H. Smith, "Conflict and Corruption: The Dallas Establishment vs. the Freedmen's Bureau Agent," *Legacies: A History Journal for Dallas and North Central Texas* 1, no. 2 (fall 1989): 25.

24. William H. Horton, letter to Lieutenant J. T. Kirkman, August 15, 1867, Roll 6, Freedmen's Bureau Records.

25. Ibid.; "Killed," *Dallas Herald,* August 17, 1867, p. 1.

26. "Report for the month ending January, 1868," Roll 24, Freedmen's Bureau Records. It seems that Alderman survived the shoot-out.

27. Thomas Smith, "Conflict and Corruption," 29.

28. Ibid.

29. Ibid.

30. For examples of this myth-weaving see John Henry Brown, *History of Dallas County,* 104; Lindsley, *History of Greater Dallas,* 75; and Frank M. Cockrell, *History of Early Dallas,* 66–67.

31. For one of the best recent depictions of Reconstruction-era political figures in the South see Richard Nelson Current, *Those Terrible Carpetbaggers: A Reinterpretation* (New York: Oxford University Press, 1988). Current notes the deep commitment of many so-called carpetbaggers to their new Southern homes and their frequent idealism. Reconstruction historiography will be discussed in greater detail in Chapter 3.

32. Randolph B. Campbell, *Grass-Roots Reconstruction,* 69; Connor, *Peters Colony,* 142. Bledsoe used no first name, only a first initial. The 6-foot 4-inch, 260-pound man was known as "Big A" and "Honest A." Though a slaveowner, he declined to serve in the Confederate Army. See Melinda Smith, "Congressional Reconstruction," 25. Bledsoe selected the site of and laid out the city of Lancaster near Dallas. See Cochran, *Dallas County,* 69.

33. Michael V. Hazel, "From Distant Shores: European Immigrants in Dallas," *Heritage News: A Journal Devoted to the History of North Central Texas* 10, no. 1 (spring 1985): 13–14.

34. Hazel, "From Distant Shores," 16; Thomas Smith, "Conflict and Corruption," 26; Melinda Smith, "Congressional Reconstruction," 103–104.

35. "Petition to Major Genl. [Charles] Griffin from Dallas, Texas, June 9, 1867," Roll 6, Freedmen's Bureau Records.

36. Thomas Smith, "Conflict and Corruption," 29–30; Randolph B. Campbell, *Grass-Roots Reconstruction,* 80.

37. Randolph B. Campbell, *Grass-Roots Reconstruction,* 94–95; Melinda Smith, "Congressional Reconstruction," 95–97.

38. Payne, *Dallas*, 46.

39. Ibid., 64–65, 73; Melinda Smith, "Congressional Reconstruction," 83.

40. Payne, *Dallas*, 70.

41. Randolph B. Campbell, *Grass-Roots Reconstruction*, 94–95; Patricia Evridge Hill, *Dallas*, xxii.

42. Payne, *Dallas*, 61; Herbert Gambrell, "Birthplace of Inhabitants of Dallas County [from] United States Census Data," Herbert Gambrell Collection, A40.183, DHS.

43. Lindsley, *History of Greater Dallas*, 128.

44. Gerry Cristol, *A Light in the Prairie: Temple Emanu-El of Dallas, 1872–1997* (Fort Worth: Texas Christian University, 1998), 6.

45. Payne, *Dallas*, 70; Gerry Cristol, *Light in the Prairie*, 6–10.

46. Hazel, "From Distant Shores," 10–13; Patricia Evridge Hill, *Dallas*, xxv.

47. *Dallas Daily Herald*, April 27, 1878, p. 2.

48. "Crime in Texas," *Dallas Daily Herald*, April 17, 1878, p. 2.

49. *Dallas Daily Herald*, May 22, 1878, p. 2.

50. *Dallas Daily Herald*, April 30, 1878, p. 2.

51. "The Confederate Bloody Shirt," *Dallas Daily Herald*, May 7, 1878, p. 2.

52. Edward L. Ayers, *The Promise of the New South: Life After Reconstruction* (Oxford, England: Oxford University Press, 1992), 21.

53. Roediger, *Towards the Abolition of Whiteness*, 13.

54. The most compelling analysis of how the cult of the Lost Cause evolved in the South can be found in Charles Reagan Wilson, *Baptized in Blood: The Religion of the Lost Cause, 1865–1920* (Athens: University of Georgia Press, 1980).

55. *Memorial and Biographical History of Dallas County, Texas* (Chicago: Lewis Publishing Co., 1892), 214.

56. Lindsley, *History of Greater Dallas*, 241–242.

57. *Memorial and Biographical History*, 213, 221.

58. Ibid., 212.

59. Ibid., 223.

60. Lindsley, *History of Greater Dallas*, 242.

61. *Memorial and Biographical History*, 231–232.

62. Ibid., 235–236.

63. Ibid., 236.

64. David G. McComb, *Houston*, 65–114; Robert Calvert and Arnoldo de León, *The History of Texas* (Wheeling, Ill.: Harlan Davidson, 1996), 192–194, 262–263.

65. Tony Horwitz, *Confederates in the Attic: Dispatches from the Unfinished Civil War* (New York: Vintage Books, 1998), 283–285; Mark Bauerlein, *Negrophobia: A Race Riot in Atlanta, 1906* (San Francisco: Encounter Books, 2001), 24–25.

66. Andrew Marshall Hamer, "Urban Perspectives for the 1980s," in Hamer, ed., *Urban Atlanta*, 5.

67. *Memorial and Biographical History*, 234–236.

68. For as important a figure in American Christianity as Scofield, there are surprisingly few scholarly appraisals of the man and his works. There are three full-length biog-

raphies, only one of which was widely published: Charles Gallaudet Trumbull, *The Life Story of C. I. Scofield* (New York: Oxford University Press, 1920); William A. Be Vier, *A Biographical Sketch of C. I. Scofield* (master's thesis, Southern Methodist University, 1960); and Joseph M. Canfield, *The Incredible Scofield and His Book* (Asheville, N.C.: Privately published, 1984). Scofield continues to be a polarizing figure, especially among conservative Christians, and this is reflected in these three works. Trumbull wrote his biography with Scofield's assistance, and the short book borders on hagiography. Trumbull either did not know about or ignored the scandals surrounding the minister in Kansas. Canfield's work is as excessively hostile as Trumbull's is gushing. Be Vier's work is the most balanced but lacks Canfield's extensive research and critical eye. Be Vier largely overlooks serious questions about Scofield's pre-Dallas background. A brief secular historical evaluation of the minister can be found in Boyer, *When Time Shall Be No More*, 97–99, and in the *Memorial and Biographical History*, 985–986. Hostile theological appraisals from fellow Christian conservatives include: William E. Cox, *An Examination of Dispensationalism* (Philadelphia: Presbyterian and Reformed Publishing Co., 1963); John H. Gerstner, *Wrongly Dividing the Word of Truth: A Critique of Dispensationalism* (Brentwood, Tenn.: Wolgemuth and Hyatt, 1991); and Dave MacPherson, *The Great Rapture Hoax* (Fletcher, N.C.: New Puritan Library, 1983). The most famous writer in the Scofield tradition is Hal Lindsey, whose *The Late Great Planet Earth* (Grand Rapids: Zondervan Publishing House, 1970) became a surprise publishing blockbuster. A collection of Scofield's papers and related church records is available at the Scofield Memorial Church in Dallas. The author thanks Paul DeHaven, the church's former pastor of communications, for his incredible generosity with his time, his invaluable knowledge, and his extensive help in conducting research on this topic.

69. Be Vier, *Biographical Sketch*, 3; Canfield, *Incredible Scofield*, 14–16.

70. Be Vier, *Biographical Sketch*, 5.

71. Canfield, *Incredible Scofield*, 36–39, 51, 55–56, 60–67; Be Vier, *Biographical Sketch*, 9–13, 15, 19–20, 28–32; Boyer, *When Time Shall Be No More*, 97.

72. Canfield, *Incredible Scofield*, 86–87; Be Vier, *Biographical Sketch*, 23–24.

73. Be Vier, *Biographical Sketch*, 24–27, 34; Boyer, *When Time Shall Be No More*, 97; Records of the First Congregational Church in Dallas, Texas, Book One, August 20, 1882, and October 22, 1882, entries, Scofield Memorial Church Archives (hereinafter SMCA).

74. Jack L. Gritz, "Dr. Scofield's Error," *Baptist Standard*, July 13, 1960.

75. Be Vier, *Biographical Sketch*, 34–35; Trumbull, *Life Story*, 44; Canfield, *Incredible Scofield*, 108–109.

76. The First Congregational Church in Dallas ordained Scofield on October 17, 1883. See the Records of the First Congregational Church of Dallas Texas, Book One, 24, SMCA.

77. Canfield, *Incredible Scofield*, 108–109; Be Vier, *Biographical Sketch*, 38.

78. Trumbull, *Life Story*, 120–121.

79. C. I. Scofield, *The Old Scofield Study Bible* (1917; reprint, New York: Oxford University Press, 1996), title page; Canfield, *Incredible Scofield*, 134; Be Vier, *Biographical Sketch*, 65. With the 1996 edition of the Scofield Bible, Oxford University Press changed

the title. The work was originally called the *Scofield Reference Bible*. With this exception, this Bible is identical to the 1917 edition, the second printing of this work.

80. Originally called the *Cedar Snag*, the *Dallas Herald* was established in 1849 by James W. Latimer and William Wallace. On June 21, 1873, the paper was renamed the *Dallas Weekly Herald*, and by 1874 the owner, J. W. Swindells and Company, began printing a daily edition called the *Dallas Daily Herald*. The *Dallas Morning News*, owned by the *Galveston Daily News*, had opened on October 1, 1885, in order to drive the *Herald* out of business. The *Herald* did not last long against the *News*, which enjoyed superior financial resources. The *Herald* limped along until December 3, 1885, when it was purchased and absorbed by the *News*. The *Dallas Herald* should not be confused with the later *Dallas Times Herald*, which formed following an 1888 merger of the *Dallas Daily Times* with the *Dallas Daily Herald*. The first issue of the *Dallas Daily Times-Herald* hit the streets on January 2, 1888.

81. *New Handbook of Texas*, 1996, s.v. "George Bannerman Dealey," "Dallas Herald," and "Dallas Morning News"; Church Register, Scofield Memorial Church, 38–39, 42–43, 110, 126–127, 128–129, SMCA; Be Vier, *Biographical Sketch*, 49.

82. Pastor's annual report for 1883, delivered January 9, 1884, Records of the First Congregational Church, Book One, 32; "Manual of the First Congregational Church," (Dallas: First Congregational Church, 1901), 8–10, SMCA; Paul DeHaven, "Records of the First Congregational Church of Dallas, Texas," unpublished paper, photocopy, 19, SMCA.

83. Boyer, *When Time Shall Be No More*, ix. Pre-millennialists believe that Jesus will come to earth a second time, stop war by divine fiat, and then establish an earthly kingdom of peace and justice that will last for a thousand years. Post-millennialists believe that after the gradual conversion of the world to Christianity, perfect peace will reign on earth for a millennium, and Christ's Second Coming will occur only then.

84. C. I. Scofield, *Rightly Dividing the Word of Truth* (Dallas: Scofield Memorial Church, 1928), 20.

85. Ibid., 24–25.

86. Robert Fuller, *Naming the Antichrist: The History of an American Obsession* (New York: Oxford University Press, 1995), 196.

87. C. I. Scofield, *In Many Pulpits with Dr. C. I. Scofield* (New York: Oxford University Press, 1922), 290.

88. Boyer, *When Times Shall Be No More*, 97–98; Ernest S. Frerichs, ed., *The Bible and Bibles in America* (Atlanta: Scholars Press, 1988), 4, 52; William E. Cox, *Examination of Dispensationalism*, 14–15; Doug Campbell, "A reference Bible known the world over," *Dallas Morning News*, April 10, 1977.

89. Boyer, 98, 100; Canfield, *Incredible Scofield*, 212–213; Gerstner, *Wrongly Dividing the Word*, 54.

90. Boyer, *When Time Shall Be No More*, 5, 7, 126–129.

91. Ibid., 99.

92. Ibid., 298.

93. C. I. Scofield, *Dr. C. I. Scofield's Question Box* (Chicago: Moody Bible Institute of Chicago, 1917), 36.

94. Canfield, *Incredible Scofield*, 234.

95. Fuller, *Naming the Antichrist*, 79, 118–119.

96. Boyer, *When Time Shall Be No More*, 322.

97. Scofield, *Old Scofield Study Bible*, 901, annotation to Deut. 2:41; Bible verses in this Scofield volume refer to the Authorized (King James) Version.

98. Scofield, *In Many Pulpits*, 227.

99. Scofield, *Old Scofield Study Bible*, 16, annotation to Gen. 9:1.

100. For the "curse of Ham" and its relationship to white attitudes regarding blacks see Jordan, *White over Black*, 54, 56, 60.

101. Trumbull, *Life Story*, 128; Canfield, *Incredible Scofield*, 270.

102. Scofield was by no means the first philo-Semitic Christian thinker. In the colonial era, John Cotton called Judaism the "mother church of Christianity," and Roger Williams emphasized the special relationship between Jews and God. Cotton Mather saw the mass conversion of the Jews as a necessary prelude to mankind's salvation. Such Protestants and their theological descendents held a warm regard for Jews that contrasted sharply with their views of the Catholic Church, which they saw as the corrupt seat of apostasy. "Israel's cherished contributions to Christianity, combined with the greater fear and threat of Catholics, made Jews the less hated minority in Protestant America," historian Frederic Cople Jaher observes in *A Scapegoat in the New Wilderness: The Origins and Rise of Anti-Semitism in America* (Cambridge, Mass.: Harvard University Press, 1994), 92–93. Scofield went much further than these earlier philo-Semites and broke with centuries of Christian tradition by suggesting that Jews need not accept Jesus as savior to reach Heaven. Scofield saw Judaism and Christianity as virtually equal religions. One of the best works describing the origins of Christian anti-Semitism is Paula Fredriksen's *From Jesus to Christ: The Origins of the New Testament Images of Jesus* (New Haven: Yale University Press, 1988). The two most important works on American anti-Semitism are Louise A. Mayo, *The Ambivalent Image: Nineteenth-Century America's Perception of the Jew* (London: Associated University Press, 1988), and Leonard Dinnerstein, *Anti-Semitism in America* (New York: Oxford University Press, 1994). Jaher's *Scapegoat* is particularly ambitious and informative in tracing American anti-Semitism back to pagan Rome and putting the American Gentile image of Jews in a trans-Atlantic context. Leon Harris, *Merchant Princes, an Intimate History of Jewish Families Who Built Great Department Stores* (New York: Harper and Row, 1979).

103. For more on Jews and whiteness see Matthew Frye Jacobson, *Whiteness of a Different Color*, 62–67, 119–131, 171–199, and Karen Brodkin Sacks, *How Jews Became White Folks and What That Says about Race in America* (New Brunswick, N.J.: Rutgers University Press, 2000). On Jewish service in the Confederate Army see Robert N. Rosen, *The Jewish Confederates* (Columbia, S.C.: University of South Carolina, 2000). Two excellent studies of Jewish accommodation and resistance to Southern racial ideology are Mark K. Bauman and Berkley Kalin, eds., *The Quiet Voices: Southern Rabbis and Black Civil Rights, 1880s to 1990s* (Tuscaloosa: University of Alabama Press, 1997); and Stuart Allen Rockoff, "Jewish Racial Identity in Pittsburgh and Atlanta, 1890–1930" (Ph.D. diss., University of Texas, 2000).

104. Jonathan A. Sarna, "The 'Mythical Jew' and the 'Jew Next Door' in Nineteenth Century America," in David Gerber, ed., *Anti-Semitism in American History* (Urbana: University of Illinois Press, 1986), 58–59.

105. "Position and Influence of the Jews," *Austin State Gazette*, August 6, 1853, p. 401.

106. Cristol, *Light in the Prairie*, 3, 11, 38.

107. Cindy C. Smolovik, "A Tradition of Service: Early Synagogues in Dallas," *Heritage News: A Journal Devoted to the History of North Central Texas* 12, no. 2 (summer 1987): 12.

108. Cristol, *Light in the Prairie*, 19–25; Dinnerstein, *Anti-Semitism in America*, 177; Jonathan A. Sarna, "The Evolution of the American Synagogue," in Robert M. Seltzer and Norman J. Cohen, eds., *The Americanization of the Jews* (New York: New York University Press, 1995), 215–229.

109. Rabbi William Henry Greenburg, "History of the Jews of Dallas," *Reform Advocate*, January 24, 1914; a copy of the article is available in the Dorothy M. and Harry S. Jacobus Temple Emanu-El Archives in Dallas (hereinafter TEAD). I thank archivist Gerry Cristol for her time, her help, and her patience.

110. "The Generosity of the Jews," *Dallas Herald*, September 27, 1873. The *Herald* story is also quoted in Cristol, *Light in the Prairie*, 37–38.

111. Patricia Evridge Hill, *Dallas*, 5.

112. "Mr. And Mrs. E. M. Kahn," *Dallas Daily Herald*, April 7, 1878, p. 1.

113. Cristol, *Light in the Prairie*, 8; Leon Harris, *Merchant Princes: An Intimate History of the Jewish Families Who Built Great Department Stores* (New York: Harper and Row, 1977), 159.

114. T. R. Burnett, *Confederate Rhymes* (Dallas: Johnston Printing Co., n.d). 13–14, Sam Merrill Collection, Folder A 455, DHS.

115. Scofield, *In Many Pulpits*, 26.

116. C. I. Scofield, *The Comprehensive Bible Course: Section I. The Scriptures. Lessons I–XIV.* (East Northfield, Mass: Published by Scofield, 1896), 19.

117. Scofield, *Old Scofield Study Bible*, 943, introductory comments to the Book of Jonah.

118. C. I. Scofield, "The Millennium: A Sermon Preached At The First Congregational Church, Dallas, Texas, Oct. 29, 1893," 58–59, SMCA. See also Scofield, *Old Scofield Study Bible*, 25, annotation to Gen. 15:18.

119. Scofield, *Old Scofield Study Bible*, 956, annotation to Hab. 2:3.

120. Ibid., 250, annotation to Deut. 30:3.

121. Boyer, *When Time Shall Be No More*, 220.

122. For an example of Old Testament promises by God to Israel see Gen. 15:1–7, 18, AV.

123. Scofield, *Dr. C. I. Scofield's Question Box*, 70.

124. Be Vier, *Biographical Sketch*, 94, 95–97; "Tributes Paid to Dr. C. I. Scofield: Three Memorial Services Held By His Friends in Dallas," *Dallas Morning News*, November 28, 1921.

125. Records of the First Congregational Church, Book 2, p. 92, SMCA.

CHAPTER THREE

1. "Society's Mirror," *Dallas Daily Times-Herald,* n.d., Alex Sanger Scrapbook, A3967 MSB, DHS. The news clipping is placed loosely between pages 8 and 9 of the scrapbook and probably dates from the 1890s.

2. Payne, *Dallas,* 83.

3. "Mr. Sanger's Industrial Education Idea," *Dallas Daily Times-Herald,* February 5, 1897, p. 4.

4. Patricia Evridge Hill, *Dallas,* xxii–xxv.

5. George Clifton Edwards, "Autobiographical Notes of George Clifton Edwards," 46–47, 97, George Clifton Edwards Papers, AR 165–1, Labor Archive, University of Texas at Arlington (hereinafter LA-UTA); biographical information is from Miriam Allen De-Ford, *On Being Concerned: The Vanguard Years of Carl and Laura Brannin* (Dallas: n.p., 1969), 23. Important works on Populism, with a strong emphasis on the movement in Texas, include Roscoe Coleman Martin, *The People's Party in Texas: A Study in Third Party Politics,* University of Texas Bulletin 3308 (Austin: University of Texas, 1933); Lawrence Goodwyn, *The Populist Moment: A Short History of the Agrarian Revolt in America* (New York: Oxford University Press, 1978); and Donna A. Barnes, *Farmers in Rebellion: The Rise and Fall of the Southern Farmers Alliance and Peoples' Party in Texas* (Austin: University of Texas Press, 1984). Goodwyn's work perhaps overly romanticizes the Populists but was a necessary antidote to the work of earlier historians like Richard Hofstadter, Seymour Martin Lipset, and Earl Raab, who—in response to pseudo-populists like Joseph McCarthy in the 1950s—depicted the People's Party as filled with bigoted, regressive rubes. Goodwyn portrays Populism as a true counterculture to nineteenth-century robber baron capitalism, arguing that leaders pursued visionary reforms that anticipated much of the New Deal. The classic study of socialism in Texas and neighboring states remains James R. Green's *Grass-Roots Socialism: Radical Movements in the Southwest, 1895–1943* (Baton Rouge: Louisiana State University Press, 1978).

6. DeFord, *On Being Concerned,* 9–10.

7. Patricia Evridge Hill, *Dallas,* 23–28, 184, n. 3.

8. Census Bureau, *Twelfth Census, 1900,* vol. 2, *Population,* part 2. (Washington D.C., 1902), 694.

9. Goodwyn, *Populist Moment,* 44–53.

10. Census Bureau, *Twelfth Census, 1900,* vol. 2, *Population,* part 2, 559.

11. Goodwyn, *Populist Moment,* 6, 15, 18–19, 122–123, 131–132, 137–138, 210, 280–283.

12. Patricia Evridge Hill, *Dallas,* 38–39, 47, 59.

13. Payne, *Big D,* 38; quote is in DeFord, *On Being Concerned,* 1.

14. Edwards, "Autobiographical Notes," 48.

15. "Principles, Platform, and Program of Socialist Party," *The Laborer,* August 1, 1908, p. 2.

16. George Clifton Edwards, "Who Are the Capitalists?" *The Laborer,* April 16, 1910, p. 1.

17. Patricia Evridge Hill, *Dallas,* 67–80.

18. Ibid., 83–85; *Dallas: The Open Shop City,* pamphlet, (Dallas: Dallas Open Shop Association, 1925), Dallas AFL-CIO Collection, AR 126-28-13, LA-UTA, 1, 2. The Mosher family joined the First Congregational Church on June 14, 1885. Theodore Mosher served as a deacon from 1887 to 1893 and was one of the authors of a November 15, 1893, letter thanking Cyrus Scofield for preaching the Gospel "in its fullness and in its purity." The relationship of the powerful Mosher family to Scofield suggests the confluence of the city's conservative clergy and their anti-reform, apolitical message with the economic agenda of business elites. See Paul DeHaven, "Records of the First Congregational Church of Dallas," computer print-out, 7, 21, 24–26, SMCA.

19. Patricia Evridge Hill, *Dallas,* 86–87.

20. Barr, *Black Texans,* 79–80; 134–136. For more on the Texas "white primary" law and its impact on African Americans see Conrey Bryson, *Dr. Lawrence A. Nixon and the White Primary* (El Paso: Texas Western Press, 1992), and Darlene Clark Hine, *Black Victory: The Rise and Fall of the White Primary in Texas* (Millwood, N.Y.: KTO Press, 1979). Hine does a particularly good job of explaining black disenfranchisement as an elite response to the challenge of Populism and of describing how elites modified franchise restrictions to allow voting by the state's significant Mexican American population in South Texas.

21. Patricia E. Gower, "Creating Consensus, Fostering Neglect: Municipal Policy in the Progressive Era," paper presented at the 104th annual meeting of the Texas State Historical Association, March 2, 2000, 2–28. The quote is on page 7.

22. Ibid., 8–11; the quotes are on pages 8 and 9.

23. David G. McComb, *Houston,* 93, 96–97; David Andrew Harmon, *Beneath the Image of the Civil Rights Movement and Race Relations: Atlanta, Georgia, 1946–1981* (New York: Garland Publishing, 1996), 3–37. Other important works on race and its impact on Atlanta's development include Hamer, *Urban Atlanta;* Robert D. Bullard, Glenn S. Johnson, and Angel O. Torres, eds., *Sprawl City: Race, Politics, and Planning in Atlanta* (Washington, D.C.: Island Press, 2000), and Clarence N. Stone, *Regime Politics: Governing Atlanta, 1946–1988* (Lawrence: University Press of Kansas, 1989).

24. Prince, *History of Dallas,* 29–30; Fairbanks, *For the City,* 29–30, 151–152; Barr, *Black Texans,* 140; Dulaney, "Whatever Happened," 69; David G. McComb, *Houston,* 108, 159. The best study on how African Americans dealt with segregation and racism in Houston is Howard Beeth and Cary D. Wintz, *Black Dixie: Afro-Texan History and Culture in Houston* (College Station: Texas A&M Press, 1992).

25. Payne, *Dallas,* 83.

26. Payne, *Big D,* 204, 214; quotes are in Joel Gregory, *Too Great A Temptation,* 38.

27. López, *White by Law,* 120–121, 132.

28. Fairbanks, *For the City,* 39–40.

29. Govenar and Brakesfield, *Deep Ellum,* xi, xix.

30. Prince, *History of Dallas,* 68.

31. Govenar and Brakesfield, *Deep Ellum,* xv, xix.

32. Lee Ballard, "The Rise and Decline of Deep Ellum," *Westward,* Sunday magazine of the *Dallas Times Herald,* September 25, 1983, 30.

33. Lewis Meriwether Dabney, *A Memoir and Letters* (New York: privately printed by J. J. Little and Ives Company, 1924), ix, 12, 16–17, 22–24.

34. Valentine J. Belfiglio, "Early Italian Settlers in Dallas: A New Life with Old Values," *Heritage News: A Journal Devoted to the History of North Central Texas* 10, no. 4 (winter, 1985–1986) 4–7; quotes are in Dabney, *Memoir and Letters,* 218. The Dallas Critic Club was founded by Rabbi William Henry Greenburg of Temple Emanu-El, George Bannerman Dealey, who by the 1930s was owner of the *Dallas Morning News,* and Cesar Lombardi, president of the A. H. Belo Corporation, parent company of the newspaper. For more on the influence of the Critic Club on Dallas history consult Michael V. Hazel, "The Critic Club: Sixty Years of Quiet Leadership," *Legacies: A History Journal for Dallas and North Central Texas* 2, no. 2 (fall 1990): 9–17. For a classic study on the reaction of "native" Anglo-Saxons to immigrants from southern and eastern Europe and the resulting immigration restrictions imposed on these groups in the 1920s see John Higham, *Strangers in the Land: Patterns of American Nativism, 1860–1925* (1955; reprint, New Brunswick, N.J.: Rutgers University Press, 1994), especially pages 234–330. Other key works on American nativism include Thomas Curran, *Xenophobia and Immigration, 1820–1930* (Boston: Twayne Publishers, 1975), and David M. Reimers, *Unwelcome Strangers: American Identity and the Turn against Immigration* (New York: Columbia University Press, 1998).

35. Dabney, *Memoir and Letters,* 214–215.

36. Ibid., 224.

37. Ibid., 147.

38. Ibid., 148.

39. *Texas Almanac for 1857* (1856; reprint, Irving, Texas: Glen's Sporting Goods, 1986), 69; Charles Carroll, *The Negro a Beast* (1900; reprint, New York: Books for Libraries Press, 1980); Dawley, *Struggles for Justice,* 162. For more on the impact of *The Birth of a Nation* see Everett Carter, "Cultural History Written with Lightning: The Significance of *The Birth of a Nation,*" *American Quarterly* 12 (fall 1960); Thomas Cripps, *Slow Fade to Black: The Negro in American Film, 1900–1942* (New York: Oxford University Press, 1993), especially pages 41–69; and John Hope Franklin, "*Birth of a Nation*—Propaganda as History," *Massachusetts Review* 20 (autumn 1979).

40. Albert E. McKinley, Arthur C. Howland, and Matthew L. Dann, *World History in the Making* (New York: American Book Co., 1927), 20. The Dallas Independent School District (DISD) Board approved this text for use May 20, 1930. See the DISD board minutes, vol. 20, p. 50. The minutes are archived at the DISD central administration building.

41. Carlton J. H. Hayes, Parker Thomas Moon, and John W. Wayland, *World History* (New York: MacMillan, 1935), 748–749. The Dallas Independent School District Board approved this text February 24, 1939. See the DISD Board minutes, vol. 25, p. 390.

42. Hayes, Moon, and Wayland, *World History,* 729.

43. Tera W. Hunter, *To 'Joy My Freedom: Southern Black Women's Lives and Labors after the Civil War* (Cambridge, Mass.: Harvard University Press, 1997), 187.

44. Justin F. Kimball, *Our City—Dallas: A Community Civics* (Dallas: Kessler Plan Association of Dallas, 1927), 197.

45. "A Stretcher," *Dallas Daily Herald,* August 30, 1874, p. 4.

46. John Henry Brown, *History of Dallas County*, 3–4, and Lindsley, *History of Greater Dallas*, 29.

47. De León, *They Called Them Greasers*, 17.

48. Ibid., 17, 67–68, 73–74. A Tejano is a person of Mexican heritage living in Texas.

49. Rodolfo Acuña, *Occupied America: A History of Chicanos* (New York: Harper-Collins Publishers, 1988) 10–11; Holly Beachley Brear, *Inherit the Alamo: Myth and Ritual at an American Shrine* (Austin: University of Texas Press, 1995), 35–37.

50. John Rosenfield Jr. and Jack Patton, illustrator, "Texas History Movies" (Dallas: PJM Publishers, n.d)., 1. The Magnolia Petroleum Company provided booklet versions of the cartoon series to the DISD, which the school board accepted on November 22, 1932. See the DISD Board minutes, vol. 22, 7.

51. Rosenfield and Patton, "Texas History Movies," 170.

52. Ibid., 174; Brear, *Inherit the Alamo*, 37–38.

53. López, *White by Law*, 61–62; Guadalupe San Miguel Jr., *Brown, not White: School Integration and the Chicano Movement in Houston* (College Station: Texas A&M University Press, 2001), 24.

54. Robert Ryer Schermerhorn, "An Occupational History of Mexican Americans in Dallas, 1930–1950," (master's thesis, Southern Methodist University, 1973), 13–14, 20–21; Walter T. Watson, "Mexicans in Dallas," *Southwest Review* 22, no. 4 (July 1937): 406, 408, 410; Payne, *Big D*, 72.

55. James Diego Vigil, *From Indians to Chicanos: The Dynamics of Mexican American Culture* (Prospect Heights, Ill.: Waveland Press, 1980), 129. In addition to Arnoldo de León's earlier cited work, important recent monographs on Mexican Americans in Texas and the development of racial identity within that community include Douglas E. Foley, Clarice Mota, Donald E. Post, and Ignacio Lozano, *From Peones to Politicos: Ethnic Relations in a South Texas Town, 1900–1977* (Austin: University of Texas Center for Mexican American Studies, 1977); Douglas E. Foley, *Learning Capitalist Culture: Deep in the Heart of Tejas* (Philadelphia: University of Pennsylvania Press, 1990); Neil Foley, *White Scourge;* and Montejano, *Anglos and Mexicans*.

56. Montejano, *Anglos and Mexicans*, 160.

57. Watson, "Mexicans in Dallas," 406–407, 410; Gwendolyn Rice, "Little Mexico and the Barrios of Dallas," *Legacies: A History Journal for Dallas and North Central Texas* 4, no. 2 (fall 1992): 22.

58. Kimball, *Our City*, 198–199.

59. Ibid., 199.

60. Gwendolyn Rice, "Little Mexico," 23–24; Shirley Achor, *Mexican Americans in a Dallas Barrio* (Tucson: University of Arizona Press, 1991), 62–63. City leaders routed the North Dallas Tollway through Little Mexico in the 1960s, splintering the barrio. Construction of Woodall Rodgers Freeway destroyed the southern end of the neighborhood in the 1970s. The neighborhood's population declined from a high of 8,000 to about 1,700, but the few remaining residents, ironically, became relatively wealthy in the 1980s when they sold their land to real estate developers bent on gentrification. See Payne, *Big D*, 344, and Gwendolyn Rice, "Little Mexico," 27.

61. Medrano quoted in Williams and Shay, *Time Change*, 63.

62. Ibid., 64.

63. "Civic Responsibility: An Appeal Addressed to the Thoughtful Citizen for Better Housing Conditions and Environment of the Poor in Dallas," George Dealey Papers, A6667, Folder 332, 2–3, DHS.

64. Ibid., 3.

65. Ibid., 4.

66. López, *White by Law*, 38; Edward J. Larson, *Sex, Race, and Science: Eugenics in the Deep South* (Baltimore: Johns Hopkins University Press, 1995), 1, 17, 33–39, 100. In addition to Larson's excellent monograph, the best historical treatments of eugenics are Elazar Barkan, *The Retreat of Scientific Racism: Changing Concepts of Race in Britain and the United States between the World Wars* (New York: Cambridge University Press, 1992), and Stephen Jay Gould, *The Mismeasure of Man* (New York: W. W. Norton, 1981).

67. For newspaper coverage leading up to the contest see "Better Babies Show," advertising copy, *Dallas Daily Times-Herald*, October 11, 1914, sec. 1, p. 14; "Prizes Offered for The Baby Show," *Dallas Daily Times-Herald*, October 26, 1914, sec. 1, p. 1; "Wednesday Is Big Day for Baby Contest," *Dallas Daily Times-Herald*, October 27, 1914, sec. 1, p. 3; "Bright Sunshine and Varied Features Bring Big Crowd to the Fair: Better Baby Contest Is Drawing Card," *Dallas Daily Times-Herald*, October 28, 1914, sec. 1, p. 1. For more on the contest see Nancy Wiley, *The Great State Fair of Texas: An Illustrated History* (Dallas: Taylor Publishing Co., 2000), 73.

68. Chip Berlet and Matthew N. Lyons, *Right-Wing Populism in America: Too Close for Comfort* (New York: Guilford Press, 2000), 94.

69. "Girl Child Makes Best Test Marks: Grace Gulden, Dallas County, Winner of Sweepstakes. Two Perfect Boys," *Dallas Daily Times-Herald*, October 28, 1914, sec. 1, p. 4.

70. Grant, *Passing of the Great Race*, 12.

71. Ibid., 6.

72. Ibid., 7; Larson, *Sex, Race, and Science*, 1.

73. Kimball, *Our City*, 218.

74. Dabney, *Memoir and Letters*, 195–196.

75. Ibid., 88.

76. Ibid., 215.

77. Ibid., 214.

78. Ibid., 216.

79. Ibid., 177.

80. Ibid., 232.

81. James Truslow Adams and Charles Garrett Vannest, *The Record of America* (Dallas: Charles Scribner's Sons, 1935), 12–14. The DISD Board approved this text February 24, 1939. See DISD Board minutes, vol. 25, 390. Other Dallas-approved textbooks openly praised authoritarian regimes such as the fascist government led by Benito Mussolini for crushing labor unrest and restoring law and order. See James Harvey Robinson and Emma Peters Smith with James Breasted, *Our World Today and Yesterday: A History of*

Modern Civilization (Dallas: Ginn and Co., 1924), 620. This text was approved by the Dallas Independent School Board on May 20, 1930. See the DISD Board minutes, vol. 20, p. 50.

82. Adams and Vannest, *Record of America,* 702.

83. Eric Foner, *Reconstruction: America's Unfinished Revolution, 1863–1877* (New York: Harper and Row, Perennial Library, 1988), 609–610. These textbooks were written, in part, by a clique of historians born in the South and trained by Confederate apologist William Dunning of Columbia University. Such textbooks, Foner writes, reinforced Southern opposition to desegregation and rationalized violence against blacks as necessary to keep African Americans in their place. Among the Dunningite textbooks used by the Dallas School District was David Saville Muzzey's *History of the American People* (Dallas: Ginn and Co., 1929). The Dallas School Board approved the Muzzey text April 23, 1929. See the DISD Board minutes, vol. 19, 12. W. E. B. DuBois effectively demolished the racist mythology created by the Dunningites concerning Reconstruction with his *Black Reconstruction in America, 1860–1880* (1935; reprint, New York: Simon and Schuster, Touchstone, 1995). Sadly, white academics ignored this black scholar's groundbreaking work for almost two decades. Kenneth M. Stampp began in earnest the deconstruction of Reconstruction with *The Era of Reconstruction: 1865–1877* (New York: Random House, Vintage Books, 1965). Significant recent works include Foner's masterful study, *Reconstruction,* and Leon F. Litwack's *Been in the Storm So Long: The Aftermath of Slavery* (New York: Random House, Vintage Books, 1979). For a good local study of Texas under Reconstruction see Randolph B. Campbell, *A Southern Community in Crisis: Harrison County, Texas, 1850–1880* (Austin: Texas State Historical Association, 1983).

84. Ivan Hannaford, *Race: The History of an Idea in the West* (Baltimore: Woodrow Wilson Center Press for Johns Hopkins University Press, 1996).

85. See the DISD Board minutes, vol. 15, 268–269.

86. A. W. Castle, *Reader and Guide for New Americans,* book 2 (New York: MacMillan, 1924), 12.

87. Ibid., 131.

88. Watson, "Mexicans in Dallas," 418.

CHAPTER FOUR

1. Payne, *Big D,* 39; Todd Bensman, "'The Time Is Right': Truth sought in 1910 mob killing of black man," *Dallas Morning News,* March 3, 1999, sec. A.

2. Payne, *Big D,* 39; Bensman, "'Time Is Right,'" *Dallas Morning News;* quotes are from Edwards, "Autobiographical Notes," 106–107; David William Livingston, "The Lynching of Negroes in Texas, 1900–1925" (master's thesis, East Texas State University, 1972), 87–88.

3. Payne, *Big D;* Bensman, "'Time Is Right'"; quotes are from Edwards, "Autobiographical Notes," 106–107; Livingston, "Lynching of Negroes."

4. Willie Newbury Lewis, *Willie, a Girl from a Town Called Dallas* (College Station: Texas A&M University Press, 1984); Payne, *Big D*, 39.

5. Hale, *Making Whiteness*, 168–230.

6. Patricia Evridge Hill, *Dallas*, 91–100; Census Bureau, *Fourteenth Census, 1920* (Washington, D.C., 1921), vol. 1, *Population*, 72, and vol. 4, *Population—Occupations*, 150, 152, 154, 156, 158, 160, 162, 164, 166, 173.

7. Jacquelyn Dowd Hall, *Revolt against Chivalry: Jessie Daniel Ames and the Women's Campaign against Lynching* (New York: Columbia University Press, 1993), 134–135.

8. Jacquelyn Dowd Hall, "'The Mind that Burns in Each Body': Women, Rape, and Racial Violence," *Southern Exposure* 12, no. 6 (1984): 62.

9. Ibid., 64.

10. Sumners quoted in Livingston, "Lynching of Negroes," 104–105.

11. Jacquelyn Dowd Hall, "'Mind that Burns,'" 64.

12. Ibid. Besides Jacquelyn Dowd Hall's monographs, important studies on how sexual and racial ideology in the United States reinforce each other include Paula Giddings, *When and Where I Enter: The Impact of Black Women on Race and Sex in America* (New York: Bantam Books, 1985); Martha Elizabeth Hodes, *White Women, Black Men: Illicit Sex in the Nineteenth-Century South* (New Haven: Yale University Press, 1997); Martha Elizabeth Hodes, ed., *Sex, Love, Race: Crossing Boundaries in North American History* (New York: New York University Press, 1999); and Nancy MacLean, *Behind the Mask of Chivalry: The Making of the Second Ku Klux Klan* (New York: Oxford University Press, 1994). See also Neil Foley's chapter "The Whiteness of Manhood: Women, Gender Identity, and 'Men's Work' on the Farm" in his *White Scourge*, 141–162. Hodes argues that that prior to Emancipation the gap between black slavery and white freedom reinforced the semiotic meanings attached to color, thus sustaining white supremacy. With the end of the "Peculiar Institution," categories of color alone bore the burden of maintaining racial hierarchy. An ambiguously defined mixed-race population thus appeared particularly threatening in the post-Emancipation age. The political need for clear black and white racial groupings encouraged the use of violence to suppress miscegenation. See Hodes, *White Women*, 147.

13. Ayers, *Promise of the New South*, 158.

14. "Will The Federal Suffrage Amendment Complicate the Race Problem?," leaflet distributed by the National Literature Headquarters, Congressional Union for Woman Suffrage, n.d. Negative Collection, Box 11, DHS, A42.200.

15. Sigmund Freud, *Civilization and Its Discontents* (New York: W. W. Norton, 1961), 38. The literature on American industrialization's impact on working-class identity and culture is vast. In addition to Saxton's *Rise and Fall*, the most important works are Lawrence W. Levine's *Highbrow/Lowbrow: The Emergence of Cultural Hierarchy in America* (Cambridge: Harvard University Press, 1988) and Eric Lott's *Love and Theft: Blackface Minstrelsy and the American Working Class* (New York: Oxford University Press, 1993).

16. Vivian Anderson Castleberry, *Daughters of Dallas: A History of Greater Dallas through the Voices and Deeds of Its Women* (Dallas: Odenwald Press, 1994), 39–47; Evelyn Miller Pierce, *Hilltop* (New York: Alfred H. King, 1931), 37–39. Two of W. B. Miller's slaves

were implicated in the 1860 fire that destroyed much of downtown Dallas. See Chapter One for more details.

17. Will Accoe, *Ma Dandy Soldier Coon* (New York: Jos. W. Stearn and Co., 1900); John T. Hall, *Looney Coons* (New York: John T. Hall Music Publishing Company, 1900); J. M. Scales, *Coon Time Rag* (Dallas: Thos. Goggan and Bro., 1903); Andrew Sterling and Howard and Emerson, *My Georgia Lady Love* (New York: T. B. Harms and Co., 1899). The music sheets were recovered from 438 South Westmoreland Avenue in Oak Cliff (Becky Spicer, telephone interview by author, October 24, 2000; the author thanks Ms. Spicer for her invaluable insight and help in recovering this material). For an example of minstrelsy in the area in the late 1950s and early 1960s see "Club Activities," *Dallas Morning News,* February 24, 1959, sec. 4. The Kiwanis Club in Richardson was reported as continuing rehearsals for a minstrel show. Richardson is a suburb just north of Dallas. For more on the mixture of hate and envy African Americans inspired in white America see Lott, *Love and Theft*, and Saxton, *Rise and Fall*, particularly pages 118, 123, 165–180, 170–171, 184 and 325.

18. Payne, *Big D,* 73–74.

19. Wyn Craig Wade, *The Fiery Cross: The Ku Klux Klan in America* (New York: Simon and Schuster, Touchstone, 1987), 57–59, 80–111; David M. Chalmers, *Hooded Americanism: The History of the Ku Klux Klan* (Durham, N.C.: Duke University Press, 1987), 19; Jack Hurst, *Nathan Bedford Forrest: A Biography* (New York: Alfred A. Knopf, 1993), 286–287.

20. Williamson, *Rage for Order,* 240–241.

21. Rockoff, "Jewish Racial Identity," 266–277.

22. Williamson, *Rage for Order,* 243–244.

23. Ibid., 244.

24. Wade, *Fiery Cross,* 140–145.

25. Chalmers, *Hooded Americanism,* 22–38; Wade, *Fiery Cross,* 119–166. Wade's and Chalmers' works extensively treat the impact of the Mary Phagan murder on the development of the "second" Klan. For more on the Mary Phagan case and its impact on American anti-Semitism and black-Jewish relations see Leonard Dinnerstein, *The Leo Frank Case* (1968; reprint, Athens: University of Georgia Press, 1987); Robert Seitz Frey and Nancy Thompson-Frey, *The Silent and the Damned: the Murder of Mary Phagan and the Lynching of Leo Frank* (Lanham, Md.: Madison Books, 1988); and Jeffrey Paul Melnick, *Black-Jewish Relations on Trial: Leo Frank and Jim Conley in the New South* (Jackson: University Press of Mississippi, 2000).

26. Chalmers, *Hooded Americanism,* 31–35, 39, 162–174, 291. In addition to Chalmers' and Wade's classic studies of the Ku Klux Klan phenomena, consult Patsy Sims' *The Klan* (Lexington: University Press of Kentucky, 1996) for a more contemporary treatment. Nancy MacLean offers a study of the Klan's gender ideology in *Behind the Mask of Chivalry*. Charles C. Alexander authored two important regional studies of the Klan—*Crusade for Conformity: The Ku Klux Klan in Texas, 1920–1930* (Houston: Texas Gulf Coast Historical Association, 1962) and *The Ku Klux Klan in the Southwest* (Lexington: University of Kentucky Press, 1966). Norman D. Brown produced the best study of the impact of the Ku Klux Klan on 1920s Texas politics in his *Hood, Bonnet, and Little Brown Jug: Texas Poli-*

tics. 1921–1928 (College Station: Texas A&M University Press, 1984). The Dallas Klan also gets considerable attention in Kenneth T. Jackson, *The Ku Klux Klan in the City, 1915–1930* (New York: Oxford University Press, 1967).

27. "Klan Lecture at Palace Sunday Drew Capacity Audience," *Corsicana (Texas) Daily Sun*, May 1, 1922.

28. David Ritz, "Inside the Jewish Establishment," *D: The Magazine of Dallas*, November 1975, 53–54.

29. Payne, *Big D*, 75–77; Patricia Evridge Hill, *Dallas*, 101.

30. Payne, *Big D*, 75–77. One of the city's highways is now named after former Klansman R. L. Thornton.

31. Norman D. Brown, *Hood, Bonnet*, 53.

32. Payne, *Big D*, 93; Kenneth T. Jackson, *Ku Klux Klan*, 77.

33. *Dallas Daily Times-Herald* quoted in Payne, *Big D*, 79; Patricia Evridge Hill, *Dallas*, 101–102.

34. Lois E. Torrence, "The Ku Klux Klan in Dallas (1915–1928): An American Paradox" (master's thesis, Southern Methodist University, 1948), 65.

35. Payne, *Big D*, 77–82; Torrence, "Ku Klux Klan in Dallas," 63.

36. Ernest Sharpe, *G. B. Dealey of the Dallas News* (New York: Henry Holt and Company, 1955), 198; Patricia Evridge Hill, *Dallas*, 102.

37. Norman D. Brown, *Hood, Bonnet*, 49.

38. Mary Gue, composer, and Walter Ardrell Riggs, arranger, "Ku Klux Kismet" (Aransas Pass, Texas: Walter Ardrell Riggs, 1924); Charles C. Alexander, *Ku Klux Klan in the Southwest* (Lexington: University of Kentucky Press, 1965), 93; Dave Garrett, "Battle for the Hearts and Minds," 5; Alexander, *Crusade for Conformity*, 36.

39. See for example Chalmers, *Hooded Americanism*, 5, 51, 143, 145, 155–157, 316.

40. "Klan Discovers Effort To Destroy American Unity," *Texas 100 Per Cent American*, October 6, 1922, p. 2 (DPL).

41. Cited in Norman D. Brown, *Hood, Bonnet*, 53.

42. F. L. Sherrill, letter "dedicated to the greater interest of Dallas Morning News," February 18, 1922, Greenville, Texas, George B. Dealey Collection, A6667, Folder 314, DHS.

43. "Read This: A Statement in Regard to the Candidacy of Earle B. Mayfield," George B. Dealey Collection, A6667, Folder 317, DHS.

44. Cited in Norman D. Brown, *Hood, Bonnet*, 117.

45. "To the White Laboring Men of the City of Dallas," *Texas 100 Per Cent American*, March 30, 1923, p. 4.

46. Neil Foley provides an excellent discussion of the intersection of gender and race in *White Scourge*, 141–162, as does Hale, *Making Whiteness*, 85–120.

47. Payne, *Big D*, 77.

48. Census Bureau, *Twelfth Census, 1900*, vol. 2, *Population*, part 2, 784, 787; Census Bureau, *Fourteenth Census, 1920*, vol. 2, *Population, General Report and Analytical Tables*, 732–733.

49. "Timely Advice to the Railroad Workers of Texas," *Texas 100 Per Cent American,* September 22, 1922, p. 1.

50. "Now, Perhaps, We'll Get Some Harmony," *Texas Kourier,* December 12, 1924, p. 4.

51. "Imperial Wizard Evans' Great Speech," *Texas 100 Per Cent American,* October 26, 1923, pp. 3–4.

52. Ibid.

53. For more on the Klan's manipulation of labor issues and progressive politics in other communities and its conflict with conservative organizations see Robert Alan Goldberg, *Hooded Empire: The Ku Klux Klan in Colorado* (Urbana: University of Illinois Press, 1981), 121, 129; William Pencak, *For God and Country: The American Legion, 1919–1941* (Boston: Northeastern University Press, 1989), 108; and Shawn Lay, ed., *The Invisible Empire in the West: Toward a New Historical Appraisal of the Ku Klux Klan of the 1920s* (Urbana: University of Illinois, 1992).

54. Dallas County Citizens League, "The Case against the Ku Klux Klan," pamphlet (Dallas: Venney, 1922), 6, CAH.

55. Norman D. Brown, *Hood, Bonnet,* 55; Carrie Kearney and Nora Crane, interview by Toni Perry, tape recording, June 1974 and March 6, 1976, University of Texas at Dallas Oral History Project, Texas/Dallas History and Archives Division, J. Erik Jonsson Central Library, DPL; *New Handbook of Texas,* 1996, s.v. "Martin McNulty Crane."

56. Dallas County Citizens League, "The Case against the Ku Klux Klan," 7–8.

57. Cited in Patricia Evridge Hill, *Dallas,* 101.

58. "Imperial Wizard Evans' Great Speech," *Texas 100 Per Cent American.*

59. Ibid.

60. E. Haldeman-Julius, *Is the Ku Klux Klan Constructive or Destructive? A Debate between Wizard Evans, Israel Zangwill, and Others* (Girard, Kansas: Haldeman-Julius Co., 1924), 12. Nordicism — the belief that northern Europeans were superior not only to blacks and other people of color but also superior to other Europeans — was most completely explicated in three tomes that greatly influenced American immigration policy in the 1920s and 1930s: Grant's *Passing of the Great Race* and Lothrop Stoddard's *The Rising Tide of Color* and *The Revolt Against Civilization.* Combined, these books helped persuade the U.S. Congress to sharply reduce immigration from southern and eastern Europe.

61. Sister Paul of the Cross McGrath, "Political Nativism in Texas, 1825–1860" (Ph.D. diss., Catholic University of America, 1930), 99, 162, 177.

62. "THE AMERICAN PARTY," *Texas State Times,* September 15, 1855, p. 1.

63. Riley, *History of the Baptists,* 222–223. Baptists ranked a distant second in number to the Methodist Church at the time of the Civil War but had become the state's largest denomination by 1906. Baptists remained Texas' largest religious group until 1990, when the Catholic Church overtook their ranking. See *New Handbook of Texas,* 1996, s.v. "Baptist Church."

64. Scofield, *Old Scofield Study Bible,* 18, footnote to Gen. 11:1, 1332, footnote to Rev. 1:20, 1332, footnote to Rev. 18:2, 1346.

65. "The Great Scarlet Woman Is Trying To Seduce America," *Texas 100 Per Cent American,* June 16, 1922, p.1.

66. H. W. Evans, "The Public School Problem in America," pamphlet (United States: Ku Klux Klan, 1924), 15–16, CAH.

67. "Klan Lecture at Palace," *Corsicana (Texas) Daily Sun,* May 1, 1922.

68. Steve Landregan, interview by author, Dallas, Texas, August 3, 1999; Ken Eppes, "St. Peter the Apostle Parish: Marker to Honor History of Service to the Disenfranchised," *Parish,* September 20, 1996, 5; "Background Information—St. Peter Academy," Roman Catholic Diocese of Dallas archives (hereinafter RCD). Steve Landregan has long been a press spokesperson and archivist for the Roman Catholic Diocese in Dallas. The author thanks him for his vast knowledge and openness.

69. "Canonical Report of St. Peter's Church, Dallas, Texas, November 15, 1924," RCD.

70. Leo Lacone and others, letter to the Most Rev. Joseph P. Lynch, D.D., January 22, 1940, Dallas, Texas, RCD.

71. "Black Priests of Rome," *Texas 100 Per Cent American,* June 23, 1922, p. 1.

72. "The 'Social Equality Tree' Is Bearing Its Fruit," *Texas 100 Per Cent American,* June 2, 1922, p. 1.

73. Landregan interview.

74. Ibid.; Sister Mary Paul Valdez, *Hispanic Catholics in the Diocese of Dallas, 1890–1990* (Dallas: 1991?), 5–7, 12–15.

75. "Can It Be Possible the Sharp Jew Is Being Hoodwinked?" *Texas 100 Per Cent American,* December 1, 1922, p. 4.

76. Marilynn Wood Hill, "A History of the Jewish Involvement in the Dallas Community," (master's thesis, Southern Methodist University, 1967), 45.

77. Ibid., 51–54; Payne, *Big D,* 80–82.

78. Designating dates as B.C. (Before Christ) or A.D. (Anno Domini, or Year of Our Lord) privileges Christianity and is increasingly inappropriate for scholars as non-Christian groups such as Buddhists, Muslims, and Jews become more numerous. Non-Christian writers in the United States often substitute the phrase B.C.E. (Before Common Era) for B.C. and C.E. (Common Era) for A.D.; otherwise, the dating system is identical. In this system, for instance, the Declaration of Independence would be dated July 4, 1776 C.E. rather than 1776 A.D. For more on this usage see Chaim Potok, *Wanderings: Chaim Potok's History of the Jews* (New York: Fawcett Crest, 1978), 20.

79. Michael Barkun has written an excellent history of British Israelism, a theology that spawned the so-called Christian Identity movement common among later American racist right-wing groups such as Aryan Nations; see Barkun, *Religion and the Racist Right: The Origins of the Christian Identity Movement* (Chapel Hill: University of North Carolina Press, 1994).

80. "The Slick Propaganda Work of Rome," *Texas 100 Per Cent American,* August 18, 1922, p. 4. For another example of British Israelism in the 1920s Dallas Klan see "Our Flag in Prophecy Or the Number Thirteen," *Texas 100 Per Cent American,* February 9, 1923, p. 3.

81. S. Webb, letter to Colonel G. B. Dealey, Albany, Texas, April 25, 1922, George B. Dealey Collection, A6667, Folder 314, DHS.

82. Torrence, "Ku Klux Klan in Dallas," 53–54.

83. Marilynn Wood Hill, "History," 51–54; Payne, *Big D*, 80–82, 163; Norman D. Brown, 215; Ritz, "Inside the Jewish Establishment," *D: The Magazine of Dallas*, 53.

84. Cited in Norman D. Brown, *Hood, Bonnet*, 215.

85. Mark Bauman, introduction to Bauman and Kalin, *Quiet Voices*, 8–9; Mark Dollinger, " 'Hamans' and 'Torquemadas': Southern and Northern Jewish Responses to the Civil Rights Movement, 1945–1965," in *Quiet Voices;* 67–75.

86. Marilynn Wood Hill, "History of the Jewish Involvement," 85–87.

87. Cristol, *Light in the Prairie*, 85–91.

88. Ritz, "Inside the Jewish Establishment," *D: The Magazine of Dallas*, 54.

89. Ibid.

90. Marilynn Wood Hill, "History," 115.

91. John William Rogers Jr., *Judge Lynch, A Drama in One Act* (New York: Samuel French, 1924), 7–8.

92. Ibid., 15–16.

93. Ibid., 16.

94. Ibid., 19.

95. Ibid., 19.

96. Ibid., 21.

97. Payne, *Big D*, 123.

98. Ibid., 82–87, 90–93.

99. Norman D. Brown, *Hood, Bonnet*, 231.

100. Payne, *Big D*, 95.

101. Norman D. Brown, *Hood, Bonnet*, 252.

102. Patricia Evridge Hill, *Dallas*, 105.

103. Payne, *Big D*, 96.

104. *New Handbook of Texas*, 1996, s.v. "Jessie Harriet Daniel Ames."

105. Jacquelyn Dowd Hall, " 'Mind that Burns,' " 66.

CHAPTER FIVE

1. Bill Neff, telephone interview by author, September 28, 1999. The author is indebted to Bill Neff, a Dallas-area wood sculptor of considerable talent, for his poetic description of the bois d'arc tree.

2. Schutze, *Accommodation*.

3. Black schools and educators played a contradictory role in the development of the African American community. The segregated school sometimes served as a training ground for dissent and sometimes as an indoctrination center for collaboration with Jim Crow. For more on the history of black education in America and the role of the pre-

desegregation schools in African American politics and culture see James D. Anderson, *The Education of Blacks in the South, 1860–1935* (Chapel Hill: University of North Carolina Press, 1988); Allen B. Ballard, *The Education of Black Folk: The Afro-American Struggle for Knowledge in White America* (New York: Harper and Row, 1973); and Donald Spivey, *Schooling for the New Slavery: Black Industrial Education, 1868–1915* (Westport, Conn.: Greenwood Press, 1978).

4. John Mason Brewer, "Apostolic," *Heralding Dawn: An Anthology of Verse* (Dallas: June Thomason Printing, 1936), 6.

5. Michael Lowery Gillette, "The NAACP in Texas, 1937–1957" (Ph.D. diss., University of Texas at Austin, 1984), 2; *New Handbook of Texas*, 1996, s.v. "Longview, Texas (Gregg County)"; Barr, *Black Texans*, 138–139.

6. Dulaney, "Whatever Happened," 69; Gillette, "NAACP in Texas," 3.

7. Peter Kurilecz, compiler, and Cindy C. Smolovik, archivist, *Dallas Negro Chamber of Commerce Collection Register and Researcher's Guide*, 1985, p. 1, Texas/Dallas History and Archives Division, DPL.

8. Ibid.

9. Tyler and Murphy, *Slave Narratives*, 83. The biographical information comes from page 128.

10. Ibid., 84.

11. Melville J. Herskovits virtually pioneered the study of West African culture and its enduring influence on African American society and religion in *The Myth of the Negro Past* (Boston: Beacon Press, 1941). Responding to racist history and anthropology that portrayed slaves as culturally empty vessels shaped almost entirely by the civilization of their white masters, Herskovits launched a debate among scholars concerning the degree to which black culture in the United States is "African" or "American." Sterling Stuckey's *Slave Culture: Nationalist Theory and the Foundations of Black America* (New York: Oxford University Press, 1987) brilliantly outlines the similarities between West African societies and American slave culture. Other important studies of African American religion are Eugene D. Genovese, *Roll, Jordan, Roll: The World the Slaves Made* (New York: Vintage Books, 1976); Lawrence W. Levine, *Black Culture and Black Consciousness: Afro-American Folk Thought from Slavery To Freedom* (New York: Oxford University Press, 1977); Albert J. Raboteau, *Slave Religion: The "Invisible Institution" in the Antebellum South* (New York: Oxford University Press, 1978); and Mechal Sobel, *Trabelin' On: The Slave Journey to an Afro-Baptist Faith* (Princeton, N.J.: Princeton University Press, 1988).

12. Tyler and Murphy, *Slave Narratives*, 83. The biographical information is available on 135–136.

13. Stuckey, *Slave Culture*, 11.

14. Ibid., 11–12, 15–16.

15. Ibid., 11.

16. Tyler and Murphy, *Slave Narratives*, 71. Biographical information is available on page 134.

17. Stuckey, *Slave Culture*, 21, 67. Walter F. Pitts suggests that the structure of twentieth-century Afro-Texan Baptist church services not only reflects African origins but

also provides a catharsis for adherents. Worshippers pass from a constraining portion of the service dominated by European music motifs that Pitts labels the "Devotion" ritual frame to the emotional release of the "Service" ritual frame, which is dominated by ring shouts, African-style chants, and black folk music. The weekly church experience thus recapitulates for Afro-Texans the experience of passing from slavery and white control to freedom. See Walter F. Pitts Jr., *Old Ship of Zion: The Afro-Baptist Ritual in the African Diaspora* (New York: Oxford University Press, 1993).

18. Payne, *Big D*, 41, 175.

19. Prince, *History of Dallas*, 97.

20. James Byrd, *J. Mason Brewer: Negro Folklorist* (Austin: Steck-Vaughn Co., 1967), 1–4; *New Handbook of Texas*, 1996, s.v. "John Mason Brewer"; Brewer, *Heralding Dawn*, 3.

21. Brewer's collections include *The Word on the Brazos: Negro Preacher Tales from the Brazos Bottoms of Texas* (Austin: University of Texas Press, 1953); *Aunt Dicy Tales: Snuff-Dipping Tales of the Texas Negro* (Austin: privately published, 1956); *Dog Ghosts and Other Texas Negro Folk Tales* (Austin: University of Texas Press, 1958); and *American Negro Folklore* (Chicago: Quadrangle Books, 1968). See also John Mason Brewer, "John Tales," in J. Frank Dobie, ed., *Mexican Border Ballads and Other Lore*, vol. 31 (Austin: Texas Folklore Society, 1946), 101.

22. Brewer, "The Hays County Courthouse Janitor," *Dog Ghosts*, 25–26.

23. Patricia Evridge Hill, *Dallas*, xxiv.

24. Glenn M. Linden, *Desegregating Schools in Dallas: Four Decades in the Federal Courts* (Dallas: Three Forks Press, 1995), 2–3; Dulaney, "Whatever Happened," 70.

25. "In Loving Memoriam of Dr. John Leslie Patton, Jr.," funeral card, Dallas Independent School District Central Administration Office.

26. Larry Grove, "Poor Larry's Almanack: Dr. J. L. Patton To Be Honored," *Dallas Morning News*, December 13, 1962, sec. 1.

27. Ibid.

28. John Leslie Patton, *Negro History: Outline for Pupils* (Dallas: Dallas Public Schools, 1939), Forward, A86.50, DHS.

29. John Leslie Patton, *Negro History*, 12.

30. Ibid., 15.

31. Ibid., forward.

32. Ibid., 38.

33. Jesse O. Thomas, *Negro Participation in the Texas Centennial Exposition* (Boston: Christopher Publishing House, 1938), 17.

34. William Douglas Turner Jr., "The *Dallas Express* as a Forum on Lynching, 1919–1921" (master's thesis, East Texas State University, 1974), 38–40.

35. Ibid., 25. For another history of the *Express* consult Louis Margot III, "The *Dallas Express*: A Negro Newspaper. Its History, 1892–1971, and Its Point of View," (master's thesis, East Texas State University, 1971).

36. William Douglas Turner, "*Dallas Express*," 124–125.

37. Payne, *Big D*, 71–72. For more on the condition of black housing in this period see Chapter Three.

38. Prince, *History of Dallas,* 95.

39. Payne, *Big D,* 144.

40. Fairbanks, *For the City,* 90; Roger Biles, "The New Deal in Dallas," *Southwestern Historical Quarterly* 95, no. 1 (July 1991): 7–8, 15; Prince, *History of Dallas,* 87–88; DeFord, *On Being Concerned,* 29; Patricia Evridge Hill, *Dallas,* 129.

41. Williams and Shay, *Time Change,* 62; DeFord, *On Being Concerned,* 30.

42. Carl Brannin, interview by Dr. George Green, Dallas, April 12, 1967, transcription, pp. 4–5, 14, Oral History Project, OH1, Division of Archives and Manuscripts, LA-UTA.

43. Brannin interview, 5–11; Patricia Evridge Hill, *Dallas,* 146.

44. Walter C. Reilly, interview by Dr. George Green, Dallas, Texas, July 29, 1971, transcription, p. 38, OH10, LA-UTA.

45. John W. "Preacher" Hays, interview by unknown person, Mabank, Texas, August 1 and August 7, 1976, transcription, p. 38, OH67, LA-UTA. Key scholarly works on the obstacles to successful biracial unions include James R. Green, "The Brotherhood of Timber Workers, 1910–1913: A Radical Response to Industrial Capitalism in the Southern U.S.A.," *Past and Present* 60 (August 1973); Herbert G. Gutman, "The Negro and the United Mine Workers of America: The Career and Letters of Richard L. Davis and Something of Their Meaning: 1890–1900," in Julius Jacobson, ed., *The Negro and the American Labor Movement* (Garden City, N.Y.: Anchor Books, 1968); and Paul B. Worthman and James R. Green, "Black Workers in the New South," in Nathan Higgins, Martin Kilson, and Daniel Fox, eds., *Key Issues in the Afro-American Experience,* vol. 2 (New York: Harcourt, Brace, Jovanovich, 1971).

46. Hays interview, 37.

47. Payne, *Big D,* 177–179; A. Maceo Smith, interview by Gayle Tomlinson, tape recording, Dallas, January 12, 1978, Dallas Public Library Oral History Project, DPL; W. Marvin Dulaney, "The Progressive Voters League: A Political Voice for African Americans in Dallas," *Legacies: A History Journal for Dallas and North Central Texas* 3, no. 1 (spring 1991): 28–29; Gillette, "NAACP in Texas," 5–6.

48. A. Maceo Smith interview.

49. Barr, *Black Texans,* 135–136.

50. Dulaney, "Progressive Voters League," 27–29.

51. Ibid., 29; Fairbanks, *For the City,* 105–106.

52. A. Maceo Smith interview; Payne, *Big D,* 179–180; Ragsdale, *Centennial '36,* 70–71.

53. James David Boswell, "Negro Participation in the 1936 Texas Centennial Exposition," (master's report, University of Texas, 1969), 8–14; A. Maceo Smith interview. How racial ideology shapes fairs and expositions is considered in Raymond Corbey, "Ethnographic Showcases, 1870–1930," *Cultural Anthropology* 8 (1993); Robert Rydell, *All the World's a Fair: Visions of Empire. International Expositions, 1876–1916* (Chicago: University of Chicago Press, 1984); Paul A. Tenkotte, "Kaleidoscopes of the World: International Exhibitions and the Concept of Cultural Space, 1851–1915," *American Studies* 28, no. 1 (1987); and Mauricio Tenorio-Trillo, *Mexico at the World's Fairs: Crafting a Modern Nation* (Berkeley: University of California Press, 1996).

54. Ragsdale, *Centennial '36*, 232.

55. The most useful studies on Dallas and the 1936 Texas Centennial Exposition are Boswell, "Negro Participation"; Ragsdale, *Centennial '36;* Thomas, *Negro Participation;* and Wallace Owen Chariton, *Texas Centennial: The Parade of an Empire* (Plano, Texas: Texas Centennial, 1979). The centennial gets extensive coverage in Payne, *Big D*, 159–174. An informative general history of the Texas State Fair is Wiley, *Great State Fair.*

56. Steve Butler, "Honoring the Past: Confederate Monuments in Dallas," *Legacies: A History Journal for Dallas and North Central Texas* 1, no. 2 (fall 1989): 33–35.

57. Ragsdale, *Centennial '36*, 251.

58. Boswell, "Negro Participation," 23.

59. Ragsdale, *Centennial '36*, 242, 253, 255.

60. Thomas, *Negro Participation*, 26; Boswell, "Negro Participation," 15–20.

61. Thomas, *Negro Participation*, 64.

62. Ibid., 87.

63. Ibid., 108–109.

64. Boswell, "Negro Participation," 29–30.

65. Charles H. Bynum, "The Centennial in Retrospect," *Dallas Express*, October 31, 1936, p. 2; Boswell, "Negro Participation," 33–35.

66. Ragsdale, *Centennial '36*, 305.

67. Dulaney, "Progressive Voters League," 30–31; Payne, *Big D*, 182–183.

68. A. Maceo Smith interview.

69. Dulaney, "Progressive Voters League," 31–32; "Platform of Voters League," *Dallas Express*, March 27, 1937, p. 1.

70. Dulaney, "Progressive Voters League," 29–30, 32–33; A. Maceo Smith interview; Payne, *Big D*, 184–190.

71. Harmon, *Beneath the Image*, 59–64, 66–67, and the documentary *The Strange Demise of Jim Crow: How Houston Desegregated Its Public Accommodations, 1959–1963*, created and executive produced by Thomas R. Cole and directed by Tom Curtis, capture this behind-the-scenes activism. Guadalupe San Miguel Jr. provides a perceptive analysis of the "Mexican American" generation and its accommodationist approach to Mexican American civil rights in mid-twentieth-century Houston in *Brown, not White.*

72. Dulaney, "Progressive Voters League," 27.

73. Ibid., 29–30; Payne, *Big D*, 184–190.

74. "A Service of Thanksgiving and Dedication on the Occasion of the Hundredth Anniversary of the Founding of the City of Dallas," program, November 23, 1941, 7, Texas State Library, Archives Division, Austin.

75. "A Service of Thanksgiving," 8–9.

76. "A Service of Thanksgiving," 9.

77. Payne, *Big D*, 201; William H. Wilson, *Hamilton Park*, 10–11; Fairbanks, *For the City*, 153.

78. Payne, *Big D*, 200–201.

79. Ibid., 201–203; Fairbanks, *For the City*, 159–160.

80. Payne, *Big D*, 185, "Streets or Mudholes," *Dallas Express*, January 15, 1938, p. 10.

CHAPTER SIX

1. Rabbi David Lefkowitz, Dallas, letter to Dr. J. M. Dowis, Acting Director, Department of Public Health, City Hall, Dallas, Texas, May 7, 1942, Anti-Semitism in Dallas/ Anti-Defamation League, B'nai B'rith folder, TEAD.

2. H. S. Linfield, director, Jewish Statistical Bureau, Auspices of National Council for Statistics of Jews, letter to Miss Aline Rutland, Secretary Congregation Emanu-El, Dallas, March 7, 1944, Anti-Semitism folder, TEAD.

3. For a discussion of this social class see George Norris Green, "The Far Right Wing in Texas Politics, 1930's–1960's" (Ph.D. diss., Florida State University, 1967).

4. "Old Testament: The Dallas High Schools, March 1952," Bulletin 150. Authorized by the Board of Education, January 22, 1952, DISD, 1952, 3–4, TSL.

5. "Old Testament," DISD, 9.

6. For more on the intensely racist tone of America's war against the Japanese in World War II's Pacific theater, as opposed to combat against the Germans, see John W. Dower, *War without Mercy: Race and Power in the Pacific War* (New York: Pantheon Books, 1986). For more on dehumanizing discourse regarding Asians see Edward W. Said, *Orientalism* (New York: Random House, Vintage Books, 1978). An analysis of anti-Semitic myths regarding Jews, including their Asian origins, can be found in George L. Mosse, *Toward the Final Solution: A History of European Racism* (New York: H. Fertig, 1978).

7. Gillette, "NAACP in Texas," 14–15, 28–29; *New Handbook of Texas,* 1996, s.v. "Juanita Jewel Shanks Craft"; Payne, *Big D,* 252–253; Dulaney, "Whatever Happened," 75; "Longtime Dallas black leader A. Maceo Smith dies at age 74," *Dallas Morning News,* December 20, 1977, sec. D.

8. Gillette, "NAACP in Texas," 111.

9. "Lovelier Hair in 7 days or your money back," advertisement for Gold Medal Hair Products, *Dallas Express,* May 6, 1961, 3; "Enjoy the Light Side of Life," advertisement for New Palmer's Skin Success Bleach Cream, *Dallas Express,* June 10, 1961, 4.

10. Patricia Evridge Hill, *Dallas,* 164; Fairbanks, *For the City,* 191.

11. Fairbanks, *For the City,* 191–192; Payne, *Big D,* 256.

12. Schutze, *Accommodation,* 9–10; Fairbanks, *For the City,* 192; Dennis Hoover, "Razing Slums Would Leave Many Homeless," *Dallas Morning News,* January 21, 1962, sec. 1.

13. Fairbanks, *For the City,* 192–193; Schutze, *Accommodation,* 13; Juanita Craft, letter to Walter White, August 7, 1951, Juanita Craft Papers, Box 1, Folder 1, DPL.

14. Payne, *Big D,* 257–260.

15. Ibid., 261–262; Schutze, *Accommodation,* 21–26, 70–72.

16. Census Bureau, *Eighteenth Census, 1960,* vol. 1, part 45, Texas, 565, 593.

17. Montejano, *Anglos and Mexicans,* 231, 265.

18. Randolph B. Campbell, *Gone to Texas: A History of the Lone Star State* (New York: Oxford University Press, 2003), 428.

19. Ibid.

20. Linden, *Desegregating Schools,* 4–5.

21. Arnoldo de León, *Mexicans Americans in Texas: A Brief History* (Wheeling, Ill.: Harlan Davidson, 1999), 111; Payne, *Big D*, 343.

22. Achor, *Mexican Americans in a Dallas Barrio*, 138.

23. De León, *Mexicans Americans in Texas*, 79, 111.

24. Neil Foley, *White Scourge*, 61.

25. San Miguel, *Brown, not White*, 36–39.

26. Neil Foley, *White Scourge*, 209.

27. Matthew Frye Jacobson, *Whiteness of a Different Color*, 246–280.

28. San Miguel, *Brown, not White*, 40–42.

29. Cynthia E. Orozco, "The Origins of the League of United Latin American Citizens (LULAC) and the Mexican American Civil Rights Movement in Texas with an Analysis of Women's Political Participation in a Gendered Context, 1910-1929," (Ph.D. diss., University of California at Los Angeles, 1992), 1, 7.

30. O. Douglas Weeks, "The League of United Latin American Citizens: A Texan-Mexican Civic Organization," *Southwestern Political and Social Science Quarterly* 10, no. 3 (December 1929): 264–265; *New Handbook of Texas*, 1996, s.v. "League of United Latin American Citizens."

31. More can be found on LULAC's history, its ideology, and its campaign against anti-Latino segregation in Richard A. García, *Rise of the Mexican American Middle Class: San Antonio, 1929–1941* (College Station: Texas A&M University Press, 1991); Benjamin Marquez, *LULAC: The Evolution of A Mexican American Political Organization* (Austin: University of Texas Press, 1993); Guadalupe San Miguel Jr., *"Let All of Them Take Heed": Mexican Americans and the Campaign for Educational Equality in Texas, 1910–1981* (Austin: University of Texas Press, 1987).

32. Neil Foley, *White Scourge*, 209–210.

33. Achor, *Mexican Americans in a Dallas Barrio*, 122–123.

34. Libby Averyt and Ron George, "Dr. Hector: 1914-1996—Legacy Endures in the Hearts Left Behind; Loved by Poor, Courted by the Mighty," *Corpus Christi Caller-Times*, August 11, 1996, special section, 3; Linden, *Desegregating Schools in Dallas*, 11. For more on the American GI Forum see Carl Allsup, *The American GI Forum: Origins and Evolution*, Monograph no. 6, Center for Mexican American Studies (Austin: University of Texas Press, 1982), and Henry Ramos, *The American G.I. Forum: In Pursuit of the Dream, 1948–1983* (Houston: Arte Público Press, 1998).

35. Paul Andow, "Civil Rights Quid Pro Quo." Statement of National Policy issued by the "Nat'l Supreme Council," 1963, LULAC archives, William Flores Subcollection, Box 1, Folder 3. Benson Latin American Collection (hereinafter BLAC).

36. Jacob I. Rodriguez, "Americans—Not 'Mejicas,'" letter to the *San Antonio Express*, May 16, 1963, LULAC archives, Jacob I. Rodriguez Subcollection, Box 7, Folder 3, BLAC.

37. Dr. Hector B. Garcia, M.D., Corpus Christi, letter to the Honorable Homer Garrison, Austin, April 17, 1950, Garcia Archives, Box 113, Folder 30, Texas A&M University at Corpus Christi (hereinafter TAMU-CC).

38. Ibid.

39. Gerald Saldaña, Crystal City, Texas, letter to Dr. Hector P. Garcia, Corpus Christi,

March 9, 1954, Garcia Archives, Box 141, Folder 13, TAMU-CC; Dr. Hector P. Garcia, Corpus Christi, letter to Gerald Saldaña, Crystal City, Texas, March 13, 1954, Garcia Archives Box 141, Folder 13, TAMU-CC.

40. Manuel Avila Jr., Caracas, Venezuela, letter to Dr. Hector P. Garcia, Corpus Christi. February 7, 1956, Hector P. Garcia Archives, Box 46, Folder 28, TAMU-CC.

41. "Resignation of Hector P. Garcia is demanded by P. R. Ochoa," *Kingsville Americano*, August 13, 1969, p. 1; *Greater Dallas Alphabetical Telephone Directory, 1960* (Dallas: Southwestern Bell, 1960); "Ochoa Commercial Academy," advertisement, *Dallas Americano*, October 20, 1954, p. 1; "Ochoa Auto Parts," advertisement, *Dallas Americano*, August 20, 1958, p. 4; *Polk's Greater Dallas City Directory, 1962*, part 2 (Dallas: R. L. Polk and Co., 1962).

42. "To You: Please use the word Americano or Texano," *Dallas Americano*, August 20, 1958, p. 4. Copies of the *Dallas Americano* are available at the J. Erik Jonsson Central Library's Texas/Dallas History and Archive Division in Dallas, DPL.

43. "News among Spaniol Readers," *Dallas Americano*, August 6, 1958, 1; "For your personal information," *Dallas Americano*, June 25, 1958, p. 1; "Organizacion de Gente Blanca," *Dallas Americano*, June 25, 1958, 6; "New from Spaniol heads," *Dallas Americano*, July 30, 1958, p. 1; "Americano: conserve su raza blanca," *Dallas Americano*, February 19, 1958, p. 1; "Americano Esta es tu Patria Americana," *Dallas Americano*, August 20, 1958, p. 5.

44. "News among Spaniol Readers," *Dallas Americano*, August 6, 1958, 1.

45. Author's translation. Ochoa's comments in the original Spanish follow: "El American GI Forum, el LULAC, el Naacp, camaras y otras agrupaciones niggerianas, repitidas veces han hecho fe integracionista para empujar alto la igualdad, inteligencia y superioridad de la raza Negra." For the complete article see "No use nopal como almohada," *Dallas Americano*, April 16, 1958, 1.

46. Montejano, *Anglos and Mexicans*, 275–276.

47. Julie Leininger Pycior, "Henry B. Gonzalez," in Kenneth E. Hendrickson Jr., Michael L. Collins, and Patrick Cox, ed., *Profiles in Power: Twentieth Century Texans in Washington* (Austin: University of Texas Press, 2004), 299–302.

48. Boles, *The South through Time*, 455–456, 467–468.

49. Calvert and de León, *History of Texas*, 362.

50. Quotes in Schutze, *Accommodation*, 91–92; Harmon, *Beneath the Image*, 109. Criswell died January 10, 2002. See Charles Richards, "Pastor Leads Baptists' 'conservative resurgence,'" *Austin American-Statesman*, January 11, 2002, sec. B.

51. Sister Mary Ignatius, "Leadership Needed in Lunch Problem," *Dallas Morning News*, March 27, 1960, sec. 3.

52. Juanita Craft, interview by David Stricklin and Gail Tomlinson, Dallas, Texas, January 23, February 5 and 20, March 20 and 29, and April 24, 1979, tape recording, Dallas Public Library Oral History Interview Project, DPL.

53. Marilynn Wood Hill, "History," 45–47.

54. Payne, *Big D*, 206, 275–276.

55. For an analysis of the right wing in America see Berlet and Lyons, *Right-Wing*

Populism; Michael Cox and Martin Durham, "The Politics of Anger: The Extreme Right in the United States," in Paul Hainsworth, ed., *The Politics of the Extreme Right: From the Margins to the Mainstream* (New York: Pinter, 2000); and Richard Hofstadter, *The Paranoid Style in American Politics and Other Essays* (1952; reprint, Cambridge: Harvard University Press, 1964). Berlet and Lyons' work bears particular relevance for this book in their analysis of how eschatology shaped the racism and anti-Semitism of the right-wing movement and its attitude toward political activism. For a case study of the far right wing in 1950s Houston see Don E. Carleton, *Red Scare! Right Wing Hysteria, Fifties Fanaticism, and Their Legacy in Texas* (Austin: Texas Monthly Press, 1985).

56. Fairbanks, *For the City*, 72.

57. Patricia Evridge Hill, *Dallas*, 116–122. The Marcus quote is from Marilynn Wood Hill, "History," 81.

58. Patricia Evridge Hill, *Dallas*, 117; Fairbanks, *For the City*, 92.

59. Payne, *Big D*, 163–174. The most complete account of the Texas Centennial Exposition and Dallas' role in the celebration can be found in Kenneth B. Ragsdale, *Centennial '36: The Year American Discovered Texas* (College Station: Texas A&M University Press, 1987).

60. Patricia Evridge Hill, *Dallas*, 122–123; Fairbanks, *For the City*, 113–116.

61. Fairbanks, *For the City*, 126.

62. Patricia Evridge Hill, *Dallas*, 123–124; Fairbanks, *For the City*, 179.

63. Patricia Evridge Hill, *Dallas*, 133–136; "Why Should Dallas Dressmakers Get Less Wages Than Northern Workers?" leaflet, International Ladies Garment Workers Union Collection, AR 167–1, LA-UTA.

64. "Strike Leader Takes Stand In Contempt Case: Perlstein, Russian-Born Jew, Says Didn't Urge Street Fighting but for Peaceful Result," *Dallas Morning News*, September 19, 1935, p. 1, sec. 1; "Hearing Number 1 before the Industrial Commission of Texas. Garment Industry in Dallas County: Statement of Facts," 262–263, George and Latane Lambert Collection, AR 127–11–1, LA-UTA.

65. "Hearing Number 1," 321.

66. Ibid., 322.

67. Patricia Evridge Hill, 131, 148–158. The NLRB quote is on page 131.

68. George Norris Green, "Some Aspects of the Far Right Wing in Texas Politics," in E. C. Barksdale, George Norris Green, and T. Harry Williams, eds., *Essays on Recent Southern Politics* (Austin: University of Texas Press, 1970), 86.

69. Ibid., 64.

70. Ibid., 86–87.

71. Calvert and de León, *History of Texas*, 360–361.

72. Carleton, *Red Scare*, 13–14, 18.

73. Ibid., 101.

74. Ibid., 160, 165–166, 172,182–186, 287–290; Payne, *Big D*, 283–285.

75. George Norris Green, "Far Right Wing in Texas," 167. For an example of how Dallas writers see the right wing of the 1950s and 1960s see Payne, *Big D*, 307–313. The Dallas role in the national right-wing movement received widespread media attention in

the early 1960s; see Keith Wheeler, "Who's Who in the Tumult of the Far Right," *Life*, February 9, 1962, 110–127.

76. DISD board minutes, vol. 41, p. 348, and vol. 42, pp. 55, 90, 102, 429.

77. J. Edgar Hoover, *Masters of Deceit: The Story of Communism in America and How to Fight It* (New York: Henry Holt and Co., 1958).

78. George Norris Green, "Far Right Wing in Texas," 284.

79. Carleton, *Red Scare*, 93.

80. Payne, *Big D*, 308; Jerome Tuccille, *Kingdom: The Story of the Hunt Family of Texas* (Ottawa, Ill.: Jameson Books, 1984), 230–231.

81. H. L. Hunt, *Alpaca*, (Dallas: H. L. Hunt Press, 1960); Tuccille, *Kingdom*, 231.

82. "Americans—Will it be Peaceful No-Existence?," leaflet distributed by Texas Christians for Freedom, Anti-Semitism in Dallas/Anti-Defamation League/B'nai B'rith folder, TEAD.

83. *New Handbook of Texas*, 1996, s.v. "John Owen Beaty"; John Beaty, *The Iron Curtain over America* (Dallas: Wilkinson, 1956), x–xii.

84. Beaty, *Iron Curtain*, 15, 16.

85. Ibid., 106.

86. Rockoff, "Jewish Racial Identity," 45.

87. Beaty, *Iron Curtain*, 27.

88. Ibid., 44–57.

89. Ibid., 77.

90. Ibid., 77–78, 134–135. For more on Holocaust denial see Deborah Lipstadt, *Denying the Holocaust: The Growing Assault on Truth and Memory* (New York: Plume, 1994).

91. Beaty, *Iron Curtain*, 197.

92. Marilynn Wood Hill, "History," 57; Barkun, *Religion and the Racist Right*, 140–141. Examples of Web sites citing Beaty's works or selling copies of *Iron Curtain over America* include Books from the Noontide Press: Zionism, Israel, and the Jewish Question, at http://www.noontidepress.com; and Institute for Historical Review, Journal of Historical Review: The "Holocaust" Put in Perspective, at http://ihr.org.

93. Hollace Ava Weiner, *Jewish Stars in Texas: Rabbis and Their Work* (College Station: Texas A&M University Press, 1999), 226; Marilynn Wood Hill, "History," 63–64.

94. Marilynn Wood Hill, "History," 65.

95. Ibid., 66–67.

96. Ibid., 70–76, 80, 85.

97. Ibid., 78–80.

98. Cristol, *Light in the Prairie*, 154–156.

99. Weiner, *Jewish Stars*, 222–223.

100. Dollinger, " 'Hamans' and 'Torquemadas,' " 58, 72.

101. Levi Olan, interview by Gerald D. Saxon, Dallas, Texas, February 4 and April 6, 1983, tape recording, Dallas Public Library Oral History Project, DPL.

102. Cristol, *Light in the Prairie*, 186.

103. Weiner, *Jewish Stars*, 229.

104. Marilynn Wood Hill, "History," 98–100.

105. William H. Wilson, *Hamilton Park*, 38–39.

106. Judge Irving Goldberg, interview by Joseph Rosenstein, Dallas, August 22, 1974, transcript, TEAD; Cristol, *Light in the Prairie*, 186.

107. Hollace Weiner, Jewish Stars in Texas: Rabbis and Their Work (College Station: Texas A&M University Press, 1999), 204.

108. F. Kenneth Jensen, "The Houston Sit-in Movement of 1960–61," in Howard Beeth and Cary D. Wintx, eds., *Black Dixie: Afro-Texas History and Culture in Houston* (College Station: Texas A&M University Press, 1992), 213–216; Thomas R. Cole, *No Color Is My Kind: The Life of Eldrewey Stearns and the Integration of Houston* (Austin: University of Texas Press, 1997), 26, 29; Weiner, *Jewish Stars*, 204–205.

109. Schutze, *Accommodation*, 87.

110. W. J. Durham, "Citizens' Committee to Abolish Discrimination Against Negro Women in Dallas Department Stores," circular letter, July 27, 1953, John O. and Ethelyn M. Chisum Collection, Box 1, Folder 2, Texas/Dallas History and Archives Division, J. Erik Jonsson Central Library (DPL); Stanley Marcus, *Minding the Store: A Memoir* (Boston: Little, Brown and Co., 1974), 368–370. Stanley Marcus died January 22, 2002. See John Kirkpatrick, "He rose to the top of retail and took Dallas along: Friends recall a great mind with a spirit to match," *Dallas Morning News*, January 23, 2002, sec. A.

111. W. J. Durham, "Citizens' Committee."

112. Juanita Craft, interview.

113. Miriam Rozen, "Price Check: Dallas' Jewish Community Gets a Close Look at John Wiley Price," *Dallas Observer*, August 12, 1993.

114. The literature on the Jewish experience with the ideology of whiteness is relatively new and growing. Notable examples include Seth Forman, *Blacks in the Jewish Mind: A Crisis of Liberalism* (New York: New York University Press, 1998); Harry Kitano, "Jews in the U.S.: The Rising Costs of Whiteness," in Becky Thompson and Sangeeta Tyagi, eds., *Names We Call Home: Autobiography on Racial Identity* (New York: Routledge, 1996); and Karen Brodkin Sacks, "How Did Jews Become White Folks?" in Steven Gregory and Roger Sanjek, eds., *Race* (New Brunswick, N.J.: Rutgers University Press, 1994).

115. Charles R. Graggs, "Attitude Has Changed," *Dallas Morning News*, January 12, 1963, sec. 4.

CHAPTER SEVEN

1. "The South Is Changed and Can Never Turn Back," *Dallas Express*, March 14, 1959, p. 1.

2. Butler, "Honoring the Past," 34.

3. Census Bureau, *Census of the Population: 1950. Special Reports. States of Birth* (Washington D.C., 1953), 4A-19–4A23; Census Bureau, *Eighteenth Census, 1960*, vol. 1, part 45, *Texas*, 45–674.

4. Calvert and de León, *History of Texas*, 414.

5. Boles, *The South through Time,* 469.

6. Ibid., 410.

7. Ragsdale, *Centennial '36,* 304. By 2002 Texas had a Republican governor and the GOP controlled all statewide offices and both houses of the legislature.

8. "Politics Hurts South's Potential," *Dallas Morning News,* March 2, 1959, sec. 4.

9. Bill McClanahan, "Somebody's Going To Get It," *Dallas Morning News,* February 18, 1961, sec. 4; Lynn Landrum, "Prejudice or Prejudgment," *Dallas Morning News,* February 16, 1961, sec. 4.

10. Davidson, *Race and Class,* 43; John R. Knaggs, *Two-Party Texas: The John Tower Era, 1961–1984* (Austin: Eakin Press, 1986), 4. For more on racial politics see Alexander P. Lamis, *The Two-Party South* (New York: Oxford University Press, 1984); Michael W. Miles, *The Odyssey of the American Right* (New York: Oxford University Press, 1980); and Raymond Wolfinger and Robert Arsenau, "Partisan Change in the South: 1952–1976," in Louis Maisel and Joseph Cooper, eds., *Political Parties: Development and Decay* (Beverly Hills.: Sage Publications, 1978).

11. Boles, *The South through Time,* 474; Williamson, *Rage for Order,* 255.

12. See Howard H. Eibling, Fred M. King, and James Harlow, *Our United States: A Bulwark of Freedom* (Dallas: Laidlaw Brothers, Publishers, 1962), 590. "Communism appeals both to some of the poor and to some of those who would like to see the poor have a better way of life," the authors wrote. The DISD Board approved this text on February 28, 1962. See the DISD Board minutes, vol. 42, 306.

13. Douglas McKibben, "Segregation Called Cause of Discord," *Dallas Morning News,* January 5, 1959, sec. 4; Mrs. J. Roland Smith, "Mississippi Shooting," *Dallas Morning News,* January 2, 1963, sec. 4. Demographic information on letter writers to the *Dallas Morning News* derives from the following sources: Donald Payton, DHS, letter to the author, Apple Valley, California, May 25, 1994; *Mapsco, Dallas: A Routing and Delivery System Combined with City of Dallas Maps and Guide to Streets* (Dallas: Mapsco, 1954); *Polk's Greater Dallas (Dallas County, Texas) City Directory,* vol. 67, 1959 (Dallas: R. L. Polk and Co., 1959), vol. 67 (1961) and vol. 71 (1963); "Family Income Data, Dallas Standard Metropolitan Statistical Area," pamphlet compiled from Advance P-1 Tables, U.S. Census (Dallas: Dallas Times Herald, 1962). The author thanks Donald Payton for his extensive help.

14. "115 Negro Ministers Join Integration Plea," *Dallas Times Herald,* May 4, 1958, sec. A.

15. "Minister Says Race Change 'Inevitable,'" *Dallas Morning News,* February 13, 1961, sec. 1. For examples of Dallas churches ending Jim Crow in their own facilities see Thomas Turner, "Episcopalians Approve Youth Camp Integration," *Dallas Morning News,* February 10, 1962, sec. 1; and Stewart Hensley, "Episcopalians OK Race Mix for Hospital," *Dallas Morning News,* February 11, 1962, sec. 1.

16. Weisbrot, *Freedom Bound,* 51; Branch, *Parting the Waters,* 222–225; William Henry Kellar, *Make Haste Slowly: Moderates, Conservatives, and School Desegregation in Houston* (College Station: Texas A&M Press, 1999), 68.

17. Gillette, "NAACP in Texas," 262–332.

18. Lynn Landrum, "Politics Lights a Fuse," *Dallas Morning News,* October 22, 1956, sec. 3.

19. Payne, *Big D,* 279–282; James R. Soukup, Clifton McCleskey, and Harry Holloway, *Party and Factional Division in Texas* (Austin: University of Texas Press, 1964), 192; Knaggs, *Two-Party Texas,* 5. Alger was the first Republican from Texas to serve a full two-year term since the 1930s.

20. Payne, *Big D,* 282; Knaggs, *Two-Party Texas,* 11.

21. Payne, *Big D,* 282.

22. Blayne Salyer, "Opening Round: Alger, Wade Trade Punches in Debate," *Dallas Morning News,* September 12, 1956, sec. 1.

23. "Alger States Position on Segregation," *Dallas Morning News,* October 25, 1956, sec. 3.

24. Payne, *Big D,* 283.

25. For example see "Racial 'Agitators' Draw Alger's Fire," *Dallas Times Herald,* June 23, 1963, sec. A.

26. Reprint of *Congressional Record,* Proceedings and Debates of the 84th Congress, 2nd session, Bruce Alger Collection, Box 7, Folder 29, Texas/Dallas History and Archives Division, J. Erik Jonsson Central Library (DPL).

27. "Setting the Record Straight on Dallas," reprint of *Congressional Record* 110, no. 822, April 27, 1964, 8920–8921; *Uniform Crime Reports for the United States* (Washington, D.C.: Federal Bureau of Investigation, 1959), Bruce Alger Collection, Box 7, Folder 30, DPL.

28. Bruce Alger, "Segregation" speech notes, Bruce Alger Collection, Box 2, Folder 4, DPL.

29. See Dan T. Carter, *From George Wallace to Newt Gingrich.* On "the Southern Strategy" see Kevin Phillips, *The Emerging Republican Majority* (New York: Arlington House, 1969).

30. "He Remembered," *Dallas Morning News,* January 23, 1960, sec. 4; Paul Casdorph, *A History of the Republican Party in Texas, 1865–1965* (Austin: Pemberton Press, 1965), 201.

31. Jimmy G. Robinson, Garland, Texas, letter to Bruce Alger, Dallas, December 10, 1962, Bruce Alger papers, Box 28, Folder 7, DPL; Marilynn Wood Hill, "History," 56; Carol Marie Hurd, Dallas, letter to Bruce Alger, Dallas, September 27, 1962, Bruce Alger papers, Box 28, Folder 7, DPL.

32. Gillette, "NAACP in Texas," 346–352; Dulaney, "Whatever Happened," 76–77; Schutze, *Accommodation,* 111.

33. Dulaney, "Whatever Happened," 78–80. The literature on the American civil rights movement is too massive to recount here, but in addition to previously cited works by Taylor Branch and Robert Weisbrot, some interesting recent works include Sean Dennis Cashman, *African Americans and the Quest for Civil Rights* (New York: New York University Press, 1991); Bettye Collier-Thomas and V. P. Franklin, *Sisters in the Struggle: African American Women in the Civil Rights-Black Power Movement* (New York: New York Univer-

sity Press, 2001); and Jack Davis, ed., *The Civil Rights Movement* (Malden, Mass.: Blackwell Publishers, 2001).

34. Dulaney, "Whatever Happened," 80; "Dallasites Picket Store: H. L. Green's Stands Firm," *Texas Observer*, October 14, 1960, 1–2; "Rev James Says Group Protests Integrating Dollar and Segregating Service," *Dallas Express*, October 8, 1960, pp. 1, 8; "Dallas Leaders Throw Weight Behind Picket Line At 'The H L Green Store," *Dallas Express*, October 29, 1960, 1.

35. "SMU Students Stage Sit-Ins," *Texas Observer*, January 14, 1961, 8; William R. Carmack and Theodore Freedman, *Dallas, Texas: Factors Affecting School Desegregation* (New York: Anti-Defamation League of B'nai B'rith, 1962?), 23, 30, Tarlton Law Library, Joseph D. Jamail Center for Legal Research, University of Texas at Austin (hereinafter T-JDJ); Payne, *Big D*, 299–300.

36. Dulaney, "Whatever Happened," 81.

37. DISD Board minutes, vol. 39, 265–266. Almost 20 percent of school employees were strongly in favor of integration, while nearly 50 percent indicated a "definite disfavoring of integration."

38. Linden, *Desegregating Schools*, 225.

39. Dulaney, "Whatever Happened," 81–82; Carmack and Freedman, *Dallas, Texas*, 15–16; Payne, *Big D*, 300–301.

40. Schutze, *Accommodation*, 128–133; *Dallas at the Crossroads* (1961), commissioned by the Dallas Citizens Council and produced by Sam Bloom (copy in author's possession).

41. Carmack and Freedman, *Dallas, Texas*, 20–21.

42. Linden, *Desegregating Schools*, 47; Carmack and Freedman, *Dallas, Texas*, 19–20.

43. Linden, *Desegregating Schools*, 48–61.

44. Davidson, *Race and Class*, 43.

45. Payne, *Big D*, 305–306; Leslie, *Dallas Public and Private*, 182.

46. Payne, *Big D*, 309–312. For examples of how the national press in 1963–1964 saw Dallas as a right-wing haven see Keith Wheeler, "Who's Who in the Tumult of the Far Right," *Life*, February 9, 1962; J. Claude Evans, "The Dallas Image Unveiled," *Christian Century*, November 20, 1963; and Richard Austin Smith, "How Business Failed Dallas," *Fortune*, July 1964.

47. Jim Bishop, *The Day Kennedy Was Shot* (New York: Funk and Wagnalls, 1968), 90, 105.

48. Ibid., 90.

49. Ibid., 112.

50. Ibid., 125.

51. Steven D. Holley, "The Dallas *Morning News* and the *Times Herald* and the Image of Dallas in the Decade after the Kennedy Assassination" (master's thesis, University of Texas, 1974), 41, 134–135.

52. Richard Austin Smith, "How Business Failed Dallas," *Fortune*, 158. For examples of how the outside world blamed Dallas, its leadership, and its right-wing atmosphere for the Kennedy assassination see "May God Forgive Dallas," *Newsweek*, December 9, 1963;

"The Shame of Dallas," *Post,* April 11, 1964; "The Dallas Rejoinder," *Nation,* May 25, 1964; and "What Makes Dallas Different," *New Republic,* June 20, 1964. A summary of press coverage of Dallas following the assassination can be found in Holley, "The Dallas *Morning News* and the *Times Herald.*"

53. Holland McCombs, "Dydamic Men," 101.

54. Fairbanks, *For the City,* 240; Payne, *Big D,* 282, 307, 323.

55. Payne, *Big D,* 324.

56. Leslie, *Dallas Public and Private,* 105.

57. Ibid., 108-109, 118.

58. George Norris Green, *The Establishment in Texas Politics: The Primitive Years, 1938-1957* (Norman: University of Oklahoma Press, 1979), 162; Carleton, *Red Scare,* 288-289.

59. Carleton, *Red Scare,* 133-134, 288-289, 295.

60. Fairbanks, *For the City,* 240-247; Payne, *Big D,* 351-355.

61. Robert F. Greenwald, *Race Relations and the Intergroup Climate in Dallas, Texas: Analysis and Comment on the Nature of Intergroup Problems and the Potential for Resolution* (Dallas: North Texas Chapter of the Association of Intergroup Relations Officials, April 1967), 1, DPL.

62. Harmon, *Beneath the Image,* 46, 49-51; Bauerlein, *Negrophobia,* 30.

63. Harmon, *Beneath the Image,* 86-87, 110, 113, 177-219.

64. Dulaney, "Whatever Happened," 86-87. Clayborne Carson's *In Struggle: SNCC and the Black Awakening of the 1960s* (Cambridge, Mass.: Harvard University Press, 1981) represents the definitive history of the SNCC organization. Other interesting works on the organization include Cheryl Lynn Greenberg, ed., *A Circle of Trust: Remembering SNCC* (New Brunswick, N.J.: Rutgers University Press, 1998), a collection of interviews of former SNCC members, and Emily Stoper, *The Student Nonviolent Coordinating Committee: The Growth of Radicalism in a Civil Rights Organization* (Brooklyn: Carlson Publishing, 1989).

65. Linden, *Desegregating Schools,* 114.

66. Achor, *Mexican Americans in a Dallas Barrio,* 77.

67. Ibid., 113; quote is from Thomas A. Neill, regional representative, Dallas Region, National Postal Union, letter [resolution] to Mrs. Doris Butts [of Frito-Lay], Washington, D.C., May 13, 1969, Hector P. Garcia Archives, Box 81, Folder 58, American GI Forum Archives, TAMU-CC; John R. McCarty, Dallas, letter to Vicente T. Ximines, Washington, D.C., February 25, 1970, Garcia Archives, Box 81, Folder 62, TAMU-CC; John R. McCarty, Dallas, letter to Dr. Hector P. Garcia, Corpus Christi, June 3, 1970, Garcia Archives, Box 81, Folder 59, TAMU-CC.

68. "Latins, Blacks Hold Vigil for Rodriguez," *Dallas Morning News,* March 7, 1971, sec. A; Terry Kliewer, "Rodriguez Rally: Protestors March in Shrine Parade," *Dallas Morning News,* March 21, 1971, sec. A.

69. Stephen Power, "Fatal Flashback: Ex-officer looks back with regret 25 years after killing boy in interrogation," *Dallas Morning News,* July 24, 1998, sec. A; Payne, *Big D,* 363-364.

70. Quote is from Payne, *Big D,* 364–365; Stephen Power and Brenda Rodriguez, "Flash point in Dallas history has faded with time," *Dallas Morning News,* July 24, 1998, sec. A.

71. Pancho Medrano, interview by George Green and Carr Winn, Dallas, Texas, August 4, 1971, transcript, OH 55, 13, 38, LA-UTA; Tony Castro, "The Medranos: Family of Activists," *Dallas Times Herald,* November 22, 1970, sec. C.

72. Medrano interview. For more on the politics of Mexican American identity in this period see Acuña, *Occupied America;* Juan Gómez-Quiñones, *Chicano Politics: Reality and Promise, 1940–1990* (Albuquerque: University of New Mexico Press, 1990); David G. Gutiérrez, *Walls and Mirrors: Mexican Americans, Mexican Immigrants, and the Politics of Ethnicity* (Berkeley: University of California Press, 1995); Montejano, *Anglos and Mexicans;* and George J. Sánchez, *Becoming Mexican American: Ethnicity, Culture, and Identity in Chicano Los Angeles, 1900–1945* (New York: Oxford University Press, 1993).

73. For more on the racial theories of José Vasconcelos consult Johns Hopkins University's recent publication of his seminal book, *La raza cósmica,* translated as *The Cosmic Race: A Bilingual Edition* (Baltimore: Johns Hopkins University Press, 1997). For an example of *chicanismo* in the Dallas–Fort Worth area in the early 1970s see *Chicano* 1, no. 1 (June 17–24, 1971). This and other issues of *Chicano* are available at the University of Texas at Arlington Library Special Collections Department.

74. José E. Limón, "The Folk Performance of 'Chicano' and the Cultural Limits of Political Ideology," in Richard Bauman and Roger D. Abrahams, eds., *And Other Neighborly Names: Social Process and Cultural Image in Texas Folklore* (Austin: University of Texas Press, 1981), 198–199.

75. Limón, "Folk Performance," 200–201.

76. San Miguel, *Brown, not White,* 22, 30, 68; Tony Castro, "The Medranos," *Dallas Times Herald;* quotes from Maurilio Vigil, *Chicano Politics* (Washington, D.C.: University Press of America, 1978), 71–73; Alan Knight, "Racism, Revolution, and *Indigenismo:* Mexico, 1910–1940," in Richard Graham, ed., *The Idea of Race in Latin America, 1870–1940* (Austin: University of Texas Press, 1990), 86–88; "Las Chicanas," *Ya Basta,* AR55, Folder 1–4, LA-UTA; Juan Jose Reyna, "Where Are You in the Chicano Movement?"; and Mike Vega, "The Coming of AMAS," *El Alacran* 2, no. 16 (March 17, 1975), 1–3, AR173, Folder 1–1, LA-UTA.

77. San Miguel, *Brown, not White,* 56, 59, 68.

78. Ibid., 75–76, 87, 97–98, 105.

79. Ibid., 196–197.

80. Beeth and Wintz, *Black Dixie,* 164, 261–263.

81. Linden, *Desegregating Schools,* 60, 96, 101, 141–142; Achor, *Mexican Americans in a Dallas Barrio,* 50; Payne, *Big D,* 366, 389–421.

82. George Lipsitz, *Possessive Investment in Whiteness: How White People Profit from Identity Politics* (Philadelphia: Temple University Press, 1998), 6.

83. Payne, *Big D,* 336–338 359–360, 377–378; Michael Sand, "Mayor using low-drama race to tout record on big projects: Foes say Kirk alienating residents, ignoring basic services," *Dallas Morning News,* April 25, 1999, sec. A; Skip Hollandsworth, "Race Matters:

Ron Kirk is ready to be Dallas' first black mayor. But is Dallas ready for him?" *Texas Monthly*, May 1995, 92.

84. Payne, *Big D*, 345–346.

85. Ibid., 345, 355–356, 358–359, 376–378; Michael Saul and Tim Wyatt, "Lipscomb found guilty: Council member 'completely stunned,' vows to appeal," *Dallas Morning News*, January 26, 2000, sec. 1; David Flick, "Leader has long been a force for change: Outsider confronted establishment, later drew praise from it," *Dallas Morning News*, January 26, 2000, sec. 1.

86. Sand, "Mayor using low-drama race," *Dallas Morning News*. Kirk ran an unsuccessful U.S. Senate campaign in 2002.

87. David Flick, "Losing Ground: Once-vibrant black community succumbs to migration, apartments," *Dallas Morning News*, February 12, 1995, sec. A; Prince, *History of Dallas*, 29–31; Mary Ann Esquivel and Jack Booth, "Running out of time: State-Thomas residents see area swallowed by development," *Dallas Times Herald*, June 29, 1986, sec. A.

88. Kathy Cox and Pierce Allman, "State-Thomas Historic District: Dallas' Oldest Neighborhood Development Nestles in Skyscraper Shadows," *Historic Dallas*, November–December 1984, 3; Flick, "Losing Ground," *Dallas Morning News*.

89. Flick, "Losing Ground," *Dallas Morning News*; William H. Wilson, *Hamilton Park*, 104–105.

90. Flick, "Losing Ground," *Dallas Morning News*; David Dillon, "The state of State-Thomas: A once-vital downtown area is poised to come back to life. So why doesn't it?" *Dallas Morning News*, June 25, 1988, sec. C.

91. Henry Tatum, "No price on history," *Dallas Morning News*, December 30, 1983, sec. A.

92. Virginia McAlester, "State-Thomas: Prime Acreage in Dallas' Heartland Expected to Fashion City Lifestyle," *Visions of Dallas*, March 16–22, 1987, 5; Dillon, "The state of State-Thomas," *Dallas Morning News*; Flick, "Losing Ground," *Dallas Morning News*; "Approve State-Thomas Plan," *Dallas Times Herald*, December 19, 1985.

93. David Fisher, "The State-Thomas Buildup: Developers test area with small projects," *Dallas Times Herald*, August 23, 1990, sec. B; David Dillon, "State-Thomas renewal: New project creates potential for urban area," *Dallas Morning News*, April 28, 1991, sec. C; Bill Minutaglio, "The big fix-up," *Dallas Life Magazine*, Sunday magazine of the *Dallas Morning News*, June 23, 1991.

94. Payne, *Big D*, 399–400; Darwin Payne, *Big D: Triumphs and Troubles of an American Supercity in the 20th Century*, rev. ed. (Dallas: Three Forks Press, 2000), 436–442.

95. Payne, *Big D*, 399–400; Payne, *Big D*, rev. ed., 439–440; "Black Population Change," *African American Almanac*.

96. Craig Flournoy, "City's demolitions called unfair to minorities: But officials say they follow rules," *Dallas Morning News*, February 12, 1995, sec. A.

97. Flournoy, "City's demolitions," *Dallas Morning News*.

98. David Dillon, "Where we live: Dallas neighborhoods. A mix of stately grandeur, cozy pockets, and gated isolation," *Dallas Morning News*, May 2, 1999, sec C.

99. Robert Ingrassia, "Police shooting was Dallas turning point: Many believe furor

over black woman's '86 death transformed department," *Dallas Morning News,* October 27, 1996, sec. A.

100. David Dillon, "Reaching for the sky: An architectural guide to Dallas/Fort Worth," *Dallas Morning News,* May 2, 1999, sec. C.

101. *Robocop* (1987), directed by Paul Verhoeven, starring Peter Weller, Nancy Allen, Daniel O'Herlihy, Ronny Cox, Kurtwood Smith, and Miguel Ferrer; *Logan's Run* (1976), directed by Michael Anderson, starring Michael York, Jenny Agutter, Richard Jordan, Peter Ustinov, Farrah Fawcett-Majors, and Roscoe Lee Brown; *The X-Files: Fight the Future* (1998), directed by Rob Bowman, starring David Duchovny, Gillian Anderson, Martin Landau, Blythe Danner, and Armin Muehller-Stahl.

102. Coburn quoted in Samuel G. Freeman, "Reporter's Notebook: For Dallas, A Growing Cultural Identity Crisis," *New York Times,* August 6, 1984, sec. C.

103. *The Thin Blue Line* (1988), directed by Errol Morris; Dillon, "Where we live," *Dallas Morning News.*

104. Dillon, "Reaching for the sky," *Dallas Morning News.*

105. Quoted in Freeman, "Reporter's Notebook," *New York Times.*

106. Dillon, "Reaching for the sky," *Dallas Morning News.*

107. Steve Blow, "Big D in Dallas is dollar, publications say," *Dallas Morning News,* December 26, 1986, sec. A.

108. Payne, *Big D,* rev. ed., 402–404, 406.

109. Miriam Rozen, "Mr. Mellow," *Dallas Observer,* June 13–24, 1998, 19.

110. Robert Ingrassia, "Neighbors accuse city of racism: 11 from Cadillac Heights sue over floods, pollution," *Dallas Morning News,* February 2, 1999, sec. A; quote is from Rozen, "Mr. Mellow," 18–20.

111. Miriam Rozen, "One Fine Mess," *Dallas Observer,* November 20–26, 1997, 31–32; Zimmerman, "It's Our Turn," 30.

112. Chris Kelly, "Learning from Detroit: Urban Nightmare Comes True in Michigan," *Dallas Morning News,* December 6, 1995, sec. A.

113. Chris Kelly, "Learning from Detroit," *Dallas Morning News.*

114. Michael E. Young, "Army Stores Report Surplus of Y2K Business: Fear of Millennial Computer Crash Increasing Sales of Survivalist Gear," *Dallas Morning News,* February 20, 1999, sec. A.

BIBLIOGRAPHY

ABBREVIATIONS USED IN BIBLIOGRAPHY AND NOTES

BLAC   Nettie Lee Benson Latin American Collection, University of Texas at Austin

CAH   Center for American History, University of Texas at Austin

DHS   Dallas Historical Society

DISD   Archives, Dallas Independent School District Central Administration Office

DPL   Texas/Dallas History and Archives Division, J. Erik Jonsson Central Library, Dallas

LA-UTA   Labor Archive, University of Texas at Arlington Library

RCD   Roman Catholic Diocese of Dallas Archives

SMCA   Scofield Memorial Church Archives, Dallas

TAMU-CC   Dr. Hector P. Garcia Archive, Texas A&M University, Corpus Christi

TEAD   Dorothy M. and Harry S. Jacobus Temple Emanu-El Archives, Dallas

T-JDJ   Tarlton Law Library, Joseph D. Jamail Center for Legal Research, University of Texas at Austin

TSL   Texas State Library, Archives Division, Austin

ARCHIVAL AND MANUSCRIPT SOURCES

Alger, Bruce. *Congressional Record,* Proceedings and Debates of the 84th Congress, 2nd session. Reprint. Bruce Alger Collection, Box 7, Folder 29. DPL.

———. "Segregation" speech notes. Bruce Alger Collection, Box 2, Folder 4. DPL.

———. "Setting the Record Straight on Dallas." Reprint of the *Congressional Record* 110, No. 822, April 27, 1964, 8920–8921. Bruce Alger Collection, Box 7, Folder 30. DPL.

Allen, Mattie Jacoby. "Cultural Patterns Attained in a Primitive Land." Mattie Jacoby Allen Collection A37.24, 1. DHS.

"Americans—Will It Be Peaceful No-Existence?" Leaflet distributed by Texas Christians for Freedom, Anti-Semitism in Dallas/Anti-Defamation League/B'nai B'rith folder. TEAD.

Andow, Paul. "Civil Rights Quid Pro Quo." Statement of National Policy issued by the "Nat'l Supreme Council," 1963, LULAC archives, William Flores Subcollection, Box 1, Folder 3. BLAC.

Avila, Manuel. Letter, Caracas, Venezuela, to Dr. Hector P. Garcia, Corpus Christi. February 7, 1956. Hector P. Garcia Archives, Box 46, Folder 28. TAMU-CC.

"Background Information—St. Peter Academy." RCD.

Brannin, Carl. Interview by Dr. George Green, Dallas, Texas, April 12, 1967. Transcript, Oral History Project, Division of Archives and Manuscripts. OH1. LA-UTA.

Burnett, T. R. *Confederate Rhymes*. Dallas: Johnston Publishing Co., n.d. Sam Merrill Collection, Folder A455. DHS.

Canonical Report of St. Peter's Church, Dallas, Texas, November 15, 1924. RCD.

Carmack, William R., and Theodore Freedman. *Dallas, Texas: Factors Affecting School Desegregation*. New York: Anti-Defamation League of B'nai B'rith, 1962? T-JDJ.

Church Register, Scofield Memorial Church. SMCA.

"Civic Responsibility: An Appeal Addressed to the Thoughtful Citizen for Better Housing Conditions and Environment of the Poor in Dallas." George Dealey Collection, A6667, Folder 332. DHS.

Craft, Juanita. Interview by David Stricklin and Gail Tomlinson, Dallas, Texas, January 23, February 5 and 20, March 20 and 29, and April 24, 1979. Tape recording, Dallas Public Library Oral History Interview Project. DPL.

———. Letter to Walter White, August 7, 1951, Juanita Craft Papers, Box 1, Folder 1. DPL.

Dallas Independent School District. Board Minutes, Vols. 15, 19, 20, 22, 25, 41, and 42. DISD.

Dallas: The Open Shop City. Pamphlet. Dallas: Dallas Open Shop Association, 1925. Dallas AFL-CIO Collection, AR 126-28-13, LA-UTA.

DeHaven, Paul. "Records of the First Congregational Church of Dallas, Texas." Computer print-out. SMCA.

Delegates of the People of Texas. "A Declaration of the Causes which Impel the State of Texas to Secede from the Federal Union." Dallas: Basye Bros., Printer, n.d. T976.408. TSL.

Durham, W. J. "Citizens' Committee to Abolish Discrimination against Negro Women in Dallas Department Stores." Circular letter, July 27, 1953, John O. and Ethelyn M. Chisum Collection. DPL.

Edwards, George Clifton, "Autobiographical Notes of George Clifton Edwards." George Clifton Edwards Papers, AR 165-2. LA-UTA.

Federal Bureau of Investigation. *Uniform Crime Reports for the United States*. Washington, D.C.: Federal Bureau of Investigation, 1959. Bruce Alger Papers, Box 7, Folder 30. DPL.

Gambrell, Herbert. "Birth Places of Inhabitants of Dallas County [from] United States Census Data." Photocopy. Herbert Gambrell Collection, A40.183. DHS.

Garcia, Hector P. Letter, Corpus Christi, to the Honorable Homer Garrison, Austin, April 17, 1950. Hector P. Garcia Archives, Box 113, Folder 30. TAMU-CC.

———. Letter, Corpus Christi, to Gerald Saldaña, Crystal City, Texas, March 13, 1954. Hector P. Garcia Archives, Box 141, Folder 13. TAMU-CC.

Gauldin, Martin Austin. "Texas Journal, 1845," Herbert Gambrell Papers A3612. DHS.

Goldberg, Irving. Interview by John Rosenstein, Dallas, Texas, August 22, 1974. Transcript. TEAD.

Greenburg, William Henry. "History of the Jews of Dallas." *Reform Advocate*, January 24, 1914. TEAD.

Greenwald, Robert F. *Race Relations and the Intergroup Climate in Dallas, Texas: Analysis and Comment on the Nature of Intergroup Problems and the Potential for Resolution.* Dallas: North Texas Chapter of the Association of Intergroup Relations Officials, April 1967. DPL.

Hays, John W. "Preacher." Interview by anonymous person, Mabank, Texas, August 1 and August 7, 1976. Transcript, Special Collections Division, University of Texas at Arlington Libraries. OH 67. LA-UTA.

"Hearing Number 1 before the Industrial Commission of Texas. Garment Industry in Dallas County: Statement of Facts." George and Latane Lambert Collection, AR 127-11-1. LA-UTA.

Hurd, Carol Marie. Letter, Dallas, to Bruce Alger, Dallas, September 27, 1962. Bruce Alger Papers, Box 28, Folder 7. DPL.

"In Loving Memoriam of Dr. John Leslie Patton, Jr." Funeral card. DISD.

Kearney, Carrie, and Nora Crane. Interview by Toni Perry. Tape recording, June 1974 and March 6, 1976. University of Texas at Dallas Oral History Project. DPL.

Kurilecz, Peter, compiler, and Cindy C. Smolovik, archivist. *Dallas Negro Chamber of Commerce Collection Register and Researcher's Guide.* 1985. DPL.

Lacone, Leo. Letter from Lacone and others, Dallas, to the Most Rev. Joseph P. Lynch, D.D., January 22, 1940. RCD.

Lefkowitz, David. Letter, Dallas, to Dr. J. M. Dowis, Acting Director, Department of Public Health, City Hall, Dallas, May 7, 1942, Anti-Semitism in Dallas/Anti-Defamation League, B'nai B'rith Folder. TEAD.

Linfield, H. S. Letter, Director, Jewish Statistical Bureau, Auspices of National Council for Statistics of Jews, to Miss Aline Rutland, Secretary Congregation Emanu-El, Dallas, March 7, 1944, Anti-Semitism Folder. TEAD.

Manual of the First Congregation Church. Dallas: First Congregational Church, 1901. SMCA.

McCarty, John R. Letter, Dallas, to Dr. Hector P. Garcia, Corpus Christi, June 3, 1970. Garcia Archives, Box 81, Folder 59. TAMU-CC.

———. Letter, Dallas, to Vicente T. Ximines, Washington, D.C., February 25, 1970. Garcia Archives, Box 81, Folder 62. TAMU-CC.

McDermett, Addie K. Questionnaire completed for F. M. Cockrell, November 27, 1927, Sarah Horton Cockrell Collection, A4340, Folder A43155. DHS.

Medrano, Pancho. Interview by George Green and Carr Winn, Dallas, Texas, August 4, 1971. Transcript. OH 55. Division of Archives and Manuscripts. LA-UTA.

Miller, William. William Miller Family Scrapbook. Vol. 1. DPL.

Neill, Thomas A. Letter, Regional Representative, Dallas Region, N.P.U., to Mrs. Doris Butts, Washington, D.C., May 13, 1969. Hector P. Garcia Archives, Box 81, Folder 58. TAMU-CC.

Official Journal of the House of Representatives of the State of Texas at the Adjourned Session, Seventh Biennial Session. Austin: John Marshall and Co., State Printers, 1857.

Olan, Levi. Interview by Gerald D. Saxon, Dallas, February 4 and April 6, 1983. Tape recording, DPL Oral History Project. DPL.

Old Testament: The Dallas High Schools, March 1952. Bulletin 150 Authorized by the Board of Education, January 22, 1952. Dallas: Dallas Independent School District, 1952. TSL.

Patton, John Leslie. *Negro History: Outline for Pupils.* Dallas: Dallas Public Schools, 1939. A86.50. DHS.

"Read This: A Statement in Regard to the Candidacy of Earle B. Mayfield." George B. Dealey Collection, A6667, Folder 317. DHS.

Reagan, John H. Letter, Fort Warren, Boston Harbor, to the People of Texas, August 11, 1865. Transcript copy, John H. Reagan Collection, Miscellany File 2-23/1079, John H. Reagan Letters, Folder 31. TSL.

———. "Necessary Measures to Reconstruction." Letter, Fort Houston, Palestine, Texas, to Governor J. W. Throckmorton. Jefferson Davis Reagan Collection A4674, Folder 10. DHS.

Records of the Assistant Commissioner for the State of Texas, Bureau of Refugees, Freedmen, and Abandoned Lands, 1865–1869, National Archives, Rolls 6 and 24. DPL.

Records of the First Congregational Church of Dallas, Books 1 and 2. SMCA.

Reilly, Walter C. Interview by Dr. George Green, Dallas, July 29, 1971. Transcript, Special Collections Division, University of Texas at Arlington Libraries. OH 10. LA-UTA.

Robinson, Jimmy G. Letter, Garland, Texas, to Bruce Alger, Dallas, December 10, 1962. Bruce Alger Papers, Box 28, Folder 7. DPL.

Rodriguez, Jacob I. "Americans—Not Mejicas." Letter to the *San Antonio Express,* May 16, 1963. LULAC archives, Jacob I. Rodriguez Subcollection, Box 7, Folder 3. BLAC.

Saldaña, Gerald. Letter, Crystal City, Texas, to Dr. Hector P. Garcia, Corpus Christi, March 9, 1954. Garcia Archives, Box 141, Folder 13. TAMU-CC.

Sanger, Alex. Alex Sanger Scrapbook, A3967 MSB. DHS.

"A Service of Thanksgiving and Dedication on the Occasion of the Hundredth Anniversary of the Founding of the City of Dallas." Program, November 23, 1941. TSL.

Sherrill, F. L. Letter "dedicated to the greater interest of the Dallas Morning News," Greenville, Texas, February 18, 1922. George B. Dealey Collection A6667, Folder 314. DHS.

Smith, A. Maceo. Interview by Gayle Tomlinson. Tape recording, January 12, 1978. Dallas Public Library Oral History Project. DPL.

Webb, S. Letter, Albany, Texas, to Colonel G. B. Dealey, April 25, 1922. George B. Dealey Collection, A6667, Folder 314. DHS.

"Why Should Dallas Dressmakers Get Less Wages than Northern Workers?" Leaflet. International Ladies Garment Workers Union Collection, n.d. AR 167-1. LA-UTA.

"Will The Federal Suffrage Amendment Complicate the Race Problem?" Leaflet. National Literature Headquarters, Congressional Union for Woman Suffrage, n.d. Negative Collection, Box 11, A42.200. DHS.

OTHER SOURCES

Accoe, Will. "Ma Dandy Soldier Coon." New York: Jos. W. Stearn and Co., 1900.

Acheson, Sam. *Dallas Yesterday*. Dallas: Southern Methodist University Press, 1977.

Achor, Shirley. *Mexican Americans in a Dallas Barrio*. Tucson: University of Arizona Press, 1991.

Acuña, Rodolfo. *Occupied America: A History of Chicanos*. New York: HarperCollins Publishers, 1988.

Adams, James Truslow, and Charles Garrett Vannest. *The Record of America*. Dallas: Charles Scribner's Sons, 1935.

Addington, Wendell G. "Slave Insurrections in Texas." *Journal of Negro History* 35, no. 4 (October 1950).

African American Almanac. 7th ed. Detroit: Gale Research, 1994.

Alexander, Charles C. *Ku Klux Klan in the Southwest*. Lexington: University of Kentucky Press, 1965.

Allen, Theodore W. *The Invention of the White Race*. Vol. 1, *Racial Oppression and Social Control*. New York: Verso, 1990.

Alexander, Charles C. *Crusade for Conformity: The Ku Klux Klan in Texas, 1920–1930*. Houston: Texas Gulf Coast Historical Association, 1962.

———. *The Ku Klux Klan in the Southwest*. Lexington: University of Kentucky Press, 1966.

Allsup, Carl. *The American GI Forum: Origins and Evolution*. Monograph No. 6, Canter for Mexican American Studies. Austin: University of Texas Press, 1982.

Anderson, James D. *The Education of Blacks in the South, 1860–1935*. Chapel Hill: University of North Carolina Press, 1988.

Aptheker, Herbert. *American Negro Slave Revolts*. New York: Columbia University Press, 1943.

Arnesen, Eric. "Whiteness in the Historians' Imagination." *International Labor and Working Class History*, no. 60, fall 2001.

Ayers, Edward L. *The Promise of the New South: Life After Reconstruction*. Oxford, England: Oxford University Press, 1991.

Baker, T. Lindsay, and Julie P. Baker, eds. *Till Freedom Cried Out: Memories of Texas Slave Life*. College Station: Texas A&M University Press, 1997.

Ballard, Allen B. *The Education of Black Folk: The Afro-American Struggle for Knowledge in White America*. New York: Harper and Row, 1973.

Ballard, Lee. "The Rise and Decline of Deep Ellum." *Westward,* Sunday magazine of *Dallas Times Herald,* September 25, 1983.

Barkan, Elazar. *The Retreat of Scientific Racism: Changing Concepts of Race in Britain and the United States between the World Wars.* New York: Cambridge University Press, 1992.

Barker, Eugene C. "The Influence of Slavery on the Colonization of Texas," *Mississippi Valley Historical Review* 11 (June 1924).

Barkun, Michael. *Religion and the Racist Right: The Origins of the Christian Identity Movement.* Chapel Hill: University of North Carolina Press, 1994.

Barnes, Donna A. *Farmers in Rebellion: The Rise and Fall of the Southern Farmers Alliance and Peoples' Party in Texas.* Austin: University of Texas Press, 1984.

Barr, Alwyn. *Black Texans: A History of African Americans in Texas, 1528–1995.* Norman: University of Oklahoma Press, 1996.

Bauerlein, Mark. *Negrophobia: A Race Riot in Atlanta, 1906.* San Francisco: Encounter Books, 2001.

Bauman, Mark K., and Berkley Kalin, eds. *The Quiet Voices: Southern Rabbis and Black Civil Rights, 1880s to 1990s.* Tuscaloosa, Ala.: University of Alabama Press, 1997.

Beaty, John. *The Iron Curtain over America.* Dallas: Wilkinson Publishing Co., 1956.

Beeth, Howard, and Carl D. Wintz, eds. *Black Dixie: Afro-Texas History and Culture in Houston.* College Station: Texas A&M University Press, 1992.

Belfiglio, Valentine J. "Early Italian Settlers in Dallas: A New Life with Old Values." *Heritage News: A Journal Devoted to the History of North Central Texas* 10, no. 4 (winter 1985–1986).

Berlet, Chip, and Matthew N. Lyons. *Right-Wing Populism in America: Too Close for Comfort.* New York: Guilford Press, 2000.

Be Vier, William A. "A Biographical Sketch of C. I. Scofield." Master's thesis, Southern Methodist University, 1960.

Biles, Roger. "The New Deal in Dallas." *Southwestern Historical Quarterly* 95, no. 1 (July 1991).

Bishop, Jim. *The Day Kennedy Was Shot.* New York: Funk and Wagnalls, 1968.

Boles, John. *The South through Time: A History of an American Region.* Englewood Cliffs, N.J.: Prentice Hall, 1995.

Bomar, George W. *Texas Weather.* Austin: University of Texas Press, 1983.

Boswell, James David. "Negro Participation in the 1936 Texas Centennial Exposition." Master's report, University of Texas, 1969.

Boyer, Paul. *When Time Shall Be No More: Prophecy Belief in Modern American Culture.* Cambridge, Mass.: Harvard University Press, Belknap Press, 1992.

Branch, Taylor. *Parting the Waters: America in the King Years, 1954–1963.* New York: Simon and Schuster, 1988.

Brear, Holly Beachley. *Inherit The Alamo: Myth and Ritual at an American Shrine.* Austin: University of Texas Press, 1995.

Brewer, J. Mason. *American Negro Folklore.* Chicago: Quadrangle Books, 1968.

———. *Aunt Dicy Tales: Snuff-Dipping Tales of the Texas Negro.* Austin: Privately published, 1956.

———. *Dog Ghosts and Other Texas Negro Folk Tales*. Austin: University of Texas Press, 1958.

———. *Heralding Dawn: An Anthology of Verse*. Dallas: June Thomason Printing, 1936.

———. "John Tales." In J. Frank Dobie, ed., *Mexican Border Ballads and Other Lore*, vol. 31. Austin: Texas Folklore Society, 1946.

———. *The Word on the Brazos: Negro Preacher Tales from the Brazos Bottoms of Texas*. Austin: University of Texas Press, 1953.

Brown, John Henry. *A History of Dallas County, Texas: From 1837 to 1887*. Dallas: Milligan, Cornett and Farnham, Printers, 1887.

———. "A Report and Treatise on Slavery and the Slavery Agitation." Austin: John Marshall and Co., State Printers, 1857. CAH.

Brown, Norman D. *Hood, Bonnet, and Little Brown Jug: Texas Politics. 1921–1928*. College Station: Texas A&M University Press, 1984.

Bryson, Conrey. *Dr. Lawrence A. Nixon and the White Primary*. El Paso: Texas Western Press, 1992.

Bugbee, Lester G. "Slavery in Early Texas." *Political Science Quarterly* 13, parts 1 (September 1898) and 2 (December 1898).

Bullard, Robert D., Glenn S. Johnson, and Angel O. Torres, eds. *Sprawl City: Race, Politics, and Planning in Atlanta*. Washington, D.C.: Island Press, 2000.

Butler, Steve. "Honoring the Past: Confederate Monuments in Dallas." *Legacies: A History Journal for Dallas and North Central Texas* 1, no. 2 (fall 1989).

Byrd, James. *J. Mason Brewer: Negro Folklorist*. Austin: Steck-Vaughn Co., 1967.

Calvert, Robert, and Arnoldo de León. *The History of Texas*. Wheeling, Ill.: Harlan-Davidson, 1996.

Campbell, Randolph B. *An Empire for Slavery: The Peculiar Institution in Texas, 1821–1865*. Baton Rouge: Louisiana State University Press, 1989.

———. *Gone to Texas: A History of the Lone Star State*. New York: Oxford University Press, 2003.

———. *Grass-Roots Reconstruction in Texas, 1865–1880*. Baton Rouge: Louisiana State University, 1997.

———. *A Southern Community in Crisis: Harrison County, Texas, 1850–1880*. Austin: Texas State Historical Association, 1983.

Campbell, Randolph B., and Richard G. Lowe. *Wealth and Power in Antebellum Texas*. College Station: Texas A&M University Press, 1977.

Canfield, Joseph M. *The Incredible Scofield and His Book*. Asheville, N.C.: Privately published, 1984.

Carleton, Don E. *Red Scare! Right Wing Hysteria, Fifties Fanaticism, and Their Legacy in Texas*. Austin: Texas Monthly Press, 1985.

Carpenter, V. K., transcriber. *The State of Texas Federal Population Schedules, Seventh Census of the United States, 1850*. Vol. 2. Huntsville, Ark.: Century Enterprises, 1969.

Carroll, Charles. *The Negro a Beast*. 1900. Reprint, New York: Books for Libraries Press, 1980.

Carroll, Joseph Cephas. *Slave Insurrections in the United States, 1800–1865.* Boston: Chapman and Grimes, 1938.

Carroll, Mark M. "Families, Sex, and the Law in Frontier Texas." Ph.D. diss., University of Houston, 1996.

Carson, Clayborne. *In Struggle: SNCC and the Black Awakening of the 1960s.* Cambridge, Mass.: Harvard University Press, 1981.

Carter, Dan T. *From George Wallace to Newt Gingrich: Race in the Conservative Counterrevolution, 1963–1994.* Baton Rouge: Louisiana State University Press, 1996.

———. *The Politics of Rage: George Wallace, the Origins of the New Conservatism, and the Transformation of American Politics.* Baton Rouge: Louisiana State University Press, 1995.

Carter, Everett. "Cultural History Written with Lightning: The Significance of *The Birth of a Nation.*" *American Quarterly* 12 (fall 1960).

Casdorph, Paul. *A History of the Republican Party in Texas, 1865–1965.* Austin: Pemberton Press, 1965.

Cashman, Sean Dennis. *African Americans and the Quest for Civil Rights.* New York: New York University Press, 1991.

Castle, A. W. *Reader and Guide for New Americans.* Book 2. New York: MacMillan Co., 1924.

Castleberry, Vivian Anderson. *Daughters of Dallas: A History of Greater Dallas through the Voices and Deeds of Its Women.* Dallas: Odenwald Press, 1994.

Chalmers, David M. *Hooded Americanism: The History of the Ku Klux Klan.* Durham, N.C.: Duke University Press, 1981.

Chariton, Wallace Owen. *Texas Centennial: The Parade of an Empire.* Plano, Texas: Texas Centennial, 1979.

Cochran, John H. *Dallas County: A Record of Its Pioneers and Progress.* Dallas: Arthur S. Mathis Service Publishing Co., 1928.

Cockrell, Frank M. *History of Early Dallas.* Chicago: Privately published, 1944.

Cockrell, Monroe F. *Sarah Horton Cockrell in Early Dallas.* Chicago: Privately published, 1944.

Collier-Thomas, Bettye, and V. P. Franklin. *Sisters in the Struggle: African American Women in the Civil Rights–Black Power Movement.* New York: New York University Press, 2001.

Connor, Seymour V. *The Peters Colony of Texas: A History and Biographical Sketches of the Early Settlers.* Austin: Texas State Historical Association, 1959.

Corbey, Raymond. "Ethnographic Showcases, 1870–1930." *Cultural Anthropology* 8 (1993).

Cox, Kathy, and Pierce Allman. "State-Thomas Historic District: Dallas' Oldest Neighborhood Development Nestles in Skyscraper Shadows." *Historic Dallas* (November–December 1984).

Cox, Michael, and Martin Durham. "The Politics of Anger: The Extreme Right in the United States." In Paul Hainsworth, ed., *The Politics of the Extreme Right: From the Margins to the Mainstream.* New York: Pinter, 2000.

Cox, William E. *An Examination of Dispensationalism.* Philadelphia: Presbyterian and Reformed Publishing Co., 1963.

Cripps, Thomas. *Slow Fade to Black: The Negro in American Film, 1900–1942*. New York: Oxford University Press, 1993.

Cristol, Gerry. *A Light in the Prairie: Temple Emanu-El of Dallas, 1872–1997*. Fort Worth: Texas Christian University, 1998.

Croly, David G. *Miscegenation: The Theory of the Blending of the Races, Applied to the American White Man and Negro*. New York: H. Dexter, Hamilton and Co., 1864.

Crook, Carland Elaine. "San Antonio, Texas, 1846–1861." Master's thesis, Rice University, 1964.

Crouch, Barry. *The Freedmen's Bureau and Black Texans*. Austin: University of Texas Press, 1992.

———. "A Spirit of Lawlessness: White Violence, Texas Blacks, 1865–1868." *Journal of Social History* 18 (winter 1984).

Curlee, Abigail. "The History of a Texas Slave Plantation, 1861–63." *Southwestern Historical Quarterly* 26 (October 1922).

Curran, Thomas. *Xenophobia and Immigration, 1820–1930*. Boston: Twayne Publishers, 1975.

Current, Richard Nelson. *Those Terrible Carpetbaggers: A Reinterpretation*. New York: Oxford University Press, 1988.

Curtis, Gregory. "A Book's Improper Burial." *Texas Monthly,* November 1986.

Dabney, Lewis Meriwether. *Memoirs and Letters*. New York: Privately published by J. J. Little and Ives Co., 1924.

Dallas at the Crossroads. Film. 1961. Commissioned by the Dallas Citizens Council and produced by Sam Bloom. Copy in author's possession.

Dallas County Citizens League. "The Case against the Ku Klux Klan." Pamphlet. Dallas: Venney Co., 1922.

"The Dallas Rejoinder." *Nation,* May 25, 1964.

"Dallasites Picket Store: H. L. Green's Stands Firm." *Texas Observer,* October 14, 1960.

Davidson, Chandler. *Race and Class in Texas Politics*. Princeton, N.J.: Princeton University Press, 1990.

Davis, Jack, ed. *The Civil Rights Movement*. Malden, Mass.: Blackwell Publishers, 2001.

Davis, Mike. *City of Quartz: Excavating the Future in Los Angeles*. New York: Vintage Books, 1992.

Dawley, Alan. *Struggles for Justice: Social Responsibility and the Liberal State*. Cambridge, Mass.: Harvard University Press, Belknap Press, 1991.

DeFord, Miriam Allen. *On Being Concerned: The Vanguard Years of Carl and Laura Brannin*. Dallas: n.p., 1969.

de León, Arnoldo. *Mexican Americans in Texas: A Brief History*. Wheeling, Ill.: Harlan Davidson, 1999.

———. *They Called Them Greasers: Anglo Attitudes Toward Mexicans in Texas, 1821–1900*. Austin: University of Texas Press, 1983.

Diamond, Sara. *Roads to Dominion: Right-Wing Movements and Political Power in the United States*. New York: Guilford Press, 1995.

Dinnerstein, Leonard. *Anti-Semitism in America*. New York: Oxford University Press, 1994.

————. *The Leo Frank Case.* 1968. Reprint, Athens: University of Georgia Press, 1987.

Dollinger, Mark. "'Hamans' and 'Torquemadas': Southern and Northern Jewish Responses to the Civil Rights Movement, 1945–1965." In Mark Bauman and Berkley Kalin, eds., *The Quiet Voices: Southern Rabbis and Black Civil Rights, 1880s to 1990s.* Tuscaloosa, Ala.: University of Alabama Press, 1997.

Dorsett, Jesse. "Blacks in Reconstruction Texas, 1865–1877." Ph.D. diss., Texas Christian University, 1981.

Dower, John W. *War without Mercy: Race and Power in the Pacific War.* New York: Pantheon Books, 1986.

Dozier, Richard K. "A Historical Survey: Black Architects and Craftsmen." *Black World,* May 1974.

DuBois, W. E. B. *Black Reconstruction in America, 1860–1880.* 1935. Reprint, New York: Simon and Schuster, Touchstone, 1995.

Dulaney, W. Marvin. "The Progressive Voters League: A Political Voice for African Americans in Dallas." *Legacies: A History Journal for Dallas and North Central Texas* 3, no. 1 (spring 1991).

————. Review of *The Accommodation: The Politics of Race in An American City* by Jim Schutze. *Southwestern Historical Quarterly* 93, no. 3 (January 1990).

————. "Whatever Happened to the Civil Rights Movement in Dallas, Texas?" In Dulaney and Kathleen Underwood, eds., *Essays on the American Civil Rights Movement.* College Station: Texas A&M University Press for University of Texas at Arlington, 1993.

Eibling, Howard H., Fred M. King, and James Harlow. *Our United States: A Bulwark of Freedom.* Dallas: Laidlaw Brothers, Publishers, 1962.

Elliott, Claude. "The Life of James W. Throckmorton." Ph.D. diss., University of Texas at Austin, 1934.

Eppes, Ken. "St. Peter the Apostle Parish: Marker to Honor History of Service to the Disenfranchised." *Parish,* September 20, 1996.

Evans, H. W. "The Public School Problem in America." Pamphlet. United States: Ku Klux Klan, 1924.

Evans, J. Claude Evans. "The Dallas Image Unveiled," *Christian Century,* November 20, 1963.

Fairbanks, Robert. *For the City as a Whole: Planning, Politics and the Public Interest in Dallas, Texas, 1900–1965.* Columbus: Ohio State University Press, 1998.

Farmer, William R. Interview by author, Dallas, Texas, January 1999.

————. "Samuel, Patrick and Cato: A History of the Dallas Fire of 1860 and Its Tragic Aftermath." N.p., n.d. Photocopy in author's possession.

Fields, Barbara Jeanne. "Slavery, Race, and Ideology in the United States of America." *New Left Review* 181 (May–June 1990).

————. "Whiteness, Racism and Identity." *International Labor and Working Class History,* no. 60 (fall 2001).

Foley, Douglas E. *Learning Capitalist Culture: Deep in the Heart of Tejas.* Philadelphia: University of Pennsylvania Press, 1990.

Foley, Douglas E., Clarice Mota, Donald E. Post, and Ignacio Lozano. *From Peones to Politicos: Ethnic Relations in a South Texas Town, 1900–1977.* Austin: University of Texas Center for Mexican American Studies, 1977.

Foley, Neil. *The White Scourge: Mexicans, Blacks, and Poor Whites in Texas Cotton Culture.* Berkeley: University of California Press, 1997.

Foner, Eric. *Reconstruction: America's Unfinished Revolution, 1863–1877.* New York: Harper and Row, Perennial Library, 1989.

Forman, Seth. *Blacks in the Jewish Mind: A Crisis of Liberalism.* New York: New York University Press, 1998.

Franklin, John Hope. *"Birth of a Nation—*Propaganda as History." *Massachusetts Review* 20 (autumn 1979).

Fredriksen, Paula. *From Jesus to Christ: The Origins of the New Testament Images of Jesus.* New Haven: Yale University Press, 1988.

Frerichs, Ernest S., ed. *The Bible and Bibles in America.* Atlanta: Scholars Press, 1988.

Freud, Sigmund. *Civilization and Its Discontents.* New York: W. W. Norton, 1961.

Frey, Robert Seitz, and Nancy Thompson-Frey. *The Silent and the Damned: The Murder of Mary Phagan and the Lynching of Leo Frank.* Lanham, Md.: Madison Books, 1988.

Fuller, Robert. *Naming the Antichrist: The History of an American Obsession.* New York: Oxford University Press, 1995.

Gallaway, B. P. *The Ragged Rebel: A Common Soldier in W. H. Parsons' Texas Cavalry, 1861–1865.* Austin: University of Texas Press, 1988.

Gammel, H. P. N., ed. *The Laws of Texas: 1822–1897.* 4 vols. Austin: Gammel Book Co., 1898.

García, Richard A. *Rise of the Mexican American Middle Class: San Antonio, 1929–1941.* College Station: Texas A&M University Press, 1991.

Genovese, Eugene D. *Roll, Jordan, Roll: The World the Slaves Made.* New York: Vintage Books, 1976.

Gerstner, John H. *Wrongly Dividing the Word of Truth: A Critique of Dispensationalism.* Brentwood, Tenn.: Wolgemuth and Hyatt, 1991.

Giddings, Paula. *When and Where I Enter: The Impact of Black Women on Race and Sex in America.* New York: Bantam Books, 1985.

Gillette, Michael Lowery. "The NAACP in Texas, 1937–1957." Ph.D. diss., University of Texas at Austin, 1984.

Goldberg, Robert Alan. *Hooded Empire: The Ku Klux Klan in Colorado.* Urbana: University of Illinois Press, 1981.

Gómez-Quiñones, Juan. *Chicano Politics: Reality and Promise, 1940–1990.* Albuquerque: University of New Mexico Press, 1990.

Goodwyn, Lawrence. *The Populist Moment: A Short History of the Agrarian Revolt in America.* New York: Oxford University Press, 1978.

Gould, Stephen Jay. *Ever since Darwin: Reflections in Natural History.* New York: W. W. Norton, 1977.

———. *The Mismeasure of Man.* New York: W. W. Norton, 1981.

Gourevitch, Philip. *We Regret to Inform You That Tomorrow We Will Be Killed with Our Families: Stories from Rwanda.* New York: Picador USA, 1999.

Govenar, Alan B., and Jay F. Brakesfield. *Deep Ellum and Central Track: Where the Black and White Worlds of Dallas Converged.* Denton: University of North Texas Press, 1998.

Gower, Patricia E. "Creating Consensus, Fostering Neglect: Municipal Policy in the Progressive Era." Paper presented at the 104th annual meeting of the Texas State Historical Association, Austin, March 2, 2000.

Graff, Harvey J. "How Can You Celebrate a Sesquicentennial If You Have No History? Reflections on Historical Consciousness in the Dallas Area." Sesquicentennial essay, *Dallas Morning News,* 1986. Computer print-out in author's possession.

Gramsci, Antonio. *Prison Notebooks.* Vol. 1. New York: Columbia University Press, 1992.

Grant, Madison. *The Passing of the Great Race or the Racial Basis of European History.* New York: Charles Scribner's Sons, 1923.

Green, George Norris. *The Establishment in Texas Politics: The Primitive Years, 1938–1957.* Norman: University of Oklahoma Press, 1979.

———. "The Far Right Wing in Texas Politics, 1930's–1960's." Ph.D. diss., Florida State University, 1967.

———. "Some Aspects of the Far Right Wing in Texas Politics." In E. C. Barksdale, George Norris Green, and T. Harry Williams, eds., *Essays on Recent Southern Politics.* Austin: University of Texas Press for University of Texas at Arlington, 1970.

Green, James R. "The Brotherhood of Timber Workers, 1910–1913: A Radical Response to Industrial Capitalism in the Southern U.S.A." *Past and Present* 60 (August 1973).

———. *Grass-Roots Socialism: Radical Movements in the Southwest, 1895–1943.* Baton Rouge: Louisiana State University Press, 1978.

Greenberg, Cheryl Lynn. *A Circle of Trust: Remembering SNCC.* New Brunswick, N.J.: Rutgers University Press, 1998.

Greene, A. C. *Dallas, U.S.A.* Austin: Texas Monthly Press, 1984.

Gregory, Joel. *Too Great a Temptation: The Seductive Power of America's Super Church.* Fort Worth: Summit Group, 1994.

Gritz, Jack L. "Dr. Scofield's Error." *Baptist Standard,* July 13, 1960.

Gue, Mary, composer, and Walter Ardrell Riggs, arranger. "Ku Klux Kismet." Aransas Pass, Texas: Walter Ardrell Riggs, 1924.

Gutiérrez, David G. *Walls and Mirrors: Mexican Americans, Mexican Immigrants, and the Politics of Ethnicity.* Berkeley: University of California Press, 1995.

Gutman, Herbert George. "The Negro and the United Mine Workers of America: The Career and Letters of Richard L. Davis and Something of Their Meaning: 1890–1900." In Julius Jacobson, ed., *The Negro and the American Labor Movement.* Garden, City, N.Y.: Anchor Books, 1968.

Haldeman-Julius, E. *Is the Ku Klux Klan Constructive or Destructive? A Debate between Wizard Evans, Israel Zangwill, and Others.* Girard, Kansas: Haldeman-Julius Co., 1924.

Hale, Grace Elizabeth. *Making Whiteness: The Culture of Segregation in the South, 1890–1940.* New York: Pantheon Books, 1998.

Hall, Jacquelyn Dowd. " 'The Mind that Burns in Each Body': Women, Rape, and Racial Violence." *Southern Exposure* 12, no. 6 (1984).

———. *Revolt against Chivalry: Jessie Daniel Ames and the Women's Campaign against Lynching.* New York: Columbia University Press, 1993.

Hall, John T. "Looney Coons." New York: John T. Hall Music Publishing Company, 1900.

Hall, Stuart. "Gramsci's Relevance for the Study of Race and Ethnicity." *Journal of Communication Inquiry* 10, no. 2 (1986).

Hamer, Andrew Marshall. "Urban Perspectives for the 1980s." In Andrew Marshall Hamer, ed., *Urban Atlanta: Redefining the Role of the City.* Atlanta: Georgia State University, 1980.

Hannaford, Ivan. *Race: The History of an Idea in the West.* Baltimore: Woodrow Wilson Center Press for Johns Hopkins University Press, 1996.

Harmon, David Andrew. *Beneath the Image of the Civil Rights Movement and Race Relations: Atlanta, Georgia, 1946–1981.* New York: Garland Publishing, 1996.

Harris, Cheryl I. "Whiteness as Property." *Harvard Law Review* 106, no. 8 (June 1993).

Harris, Leon. *Merchant Princes: An Intimate History of the Jewish Families Who Built Great Department Stores.* New York: Harper and Row, 1977.

Hartigan, John. *Racial Situations: Class Predicaments of Whiteness in Detroit.* Princeton, N.J.: Princeton University Press, 1998.

Hayes, Carlton J. H., Parker Thomas Moon, and John W. Wayland. *World History.* New York: MacMillan Co., 1935.

Hazel, Michael V. "The Critic Club: Sixty Years of Quiet Leadership." *Legacies: A History Journal for Dallas and North Central Texas* 2, no. 2 (fall 1990).

———. "From Distant Shores: European Immigrants in Dallas." *Heritage News: A Journal Devoted to the History of North Central Texas* 10, no. 1 (spring 1985).

Herskovits, Melville J. *The Myth of the Negro Past.* Boston: Beacon Press, 1941.

Higham, John. *Strangers in the Land: Patterns of American Nativism, 1860–1925.* 1955. Reprint, New Brunswick, N.J., 1994.

Hill, Marilynn Wood. "A History of the Jewish Involvement in the Dallas Community." Master's thesis, Southern Methodist University, 1967.

Hill, Patricia Evridge. *Dallas: The Making of a Modern City.* Austin: University of Texas Press, 1996.

Hine, Darlene Clark. *Black Victory: The Rise and Fall of the White Primary in Texas.* Millwood, N.Y.: KTO Press, 1979.

Hodes, Martha Elizabeth. *White Women, Black Men: Illicit Sex in the Nineteenth-Century South.* New Haven: Yale University Press, 1997.

———, ed. *Sex, Love, Race: Crossing Boundaries in North American History.* New York: New York University Press, 1999.

Hofstadter, Richard. *The Paranoid Style in American Politics and Other Essays.* 1952. Reprint, Cambridge, Mass.: Harvard University Press, 1964.

Hollandsworth, Skip. "Race Matters: Ron Kirk Is Ready to Be Dallas' First Black Mayor. But Is Dallas Ready for Him?" *Texas Monthly,* May 1995.

Holley, Steven D. "The Dallas *Morning News* and the *Times Herald* and the Image of Dallas in the Decade after the Kennedy Assassination." Master's thesis, University of Texas, 1974.

Hoover, J. Edgar. *Masters of Deceit: The Story of Communism in America and How to Fight It.* New York: Henry Holt and Co., 1958.

Horwitz, Tony. *Confederates in the Attic: Dispatches from the Unfinished Civil War.* New York: Vintage Books, 1998.

Howard, James. *Big D Is for Dallas: Chapters in the Twentieth Century History of Dallas.* Ann Arbor: Edward Brothers, 1957.

Hunt, H. L. *Alpaca.* Dallas: H. L. Hunt Press, 1960.

Hunter, Tera W. *To 'Joy My Freedom: Southern Black Women's Lives and Labors after the Civil War.* Cambridge, Mass.: Harvard University Press, 1997.

Hurst, Jack. *Nathan Bedford Forrest: A Biography.* New York: Alfred A. Knopf, 1993.

Institute for Historical Review. Journal of Historical Review: The "Holocaust" Put in Perspective. http://ihr.org.

Jackson, Kenneth T. *The Ku Klux Klan in the City, 1915–1930.* New York: Oxford University Press, 1967.

Jackson, Susan. "Slavery in Houston: The 1850s." *Houston Review* 2 (1980).

Jacobson, Matthew Frye. *Barbarian Virtues: The United States' Encounters With Foreign Peoples at Home and Abroad, 1876–1917.* New York: Hill and Wang, 2000.

———. *Whiteness of a Different Color: European Immigrants and the Alchemy of Race.* Cambridge, Mass.: Harvard University Press, 1999.

Jaher, Frederic Cople. *A Scapegoat in the Wilderness: The Origins and Rise of Anti-Semitism in America.* Cambridge, Mass.: Harvard University Press, 1994.

Jordan, Winthrop D. *White over Black: American Attitudes Towards the Negro, 1550–1812.* New York: W. W. Norton, 1968.

Junkins, Enda. "Slave Plots, Insurrections, and Acts of Violence in the State of Texas, 1828–1865." Master's thesis, Baylor University, 1969.

Kellar, William Henry. *Make Haste Slowly: Moderates, Conservatives, and School Desegregation in Houston.* College Station: Texas A&M University Press, 1999.

Kimball, Justin F. *Our City—Dallas: A Community Civics.* Dallas: Kessler Plan Association of Dallas, 1927.

Kitano, Harry. "Jews in the U.S.: The Rising Costs of Whiteness." In Becky Thompson and Sangeeta Tyagi, eds., *Names We Call Home: Autobiography on Racial Identity.* New York: Routledge, 1996.

Knaggs, John R. *Two-Party Texas: The John Tower Era, 1961–1984.* Austin: Eakin Press, 1986.

Knight, Alan. "Racism, Revolution, and *Indigenismo:* Mexico, 1910–1940." In Richard Graham, ed., *The Idea of Race in Latin America, 1870–1940.* Austin: University of Texas Press, 1990.

Kohn, Marek. *The Race Gallery: The Return of Racial Science.* London: Vintage, 1996.

Ladd, Jerrold. *Out of the Madness: From the Projects to a Life of Hope.* New York: Warner Books, 1994.

Lamis, Alexander P. *The Two-Party South.* New York: Oxford University Press, 1984.

Landregan, Steve. Interview by author, Dallas, Texas, August 3, 1999.

Larson, Edward J. *Sex, Race, and Science: Eugenics in the Deep South.* Baltimore: Johns Hopkins University Press, 1995.

Lay, Shawn, ed. *The Invisible Empire in the West: Toward a New Historical Appraisal of the Ku Klux Klan of the 1920s.* Urbana: University of Illinois, 1992.

Leslie, Warren. *Dallas Public and Private: Aspects of an American City.* New York: Grossman Publishers, 1964.

Levine, Lawrence W. *Black Culture and Black Consciousness: Afro-American Folk Thought From Slavery To Freedom.* New York: Oxford University Press, 1977.

———. *Highbrow/Lowbrow: The Emergence of Cultural Hierarchy in America.* Cambridge, Mass.: Harvard University Press, 1988.

Lewis, Willie Newbury. *Willie, a Girl from a Town Called Dallas.* College Station: Texas A&M University Press, 1984.

Limón, José E. "The Folk Performance of '*Chicano*' and the Cultural Limits of Political Ideology." In Richard Bauman and Roger D. Abrahams, eds., *And Other Neighborly Names: Social Process and Cultural Image in Texas Folklore.* Austin: University of Texas Press, 1981.

Linden, Glenn M. *Desegregating Schools in Dallas: Four Decades in the Federal Courts.* Dallas: Three Forks Press, 1995.

Lindsey, Hal. *The Late Great Planet Earth.* Grand Rapids: Zondervan Publishing House, 1970.

Lindsley, Philip. *A History of Greater Dallas and Vicinity.* Vol. 1. Chicago: Lewis Publishing Co., 1909.

Lipsitz, George. *Possessive Investment in Whiteness: How White People Profit from Identity Politics.* Philadelphia: Temple University Press, 1998.

Lipstadt, Deborah. *Denying the Holocaust: The Growing Assault on Truth and Memory.* New York: Plume, 1994.

Litwack, Leon F. *Been in the Storm So Long: The Aftermath of Slavery.* New York: Random House, Vintage Books, 1979.

Livingston, David William. "The Lynching of Negroes in Texas, 1900–1925." Master's thesis, East Texas State University, 1972.

Lonn, Ella. *Desertion during the Civil War.* 1928. Reprint, Gloucester, Mass.: P. Smith, 1966.

López, Ian F. Haney. *White by Law: The Legal Construction of Race.* New York: New York University Press, 1996.

Lott, Eric. *Love and Theft: Blackface Minstrelsy and the American Working Class.* New York: Oxford University Press, 1993.

MacLean, Nancy. *Behind the Mask of Chivalry: The Making of the Second Ku Klux Klan.* New York: Oxford University Press, 1994.

MacPherson, Dave. *The Great Rapture Hoax.* Fletcher, N.C.: New Puritan Library, 1983.

Marcus, Stanley. *Minding the Store: A Memoir.* Boston: Little, Brown and Co., 1974.

Margot, Louis III. "The *Dallas Express*: A Negro Newspaper. Its History, 1892–1971, and Its Point of View." Master's thesis, East Texas State University, 1971.

Marquez, Benjamin. *LULAC: The Evolution of A Mexican American Political Organization.* Austin: University of Texas Press, 1993.

Martin, Roscoe Coleman. *The People's Party in Texas: A Study in Third Party Politics,* University of Texas Bulletin 3308. Austin: University of Texas, 1933.

"May God Forgive Dallas." *Newsweek,* December 9, 1963.

Mayo, Louise A. *The Ambivalent Image: Nineteenth Century America's Perception of the Jew.* London: Associated University Press, 1988.

McAlester, Virginia. "State-Thomas: Prime Acreage in Dallas' Heartland Expected to Fashion City Lifestyle." *Visions of Dallas,* March 16–22, 1987.

McCaslin, Richard B. *Tainted Breeze: The Great Hanging at Gainesville, Texas, 1862.* Baton Rouge: Louisiana State University Press, 1994.

McComb, David G. *Houston: A History.* Austin: University of Texas Press, 1981.

McCombs, Holland. "The Dydamic Men of Dallas." *Fortune,* February 1949.

McGrath, Sister Paul of the Cross. "Political Nativism in Texas, 1825–1960." Ph.D. diss., Catholic University of America, 1930.

McKinley, Albert E., Arthur C. Howland, and Matthew L. Dann. *World History in the Making.* New York: American Book Co., 1927.

Meinig, Donald W. *Imperial Texas: An Interpretive Essay in Cultural Geography.* Austin: University of Texas Press, 1969.

———. *The Shaping of America: A Geographical Perspective on 500 Years of History.* Vol. 2, *Continental America, 1800–1867.* New Haven, Conn.: Yale University Press, 1993.

———. *Southwest: Three Peoples in Geographical Change, 1600–1970.* New York: Oxford University Press, 1971.

Melnick, Jeffrey Paul. *Black-Jewish Relations on Trial: Leo Frank and Jim Conley in the New South.* Jackson: University Press of Mississippi, 2000.

Memorial and Biographical History of Dallas County, Texas. Chicago: Lewis Publishing Co., 1892.

Miles, Michael W. *The Odyssey of the American Right.* New York: Oxford University Press, 1980.

Minutaglio, Bill, and Holly Williams. "The Big Fix-up." *Dallas Life Magazine,* Sunday magazine, *Dallas Morning News,* June 23, 1991.

Montejano, David. *Anglos and Texans in the Making of Texas, 1836–1986.* Austin: University of Texas Press, 1987.

Morgan, Edmund S. *American Slavery/American Freedom: The Ordeal of Colonial Virginia.* New York: W. W. Norton, 1975.

Mosse, George L. *Toward the Final Solution: A History of European Racism.* New York: H. Fertig, 1978.

Muzzey, David Saville. *History of the American People.* Dallas: Ginn and Co., 1929.

Neff, Bill. Telephone interview by author, September 28, 1999.

Noontide Press. Zionism, Israel and the Jewish Question. http://www.noontide press.com.

Norton, Wesley. "The Methodist Episcopal Church and the Civil Disturbances in North Texas in 1859 and 1860." *Southwestern Historical Quarterly* 68, no. 3 (January 1965).

Olmsted, Frederick Law. *A Journey through Texas: Or, a Saddle Trip on the Southwestern Frontier*. 1857. Reprint, Austin: University of Texas Press, 1978.

Omi, Michael and Howard Winant. *Racial Formation in the United States from the 1960s to the 1990s*. New York: Routledge, 1994.

Orozco, Cynthia E. "The Origins of the League of United Latin American Citizens (LULAC) and the Mexican American Civil Rights Movement in Texas with an Analysis of Women's Political Participation in a Gendered Context, 1910–1929." Ph.D. diss., University of California—Los Angeles, 1992.

Pascoe, Peggy. "Miscegenation Law, Court Cases, and Ideologies of 'Race' in Twentieth-Century America." *Journal of American History* 83 (June 1996).

Payne, Darwin. *Big D: Triumphs and Troubles of an American Supercity in the 20th Century*. Dallas: Three Forks Press, 1994.

———. *Big D: Triumphs and Troubles of an American Supercity in the 20th Century*. Rev. ed. Dallas: Three Forks Press, 2000.

———. *Dallas: An Illustrated History*. Woodland Hills, Calif.: Windsor Publications, 1982.

Payton, Donald. Letter, Dallas, Texas, to the author, Apple Valley, Calif., May 25, 1994.

Peck, Gunther. *Reinventing Free Labor: Padrones and Immigrant Workers in the North American West, 1880–1930*. New York: Cambridge University Press, 2000.

Pencak, William. *For God and Country: The American Legion, 1919–1941*. Boston: Northeastern University Press, 1989.

Phillips, Michael. "White Violence, Hegemony, and Slave Rebellion in Dallas, Texas, before the Civil War." *East Texas Historical Journal* 37, no. 2 (1999).

Pierce, Evelyn Miller. *Hilltop*. New York: Alfred H. King, 1931.

Pitre, Merline. *Through Many Dangers, Toils and Snares: The Black Leadership of Texas, 1868–1900*. Austin: Eakin Press, 1985.

Pitts, Walter F. Jr. *Old Ship of Zion: The Afro-Baptist Ritual in the African Diaspora*. New York: Oxford University Press, 1993.

Potok, Chaim. *Wanderings: Chaim Potok's History of the Jews*. New York: Fawcett Crest, 1978.

Pratt, James. "Our European Heritage: The Diverse Contributions of La Réunion." *Legacies: A History Journal for Dallas and North Central Texas* 1, no. 2 (fall 1989).

Prince, Robert. *A History of Dallas: From A Different Perspective*. Dallas: Sunbelt Media, Nortex Press, 1993.

Proctor, Ben H. *Not without Honor: The Life of John H. Reagan*. Austin: University of Texas Press, 1962.

Proud Heritage: Pioneer Families of Dallas County. Dallas: Dallas County Pioneer Association, 1986.

Pycior, Julie Leininger. "Henry B. Gonzalez." In Kenneth E. Hendrickson Jr., Michael L. Collins, and Patrick Cox, eds., *Profiles in Power: Twentieth-Century Texans in Washington*. Austin: University of Texas Press, 2004.

Raboteau, Albert J. *Slave Religion: The "Invisible Institution" in the Antebellum South*. New York: Oxford University Press, 1978.

Ragsdale, Kenneth B. *Centennial '36: The Year American Discovered Texas.* College Station: Texas A&M University Press, 1987.

Ramos, Henry. *The American G.I. Forum: In Pursuit of the Dream, 1948–1983.* Houston: Arte Público Press, 1998.

Rawick, George P., ed. *The American Slave: A Composite Autobiography,* supplement series 2. Vol. 2, *Texas Narratives,* part 1. Westport, Conn.: Greenwood Press, 1979.

Reimers, David M. *Unwelcome Strangers: American Identity and the Turn against Immigration.* New York: Columbia University Press, 1998.

Reynolds, Donald E. *Editors Make War: Southern Newspapers in the Secession Crisis.* Nashville: Vanderbilt University Press, 1966.

Rice, Gwendolyn. "Little Mexico and Barrios of Dallas." *Legacies: A History Journal for Dallas and North Central Texas* 4, no. 2 (fall 1992).

Rice, Lawrence D. *The Negro in Texas, 1874–1900.* Baton Rouge: Louisiana State University Press, 1971.

Richardson, Rupert Norval, Ernest Wallace, and Adrian N. Anderson. *Texas: The Lone Star State.* Englewood Cliffs, N.J.: Prentice-Hall, 1981.

Riley, B. F. *History of the Baptists of Texas: A Concise Narrative of the Baptist Denomination in Texas, from the Earliest Occupation of the Territory to the Close of the Year 1906.* Dallas: Privately published, 1907.

Ritz, David. "Inside the Jewish Establishment." *D: The Magazine of Dallas* (November 1975).

Robinson, James Harvey, and Emma Peters Smith, with James Breasted. *Our World Today and Yesterday: A History of Modern Civilization.* Dallas: Ginn and Co., 1924.

Rockoff, Stuart Allen. "Jewish Racial Identity in Pittsburgh and Atlanta, 1890–1930." Ph.D. diss., University of Texas, 2000.

Roediger, David R. *Towards the Abolition of Whiteness: Essays on Race, Politics, and Working Class History.* New York: Verso, 1994.

———. *The Wages of Whiteness: Race and the Making of the American Working Class.* New York: Verso, 1991.

Rogers, John William. *Judge Lynch, A Drama in One Act.* New York: Samuel French, 1924.

———. *The Lusty Texans of Dallas.* New York: E. P. Dutton and Co., 1960.

Rosen, Robert N. *The Jewish Confederates.* Columbia: University of South Carolina, 2000.

Rosenfield, Jack, and Jack Patton, illustrator. "Texas History Movies." Dallas: PJM Publishers, n.d.

Rosenzweig, Roy, and David Thelen. *The Presence of the Past: Popular Uses of History in American Life.* New York: Columbia University Press, 1998.

Rydell, Robert. *All the World's a Fair: Visions of Empire. International Expositions, 1876–1916.* Chicago: University of Chicago Press, 1984.

Sacks, Karen Brodkin. "How Did Jews Become White Folks?" In Steven Gregory and Roger Sanjek, eds., *Race.* New Brunswick, N.J.: Rutgers University Press, 1994.

———. *How Jews Became White Folks and What That Says about Race in America.* New Brunswick, N.J.: Rutgers University Press, 2000.

Said, Edward W. *Orientalism.* New York: Random House, Vintage Books, 1979.

Sánchez, George J. *Becoming Mexican American: Ethnicity, Culture, and Identity in Chicano Los Angeles, 1900–1945.* New York: Oxford University Press, 1993.

San Miguel, Guadalupe Jr. *Brown, Not White: School Integration and the Chicano Movement in Houston.* College Station: Texas A&M University Press, 2001.

———. *"Let All of Them Take Heed": Mexican Americans and the Campaign for Educational Equality in Texas, 1910–1981.* Austin: University of Texas Press, 1987.

Santerre, George H. *White Cliffs of Dallas: The Story of La Réunion the Old French Colony.* Dallas: Book Craft, 1955.

Sarna, Jonathan A. "The Evolution of the American Synagogue." In Robert M. Seltzer and Norman J. Cohen, eds., *The Americanization of the Jews.* New York: New York University, 1995.

———. "The 'Mythical Jew' and the 'Jew Next Door' in Nineteenth Century America." In David Gerber, ed., *Anti-Semitism in American History.* Urbana: University of Illinois Press, 1986.

Saxton, Alexander. *The Rise and Fall of the White Republic: Class Politics and Mass Culture in Nineteenth-Century America.* New York: Verso, 1990.

Scales, J. M. "Coon Time Rag." Dallas: Thos. Goggan and Bro., 1903.

Schermerhorn, Robert Ryer. "An Occupational History of Mexican Americans, 1930–1950." Master's thesis, Southern Methodist University, 1973.

Schutze, Jim. *The Accommodation: The Politics of Race in An American City.* Secaucus, N.J.: Citadel Press, 1986.

Schwartz, Rosalie. *Across the Rio to Freedom: United States Negroes in Mexico.* El Paso: Texas Western Press, 1975.

Scofield, C. I. *The Comprehensive Bible Course: Section I. The Scriptures, Lessons I–XIV.* Northfield, Mass.: Published by Scofield, 1896.

———. *Dr. C. I. Scofield's Question Box.* Chicago: Moody Bible Institute of Chicago, 1917.

———. *In Many Pulpits With Dr. C. I. Scofield.* New York: Oxford University Press, 1922.

———. "The Millennium: A Sermon Preached at the First Congregational Church, Dallas, Texas, Oct. 29, 1893." SMCA.

———. *Rightly Dividing the Word of Truth.* Dallas: Scofield Memorial Church, 1928.

———, ed. *The Old Scofield Study Bible.* 1917. Reprint, New York: Oxford University Press, 1996.

Seifert, Shirley. *Destiny in Dallas.* New York: J. B. Lippincott Co., 1958.

Sellers, Charles. *The Market Revolution: Jacksonian America, 1815–1846.* New York: Oxford University Press, 1991.

"The Shame of Dallas." *Saturday Evening Post,* April 11, 1964.

Sharpe, Ernest. *G. B. Dealey of the Dallas News.* New York: Henry Holt and Co., 1955.

Sims, Patsy. *The Klan.* Lexington: University Press of Kentucky, 1996.

Slotkin, Richard. *The Fatal Environment: The Myth of the Frontier in the Age of Industrialization, 1800–1890.* 1985. Reprint, Norman: University of Oklahoma Press, 1998.

———. *Gunfighter Nation: The Myth of the Frontier in Twentieth-Century America.* 1992. Reprint, Norman: University of Oklahoma Press, 1998.

————. *Regeneration through Violence: The Mythology of the American Frontier, 1600–1860.* 1973. Reprint, Norman: University of Oklahoma Press, 2000.

Smallwood, James W. *Time of Hope, Time of Despair: Black Texans during Reconstruction.* Port Washington, N.Y.: Kennikat Press, 1981.

Smith, Melinda Diane Connelly. "Congressional Reconstruction in Dallas County, Texas: Was It Radical?" Master's thesis, University of North Texas, 1992.

Smith, Richard Austin. "How Business Failed Dallas," *Fortune,* July 1964.

Smith, Thomas H. "Conflict and Corruption: The Dallas Establishment vs. the Freedmen's Bureau Agent." *Legacies: A History Journal for Dallas and North Central Texas* 1, no. 2 (fall 1989).

Smolovik, Cindy C. "A Tradition of Service: Early Synagogues in Dallas." *Heritage News: A Journal Devoted to the History of North Central Texas* 12, no. 2 (summer 1987).

"SMU Students Stage Sit-Ins." *Texas Observer,* January 14, 1961.

Sobel, Mechal. *Trabelin' On: The Slave Journey to an Afro-Baptist Faith.* Princeton, N.J.: Princeton University Press, 1988.

Soukup, James R., Clifton McCleskey, and Harry Holloway. *Party and Factional Division in Texas.* Austin: University of Texas Press, 1964.

Spivey, Donald. *Schooling for the New Slavery: Black Industrial Education, 1868–1915.* Westport, Conn.: Greenwood Press, 1978.

Stampp, Kenneth M. *The Era of Reconstruction: 1865–1877.* New York: Random House, Vintage Books, 1965.

Sterling, Andrew, and Howard and Emerson. "My Georgia Lady Love." New York: T. B. Harms and Co., 1899.

Stoddard, Lothrop. *The Rising Tide of Color against White World Supremacy.* New York: Charles Scribner's Sons, 1920.

————. *The Revolt against Civilization: The Menace of the Under Man.* New York: Charles Scribner's Sons, 1922.

Stone, Clarence N. *Regime Politics: Governing Atlanta, 1946–1988.* Lawrence: University Press of Kansas, 1989.

Stoper, Emily. *The Student Nonviolent Coordinating Committee: The Growth of Radicalism in a Civil Rights Organization.* Brooklyn: Carlson Publishing, 1989.

The Strange Demise of Jim Crow: How Houston Desegregated Its Public Accommodations, 1959–1963. Film. 1997. Created and produced by Thomas R. Cole and directed by Tom Curtis.

Stuckey, Sterling. *Slave Culture: Nationalist Theory and the Foundations of Black America.* New York: Oxford University Press, 1987.

Takaki, Ronald. *Iron Cages: Race and Culture in 19th-Century America.* Oxford, England: Oxford University Press, 1990.

Tenkotte, Paul A. "Kaleidoscopes of the World: International Exhibitions and the Concept of Cultural Space, 1851–1915." *American Studies* 28, no. 1 (1987).

Tenorio-Trillo, Mauricio. *Mexico at the World's Fairs: Crafting a Modern Nation.* Berkeley: University of California Press, 1996.

Texas Almanac for 1857. 1856. Reprint, Irving, Texas: Glen's Sporting Goods, 1986.

Thomas, Jesse O. *Negro Participation in the Texas Centennial Exposition.* Boston: Christopher Publishing House, 1938.

Thometz, Carol Estes. *The Decision-Makers: The Power Structure of Dallas.* Dallas: Southern Methodist University, 1963.

Torrence, Lois E. "The Ku Klux Klan in Dallas (1915–1928): An American Paradox." Master's thesis, Southern Methodist University, 1948.

Trumbull, Charles Gallaudet. *The Life Story of C. I. Scofield.* New York: Oxford University Press, 1920.

Tuccille, Jerome. *Kingdom: The Story of the Hunt Family of Texas.* Ottawa, Ill.: Jameson Books, 1984.

Turner, William Douglas Jr. "The *Dallas Express* as a Forum on Lynching, 1919–1921." Master's thesis, Southern Methodist University, 1974.

Tyler, Ronnie C., and Lawrence R. Murphy, eds. *The Slave Narratives of Texas.* Austin: State House Press, 1997.

U.S. Bureau of the Census. 1860 Census. *Eighth Census of the United States, 1860: Dallas County.* Vol. 1. Manuscript.

———. 1860 Census. *Population of the United States in 1860: Compiled from the Original Returns of the Eighth Census under the Direction of the Secretary of the Interior.* Washington, D.C., 1864.

———. 1860 Census. *Texas Slave Schedules, 1860.* Vol. 1. Manuscript.

———. 1900 Census. *Twelfth Census of the United States, Taken in the Year 1900. Census Reports.* Vol. 2, *Population,* part 2. Washington D.C., 1902.

———. 1920 Census. *Fourteenth Census of the United States Taken in the Year 1920.* Vol. 1: *Population.* Washington D.C., 1921.

———. 1920 Census. *Fourteenth Census of the United States Taken in the Year 1920.* Vol. 4: *Population. Occupations.* Washington D.C., 1921.

———. 1950 Census. *Census of the Population: 1950. Special Reports. States of Birth.* Washington D.C., 1953.

———. 1960 Census. *Census of the Population: 1960.* Vol. 1: *Characteristics of the Population,* part 45, *Texas.* Washington, D.C., 1961.

———. 1998. *Statistical Abstract of the United States.* 118th edition. Washington, D.C., 1998.

Valdez, Sister Mary Paul. *Hispanic Catholics in the Diocese of Dallas, 1890–1990.* Dallas: 1991.

Vasconcelos, Jose. *The Cosmic Race: A Bilingual Edition.* Baltimore: Johns Hopkins University Press, 1997.

Verrett-Carter, Calvin. "Parkland's community-oriented healthcare at the center of controversy over minority personnel." *Dallas Weekly,* December 14–21, 1994.

Vigil, James Diego. *From Indians to Chicanos: The Dynamics of Mexican American Culture.* Prospect Heights, Ill.: Waveland Press, 1980.

Vigil, Maurilio. *Chicano Politics.* Washington, D.C.: University Press of America, 1978.

Wade, Wyn Craig. *The Fiery Cross: The Ku Klux Klan in America.* New York: Simon and Schuster, Touchstone, 1987.

Warren, Robert Penn. *The Legacy of the Civil War: Meditations on the Centennial*. New York: Random House, 1961.

Watson, Walter T. "Mexicans in Dallas." *Southwest Review* 22, no. 4 (July 1937).

Weeks, O. Douglas. "The League of United Latin American Citizens: A Texan-Mexican Civic Organization." *Southwestern Political and Social Science Quarterly* 10, no. 3 (December 1929).

Weiner, Hollace Ava. *Jewish Stars in Texas: Rabbis and Their Work*. College Station: Texas A&M Press, 1999.

Weisbrot, Robert. *Freedom Bound: A History of America's Civil Rights Movement*. New York: W. W. Norton, 1990.

West, Richard. "Censorship or Business Sense? Taylor Drops a Controversial Book." *D: The Magazine of Dallas*, November 1986.

"What Makes Dallas Different." *New Republic*, June 20, 1964.

Wheeler, Keith. "Who's Who in the Tumult of the Far Right." *Life*, February 9, 1962.

White, Dana F., and Timothy J. Crimmins. "How Atlanta Grew: Cool Heads, Hot Air, and Hard Work." In Andrew Marshall Hamer, ed., *Urban Atlanta: Redefining the Role of the City*. Atlanta: Georgia State University, 1980.

White, William W. "The Texas Slave Insurrection of 1860." *Southwestern Historical Quarterly* 52, no. 3 (January 1949).

Whorton, Brenda B., and William L. Young. "Before John Neely Bryan: An Overview of Prehistoric Dallas County." *Legacies: A History Journal for Dallas and North Central Texas* 3, no. 2 (fall 1991).

Wiley, Nancy. *The Great State Fair of Texas: An Illustrated History*. Dallas: Taylor Publishing Co., 2000.

Williams, Roy H., and Kevin J. Shay. *Time Change: An Alternative View of the History of Dallas*. Dallas: To Be Publishing Co., 1991.

Williamson, Joel. *New People: Miscegenation and Mulattoes in the United States*. New York: Free Press, 1980.

———. *A Rage for Order: Black-White Relations in the American South since Emancipation*. Oxford, England: Oxford University Press, 1986.

Wilson, Charles Reagan. *Baptized in Blood: The Religion of the Lost Cause, 1865–1920*. Athens: University of Georgia Press, 1980.

Wilson, William H. *Hamilton Park: A Planned Black Community in Dallas*. Baltimore: Johns Hopkins University Press, 1998.

Winant, Howard. *Racial Conditions: Politics, Theory, Comparisons*. Minneapolis: University of Minnesota Press, 1994.

Wolfinger, Raymond, and Robert Arsenau. "Partisan Change in the South: 1952–1976," in Louis Maisel and Joseph Cooper, eds., *Political Parties: Development and Decay*. Beverly Hills: Sage Publications, 1978.

Wooster, Ralph A., and Robert Wooster. "A People at War: East Texans During the Civil War." *East Texas Historical Journal* 28, no. 1 (1990).

Worthman, Paul B., and James Green. "Black Workers in the New South." In Nathan

Higgins, Martin Kilson, and Daniel Fox, eds., *Key Issues in the Afro-American Experience,* vol. 2. New York: Harcourt, Brace, Jovanovich, 1971.

Wright, Lawrence. *In the New World: Growing Up with America, 1960–1984.* New York: Alfred A. Knopf, 1988.

Zimmerman, Ann. "It's Our Turn To Be Heard," *Dallas Observer,* April 17–23, 1997.

NEWSPAPERS

Austin American-Statesman

Austin State Gazette

Chicago Tribune

Chicano

Clarksville Northern Standard

Corpus Christi Caller-Times

Corpus Christi Times

Corsicana Daily Sun

Dallas Americano

Dallas Daily Herald

Dallas Daily Times-Herald

Dallas Express

Dallas Herald

Dallas Morning News

Dallas Observer

Dallas Times Herald

Dallas Weekly

El Alacran

Houston Telegraph

Houston Telegraph and Texas Register

Houston Weekly Telegraph

Kingsville Americano

The Laborer

New Orleans Daily Picayune

New York Times

San Antonio Express and News

San Diego Union Tribune

Texas Kourier

Texas 100 Per Cent American

Texas State Times

Ya Basta

INDEX

Rogers, John William, Jr., and *Judge Lynch,* 99, 100
Rothblum, Phillip J., and Klan violence, 95

Sanger, Alexander; and assimilation, 98; on Dallas' class structure, 57; and opposition to the 1920s Klan, 96, 100; as part of the 1870s immigrant rush, 43
Sanger, Charles, and opposition to the Dallas Klan, 96
Sanger, Eli, and the Little Theater, 98
Sanger, Morton, and segregation at the E. M. Kahn store, 146
Sanger, Philip, and "Night in Venice" party, 57; as part of the 1870s immigrant rush, 43; and service in the Confederate Army, 54; on "useful" education for the working class, 57–58
Sanger Harris Department Store: and sales of Scofield Reference Bibles, 55–56; and segregation, 146
Schachtel, Judah, and accommodation among Houston Jews, 145
Schutze, Jim (author); and Dallas historiography, 183; on Dallas' racial politics, 1, 6–7; depiction of, of Dallas African Americans, 103
Scofield, Cyrus; anti-Catholicism of, 92; background of, 47; on capitalism, 49; and conservative politics, 47, 50–51, 75; and dispensationalism, 49; and the First Congregationalist Church in Dallas, 48; and the influence of the *Scofield Reference Bible,* 50, 55–56; and Jewish whiteness, 16, 54–55, 122; and pessimism in late 20th century Dallas, 177; and philo-Semitism, 16, 47, 51–52; and regional reconciliation, 47, 48; relationship of, with Dallas elites, 48, 55
Scofield Reference Bible, influence of, on American Christianity, 48, 50–51

Segregation: African American legal victories regarding, 17; and African American relations with Jews, 144–147; and African American schools, 108–110; and the building of an African American community, 103; Catholic and Fundamentalist Protestant responses to, 133–134; and conflicts between Northerners and Southerners in Dallas, 13; and disease in poor neighborhoods, 67; and election laws regarding African Americans, 112–113, 117–118; and John Ben Shepperd's campaign against the NAACP, 153; and liberal Protestants, 152; and Mexican Americans, 70, 119, 126–127; and the 1950s bombings, 125–126; and overcrowded black housing in the 1940s and the Exline bombings, 119–120; and "property" in whiteness, 10; and the racialization of African Americans, 64; reinforced by federal policies, 168; and the State-Thomas neighborhood, 169–170; and Texas school districts' responses to the *Brown* decision, 152–153; and unions, 111–112
Shepperd, John Ben, and efforts to ban the NAACP, 153
Shillady, John, and Texas oppression of the NAACP, 105, 110
Simmons, William J., and Klan anti-Catholicism, 96; overthrow of, by Hiram Evans, 85; and the rebirth of the Ku Klux Klan, 83
Slave rebellions: and Colorado County, Texas, 25; and Denmark Vesey, 30; and Gabriel Prosser, 30; and Nat Turner, 30; in the United States, 29
Slavery: and antebellum demographics in Texas, 21–22; and calls to resume the slave trade, 25; and the color line, 18; and differences between black and Mexican American history, 8; growth

CPSIA information can be obtained
at www.ICGtesting.com
Printed in the USA
FSHW020715260620
71512FS